The Politics of Solidarity

The Politics of Solidarity

The International Working Men's Association 1873

AW Zurbrugg

MERLIN PRESS

Published in the UK in 2024 by
The Merlin Press
Central Books Building
50 Freshwater Road
Dagenham
RM8 1RX

www.merlinpress.co.uk

ISBN 978-0-85036-790-4

A CIP catalogue record for this book is available at the British Library

Illustration on page 5:
Expressing solidarity with the Paris Commune, New York, December 1871

Printed in the UK by Imprint Digital, Exeter

Contents

Chronology

(International events and events in particular countries.)

1861: *Russia* – serfs emancipated.

1862: English and French and labour representatives meet at an International Exhibition in London. Ferdinand Lassalle's *Arbeiterprogramm* published.

1863: German General Workers' Association (*Allgemeiner Deutscher Arbeiterverein*, ADAV) founded in Leipzig, led by Lassalle. Polish uprising. *USA* – Emancipation Proclamation; Anti-Black riots in New York.

1864: London, foundation of the International Working-Men's Association (IWMA). Schleswig war, Denmark defeated. Fall of Nanking, defeat of the Taiping rebels. Death of Lassalle. *France* – labour laws relaxed

1865: American civil war ends; 13th amendment abolishes slavery. Death of Proudhon. *Jamaica* – Morant Bay Rebellion.

1866: Geneva: First IWMA Congress. Austrian Empire defeated in war with Prussia and Italy. *USA* – 'Police riot' in New Orleans 34 African Americans killed.

1867: Lausanne: Second IWMA Congress. *Germany* – relaxation of laws against labour unions. *UK* – trade union reforms, right to strike.

1868: Brussels: Third IWMA Congress. *Cuba* – Ten-year war begins. *France* – IWMA officials imprisoned. Government announces toleration of unions, membership mushrooms. *Spain* – military revolt, Queen Isabella deposed. *Switzerland* – IWMA helps win strike of construction workers in Geneva. *USA* – African Americans granted citizenship. Massacre in Opelousas, Louisiana.

1869: 6-12 September, Basle: Fourth IWMA Congress. *Belgium* – massacre in Seraing, nine killed. *Cuba* – bid to set up an independent republic. *Germany* – 7th August, Eisenach congress and foundation of the Social-Democratic Workers' Party (*Socialdemokratische Arbeiterpartei*). Labour

combination laws relaxed in the north. *Mexico* – *Campensino* rights as–
serted, execution of Julio Chávez López. *USA* – Colored National Labor
Union and Knights of Labor formed.

1870: July, Franco-Prussian War. September, Napoleon III defeated
at Sedan, fall of the Third Empire; Communes declared in Lyon and
Marseilles. Paraguay war ends. *Austria-Hungary* – Oberwinder, Scheu,
Most and Pabst sentenced to five years' imprisonment. *Germany* –
January, congress of the (Lassalle) General Labour Association (ADAV);
July, congress of the Social-Democratic Workers' Party (SDWP).
Switzerland – April, split in the Francophone-Swiss IWMA regional
federation. *USA* – Some African Americans allowed to vote.

1871: January, Franco-Prussian war ends. September, London IWMA
Conference. *Algeria* – mutiny and revolt among Kabyle people and
others. *France* – March to May, Paris Commune; IWMA banned.
Germany – January, foundation of new Empire. March, elections, 60,000
votes for ADAV, 40,000 for SDWP. *Switzerland* – November, Sonvilier
Jura congress rejects London conference resolutions. *UK* – legislation:
union funds protected; picketing banned. Nine Hours League wins a
strike at Armstrong's Tyneside. *USA* – June, New York, 20,000 workers
demonstrate for eight-hour day. July, troops fire on Irish demonstration in
New York, sixty killed; December, march held to mourn Commune.

1872: Fifth IWMA congress, 2-7 September, in The Hague, the General
Council relocated to New York. 15-16 September, Saint Imier IWMA
congress repudiates the decisions taken in The Hague. November,
followers of Blanqui leave the IWMA. *Argentina* – IWMA sections formed
1872 onwards, later publishing *El Trabajador* and *Le Révolutionnaire*.
Belgium – December, Belgian IWMA congress repudiates decisions of
The Hague. *Canada* – strikes for nine-hour day, unions legalised. *Chile*
– IWMA section founded in Valparaiso. *France* – March, new law bans
organisations promoting strikes, and criminalises IWMA membership
(repealed 1901). *Germany* – March, Bebel and Liebknecht imprisoned;
May, ADAV congress; September, congress of the SDWP. *Italy* – August,
Rimini, IWMA conference, Italian federation breaks with General
Council. Death of Mazzini. *Spain* – January, IWMA banned; April –
Carlists launch reactionary insurrection in the north; Saragossa, Spanish
Federation congress. December, Spanish Federation congress in Cordoba
repudiates decisions of The Hague congress. *Switzerland* – August,
Nechaev arrested in Zürich. *UK/Ireland* – July, first Congress of the British
IWMA federation. 20,000 demonstrators support Irish Fenians. *Uruguay* –

IWMA formed. *USA* – IWMA split (Spring Street vs. Tenth Ward); several strikes demand an eight-hour day.

1873: Great economic depression (lasts five years). January/February, New York General Council suspends Jura federation. The Spring Street USA federation and the Dutch federation repudiate the decisions taken at The Hague. British IWMA federation breaks with General Council. 30 May – New York General Council declares that all the IWMA bodies that have rejected the resolutions of The Hague have 'placed themselves outside' the IWMA; international exhibition in Vienna. 1-6 September, Geneva, Sixth IWMA Congress; 8-13 September, General-council-congress, Geneva. *Argentina* – two Italian anarchists attempt to assassinate President Sarmiento. *Austria-Hungary* – split between moderate and radical Social-Democrats. *Canada* – Labour union created. *France* – a list of IWMA members is revealed to the police, two emissaries appointed by the New York IWMA General Council give evidence to the state. June, congress in Saint-Etienne; August, regional congress in Lyon. *Germany* – March, printers' strike; May, ADAV congress; June, weavers' strike; 23 August, SDWP congress (banned in Nuremburg, relocated to Eisenach). *Italy* – March, Bologna, second federal congress. *Portugal* – IWMA members detained for promoting strikes. *Russia* – engenders revolt. *Spain* – January, IWMA congress in Cordoba; 11 February – republic proclaimed. June-July, cantonalist regional movements and risings; IWMA prominent in events in Alcoy, Sanlúcar de Barrameda (Cadiz); general strike in Barcelona; repression; 300 shot in Seville. *Switzerland* – June, a labour congress in Olten creates an ephemeral Labour League (*Schweizerische Arbeiterbund*). *UK* – Public protests demand reform of laws affecting trade unions. *USA* – collapse of the National Labor Union. Colfax, Louisiana, over 100 African American ex-soldiers killed.

1874: Brussels, September, Seventh IWMA congress. Portuguese end coolie transportations from Macao. *Belgium* – May, regional congress in Liège. *Austria-Hungary* – Neudörfl socialist congress, Czech and German structures created. Treason trials and arrests. *France* – April, trial of Internationalists in Lyon. *Germany* – January, Socialists (ADAV and SDWP) win 350,000 votes, (6.8%) in national elections; persecution of socialists increased; March, government seeks to enforce law banning propaganda for class hatred. May, Johann Most imprisoned; ADAV congress, 15,000 members represented; June, ADAV banned in Prussia; July, SDWP congress, 8,700 members represented; September, SDWP banned in Munich, repression encourages moves towards unity of the ADAV and SDWP. *Italy* – August, attempted insurrection in Bologna, IWMA banned. *Russia* – mass arrests. *Spain* – January, military coup d'état, attempted general strike in Barcelona, defeat of last rebel administration in Cartagena, labour associations banned; June, (clandestine) 4th Spanish Federation congress in Madrid. IWMA banned (allowed to re-emerge only in 1881); ongoing civil war against the Carlists. *Switzerland* – April, Jura federation congress. Economic recession in watch and clock-making. *UK/Ireland* – Women's Protective and Provident League formed; 20,000 linen workers strike in Belfast (Catholic and Protestant). *USA* – January, defeat of protests in New York, April, congress of the centralist federation. White League organised in Louisiana against African Americans. Vicksburg massacre (300? African Americans killed). November: Democrats win congressional election.

1875: IWMA international congress unable to meet. *Austria-Hungary* – police prevent labour congress taking place; Malatesta supports revolt in Bosnia-Herzegovina. *Germany* – May, congress in Gotha, merger of ADAV and SDWP and formation of the Socialist Workers' Party. October, renewed repression of labour organisations. *Italy* – trials against insurrectionists in Rome, Florence and Puglia; many of the accused are acquitted. *Portugal* – Socialist Party formed. *Russia* – revolts. *Spain* – regional (*comarca*) IWMA conferences. *UK* – relaxation of labour law, allows peaceful picketing. *Uruguay* – Montevideo labour federation formed. *USA* – Pinkertons target Molly Maguires in the Pennsylvania coalfields.

1876: July, death of Bakunin; world exhibition in Philadelphia; dissolution of the General-Council-IWMA. October, Bern, 8th IWMA congress. Rebellions in European parts of Ottoman empire. *Argentina* – *Centro de Propaganda Obrera* formed. *France* – labour congress in Paris. *Germany* – congress of the Socialist Workers' Party. *India* – Mass famine. *Italy* – October, Italian federation reorganises; congress in Florence/Tosi, mass arrests. Bologna mass trial, acquittals. *Mexico* – Labour congress, conflict between statists and ant-statists. *Russia* – demonstration in Kazan square, St. Petersburg.

1877: Russo-Turkish War, ends 1878. September, 9th international IWMA Congress, in Verviers; and 'Universal' Socialist Congress, in Ghent. *Italy* – April, IWMA members attempt to spark a rebellion in the Matese mountains. *Russia* – trial of 193 revolutionary-socialists in St Peterburg. *France/Switzerland*– March, Bern, police forces attack a demonstration carrying a red flag. August, delegates from 12 French sections hold congress in La Chaux-de-Fonds. *Spain* – regional (*comarca*) IWMA conferences. *UK* – 200 miners killed in Blantyre. *USA* – troops withdrawn from the former confederate states. June, execution of ten Molly Maguires. July-August, a hundred workers killed in the course of railway strikes, general strike in St Louis.

1878: *Cuba* – end of the ten years' war. *France* – labour congress in Lyon; *Fédération des travailleurs socialistes de France* formed. *Germany* – Antisocialist laws. (Austria-Hungarian and Italian governments also target radicals). *Italy* – congress of the Italian federation in Pisa; trial of the Matese insurrectionists. *Spain* – summer, regional (*comarca*) IWMA conferences. *Switzerland*– James Guillaume takes a job in Paris.

Introduction

On Sunday 17 December 1871, ten thousand men, women and children gathered on the streets of New York. A silent but dignified march expressed solidarity and support for the people of Paris, mourning the recently defeated Commune and the execution of thousands of Parisians.[1] Radical people viewed the Commune as an experiment in popular, accountable democracy. Many Americans had shown their sympathy in practical ways, sending funds to provide relief for rebels, disregarding conservatives who sought to portray the people of Paris as bloodthirsty terrorists.[2] The marchers came together in response to a broad appeal addressed to 'people of all nations, regardless of sex, color or religion'.

The procession was led by six funeral horses, a band, a group of 38 white men selected from various sections of the International Working Men's Association (IWMA), and a company of 'colored' (African American) Skidmore Light Guards.[3] It drew in African Americans, Cubans, Czechs, Irish Fenians, French refugees and communards, Labour Leaguers, others from the IWMA (displaying red ribbons), Germans, Italians and Swiss, and members of various unions: bricklayers, cabinet makers, painters and printers.

Just behind the guards came twenty-three women on foot, one carrying a child. Tennie Claflin carried a red flag with the motto 'Complete Political and Social Equality for Both Sexes'. There followed a hundred or so Cubans (with a *Lanzeros del Camaguey* flag), sixty Swiss with their flag, a catafalque and a motto, 'To the martyrs of the Universal Republic'(a reference to persons killed in Paris and Cuba).[4] There followed other of IWMA sections with various flags – including the American flag – and Garibaldi guards. They were joined by 'a vast body of citizens of every color, creed, and nationality'.

50,000 to 100,000 people looked on.[5] One conservative paper remarked that by half-past one, all the streets near the Cooper Institute were fairly filled with people, ... the marchers walked straight along, at a rapid pace and in perfect silence ... the police, apparently in pursuance of orders let the procession severely alone … in going up Broadway, for example, the Internationals were fairly jammed together by the pressure of the crowd into a confused mass … The internationals had friends in the crowd of watchers, but the *New York Daily Herald* (18 December 1871) wrote: 'at no part of the route was there even the faintest cheer of sympathy and support'. It estimated 1,500 to 2,000 marchers. The *Herald* went on to describe the background to the International, the membership of its General Council, and its regulations for decision-making at national and international levels.

This was an inspiring moment for internationalists. The coloured Skidmore Guards were loudly cheered. For a few hours, an international spirit was celebrated, involving men and women, Black and white, African Americans, Cubans* and peoples of European extraction all joined together. It was trans-continental, convivial and communist; it called for 'Liberty, Equality, Fraternity'.[6] The *World* (New York, 18 December 1871), told how communities mixed amicably. The Cubans (black, mulatto and white) voiced calls for independence from Spain.[7]

The demonstration had been called on an appeal from Benoît Hubert[8] and other French-speakers; some hundreds of them marched. They were supported by the wing of the IWMA based at Spring Street, New York. Friedrich Sorge, a leader of a rival IWMA network based at the Tenth Ward Hotel, opposed it, because he thought the moment was inopportune; he mentioned workers might lose a day's pay. His opposition restricted support from the substantial local German community, but he was compelled to acknowledge that the march had brought good results.[9]

Was the energy present in this march something to build on? Did this march portend something new or was it an isolated event? Was a turn to electoral politics the best way forward? Could a broad, multi-national coalition be built, demanding rights for waged workers and all working people? Did the International have means to help build such a coalition – a press and an organisation (within itself and/or in coalition with others)?[10] Questions such as these may have been on the minds of marchers.

This book considers these matters, focusing on how such questions were discussed before and after the congresses of the IWMA, held in September 1873. It has five parts: the first considers context, circumstances, and perspectives. Why did socialism mean different things to different people? What were the underlying conflicts in the IWMA? What sorts of politics were being promoted or sidelined? How did issues of class, race and gender affect labour organisations? It concludes with an overview of the history

---

* A ten-year war for independence was ongoing in Cuba; many Cubans had fled to Florida and New York, and some became tobacco workers.

of the IWMA written by an occasional correspondent for *The Times* of London.

The second part presents a translation of the *Official Report* of the congress attended by six Federations of the federalist IWMA, held between the first and sixth September. There are day-by-day records, notes on delegates and the revision of the IWMA statutes, reports from various federations and sections, and details of several debates.

The third part consists of newspaper reports of the centralist congress convened by the New York General Council and held between 8 -13 September. Part four considers the impact, aftermath, and consequences of these two congresses. There are brief notes on particular countries and political networks.

Lastly, there are five appendices, each providing contemporary perspectives about IWMA politics. Firstly, the speech of Hermann Jung at the British Federation congress of 26 January 1873 commenting on the workings of the General Council in London in 1871 and 1872. The second appendix is a report on the public meeting of 4 September 1873, a meeting organised by the 'federalists', but also attended by 'centralists'. The third reports on the discussion of the general strike, a discussion that was deliberately omitted from the federalists' *Official Report*. Appendix four consists of a review of the two congresses, published in the *Bulletin de la Fédération Jurassienne*. The final appendix, published the *Volksstaat*, illustrates another viewpoint.

Most translations are my own. The names of speakers are often given in italics. Most footnotes and endnotes have been added. The title of the International Working Men's Association is generally abbreviated to IWMA.

Part 1

Circumstances, Perspectives, Contexts, Politics

In September 1873, two distinct and rival congresses of the IWMA met in Geneva, a turn of events that came about after regional federations rejected the proceedings of the international or 'general' congress held at The Hague in 1872.[11] Seven regional IWMA federations supported the congress that met on 1 September 1873. The second congress, which met on the 8th, had no delegates appointed by regional federations.

Two IWMA networks committed to some form of socialism met in Geneva; both cherished sentiments expressed in the first words of the IWMA's statutes, a text that set out that 'the emancipation of workers should be the accomplishment of workers themselves'. Both subscribed to the view that 'hitherto all struggles have failed, for want of solidarity between workers of various trades within each country, and for the lack of fraternal unity between the workers of different regions'.[12] Nonetheless, there were conflicting visions as to how to move forward.

The *Official Report of the Sixth Congress of 1873* documents the workings of the thirty delegates who represented the great majority of the IWMA. Twelve of its thirty delegates had attended previous IWMA international congresses.[13] Among them was James Guillaume,[14] an IWMA veteran who had been targeted for expulsion by the previous year's congress.[15] Also present were former members of the General Council of London, (George Eccarius[16] and John Hales[17]) now representing the British IWMA Federation. Jean-Louis Pindy was another remarkable figure: he had attended IWMA congresses in 1868 and 1869, had served time in prison, and had been a colonel in the forces of the Paris commune; fleeing a death sentence he had taken refuge in Switzerland and joined the Jura federation.[18] Several other Paris Commune activists were present, representing sections in France, the Jura and Spain.[19] The *Official Report* of this first congress, translated in full below, offers an overview of activity in the ongoing, federalist IWMA. It tells of the composition of the various federations and lists delegates and their sections. Delegates held different views on means and priorities, but all were determined to construct democratic, accountable, federalist* structures.

A second congress met between 8 and 13 September, bringing together persons in touch with Friedrich Sorge and the IWMA General Council in New York, and Karl Marx and Friedrich Engels in London. It drew support from Social-Democratic electoral parties in Germany, Austria and Switzerland. Six delegates had travelled from Germany to the fifth IWMA congress at The Hague in 1872,[20] but only one German-based delegate came to Geneva in 1873. Many of the key movers and shakers who had shaped proceedings before and after the congress at The Hague (Engels, Marx, Auguste Serraillier,[21] Friedrich Sorge[22] and Nikolai Utin)[23] were absent. However, four people who had attended the 1872 event did play key roles in 1873: three were based in Geneva: Theodor Duval and Henri Perret, (members of the Geneva central IWMA section) and Johann Philipp Becker,[24] a German exile and a long-standing activist. The fourth key man was Heinrich Oberwinder. He had sailed under the alias 'Ludwig Heim' at The Hague, now, in 1873, he came as 'Schwartz'; he was a correspondent for the *Neue Freie Presse* and was a leading figure in the labour movement in Vienna and the journal *Volkswille*.[25] National and regional newspapers carried anecdotes and some very extensive reports about the two congresses. Journalists described the second event sponsored by the General Council as a congress of 'centralists', 'authoritarians' or 'Marxists'. The organisers of that second congress did not publish an official report, so the newspaper accounts below are the best source of information on what happened there.

Several other notable IWMA figures took no part in these September congresses; the absentees included Andreas Scheu (Austria), César De Paepe, Eugène Hins and Paul Robin (Belgium), Jules Guesde, Benoît Malon (France), August Bebel and Wilhelm Liebknecht, (Germany), Tomáz González Morago (Spain), Bakunin, Herman Greulich (editor of the *Tagwacht*), Hermann Jung and Adhémar Schwitzguébel, (Switzerland).

CIRCUMSTANCES

The 1873 congresses met in the aftermath of the Paris Commune; some twenty thousand rebels had been killed or executed, thousands were deported or imprisoned, and perhaps as many as 100,000 people had left or fled Paris. The IWMA in France was smashed and banned.

These events elicited contrasting reactions.[26] Certain British trade union

* The term 'federalism' is explored below – see 'Federalism and decentralised organisation'.

leaders had resigned from the General Council of the IWMA when the latter supported the Commune. (Persons such as these) They hoped to obtain reforms by quieter and respectable means, lobbying the liberal government of William Gladstone. In Belgium, there was some contentment, wages among miners had risen by 60 per cent since 1869 and workplace action seemed unnecessary.[27] Other liberals also thought that opportunities were open for peaceful, individual progress: for example, *The Word – a monthly journal of Reform,* of Princeton, Massachusetts, regarded 'all claims to property, not founded on labor title, as morally void'. One contributor also wrote in its May 1873 edition: 'With industry, prudence, sobriety and self-culture, the laboring man of the United States can always make has way, and he needs no trades-unions or leagues to trammel his action or direct his form of thought. He is a free citizen ...'

The Catholic Church portrayed communards as prisoners escaped from Hell. In the USA, bishops told their flock that the Commune was anti-Christ. *Woodhull & Claflin's Weekly* (13 September 1873), reported on a meeting of the American Spring Street Federal Council, on 31 August. The Bishop of Montreal had ruled: 'your Society [a union affiliated to the IWMA] is interdicted, because it engages in things unjust and condemned; for example, to make strikes ...' One priest refused to bury a worker who died in the course of a strike. William West, a key figure in that Spring Street Council, told this 'lordship' that it was not right for him to boss workers. In Belgium, some workers had won a reduction of the working day to ten hours, but after 1872 there was little success; many workers left the unions, and many union branches disaffiliated from the International.[28]

In Ireland, the IWMA was portrayed as irreligious and barbaric, so much so that support for the IWMA had dissipated.[29] In many countries, catholic priests worked to shape catholic labour networks, largely inimical to the International. In Austria-Hungary, the Catholic church harboured anti-Semitic priest-journalists. In Italy, radicals were able to organise in cities, but not so much beyond them. Fearful governments recruited armed forces from rural areas. Urban rebels would seek to influence rural people, but cultural and religious differences might keep them apart. Darwin's theory of evolution might scare religious forces, who feared that their authority and traditions were being challenged. Radicals had to tread carefully. Many working people rejected atheism. Internationalists were slandered and imprisoned. Supporters of Commune, forcibly dispersed, spread their experience, learnt about new places and cultures, and acquired a more global awareness. Police forces kept a wary eye on rebels.

Thousands of French prisoners were held on the other side of the world in New Caledonia. Back in France, sections of the IWMA struggled to survive, defying poverty, police spies, turncoats, and banning orders. Strikes petered out. Some activists thought under prevailing conditions, and with the International banned, it would be foolish to attempt to reorganise. A state of siege was kept in place until April 1876. In France, and in much of continental Europe, the IWMA was an illegal organisation.[30]

Although the Commune provoked the decline of the IWMA in Britain, Ireland and France, this was not the case in several other countries. The Commune met with new or renewed enthusiasm and shaped a new radical movement in Belgium, Spain and Italy.[31] Italian internationalists broke with the veteran radical, Giuseppe Mazzini,[32] and his concept of *dio e populo* (God and the people).[33] In Spain, the growth of the IWMA had not alarmed the government hitherto, but the Commune did, and counter-measures were implemented. Some key figures (Francisco Mora, Anselmo Lorenzo and Tomáz González Morago) took sanctuary in Lisbon in 1871, and met counterparts (A. de Quental, José Fontana, Francisco Lopes, and others).[34] Portuguese internationalists drew on both Proudhon and Marx, looking for a mutualist state as against the capitalist and authoritarian state.

Support for workplace organising and the building of strike funds was the pressing, everyday task of the IWMA. Some international trade organisations were being organised. The *Bulletin de la Fédération Jurassienne* of 20 July 1873 reported on the convening of a European congress of workers in tailoring, to be held in Liège, and on the first international federation of shoemakers, meeting in Brussels on 1 and 2 June. Twenty delegates had taken part, mostly Belgians, and one French. A shoemakers' association in Germany sent support, as also did a Spanish shoemakers' federation. Regulations were adopted and another congress was scheduled to meet in Antwerp, in September.

Many IWMA activists, both centralists and federalists, sought to understand economics and statistics. Marx's economic research was widely admired. The journal of the Jura federation viewed *Capital* as a valuable but one-sided work.[35] In 1878, Carlo Cafiero wrote a summary or abridgement, *Il Capitale di Carlo Marx*.[36] Cafiero had lived in London and had corresponded with Engels. For a time he had sought to promote support for Marx and the General Council, but he became alienated by the arrogance he encountered. He rejected the project of change through a strong state, saw an 'evil spirit'[37] in Engels, and became one of Italy's foremost anarchists.[38]

While campaigns to reduce the working day or ban child labour attracted broad support across the world of labour, other political perspectives were less well defined and quite diverse. When governments persecuted rebels, working people might instinctively express solidarity with each other, whatever their views. Many perspectives were fluid and flexible.[39] Diverse circumstances helped foster diverse politics. In the USA more than half of Americans lived outside cities and many hoped to get land from the state. Except in a few locations in Spain and the USA, there were few rural IWMA sections.

Many currents of opinion had some presence. There were radicals, revolutionaries, liberals and conservatives, many religious groups, associations with ethnic identities (Hibernians, Molly Maguires), and others tied to racist and/or nationalist perspectives. The Swiss nationalist *Grütli Verein* and the German Hirsch-Duncker unions both sought harmony between workers and managers (sometimes through no-strike agreements). The British trade unions, the largest labour organisations of this era, had many leaders working in tandem with the Liberal Party rather than with the International. Union leaders and ambitious would-be politicians had particular interests. Legal pressures were applied to foster neutral and apolitical unions. Many radicals looked back to the past, to the ideas of the great French Revolution. Some looked back to Chartism, the legacy of 1848, or to figures such as Blanqui,[40] Garibaldi or Mazzini.

CONTEXTS

Belgium, Britain, and parts of the north-eastern USA were predominantly urban societies in the early 1870s; industrialisation and machine production were gathering pace, but in most of Europe and North America, artisan production, and putting-out were common, with most people living in rural locations. Expanding cities created miserable conditions and unhealthy overcrowded districts. Worldwide cholera and smallpox epidemics killed hundreds of thousands. Some radical political parties existed, representing the more prosperous, urban, male artisans, but not many women, the unskilled, the peasant, the domestic servant, or other layers of working people. Many IWMA members were concerned with disparities between 'middlemen' and manual workers and the issue would be debated at both September congresses.* Class was seen not as a binary identity, but as something more complex. Many labour parties were shaped by particular interests and trades and were not representative bodies.

---

* *The Times*, 16 September noted: 'Medical men, lawyers, writers, possessors of capital in one form or another, and a good many others that could be named, work hard enough, but, as they live on the proceeds of other people's labour and professedly occupy a distinct position over the great working class, they are alien, and cannot be trusted. They are middlemen, having a game of their own and that not the people's'.

Workplace organisations were growing, but many working people were unorganised. The International Working Men's Association was strongest where it brought workplace organisations into its web directly, as sections or resistance societies or indirectly as affiliated bodies. In France membership had grown, and some writers claim that it peaked at 200,000 to 300,000 before the defeat of the Commune.[41] In Spain, membership in the regional IWMA peaked at around 60,000. In Britain, in 1874, the Trade Union Congress claimed a million members, but IWMA membership was a few hundred. In Germany, in 1870, the 'liberal' Hirsch-Duncker unions had 35,000 members and were the largest organised labour network; there were smaller numbers in other organisations, but membership numbers were declining.[42]

Hardship increased with the worldwide economic downturn of 1873. There was a stock exchange crash that May, in Vienna. An economic downturn began in the USA in September. Britain entered a period of depression. In Italy, some workers had to spend a third of their daily wages to buy just one kilogram of bread; bread riots were not uncommon.[43] Economic crisis sparked mass protests, and state violence. Many labour associations were weakened,[44] and fewer strikes were attempted or won. Some conservatives blamed Jews and stirred anti-Semitism in France, Germany and elsewhere.

The success or failure of a strike often entailed the expansion or contraction of a labour organisation. The IWMA was strongest among artisans and waged workers in craft sectors – typesetters, jewellery workers, watchmakers – and much weaker among the casual and unskilled, in building, construction, and textile industries, and among women workers. The latter might win occasional strikes but were less able to sustain ongoing organisations. Peter Kropotkin noted:

Outsiders never realise the sacrifices which are made by the workers in order to keep their labour movements alive. No small amount of moral courage was required to join openly a section of the International Association, and to face the discontent of the master and a probable dismissal at the opportunity, with the long month out of work which usually followed. But even under the best circumstances, belonging to a trade union, or to any advanced party, requires a series of uninterrupted sacrifices. Even a few pence given for the common cause represent a burden on the meagre budget of the European worker, and many pence had to be disbursed every week.[45]

In geographical terms the International was weakest in Britain, Germany, and the USA, where unions had organised before the IWMA formed, and organised outside the International. In such places individual union members might join, and odd unions might affiliate, but most links were loose and /or distant. The General Council had boasted, in September 1872, that 'the International has been extended to the Irish in England and to Ireland itself, to Holland, Denmark, and Portugal, that it has been firmly organised in the United States, and that it has established ramifications in Buenos Aires, Australia, and New Zealand',[46] but these claims were ephemeral, exaggerated and fallacious.

The weight of the International as against other labour organisations, and as against unorganised economic sectors varied greatly from place to place. In Britain, the IWMA presence was among the weakest bodies as compared with various radical political bodies, and an organised labour movement approaching a million members, numbers far greater than in any other country. Accounts of labour organisations and strikes peppered the federalist IWMA press. The Spanish IWMA reported 115 successful strikes in 62 places, between September 1872 and August 1873.[47] The International was valued as a forum for sharing news and for the analysis of wage-rates,[48] there were requests for support when strikes broke out, and frequent warnings to journeymen not to take up the jobs of strikers.

In Italy, a federation came together in 1871-2, gaining strength in some urban areas, and among artisans and small traders. Italy had gradually emerged as a new, monarchical nation state. One of the leaders of the Italian federation was Carlo Cafiero, a man once sympathetic to Marx and Engels, who moved over to support Mikhail Bakunin.[49] The federation claimed a membership of 26,704 in February 1871, organised in 129 sections.[50] More might have joined but for the fear of a loss of employment. The great majority worked as bakers, blacksmiths, book-keepers, butchers, and similar occupations. *La Federazione Italiana dell'Associazione Internazionale dei Lavoratori*, published many periodicals.[51] Costa would report to the federalist congress that they had suffered much from persecution. Enrico Bignami, editor of the left-wing journal *La Plebe* of Lodi, was arrested in November 1872 and only released in February of the following year. Several issues of the libertarian *Il Martello* of Milan were seized. Celso Ceretti[52] was arrested on 11 March 1873. Regional congresses were held, and the police arrested several delegates to the second (countrywide) federation congress on the 16th. The federation consolidated and expanded despite this repression.[53]

Andrea Costa, a twenty-one-year-old delegate from Bologna,* thought numbers would soon increase further. The work was very difficult; the International now had to contend not just with the government, but also with followers of Garibaldi and Mazzini. In Costa's view the Garibaldians opposed the International because it was not prepared to fight on every occasion; they had less use for an international movement, though they were good for a national one and they had no idea of science or theory. The Mazzinians, said Costa, opposed the International because it did not sufficiently reverence authority and religion.[54] The Italian federation had a mind of its own and rejected advice from James Guillaume and Bakunin to attend the congress in The Hague.[55] It repudiated Engels, (General Council correspondent for Italy) and declared its support for federalism and anarchism, and perhaps also for female equality. It made progress in a period when other Internationalists were not doing so well. It sought, 'the creation of a new civilisation, moral improvement, and material progress … '.[56]

A republic was proclaimed in Spain in February 1873. There were hopes that it would bring in a new era. Conditions varied, there was some industrial and urban development in the Basque country and Catalonia, but bitter poverty, landlessness, and quasi-feudal conditions in Andulacía and other rural areas. Elisée Reclus[57] saw the fall of the monarchy as great news, hopefully bringing 'most happy consequences'. He speculated about some eventual confederation on both sides of the Mediterranean (Spain ruled over parts of north-west Africa). He wanted the abolition of slavery in Cuba, a definitive liberation in the Caribbean, reconciliation between former colonies and the mother country, and a common freedom. He hoped Brazil, a slave-holding empire, would soon be isolated.

The new Spanish republic faced enemies and internal conflict. Some liberals sought power in Madrid while others looked towards decentralised regional or cantonal administrations. In the Basque country and to the south of Barcelona there were risings by Carlist armies – Carlism represented traditionalist, Catholic reaction. The IWMA criticised the Madrid central government and condemned it for preferring to fight radicals and devolutionists rather than the reactionary Carlists: 'the government dissolves our sections and imprisons the most active of our brothers; … and if that is not enough for you, look at the executions in Seville and of soldiers, and in the recent ones of insurgents in Cuba and I ask later: Where has a Carlist been shot? Nowhere.'[58] Spain was the strongest region of the

* There are notes on the occupations and affiliations of Costa and other delegates to the federalist congress in the official congress report below.

International in 1872-73, organising hundreds of workplaces and trades as IWMA sections and publishing many journals.[59]

In 'Latin' Europe, IWMA organisations worked hard to develop mass, active federations – often having to work discretely against state repression. A network of branches, and a substantial IWMA presence emerged in Alcoy, Geneva, Lyon, Paris, and Verviers,[60] albeit sometimes only briefly. Naturally, participation had its ups and downs, and was beset by problems, but from time to time there was open, mass activity. Large numbers might come together in regular club events and meetings, or occasional banquets, and social evenings (perhaps with singing or picnics). General assemblies of IWMA members might begin to take on the features of participatory mass democracy, so much so that the International had weight and substance; in short, in a few places the labour movement and the IWMA were largely one and the same.[61] IWMA sections or unions grew in diverse trades, supporting workplace organisation, raising strike funds, holding meetings of political and educational clubs, networking with exile groups, and occasionally, when they could do so, holding mass local general assemblies, perhaps discussing the agenda of the next IWMA congress and publishing IWMA newspapers addressing issues in and beyond the workplace. These newspapers helped bind together local, regional, and public IWMA bodies, and helped to shape movements of working peoples *in* the IWMA. This was something qualitatively different compared to the more limited 'cosy' doings of committees working behind closed doors, while mass movements of working peoples organised beyond them.

Beyond the workplace, the International had other forms: educational clubs, city centre propaganda sections; even delegations to an exhibition might disguise an IWMA assembly. For many years after its foundation the IWMA might first organise in 'central sections' – bodies that supported the formation of workplace organisations. Sometimes, as in Geneva, the central section might come to be almost a trades' council, it might help develop new workplace sections, and conversely members of local unions might attend meetings of this central body. The historian Max Nettlau commented:

In 1872, the British trade unions were no longer concerned with the International; on the continent, the German unions and the French syndicates were legally obliged to keep away; the Belgian and Swiss syndicates were minimal, the Italians nil; only Spain showed hundreds of resistance sections and sections by the hundred in various trades. These sections were, it is true, scattered all over the breadth of the land and often the number of members was so poor that they had little material influence bar places where those few members had acquired a moral influence. But, it was always one might say infinitely greater than what then obtained in many other countries because, perhaps with the only exceptions of a few small places in the Jura and some towns in the Romagna, the International no longer had any local influence – not even in Belgium or in Geneva.[62]

In New York city, IWMA section No. 1 had substantial influence within the skilled German-language community, but little elsewhere. In London, the key decision makers on the General Council comprised correspondence secretaries and a sub-committee that worked without effective oversight. For the first five years of its life the IWMA General Council in London relied on working through a few trade union leaders. Before refugees from the Commune arrived in London, the IWMA in Britain was mainly an advice committee, translating documents and facilitating contacts. It was supported by German-language educational clubs and had few union affiliations but had no great weight in the unions. When, because of the Paris Commune, key British leaders parted company with it, much of the indirect influence that it had was lost. Some IWMA members dabbled in the major parties (liberals and conservatives), while others supported the Land and Labour League, and/or other republican and radical bodies.

In Geneva, critics saw the centralist IWMA working behind closed doors; several workplace sections took on the form of committees, meeting infrequently, and lacking activity and vitality, with committee members subordinating workplace activity to the task of getting themselves elected to local government.[63] Workers in the local luxury trades, some of them IWMA members were intent on working with liberals to win positions in local government. The organisation of workers in the building trades had declined. Some federalists had sought to reverse this committee-based mould, by initiating a discussion circle where, speech-making was banned, and chatting encouraged, all to promote participation. Federalists facilitated the development of union networks and sought to involve not just citizen-artisans, but also the unskilled and the non-Swiss. Although these efforts met with little success; a radical presence remained supported by many exiles.

Radicals from eastern Europe and Russia, some Jews among them, were coming to western Europe to study, and some were attracted to the International. Later, many would return to agitate against autocracy and the Tsar, braving dangers to 'go among the people'.[64] In Zurich there were networks of Russians and Slavs where both Bakunin and Peter Lavrov[65] had been active. At least seven Russian women attended the Saint Imier congress of September 1872,* (Warwara Iwanowna Alexandrowa, Sophia Illarionowna Bardina, Katioussa Hardina, Olga Ljubatowitsch, Adelaida Ikolajewna Lukanina, Maroussia Pototskaja and Warwara Iwanowna Wachowskaja), several were medical students in Zurich. They formed a women's group reading Bakunin, Louis Blanc, Cabet, Fourier, Lassalle, Marx, Thomas More, Proudhon, Saint Simon, and others, and studying the development of labour movements.[66] Alarmed by their radicalisation, the Russian government issued a decree in May 1873, that all female students had to return to Russia. These women would have had no opportunity to participate in electoral politics in Switzerland.

Switzerland was chosen as a venue for several IWMA congresses because it allowed a freedom of speech and assembly that was not so common in continental Europe. However, several teachers were dismissed because they held radical views. Also, all meetings had to end by 11 p.m. or risk being broken up by the police.[67] Geneva offered a relatively accessible, safe meeting place, but police permission might have to be obtained before posters were put up. Working people were invited to public sessions of the congress but a hundred or so rowdy folk showed what they thought of radicals and Paris Commune refugees by joining in the singing of the Swiss national anthem outside the congress hall, making such a din that discussion became impossible. The threat of extradition remained very serious. A French military tribunal had passed a death sentence *in absentia*, on Pindy, the correspondence secretary of the Jura Federation, in January 1873.[68] Gustave Lefrançais[69] had also been sentenced to death. The French *Préfecture de Police* employed agents to report on 200 exiled rebels.[70] IWMA members might be arrested on their travels.** An Italian delegate to the federalist congress was sought by the police.[71] Oberwinder, used the pseudonym Schwartz at the centralist congress, presumably to avoid prosecution back in Vienna.

Sometimes, Russian, Belgian, and French authorities prevailed on Swiss counterparts to take action. In January 1872, Geneva authorities conducted a lengthy search at the home of Nikolai Utin looking for incriminating evidence. In March 1873, a member of the Zurich Slav section, Zamfir Ralli,[72] was arrested in the Swiss capital after being denounced by a Russian spy; he was held overnight in prison and had his papers seized.[73] Another

---

* This congress was held on 15-16 September 1872, and was attended by delegates from American, French, Italian, Jura and Spanish federations and sections, and others, It rejected electoral politics and the proceedings of the congress at The Hague, it asserted: 'That the destruction of all political power is the first duty of the proletariat.'
** The Dutch delegate Henri Van den Abeele had been arrested and expelled from France recently.

Russian radical, Nechaev, had been arrested in Zurich on 14 August 1872, betrayed by a one-time Polish revolutionary, Adolph Stempkowski working as a spy for the Russians,[74] and extradited to Russia, despite protests.[75] The Swiss confederal government had been restrained from extraditing other radicals by campaigns mobilising support for Switzerland's then more habitual policy of granting political asylum.[76]

Some Italian internationalists were working to create a clandestine Committee for Social Revolution.[77] Andrea Costa had already been imprisoned twice for promoting the International.[78] The Italian government warned its Swiss counterpart of plots against state security and social order and suggested that the congress would incite strikes.[79] Italian delegates thought that it was sensible to avoid compiling membership lists, in case these fell into the hands of the police. 53 delegates representing some 150 sections had been present at the second congress of the Italian Federation held in Bologna in March 1873. The congress had been convened to meet in Mirandola but was forced to relocate. Carlo Cafiero, Francesco Chiarini, Andrea Costa, Alceste Faggioli, Errico Malatesta, Lodovico Nabruzzi, Abdon Negri and Antonio Saiani had been arrested, and the Italian Interior Ministry had issued orders to destroy the IWMA.[80] Delegates may have wanted to exercise some discretion when touchy subjects were addressed at the federalist congress, and a report noted:

> One young firebrand demanded that in every federation a calculation should be made of how many members could be reckoned upon with certainty to take part in a physical force revolution, so that in case of emergency it might be known what force was available. This was speedily put down as an attempt to give the International the character of a conspiracy.[81]

The federalist delegates did not rise to this suggestion.[82] This sort of realism was not unusual. Earlier Belgian workers had asked counterparts in Spain if they thought it sensible to begin an uprising. Francisco Tomás replied for the Spanish region in May-June 1873, advising that his organisation considered any isolated movement premature, with little chance of success.[83]

Russians were present at the federalist congress, but Russia did not figure in public discussions, perhaps for reasons of personal safety; the names of French IWMA members may have gone unrecorded for similar reasons. The delegate from Germany to the centralist congress, insisted that his party would do nothing illegal.

There was great diversity within both International networks. Their strength, shape, resonance, and political culture varied from place to place, and from time to time. IWMA bodies had weight in some places but might be ephemeral elsewhere. The article below, from the London *Times* (4th of September 1873), surveyed developments in the International, since its foundation.[84]

SIXTH INTERNATIONAL WORKING MEN'S CONGRESS,
The Times (FROM AN OCCASIONAL CORRESPONDENT)
Geneva, 1 September

Seven years ago, on the first Monday of September 1866, the representatives of the working classes of Europe assembled in their first Congress for the purpose of proclaiming their common aspirations to the world and concerting measures to carry their principles into effect. They set out full of courage, full of hope and brotherly love, and determined to achieve their aim – the complete emancipation of the proletariat from the domination of capital – by united action. Since then, the International Working Men's Congresses have made the tour of the most available places, and this year the annual congress is once more held in Geneva; but where are those ardent spirits of 1866, who hoped so much and were so ready and eager to work so hard? Certainly not here.

One of the English delegates of 1866, Matthew Lawrence, President of the London Co-operative Tailors' Association, some time since departed this life. Mr. George Odger and Mr. W. Cremer, who, with Lawrence, may be said to have represented English Unionism in 1866, have long since severed their connexion with the society, though they are more than ever active in the cause of social and political reforms, the ultimate end of which is the complete emancipation of the work people.[85] Of those delegates who represented the International pure and simple, such as Carter, Dupont, Eccarius, and Jung, the first also has long since left the society, and the latter two have taken side with the Federalists against their old leader, Dr Marx, and his co-workers, who are bent upon a strong centralisation as a means of regenerating mankind.

Of the French delegates who took part in the first Congress, some, like Varlin, the financial secretary under the Commune, have paid for their principles with their lives; others, like Murat, who represented the Paris engineers at every Congress up to 1869, have turned their backs upon the society. After the 4th September Murat became Maire of the 10th arrondissement, and was accused during the siege of unfair dealings in the distribution of provisions. After the memorable 18th of March [The first day of the Paris Commune] he turned against his old companions. Fribourg, who was one of the originators of the International, remained but a short time with his old companions after the first Congress, finding it more profitable to become a regular contributor to La Liberté, the paper of M. Emile de Girardin, than following his trade. He has written a history of the International. Partially to cover and excuse his retreat,*

---

* A French royalist newspaper: a similar title but with different views, was published in Brussels.

the substance of it has been reproduced in an English history of the International, by Houndslow York – a fictitious name. Perrachon, who in the Spring of 1867 was one of the leading spirits in the first Paris strike of any importance – the bronzeworkers' strike – and companion of Camelinat at the Mint under the Commune, where holy vessels were coined into money for bread, has since his exile in Belgium, strictly abstained from agitation of any kind, simply minding his business as a bronze-worker. Chemalé, a young enthusiastic Proudhonist, became disgusted with the International when it adopted the abolition of private property in land, but he did not on that account sever his connexion. Good luck would have it that his business as an architect called him into the provinces shortly before the siege, in consequence of which he kept out of all scrapes. He, too, I am credibly assured, has a regular engagement on a Paris paper, but others say he is dead. He was a considerable time at the sea-side on account of illness, but, dead or alive, he has no longer anything to do with the International. There remains Tolain, who, at Geneva, in 1866, was decidedly the spokesman of the French International, and he was Proudhonism incarnate. At Basle, however, he no longer commanded the confidence of his old friends; all the votes he could command on the land question were those of Chemalé, Murat and Langlois; the last of whom has since made himself conspicuous by his eccentricities in the National Assembly in Versailles. Tolain was expelled by the Paris Federation during the war, and his expulsion was ratified by the London General Council and published throughout the world. Since then, he has sat in the National Assembly, where he vexes the Ultramontanes [Clerical reactionaries] occasionally; for the Labour movement he is practically dead.

Among the provincial French delegates, a very young silk worker from Lyons, Albert Richard, attracted a good deal of attention. He, too, was a Proudhonist, but slowly turned round, and at Basle, in 1869, he was very strongly in favour of the abolition of private property in land. He was the leading spirit of Lyons, was prosecuted and imprisoned several times, and at last unable to get work at his trade. He took a leading part in the proclamation and establishment of the Republic, and, like many others, repaired to Paris to assist in the regeneration of France; but his heart failed him when it became necessary to take up arms in defence of his principles. He suddenly turned a man of peace, paid a visit to Chislehurst, and has since founded the French Union of the Friends of Social Peace, whose head-quarters are at Turin. In a recent appeal to the good sense of the French workmen, which he has sent out in bundles, on fine paper, to his old associates, he says:*

The Empire is the revolution under the only possible and durable form; it is the pacific, intelligent, and rational revolution; the Empire of the legend and

---

* Napoleon III resided there from 1871 until his death in January 1873..

also the Empire of right – in one word, the orthodox Empire.

In another part he says:

Were Napoleon III. still alive we might say more, for then we should not displease the eclectics of the Imperial party. Napoleon at Chislehurst thought as we do; are in a position to prove it. But if the situation has been changed by the death of the Emperor the alliance between the people and the Empire has been rendered still more necessary. We simply affirm that without enlarging upon it.

That everybody – Legitimists, Orleanists, Republicans, and his old associates – should come in for a very large share of strong expressions is but natural, but his profession of faith is exceedingly mild:*

With the members of the Union, Socialism is completely disregarded from the slough of the mad theories of other days. They neither attack religion, family, nor private property; they only hope by the force of patience and perseverance to introduce into our economical relations an established right, by virtue of which the workmen many become independent, more powerful, more respected, better educated, and better paid. They will not then have any reason whatever to favour the disturbers of the public peace.

The Swiss delegates of 1866 consisted of three different kinds. There were first the resident and native artisans of Geneva, in sympathy with the Mountaineers of the Jura, who are mainly employed in the various branches of the watch trade. There were the native German Swiss, and the resident German workmen, who are mainly engaged in shoe-making, tailoring, and the various branches of the building trades – the low paying trades. At the first congress the principal spokesman of the Genevese was Dupleix, a bookbinder, well-to-do and somewhat advanced in years, but without any particular doctrine – simply a humanitarian. The Mountaineers had Dr Coullery, a Radical physician, of La Chaux-de-Fonds, for their spokesman, who was also a simple humanitarian, without any defined social or political doctrine. Besides him there was a very young man, James Guillaume, a professor [school master], and a watchmaker named Schwitz Guebel[86] [sic]. These were the most prominent members of the French Swiss, with a leaning towards the French rather than to the Germans, but frequently in a fog which side to take. Dr Coullery, fully conversant with both French and German, gave the cue how to vote, and on the whole helped the London programme, which was accepted by the Germans without reserve, to become the programme of the International. The native German Swiss were represented by Bürkly, of Zurich, a stone-mason and by Frey, a riband weaver, of Basle. The German residents, under the leadership of Jn. Ph. Becker, an old German Communist. were numerously represented but had not furnished a man of note besides their leader. They had a strong political Socialist section

---

* Rival French royalists.

at Geneva, with a paper of their own, and some members of the section had credentials from other places.

Dr Coullery became offended when private property in land was attacked at the Lausanne Congress in 1867, and has gradually vanished from the scene, partly voluntarily and partly elbowed out. He is now in a Government situation, which he is said to have obtained by the favour of the Conservative party of Neufchâtel. Dupleix belongs to a loan society, which was affiliated some years ago, and which is said still to belong to the old society; but Dupleix has ceased to play an active part. Jn. Ph. Becker's German section is scattered to the winds, his paper, the Vorbote, has ceased to exist. He adheres to the New York Council. Bürkly is managing director of the Co-operative establishment at Zurich, and adheres to the New York Council, believing that centralisation and a proletarian dictatorship will be necessary to regenerate society. This is all that is left of the sanguinary reconstruction of society who met her seven years ago. With the vanished spokesman, their following has either also vanished or changes its principles and opinions. The delegates who assembled here this morning are to all intents and purposes a new association. The youngster of 1866, James Guillaume, has become the leader of the Mountaineers, and has a following of nothing but ardent young men. He is the only active man today who was present here seven years ago, but his name does not occur in the compte-rendu of that Congress; he was the spokesman of the Federalists at the Hague.

The Congress of 1873, which was opened this morning at the Brasserie Schiess, may justly be termed the new departure of the International Labour Combination – at least as far as the Latin races are concerned. There is a sprinkling of Flemish and English blood among the delegates, but the Germans are entirely unrepresented. All is swarthy and black-haired, and they seem to mean work. They commenced at 8 o'clock this morning and have allowed an hour for dinner.

The sitting was opened at 8 o'clock by Citoyen Fulligcet, [Fuliquet] the President of the local section, which is no other than the alliance which brought the split that had been brewing for some time in Switzerland to a head last year at the Hague, and which has rent the old International in two – that is to say, has separated the German from the Latin element. In his opening remarks, the President warned the delegates against indulging in personalities of any sort, even against adversaries, as the cause for the promotion of which the Congress had met was so just that it would not require such undignified means to make it succeed. A list of delegates was then read, and each Federation represented had to select its man for the committee on credentials, which was but the work of a few minutes, and then the committee retired. On its return M. Van den

Abeele, of Antwerp, announced that he had been commissioned to report, and the report was to the effect that the credentials of three Italian, ten Spanish, four Belgian, one Dutch, two French, ten Swiss, and three English delegates should be accepted, but that those of an Italian, delegated by a section of Intransigentes of Turin, who were not in relation with the Internationals anywhere, should be rejected. The acceptance of the credentials recommended by the committee having been voted en bloc, Signore Tergati obtained 'the word' to defend his claim. He had to admit that his society was hardly a month old; that it had not been in relation with the Italian Federation, or any other section or federation of the International; and he was met by a reproach that his society had only been formed to work against the Italian Federation, which had been denounced and libelled in a paper published by his society. His reply was that they could not join the Italian Federation for two reasons – the first was that the leaders were Mazzinists and Garibaldians, and the second was that by joining it the society would have laid itself open to police prosecutions. As to the libelling, that was only meant for certain persons, and had nothing whatever to do with the Federation. However, all pleading was in vain; he was not accepted. That wound up the morning session. Mr. Eccarius and Mr. John Hales have taken their seats, but Mr. Mottershead[87] has not yet arrived.

Political Conflicts in the IWMA

A variety of viewpoints and experiences were expressed at IWMA congresses, and in the press published by IWMA federations. The IWMA was a meeting place where progressive ideas of various sorts met and where perspectives evolved. These views were articulated through the IWMA press, particularly through journals published in Belgium and Switzerland, which circulated among French* and German readers in Europe and the Americas.

As the above report in *The Times* indicates, matters of property, capital and land ownership were contentious issues in the first five years of the IWMA, and were discussed over three congresses, in 1867, 1868 and 1869; they were contentious issues but did not lead to splits or expulsions. The agenda of each congress was pre-circulated, a norm that allowed the IWMA press and its federations and sections to discuss items on the agenda and choose delegates corresponding to their views. The IWMA was in large part a federation of workplace organisations and resistance societies, and these organisations had goals and programmes which might be interpreted in various ways,[88] but it was generally believed that the land, the management, and the working capital of businesses should be socialised, and that thereby

---

* Censorship obstructed the publishing of a regular IWMA press in France, but the press of the Belgian and Swiss IWMA did circulate.

working people should enjoy the fruit of their labour.

At Basle, at the fourth IWMA congress in 1869, a resolution was passed without opposition that concluded: resistance (strike) funds should be built up, and workplace organisations should come together in national trades' federations, for common action, 'until such time as waged work is replaced by the Federation of Free Producers'.[89] This resolution outlined a long-term perspective, a future society shaped through the structures of Labour, alongside everyday activity in the workplace. In this perspective, organising in and around the workplace was key and it was hoped that these structures would provide a matrix in which working people would manage things, in the future. Building electoral political parties did not figure.

The Basle congress had rejected a resolution proposed by the General Council for the taxation of inherited property.[90] Bakunin helped defeat that proposal and spoke against electoral politics. A notorious figure for decades, he represented a section of women textile workers in Lyon and was already in Marx's sights as someone to expel from the IWMA.

The issue of the utility of electoral politics arose in Basle but did so only in irregular fashion. A new *Sozialdemokratische Arbeiterpartei Deutschlands,** had just been formed on 7-9 August in Eisenach, with Bebel as one of its co-chairmen, and with Heinrich Oberwinder as one of its vice-presidents, and claiming to represent 100,000 supporters in Germany, Austria-Hungary and Switzerland.[91] Its programme called for voting rights for men over twenty. Delegates of the party and others raised participation in elections and referenda when they arrived at the Basle Congress. The topic had not been placed on the congress agenda before it met and had not been discussed in IWMA sections. (The procedure at the time was for sections to suggest topics for a congress, and the General Council then set the agenda). The Basle Congress therefore discussed whether it was proper to *add* the issue to the agenda, as pressed by some delegates, and decided that it might be discussed[92] but only after other matters more properly set on the agenda were dealt with. In practice this meant that there was no substantial discussion; congress records suggest that electoral politics had only limited support.

The discussions at the Basle congress had symbolic and practical significance. For many, they indicated aspirations, and although their everyday work focused on workplace organising, their broader aspirations motivated them. For those IWMA members seeking election, these aspirations were somewhat dangerous. Few liberal voters wanted a ban on the inheritance of land or capital. Those who advocated electoral politics

* Social-Democratic Workers' Party (SDWP), (Eisenachers).

wanted to tone down such 'impractical' things. In Geneva and in Germany, a few members feared that radical ideas would frighten off liberal alliance partners. It was not immediately obvious, but there were implications in the idea that an inheritance of capital should be taxed; there was an implication that working people should cohabit with capital and tax it rather than dispense with it.

The defeat of the General Council's draft inheritance resolution challenged its key figures. It highlighted that there were divergent perspectives within the IWMA. Marx and his allies resolved on arranging things to have a majority at the next congress. The outbreak of the Franco-Prussian war in July 1870 prevented that congress meeting that September in Paris, and the next one met only in September 1872. For three years the process of IWMA congress decision-making was in abeyance. When the next congress did meet, the General Council failed to circulate the agenda two months beforehand.[93]

Meanwhile the formation of the *Sozialdemokratische Arbeiterpartei Deutschlands* had encouraged Marx and Engels to set out that: 'The conquest of political power has therefore become the great duty of the working class.'[94] The formation of labour parties and electoral participation was in this view, a general priority. The policy was widely accepted among English- and German-speakers,[95] but not much or not at all in 'Latin' Europe or among the large majority of IWMA members.*

Instead of discussing the matter in a friendly manner, and seeking to persuade, Marx, Engels and their associates had attempted to 'smash' opposition.** The congress at The Hague in 1872 ratified the position of Marx and Engels, but the congress was seen as illegitimate by most members and by seven federations. Several delegates critical of the General Council had been kept out of the congress, while 'friendly' delegates – even those with credentials that could not be verified – were allowed in. Two at least were shown to be spies. Some had acted against the wishes of those they represented; there was a delegate from Berlin – although no section existed there, and a French delegate, Vichart, who was not an IWMA member.[96]

A discussion that had extended over three months in Belgian sections and area federations was concluded at the regional (countrywide) congress of 25-26 December 1872; it rejected the workings of the congress at The Hague as 'arbitrary, authoritarian and contrary to federalist principles and the spirit of autonomy', also viewing its resolutions as 'null and void,

---

*   See also below, 'Decision-making, editing and the IWMA' on the launch of this perspective.

**   See appendix one.

fabricated by a fictional majority'.[97] Six other federations took a similar view. Former friends and associates in London (including several who favoured electoral politics) broke with Marx and Engels, antagonised by the way they had sought to manipulate decision-making.

What was the 'political power' that centralists and Social-Democrats sought? The party of Social-Democrats in Germany appeared to answer that political power would come through a nation-state conquered through elections. Meanwhile the rule of law was to be accepted. German law allowed political discussion of a restricted agenda, in restricted circles, for restricted people. Trade unions could not affiliate to political parties or discuss politics; women were not allowed to join. There would be no challenge to the nation's armed forces. The task was to build electoral support and eventually to bring the nation-state under Social-Democratic control, as a *Volksstaat* (People's State).

In practice, working for electoral politics implied accepting this very restricted framework of politics, as set by Bismarck. Perhaps, in some future, social change might come, but meanwhile, and for an indeterminate future, electoral politics accepted constraints. These electoral-political perspectives contradicted the aspirations of the Basle congress resolution calling for workplace organisation in the present and a Federation of Free Producers for the future. Contrasting strategies had emerged in and around the IWMA, and questions were being asked: were electoral politics useful? could the structures of some form of state be used to promote socialism? Some quotations from the writings of Engels and Marx indicate their perspectives. The first quotation below is from Friedrich Engels:

We have thus seen that, on the one hand, a certain authority, no matter how delegated, and, on the other hand, a certain subordination, are things which, *independently of all social organisation, are imposed upon us* together with the material conditions under which we produce and make products circulate …

… the anti-authoritarians demand that the authoritarian political state be abolished at one stroke, even before the social conditions that gave birth to it have been destroyed. They demand that the first act of the social revolution shall be the abolition of authority. Have these gentlemen ever seen a revolution? A revolution is certainly the most authoritarian thing there is; it is the act whereby one part of the population imposes its will upon the other part by means of rifles, bayonets and cannon – authoritarian means, if such there be at all; and if the victorious party does not want to have fought in vain, it must maintain this rule by means of the terror which its arms inspire in the reactionaries. Would the Paris Commune have lasted a single day if it had not made use of this authority of the armed people against the bourgeois? Should we not, on the contrary, reproach it for not having used it freely enough? Therefore, either one of two things: either the anti-authoritarians don't know what they are talking about, in which case they are creating nothing but confusion; or they do know, and in that case, they are betraying the movement of the proletariat. In either case they serve the reaction.[98]

Marx, in his text the *Civil War in France* wrote:

Instead of deciding once in three or six years which member of the ruling class was to misrepresent the people in Parliament, universal suffrage was to serve the people, constituted in Communes, as individual suffrage serves every other employer in the search for the workmen and managers in his business. And it is well-known that companies, like individuals, in matters of real business generally know how to put the right man in the right place, and, if they for once make a mistake, to redress it promptly.

So, in their thinking Marx and Engels viewed authority and subordination as flowing from material conditions, arising from forms of social organisation 'imposed upon us'. It was also suggested that universal suffrage would work much like the workings of a business, 'with the right man in the right place'. Commune democracy might be a little different in that this 'right man' might be recalled, but as for the *format* of politics, of having one man in charge, (as with managers in a business), that format was taken for granted. In this Marx/Engels view, authority in the labour movement was somewhat immutable and essential. The key task was to place authority in the hands of the 'right man'. Further, if workers became managers (in a legislature, co-op or state enterprise) these former-workers-turned-managers would retain a working-class identity – just as a factory owner remained bourgeois when they became municipal councillors.[99] In this view of authority, hierarchies and some forms of state power could be made to serve working people.

There were different shapes in labour movements, with paid full-timers forming an important layer in the leadership of co-ops, parties, and cooperatives. The Lassalle organisation even allowed presidents dictatorial powers; some German labour bodies might have *Bevollmächtigte* (plenipotentiaries). Such people had distinct interests as against other workers. Officials might negotiate for working people, and help individual workers avoid victimisation, but experience was showing already that the placing of power in the hands of individuals very often empowered layers of officials and disempowered and weakened grassroots organisation. It was widely accepted that power might corrupt, and federalists looked for forms of social power where participation rather than delegation was the priority.

Recent experience discouraged many IWMA members from placing any trust in remote electoral politics. Two cases were notorious and involved IWMA veterans. The first was the case of Dr Pierre Coullery, who formed an alliance with 'royalists' to secure his presence in a local administration in Switzerland.[100] The second case concerned Henri Tolain, elected to the French legislature (on a slate of labour organisations, Paris arrondissement bodies and the International in February 1871). Tolain had been unanimously expelled by the Paris IWMA federal council in April 1871, for abandoning workers' interest 'in the most cowardly and shameful manner'. He had sat in the Versailles assembly as it directed the suppression of the Paris Commune.

In Britain, electoral politics was widely accepted by both wings of the IWMA. British trade-union leaders had worked with the General Council since the foundation of the IWMA, but it was widely believed that these leaders were more ambitious for themselves, and by 1871 their interest in the International had died.[101] They wanted to get elected to parliament; they worked with the Liberal Party and did not prioritise a distinct labour party. Some members of the IWMA were active in radical political organisations and in radical trade union networks. Critics saw corrupt behaviour as quite common in all forms of electoral politics, and deplored the passivity that it encouraged.

Michael Maltman Barry, a member of the London General Council, was one of Marx's allies. Most British IWMA members rejected Barry; he was briefly the provisional chairman of the newly constituted English Federal Council but was expelled and for some thirty years was '[a]lmost universally distrusted in the labour movement'. He became notorious for taking money from and standing for the Conservative Party in national elections.[102] In the USA, various layers of government created positions for thousands of placemen. There was widespread cynicism concerning persons who enjoyed comfortable positions at the expense of taxpayers. There were calls for public expenditures on appointees to be reduced and for an end to grants of land to railway companies. In Switzerland, the paper of the Geneva IWMA (*L'Égalité*, 27 May 1871) had asserted: 'in Switzerland the people are able to peacefully accomplish winning labour representation, through means offered by republican institutions ...'[103] Communard refugees however were not impressed by what they saw. Gustave Lefrançais and Benoît Malon, wrote to Laurent Verrycken in Brussels on the 16 October 1871:

> The [centralist] International has no intellectual existence in practice here, despite the freedoms available to the [men of] Geneva, and despite every means that they have open to them – press freedom, rights of assembly and association. No meetings, no lectures, no discussion of principles. Most members are completely ignorant as regards the International's principles or the goals that it seeks.[104]

Bakunin had noticed such things in Geneva in 1868-69 and had described how central labour committees worked to eviscerate labour organisations. Centralists turned sections into paper entities, in practice only committees where functionaries decided what should be done.[105] In a text quoted below, Adhémar Schwitzguébel highlighted how functionaries and officials might pursue their own agenda and prioritise their own distinct interests. Experiences such as these led many radicals to believe that electoral politics was part and parcel of a strategy that empowered committee men, leaving the grassroots inactive, passive, and powerless.

No nationwide electoral parties of labour existed in Austria-Hungary, Belgium, France, Italy, Russia, Spain, and the USA at this time, and there was little prospect of fair elections in the near future. Voting was very restricted in many countries. Some men might vote, women did not. In Italy, the electorate comprised only half a million men, and the great majority of the population had no vote. Overall, there was little interest in party-building and electoral-politics within the IWMA in Europe. Three federations (Italy, the Jura, Spain) entirely rejected that project. In Belgium and the Netherlands, only a minority showed interest.

Elections focused citizens' attention on national issues, and often undermined international concerns. Where there was a broad male suffrage, in France, Switzerland and the USA, electoral politics was something carried through on the basis of nationality or race, and this lens frequently implied the marginalisation of minorities, illiterates, so-called disreputable persons and non-citizens.[106] Often, electoral politics was combined with discrimination: racist discrimination against non-whites, and discrimination against precarious people and the rural poor.

Varied circumstances engendered varied viewpoints and strategies as to how to best move towards socialism. The Belgian journal *L'Ami du Peuple* (Liège federation of the IWMA), remembered the massacre at Seraing in 1869, when iron-workers and miners resisting an increase of working hours without a pay increase were attacked by troops; nine were killed, and many wounded.

> Workers are well and truly in a state of legitimate defence; and have nothing to expect from the governmental caste …. The time has come for workers to organise, to come together, to form up in trade bodies, and to build the great federation of labour. They have only to be determined; united they are strong, and, since there is no other way to obtain justice, they have to oppose force with force. Living through work or dying through struggle. For better or worse, one returns to the same formula: bread or lead![107]

If the option of working beyond the law or 'under the radar' was chosen, it was not out of love for conspiracy, or a determination to build some self-serving, secret conspiratorial hierarchy. Most radicals, if they wanted to avoid the attentions of the police and other agencies, could only opt for some form of underground organisation. Also, beyond the IWMA, there were rebels who did not know of, or did not recognise, the IWMA as a useful matrix for change. In many countries the option of working for electoral change was not realistic and would remain so for many years to come. The IWMA was an international, multi-ethnic organisation of labour, for labour in 'civilised countries' and perhaps beyond them. In the IWMA both sexes, and both citizens and non-citizens alike might organise; but that potential often declined as party building and electoral work became the priority.

Looking to the future, the potential utility of electoral politics was in doubt. Some federalists foresaw that a people's state might be a remote and unaccountable Leviathan, ruling over working people. In part it was a matter of terrain – electoral politics seemed to be predicated on the view that if some working people (male citizens) could vote and organise a political party (organised in geographical constituencies within a nation-state) they would then acquire power vicariously – through 'their' representatives. Bakunin, Guillaume, and other libertarians looked for power on other terrains: in the workplace and the community, doubting that persons in remote legislatures would serve labour interests once they were immersed in remote, bourgeois social settings, and most likely adapting to their customs and priorities. They were less critical of elections for local community administrations: here a community was better informed and could more easily keep an eye on things; but this oversight did not prevail in remote forums. The need for broad solidarity was recognised ('hitherto all struggles have failed, for want of solidarity between workers') but there was much doubt as to whether electoral tactics that hinged on male, citizen, waged-workers could bring general progress.

The USA

In 1870 Friedrich Bolte, the secretary of the German New York branch, described developments in a letter to the London General Council. Antagonisms between Labour and Capital were becoming greater every day, but the trade unions were in 'a state of dissolution'; 'English-speaking trade unionists were for homeopathic remedies, they wanted to cure society by becoming capitalists themselves by means of co-operative societies and other little schemes, … every office was obtained for money, and those who invested money to get an office made up for it when they got it'.[108]

Huge strikes took place in northern cities in 1872 and some 100,000 workers came out in New York City alone. In parts of the building trade the eight-hour day was won. American unions organised around 300,000 workers in the 1870s. *Le Socialiste,* and *Neue Zeit,* (replaced by the *Arbeiter Zeitung* in February 1873), serviced French and German internationalists. English-language readers might have read *The World,* the *Woodhull & Claflin's Weekly* or the *Workingman's Advocate.* The *Advocate* believed that workers could advance their interests through the ballot box, which 'places him on an equality with his more aristocratic, and would-be monarchical master'.[109] 'American workers often had the option of organizing secretly or not at all.'[110] So, the National Labor Union organised in public, and the Knights of Labor began to organise in 1869, secretly at first, and growing only slowly.

Labour was able to make some progress as the northern economy prospered in and after the civil war, but most organised workers were in unions with little or no connection to, or knowledge of the IWMA.[111] Some individuals in the National Labor Union were progressive and worked for race and gender equality, but most affiliate unions were 'white only' organisations. Henry Louis Gates has remarked that anti-black racism continued and grew in the reconstruction era* in the North, even among people who had opposed slavery.[112] African Americans had established a Colored National Labor Union in 1869.

Other communities of resistance existed beyond organised labour. Maroon and similar communities existed in several marginal areas in North America. In the American civil war, some had aided runaway slaves and northern armies. In Jamaica, some former slaves chose to live away from

---

*   The dozen years following the end of the war of 1861-1865.

former slave estates in places outside the mainstream economy. In one sense such people and communities might be termed unproductive, but in another sense they might sustain a liberated culture, support traditions of resistance and foster more inclusive race relations.[113] There was no one to one coincidence between industry and progress, and working people were fractured by race and ethnicity.

There was substantial ideological divergence among American sections of the International. Most members – especially those born in the USA – stood in an abolitionist, human rights tradition, demanding equal rights for all. A minority – especially German speakers formerly organised in the *Allgemeine Deutsche Arbeiterverein* – promoted a narrower agenda which prioritised improving the status and the family wage of male artisans in skilled trades, as if their progress was tantamount to progress for all. Those born in America might be condemned as idle, unruly, and misguided and, it was alleged, they raised issues that had nothing to do with labour; it was said that about IWMA rules, essentials, and principles they had no clue – and they sought to transform the IWMA into a bourgeois organisation. It was said that they even placed themselves on 'bourgeois territory against workers' struggles'.[114] German speakers felt that their politics and influence was being marginalised as the American-born membership increased.

Several centralist German-speaking sections used sharp practice to promote their authority.* A network based at the Tenth Ward Hotel seized the treasury of the federation. It conducted a purge, expelling sections that were, they said, predominantly composed of non-workers. The Tenth Ward network insisted that: '1. Only the labor question to be treated in the organization; 2. Only new sections to be admitted, when at least two-thirds of their numbers are wage-laborers; 3. Section 12 [Spring Street] and sections formed on its appeal to be excluded.' The purge has been called 'one of the most self-destructive acts in the history of the American Left'.[115] Those expelled, and others, set up an organisation identified by its location at Spring Street. These Spring Streeters refused to submit. They recognised that the labour question came first, and that bodies with other distinct priorities could not be admitted. However, once the labour agenda was addressed there was nothing to prevent some co-operation with other reform movements.[116] The campaign for the eight-hour day found some support among bourgeois radicals.[117]

Spring Street's firm support for women's equality was anathema to the

---

* In New York, the time of a meeting was altered to prevent opponents taking part. Similar stratagems were used in London, see *Eastern Post*, 1 February 1873; *Bulletin de la Fédération Jurassienne*, 15 February and 15 March 1873; *La Federación*, 22 March 1873.

Ward Hotel network.[118] Friedrich Bolte set out that the centralists wanted nothing to do with campaigns for women's rights: 'women's female suffrage and free love, may do … in the future, but the question which interests us as workingmen is that of labor and wages.'[119] Victoria Woodhill, Spring Street's most notorious member, had advocated a revision of the US constitution. She and others (e.g., Victor Drury and Theodore Banks) had supported the work of the National Woman Suffrage Association. For them, human rights were indivisible; without rights all workers would be slaves.[120] Woodhill called for women to own and control their bodies and themselves; she defined marriage as a form of slavery; the quotation below is from the *Woodhull & Claflin's Weekly* of 13 September 1873:

> The marriage bond is merely a piece of paper or parchment, as the case may be, but it carries tons of laws on its back. By it, the young man who secures a wife feels that she must forever hold herself sacred to his will, and mentally schedules her among his other possessions. It is to be expected that he should so feel. For him the woman of his choice is called upon to surrender her very name and to accept his, as her badge of servility to him forever.

Woodhull and her sister Tennessee Claflin, (the other sponsor of the *Weekly*) called for elections by the whole people.* Woodhull wrote to *The World* (New York, 16 April 1872): 'whoever knows anything knows that two-thirds of the people of this country are not wage-laborers … that rule would exclude almost everybody west of the "Alleghenies", as well as fully one half of all the laboring peoples elsewhere in this country, from membership.' Class identities might be fluid: someone might be in turn an employer, an employee, and a part-time farmer. American society was changing: more settlers were arriving, people were moving (within states, between states and into cities), and classes were becoming more distinct. Although the Spring Street federation was attacked for not being sufficiently proletarian some branches had weight among painters, typographers, jewellers, and shoemakers (the latter within the 'Knights of St Crispin'). William West noted that there were few workers on the London General Council or among the delegates of the congress at The Hague; many centralists were not workers, and the non-recognition of Spring Street was motivated by factional interests.

* The British Congress of the IWMA had supported the formation of a party of Labour campaigning for proportional representation and women's suffrage. *Reynolds's Newspaper*, 28 July 1872.

The Spring Streeters were encouraged by the success of the New York demonstration of December 1871. The federation held a congress in February 1872 and claimed the support of forty of the fifty American sections. They had some contacts in New Orleans where the IWMA was denounced for 'wickedness absolutely unexampled'.[121] They had the support of *Neue Zeit*, the *Woodhull & Claflin's Weekly* and *Le Socialiste*. Many former members of the *Union républicaine de langue française*) supported them, and they attracted new arrivals including Marie-Louise David (Huleck), a French woman activist, who had served on the General Council in London, and later joined the Spring Street council. They celebrated the 18 March of the Paris Commune as a holiday.

Spring Streeters feared that President Grant might launch a war against Mexico. They wanted 'the I. W. A. to co-operate with all other organizations whose objects are the political, social and humanitarian enfranchisement of the people'. They came to see that they had been treated with systematic hostility by Marx and his General Council allies.[122] They joined the ongoing federalist IWMA, approving the resolutions adopted at Saint Imier but defending electoral politics and affirming that 'anyone, waged or not, who accepts the principles of the IWMA, is eligible and may become a member';[123] an inclusive formulation.

Spring Street's most famous member, Victoria Woodhull, was a dealer in financial stocks.[124] She was something of a star, toured the USA as a public speaker and attracted great attention. Her sister, Tennessee Claflin, was nominated as the colonel of the 85th regiment, composed of African Americans (seeking to be integrated into the National Guard in New York), a signal that Claflin enjoyed some respect.[125]

The Tenth Ward Hotel network did not support electoral work at this moment. Victoria Woodhull was nominated to stand for the presidency in the 1872 election, winning support from internationalists and women suffragists, at a convention of with 500 delegates from 22 states,[126] and campaigning for equal rights. She attempted to link up with Frederick Douglass, as a vice-presidential nominee, thinking that it was important that there should be a Black candidate.[127]

Douglass did not respond to that invitation, because he did not wish to abandon the Republican Party. He was the president of the Colored National Labor Union and edited *The New National Era*. Its edition of 11 September 1873 condemned the Equal Rights Party, claiming it stirred up strife between the races; with Black men running in elections in Washington DC, 'simply because they are black'… and regardless of their qualifications. His priority was to work for equal rights and for Coloured people, through the Republican Party. A prospectus, in the *Era* (15 January 1874) declared: 'Remembering the past history of the Republican party and recognizing what it has done for the colored people of the nation, the *New National Era* will give its hearty support to that party without reserve.'

The sixteen-page *Woodhull & Claflin's Weekly* carried watchwords below its title: 'Progress! Free Thought! Untrammelled Lives! Breaking the way for Future Generations.' It was more a review than a newspaper; it discussed ideas, especially spiritualist[128] and feminist ideas, and events. It recognised that material and bodily needs had to satisfied. It wrote about sex and women's rights (including the right of married women to refuse sex). It published all sorts of contributors, Marx included.[129] In an era when most editors were men, these women editors were pioneers, publishing contributions from women and addressing issues such as nurseries that other papers seldom if ever touched. Pioneering ideas confronted the forces of reaction gathering around Anthony Comstock and the New York Society for the Suppression of Vice. The Comstock Law of 1873 banned information on birth control, abortion, and lewd materials from the US mail. The *Weekly* carried occasional pieces on 'colored' (African American)[130] and Asian peoples. It had many articles on labour under the rubric 'Industrial Justice' and about the Spring Street IWMA, but not the regular reports or notices of union meetings that were found in the labour press. It was sympathetic to, but not the paper of, organised labour. Overall, this gave the *Weekly* a liberal, mainly white, eclectic profile.

For Sorge, Woodhull and her *Weekly* were beyond the pale. Her views on women's emancipation and suffrage were 'empty phrases'.[131] Atheism, 'free love' and communal living were all unacceptable if the IWMA was to draw in Irish and Catholic people. In his view, IWMA progress would be hindered if it were associated with undisciplined and un-proletarian 'quacks'. His focus on men-first (or men-only) and linking up with the Irish, obstructed a broader coalition. On 29 January 1873, a meeting at Ward Hotel, denounced critics as 'false reformers and frequently in the service of the capitalists'. It was a cruel amalgam: Victoria Woodhull and her like were not consistent socialists, but there was more to them than mere service to capitalists.[132]

Some Spring Street supporters were not wholly uncritical of Woodhull. Her views on family life were not so popular. In March 1873, Theodore Banks opposed her nomination to the Spring Street Federal council because she had a 'special mission outside of the objects of the Internationals'. Banks and another member resigned when she was elected to that body. A public meeting on the 9th was told that Woodhull would not compromise the Association with that 'special mission'. The meeting heard of communications from Chicago, New Orleans and San Francisco and was told that 35 papers were being received each week. Troubles were expected in California, where church ministers were 'protesting against the introduction of Chinese in the Pacific States'.[133]

The American IWMA may have had between 3,000 and 5,000 members before it split. After the summer of 1872, the Spring Street federation declined: 'A generous estimate would allow its thirteen sections at the utmost five hundred members ....'[134] The Tenth Ward network may have had similar numbers (perhaps a little larger, but also declining). Some sections, perhaps as many as ten French sections, remained unaffiliated.[135]

The federalist American Federal Council told its British counterpart that the relocation of the General Council to New York was a crime: 'the men who removed it preferred to destroy it, rather than see it exist free from their interference and control'.[136] *Reynolds's Newspaper* (London, 15 September 1872), had reported the comments that Arsène Sauva had made at the congress of The Hague: 'It was the German party, or more properly speaking the Marx party, that would form the council, to the exclusion of all other shades of opinion, and if accepted the general council would be more authoritative [authoritarian] than ever and keep the great bulk of the American members outside the association.'

The relocated New York Council depended on five German members: Francis J. Bertrand, Friedrich Bolte, Konrad Carl, Karl Speyer, and Sorge. The rather unpopular Sorge had not been elected to the council by the congress at The Hague but was co-opted and appointed as General Secretary. Other persons refused to serve with him. (The drop-outs included Cetti, Eduard David, Simon Dereure, Fornaccieri, E. Levièle, E. P. St. Clair and Osborne Ward).

The centralist Tenth Ward federation claimed the support of eleven or twelve German-speaking, four French-speaking, two English-speaking sections, and one section each of Irish, Italians, and Scandinavians. It had some influence in a few luxury trades, and weight in the German community in New York, and concentrated on building union branches, most especially among German migrants. Between June 1872 and the end of 1873, it lost 200 members, leaving between 500 and 750.[137] It was a small ethnic fragment often at odds with other radical bodies.

Several radical networks and parties emerged. An 1873 convention had called for an American Labor Reform party including demands for the elevation of women to equality with men, and sympathy and aid to all oppressed nations.[138] A short-lived National Industrial Congress held three conventions before it expired in 1875.[139] It adopted a 'Workingmen's platform' in Cleveland, Ohio, in July 1873, advocating an eight-hour day; support for co-operative institutions; the reserving of public lands, the heritage of *the people, for the actual settler*, and not another acre for railroads and speculators; laws that 'bear equally upon capital and labor'; strike arbitration; 'the prohibition of the importation of all servile races' and an end to the convict contract labour system.[140] (African American convicts were hired out by authorities as labourers; slaves no longer, but treated worse than slaves and suffering high mortality.) The congress demonstrated a faith in arbitration and 'equal laws'. Perspectives such as these showed thar the shape of American labour movements was coloured not just by class, but also by factors of gender, ethnicity, and race. These issues will be considered further.

Germany

In Bismarck's newly created German empire the organising of a union or a left-wing party was no easy matter; groups disliked by Bismarck (including Catholics, Danes, French-speakers, Poles) were all harassed. German law sought to enforce a division between 'economic' and 'political' organisation; it banned women from joining unions and parties, restricted discussion of politics in all sorts of associations, and forbade international affiliations; workers in trades might join unions, but not employees, officials, or agricultural workers. Trade unionists campaigning for the ten-hour day faced difficulties: activists might be imprisoned for disturbing the peace or for discussing 'political' issues. Left unions were dissolved, sometimes more than once, while the liberal Hirsch-Duncker unions were tolerated. Ferdinand Lassalle had made a huge impact and his writings were widely distributed. Left electoral politics, had a substantial following, underpinned by educational organisations and journals.

Skilled workers such as typesetters, bookbinders, and cigar makers were among the first to form trade unions. In 1873 typographical workers shaped a national convention with employers, setting tariffs (pay rates) and seeking industrial peace, through negotiation and arbitration.[141] Left or 'free' unions such as tanners and potters were created in 1872-73 but might be forced to relocate their offices or face regional bans. Left unions had some presence in Berlin, the Rhine valley, Saxony, and Silesia and among northern, skilled and Protestant workers. Unskilled Catholic workers were encouraged to join Catholic sponsored associations.

The progressive wing of the labour movement was split between the General Labour Union (*Allgemeiner Deutscher Arbeiterverein*, ADAV, founded by Lassalle) and the Social-Democratic Workers Party (SDWP – *Sozialdemokratische Arbeiterpartei*). The tension between them had arisen in part because of different perspectives on the unification of German, but after the proclamation of the new German Empire in 1871 these divisions became less meaningful. The ADAV changed direction somewhat around 1870, began to support strikes, and won increasing support. A few individuals in Germany and Austria-Hungary paid dues to New York, but the report of the General Council, below, gives no evidence of any specific IWMA workplace affiliates in Germany. The SWDP was around 9,000 strong and its leaders were close to Marx. It had emerged through a grafting of a limited social agenda onto campaigns for a post-feudal state. The SWDP demands were:

1. Granting of universal, equal, direct, and secret suffrage to all men aged 20 and over for elections to the parliaments, parliamentary deputies are to be granted adequate per diem pay.
2. Introduction of direct legislation (i.e., the right to make and reject proposals) through the people.
3. Abolition of all privileges attached to class, property, birth, and religious faith.
4. Establishment of a people's militia in place of standing armies.
5. Separation of the church from the state and of schools from the church.
6. Obligatory classes in elementary schools and free instruction at all public educational institutes.
7. Independence of the courts; introduction of trial by jury and specific trades' courts; introduction of public and oral court proceedings, as well as the administration of justice at no cost.
8. Abolition of all laws aimed against the press, associations, and labour unions; introduction of the normal workday; restriction of female labour and a ban on child labour.
9. Abolition of all indirect taxes and introduction of one progressive income tax and inheritance tax.
10. State support of the co-operative system and state loans for free producers' co-operatives subject to democratic guarantees.[142]

Social-Democrats embraced the idea of the Paris Commune but Wilhelm Liebknecht, a key party leader, was reported as saying that he opposed a federal republic. For him there was little difference between a *Volksstaat* (People's state) or a commune; critics rebuked him, saying his liking for a centralised republic showed that he and other leading Social-Democrats, misunderstood the Commune's fundamentally federalist principles.[143] Many Social-Democrats posed a choice between real organisation (hierarchical) or chaotic organisation (anarchic), a prejudicial framing of choice that obstructed discussion of accountable, devolved organisation.

There were small, regional Social-Democratic groups in parts of Austria-Hungary and Switzerland, but these parties seldom affiliated and paid IWMA dues.[144] The Social-Democrats at the second 'centralist' or 'Marxist' congress in Geneva garnered votes but had less presence in workplace organisations. Funds that flowed into national party formations were not shared with the IWMA and the construction of electoral parties did little or nothing to support the International.

The London conference of 1871 was the moment when the Marx and Engels project of building electoral-political instruments and parties was revealed to the wider IWMA. Marx and Engels sought to destroy the IWMA as a largely workplace organisation with diverse, federalist characteristics.[145] They and their allies acerbated antagonism as the applied force: disciplining the IWMA press, and expelling critics. Their project was widely condemned as 'authoritarian'.

The developing character of electoral-politics in the USA and in Germany is explored further in Part Four below.

The IWMA in Britain

London was the base of the IWMA General Council between 1864 and 1872, but it shaped no mass organisations and lived on the periphery of the labour movement. Unions had existed before the IWMA and continued after it disappeared. Proud Britons* might hope that working people would make progress through quiet, constitutional reform, and might look with disdain at unruly continentals. Marx saw the task of countering English workers' hostility to the Irish as key and wrote 'to hasten the social revolution in England is the most important object of the [IWMA]'; and viewed Irish independence as the way forward.[146] But the General Council was in no position to facilitate that project. The IWMA in the UK** had had union 'affiliations', but often affiliation amounted only to the passing of a resolution, and the allocation of some dues, and even this limited and passive involvement diminished – from 33 affiliations in 1867, to 8 in the autumn of 1872,[147] as liberal trade union leaders with parliamentary

---

* As in: 'Rule Britannia, Britannia, rule the waves / Britons never, never, shall be slaves'
** Ireland at this time was part of the United Kingdom and had members in the Westminster parliament.

ambitions deserted.[148] A demonstration supporting the Paris Commune took place in April 1871, but without any substantial input from the London General Council. As we have seen, a mass demonstration of support for the Commune was held in New York, but no coalition was formed to support such a large project in London.[149] The General Council had been present for seven years in London but was not embedded in a range of labour activities; it had done some useful work helping to put British workers in touch with foreign counterparts to extend solidarity and prevent strikebreaking, but as Eccarius observed, this role – as a bureau for international aid – had sometimes been ignored; unions might make direct contacts for themselves. Before 1871 the General Council functioned as a surrogate British Regional Council and was criticised for failing to promote a British federation.[150] John Hales and others worked to build British sections and helped form a regional Federal Council with some twenty branches.[151] Even so in the UK, IWMA membership was very low. Many sections were discussion groups rather than union branches, as on the continent, and they existed among many other clubs, leagues, and associations – Republican Clubs, the Land and Labour League, the National Reform League, Fenians, suffrage campaigns, etc – and in this milieu IWMA supporters had little specific weight. IWMA branches expanded and deflated rather rapidly, failing to build coalitions. Furthermore, the reputation and respect commanded by the IWMA diminished, and that loss was perhaps of greater importance that its loss of numbers and monetary support.

Neither the General Council nor the British regional council, when it was formed (after September 1871) published a journal such as existed on the continent. There were occasional news items in the *Bee-Hive*, *The Commonwealth*, *International Herald*, *Eastern Post* and *Reynold's News*, but coverage of the IWMA was sparse and episodic. These papers were the projects of individuals, and their outlook was inconsistent. The *Bee-Hive* had served as the main IWMA journal for a time, but later came to advocate the reconciliation of labour and capital. If a message needed airing the IWMA in Britain had to rely, not on its own press, but rather on these and/ or other editors, or on letters, circulars and pamphlets, to get their views across.

The weakness of the IWMA in Britain, and the lack of a consistent IWMA press there had consequences: a focus for organisation and discussion was lacking concerning issues from home and abroad. British and General Council perspectives were not easily and publicly accessible, and discussion with counterparts on the continent was hampered. Because the IWMA in Britain was under-developed, it was less able to support publishing and organising. For example, in 1870, funds were lacking to print an address of General Council on the Franco-Prussian War.[152] The continental IWMA press articulated labour viewpoints, but it was rarely available to English speakers.

The formation of a British IWMA fostered a space beyond the control of Marx and Engels. This was a factor motivating the relocation of the General Council from London to New York.[153] Marx was determined to avoid the IWMA coming under the control of political enemies: 'To avoid this he was prepared to use the most drastic means, including the expulsion of individuals and sections. These tactics alienated a good many people, especially in England …'[154] Marx and Engels quarrelled with Universal Federalists, Universal Republicans, long-serving colleagues (Hales, Eccarius and Jung) and refugees from the Commune.[155] Followers of Blanqui had been temporary allies of Marx and Engels, but they and many other exiles became disenchanted. Some IWMA sections with French exiles in the USA kept their distance from both federalists and centralists. *Reynold's News* (22 September 1872) carried a report on a congress of French, German and English sections in the UK that resolved:

> That considering that the International Association of Working Men has for its object the emancipation of working men by themselves; considering that the General Council of the association nominated to carry out the programme has, on the contrary, affirmed an autocratic principle contrary to the statutes of the International and the true interests of the working classes, the congress, therefore, blames the conduct of the International in its past, and proposes a revision of its statutes and rules to be based upon Communalist and Federalist principles.

The following description was published some 75 years later:

> The International Working Men's Association which revived Socialism in many countries, produced no such results in England. There it was meant to be a dignified, decorative institution, giving lustre to a number of aspiring, advanced trade unionists and politicians, who washed their hands of socialism and were not interested in the high-sounding revolutionary talk on the Continent. They left it to Marx to deal with that and Marx *con amore* applied himself to the task of browbeating and weeding out the revolutionary socialists, those who had done the real work of bringing together and hurrying up the dilatory and half-hearted elements whom legend calls the founders of the International …

His work practically meant that he felt authorized by himself to combat every form of socialism which was not of his own coinage or subservient to his purposes – a nice attitude for the trusted member and one of the administrative functionaries of an organization which was to promote the brotherhood of the workers and to respect their social creeds ... The English workers were not even allowed to form sections and a Federation of their own, as Marx only had an eye for nominally affiliated trade unions, and these would only affiliate themselves under the tacit understanding that they would not be compromised by any socialist agitation made by British sections.[156]

Little centralist support was left behind when the General Council moved to New York: some supporters in Nottingham, and some sections in London and Manchester. By the middle of 1873, both wings of the British IWMA were marginalised and with the General Council now an ocean away, whatever usefulness or prestige the IWMA might have had was gone.

Decision-making and the IWMA Press

At a General Council meeting on 9 July 1872 Hales proposed that all* IWMA meetings, except meetings of the General and Federal Councils should be open to all IWMA members. Hales spoke of openness preventing conspiracies, and, if members were disagreeing with each other 'it was far better that they should have a common platform, which they could meet to settle their differences, rather than that they should fight section against section, branch against branch.' Engels opposed him on the grounds that such democratic openness would be tiresome and inefficient.[157]

For federalists and centralists alike, the role of the press was a key issue, as choices were made concerning who should speak for an organisation, how conflicting viewpoints might be presented, over the tone of their politics, over how editors might control or be controlled, and over ownership of presses and printshops.

Continental European IWMA federations and sections sponsored a diverse IWMA press. A substantial part of the leadership of the IWMA was exercised through its regional and local press and through regional federations. The papers of the IWMA expressed the life and activity of the IWMA and provided informal leadership, in ways that the General Councils (in London or New York) might envy. The press in the Americas might print some articles from Europe, but this traffic was largely one-way.

---

* His proposal might have been limited to 'free' countries.

The IWMA press highlighted the strikes and conflicts of the day and might frame political discussions in the light of various labour organisations and perspectives. Papers provided a social nexus, and certain articles (especially those addressing broader international issues) might be translated or reprinted. Some dialogue might occur, if one paper objected to something in another, which might then be qualified and revised. Articles reported back on local and international congresses. Editorial comments and letters might address conflicting views or criticise the General Council.

The General Council depended on the goodwill of editors to have its texts printed: IWMA editors where the IWMA areas published a journal; non-IWMA editors in London and elsewhere. The London General Council might issue press releases or print a thousand copies of a leaflet against war, but its views had a far greater circulation and impact only if they accepted for publication by the *Pall-Mall Gazette*, *The Times*, etc.

The European IWMA press worked for various language communities. Political conditions might obstruct IWMA publishing in France, but papers might flow in from Belgium and Switzerland and circulate to overseas communities. The Spanish IWMA press circulated in colonies and throughout the Americas; Madrid papers advertised contact addresses in Cuba and the Philippines. There were very many smaller or local IWMA papers serving communities, towns, or trades.

In Germany, the labour press was responsible to rival party organisations and circulated in Austria, Hungary, Switzerland, the Americas, and elsewhere.

IWMA structures, languages, and national frontiers did not always coincide. In the United Kingdom (of Britain and Ireland), there were two networks – British and Irish. Before 1869, Johann Becker's journal *Vorbote* had been published in Switzerland and had helped promote the International in Germany, making Geneva an organising centre. The Jura federation came to have sections in neighbouring France and Germany. Both centralists and federalists looked for some form of co-operation between Northern and Southern Netherlands (Belgium). The attempted transformation of the IWMA into a network of national electoral-political parties had implications where community and/or language did not coincide with the frontiers of a state.

The diversity of the IWMA and labour press was not to the liking of Marx, Engels, and their allies. In their view, decision-making was something reserved for 'higher authorities' – perhaps Marx and the General Council and/ or regional Federal Councils. Marx believed that 'those who wish to deprive the General Council of the prerogatives without which the International would be nothing but a confused, disjointed and, to use the language of the Alliance, "amorphous" mass, we cannot regard them otherwise than as *traitors or dupes*'.[158] The federalist *La Federación* (Barcelona, 19 October 1872) had a very different viewpoint:

> The strength of the International, its revolutionary power is not at all based in the strength or power of some committee. It is born of workers' conscience, it is demonstrated by the activities of its sections, and it can never be anything other than the consequence of its convictions; the manifestation and result of its fertile, federal principles. To consider the International as an army, needing official directives, which should react with a single, obligatory, official programme for all Internationalists is to negate the power of the revolutionary principle, it means a constraint on progress, and it is a negation of the International itself.

The 'Sonvillier' declaration of the Jura federation congress (November 1871) had advocated decentralised participatory organisation:

> The society of the future should be nothing other than the universalisation of the organisation with which the International itself adopts. We should therefore be careful and ensure that this organisation comes as near as possible to our ideal. How could one imagine that a free and egalitarian society should emerge from an authoritarian organisation? It would be impossible. The International, being the embryo of a humane future society, has to be from the present on the faithful image of our principles of federation and freedom, casting out from itself any principle tending towards dictatorship and authority.[159]

In this view current organisations might not be perfect, but current organisations should try to prefigure a liberated future. Forms of one-man management and decision-making behind closed doors might suit armies, or current society as dominated by business-people, and capitalists, but it did not follow that such hierarchical relations would suit working people or progress to socialism. In a libertarian socialist perspective, whatever means were used needed to conform with goals; non-hierarchical means suited the goal of a non-hierarchical society. In this view, it was absurd to expect a broad-based movement such as the IWMA to adopt one viewpoint and one policy. What was wrong here was not the intention to promote strategic thinking and priorities, but rather the intention to legislate and impose one universal line. Bakunin did not shy away from such strategic thinking, he recognised that the IWMA should be a place where such problems were discussed, and action agreed – but not legislated or imposed.

International General Congresses had the statutory responsibility for directing the association but given that no congresses were held between 1869 and 1872, congress authority was in abeyance. Meanwhile Marx and his allies[160] were intent on asserting themselves – illicitly, in the view of federalists. The General Council had been placed in London because there was greater freedom there than elsewhere, but not because members wanted it to direct the association. Most IWMA members had little contact with it. Before 1872, even those who had attended a general congress, or who edited an IWMA journal, could have met only two or three of its members. Many new people had been co-opted on to the General Council and few of those elected at the Basle congress remained.[161] This largely unknown London council might be a convenience, but for most members it was not as an authority. Regions had their own experience, made decisions for themselves, sponsored a press that disseminated their opinions and worked with networks of sections. 'London' figured only as a correspondent, offering occasional advice, which might be disregarded. So, in the matter of leadership and style, profoundly different cultures were in conflict.

Marx was sensitive to criticism of the General Council. When it was criticised for failing to publish reports, he objected that it was not obliged to reply to criticism – and replied rather tetchily that communications should go through proper channels,[162] and that the poorly financed London council lacked means. The London council was poor indeed, but it might have sent regular communications to federations for them to publish in the regional IWMA press. The London IWMA conference of 1871 passed the following resolution:

> The Conference gives warning that henceforth the General Council will be bound to publicly *denounce and disavow* all would-be organs of the International which, following the precedents of the *Progrès* and the *Solidarité*, should discuss in their columns, before the middle-class public, questions *exclusively reserved* for the local or Federal Committees and the General Council, or for the private and administrative sittings of the Federal or General Congresses.

The resolution amounted to a warning shot – editors who expressed displeasing opinions were warned that they might be denounced if they did not toe the line. When it was edited by allies of Marx there was no reaction to *L'Égalité* (the Geneva IWMA paper) discussing policy, but it was seen as an enemy when it criticised the London council. The antipathy towards discussing matters before 'the middle-class public' was spurious. The General Council used the bourgeois press when it could, and of course no IWMA journal could prevent the press being read by non-members. IWMA editors naturally disregarded this warning shot and continued to discuss IWMA policies. They could do nothing else if they were not to muzzle discussion among IWMA members themselves.

The 1871 London conference sought to ban IWMA bodies from using titles with '*sectarian names* such as Positivists, Mutualists, Collectivists, Communists, etc., or to form separatist bodies under the name of sections of propaganda etc., *pretending to accomplish special missions*, distinct from the common purposes of the Association'.[163] The General Council perceived diverse bodies as 'sects' and where its writ ran, excluded them from the International. However, the General Council did not challenge other bodies with 'special missions': e.g. Social-Democrats – here again the conference was acting in a partisan fashion, sending a message that it regarded some parts of the IWMA as its *enemies.*

Hitherto, the IWMA had contained diverse views and had grown mainly as a workplace organisation, with workplace concerns largely (but never exclusively) filling its agenda.[164] For many years, Marx and Engels had hoped that 'when the next revolution comes, … we (i. e. you and I) will have this mighty instrument *in our hands*'.[165] For the first time, a substantial electoral party with Marx's friends in leadership positions had emerged. It drew on Marxist ideas, and Marx and Engels came to be seen as its leaders-in-exile. For Marx and his allies, this party was a better instrument as against an ineffective network of diverse workplace organisations with motley ideas (from Proudhon and others).[166]

In 1870 and 1871 Marx had signalled that he wished to take control of the IWMA, ending diversity. A new project was to be launched making party-building and electoral politics the priority. To obscure this move, past records needed 'editing'. A key clause in the IWMA statutes, as adopted at the first congress of the IWMA, held in Geneva in 1866, had set out that: '*the economic emancipation of workers is the great goal to which every political movement ought to be subordinated.*' [Italics in original.] The words 'as a means' were appended to that clause and the IWMA was asked to follow the lead of German Social-Democracy, in prioritising the building electoral political parties in each country. The conference declared that 'false *translations* of the original Statutes have given rise to various interpretations which were mischievous to the development and action of the International Working Men's Association.' This reference to translations misled readers of

English-language texts. No English texts had been approved at the inaugural 1866 congress – congress discussions had been conducted in French, and it was a French text of the statutes that was approved. The claim that French texts were inauthentic, bad translations was spurious, and French speakers spotted the lie.[167]

Through its resolutions the conference and the leading members of the London council sought one centralised discourse, one policy-making authority and the disempowering of those with other viewpoints. This change involved the downgrading of the International as a broad, network of mainly workplace organisations, and the transformation of the IWMA into a network of national electoral political parties. Nothing in this reorientation was sanctioned by a regular, democratic process. The 1869 congress had neither prioritised a discussion of electoral politics nor endorsed it as a priority. The 1871 conference was an unrepresentative event involving selected members. Unfriendly sections were not invited. Key final conference texts (e.g., that 'the working class cannot act, as a class, except by constituting itself into a political party')[168] were re-edited after the event, by Marx and the General Council.

Marx wrote that at this London conference – 'more was done than at all the previous congresses put together'.[169] IWMA statutes empowered only international general congresses to shape policy, but now, in violation of that norm, policies were transformed. Had the mass of IWMA members chosen to follow Marx and his allies, this might have been a decisive moment: a broad and diverse body would have been eliminated, and narrower party bodies might have emerged wherever the IWMA had been active. This was not the case. The General Council and the audience it had selected for the conference in London had only a small following in the IWMA. The mass of IWMA members were not engaged in electoral activities and did not want to endorse that new project.

Marx and his allies used methods that enflamed antagonism as they attempted to push others to accept their viewpoint. A sequence of sanctions and expulsions followed. Critics were sanctioned: Paul Robin was expelled from the General Council; communards were expelled from the Geneva central section. The Yankees in the American IWMA were expelled by Sorge and his allies. Hales and Eccarius were sanctioned by the General Council when they sympathised with dissident IWMA members. Bakunin and Guillaume were expelled at the congress at The Hague; then entire federations were expelled. Lastly, as will be shown below, Sorge and his allies expelled and suspended critics and New York Section number one – the most important section remaining in the remnant centralist IWMA.[170]

Marx and his allies also promoted character assassination. The Jura *Bulletin* (10 May 1872) noted a series of lies and slanders and commented: 'We have received communications and letters written last autumn to friends in Italy by Mr Engels, corresponding secretary of the General Council for Italy; in these letters Mr Engels embraces the most odious slanders against the spirit of our federation in general and against honourable citizen members of the *Fédération jurassienne*.' The Jura Federation condemned this venom: 'the very character of this animosity was such that any conciliation appeared to have become impossible.'[171]

César De Paepe[172] wrote to Marx in December 1872, deploring violent injurious language. Long-term friends and colleagues Eccarius and Jung[173] broke with Marx and Engels not because of disagreements as to the usefulness of electoral-political activity, but rather because they could not tolerate their disdain, bitterness and dishonesty. Franz Mehring would comment: 'At a number of congresses, they [Eccarius, Jung] had become known to the whole world as the most zealous and reliable interpreters of the opinions which Marx held, and when they now appealed to the toleration of the Jura Federation for these same opinions against the intolerance of the Hague decisions the dictatorial hankerings of Marx and Engels seemed to be proved beyond all doubt.'[174]

The vituperative spirit of Marx and Engels affronted many IWMA supporters, whose very dignity demanded respect for morality, justice, and truth.[175] Marx and Engels condemned Bakunin twice over: if he published his opinions, he was disrespecting authority and proper procedure; if he spread his views in private, he was 'conspiring'.*

Accusations of conspiracy begged a question: who was conspiring against whom? In the southern US, after the Civil War, white Democratic Party administrations and business interests schemed to dominate, criminalise, and imprison African Americans, but were never prosecuted. In the UK, in December 1872, London gas workers were imprisoned for criminal conspiracy and organising a strike for shorter hours (working a twelve-hour day in a furnace was a norm). State officials ruled that certain people were not allowed to discuss or plan for purposes that they defined as illegal. In May 1873 sixteen women at Ascott under Wychwood were sent to prison for picketing and supporting their striking husbands (English agricultural workers). They were charged with obstructing and coercing employees to desert employers (their *masters*). For the powers-that-be, collective dissent might be seen as conspiracy; whether a 'conspiracy' was prosecuted

---

* Marx discussed IWMA affairs with Friedrich Engels when the latter was a manager and not an IWMA member.

as a crime or not depended on relative levels of community power or powerlessness. Former allies and close collaborators of Marx would have been familiar with the prejudicial use of 'conspiracy' charges to intimidate, subordinate and punish working people. They recognised a pattern when Marx and Engels accused critics of conspiracy against the IWMA. They saw accusations arising from a determination to smash antagonists. John Hales came to see attacks as 'an intrigue on the part of one secret society to build itself up by the destruction of another'.[176]

Marx and Engels attacked networks of Bakunin's friends, particularly the Alliance for Social-Democracy. That association had once been headed by Bakunin and by Johann Becker. At Marx's suggestion its statutes had been amended to meet with the approval of the General Council and it had been admitted as a section of the IWMA in Geneva.[177] However, Marx and Engels were concerned by Bakunin's abilities, charisma, and influence. They accused him of wishing to become a dictator.[178] alleged that a series of papers – *L'Égalité*, *Le Progrès*, *La Solidarité*, *La Révolution Sociale* – had made 'overt attacks' on the General Council and against its allies.[179] *La Révolution Sociale*,[180] edited by Aristide Claris with help from other Paris Commune refugees, served as the weekly organ of the Jura federation for a few weeks up to 4 January 1872. It published articles by André Léo;[181] in one of them she condemned the expulsion of honest and devoted socialists from the International in Geneva, and the pretentious infallibility of German and 'Bismarckian minds' in the General Council in London. Marx, she thought,[182] was an evil genius.*

Marx and Engels cast rebel critics as nationalist reactionaries: *La Révolution Sociale*, was condemned in the following amalgam: 'From its first issue, this newspaper had striven to put itself on the same level as *Le Figaro*, *Le Gaulois*, and *Le Paris-Journal* and other filthy [bourgeois, mainstream] *rags* by republishing their scurrilous attacks on the General Council. It now considered the time ripe for fanning the flames of national hatred even within the International itself.'[183] Engels deployed another amalgam when he argued at the 1871 conference: 'To preach abstention would be to push them [workers] into the arms of bourgeois politics.'[184] Followers of Lassalle were termed 'simple instruments of the police'.[185] Amalgams such as these fanned the flames of political warfare and obscured the nature of disagreements.

Marx and Engels attacked Bakunin in private circulars, the *Konfidentielle Mitteilung* (Confidential communication, sent secretly in March 1870),

---

* James Guillaume regretted these personal remarks; other libertarians repudiated Bakunin's racist comments.

and *Les prétendues scissions dans l'Internationale* (*Fictitious Splits in the International*), a pamphlet issued in May 1872 to selected IWMA bodies. Scant IWMA funds were used mailing these factional documents. The accused were given no prior warning, nor an opportunity to refute allegations.[186]

Friends rallied to defend Bakunin. A letter from an IWMA section in Zurich (composed mostly of students and friends: Armand Ross, Alexander Oelsnitz, Vladimir Holstein, Zamfir Ralli et al.), was published in *La Liberté* (Geneva, October 1872), saying he was 'too well esteemed and known there for calumny to touch him'.[187] The *Bulletin de la Fédération jurassienne* refuted accusations in a double issue on 15 June.[188] James Guillaume, once a teacher, wrote a point by point reply; for example, he wrote that the accusation that the *Progrès* was Bakunin's *personal organ* was utterly ridiculous. The journal had always had an editorial committee, and often Bakunin's articles were printed only after considerable editing and modification; also, where possible, after editors had consulted others. Bakunin was esteemed, but he was always treated as an equal. If Marx though otherwise, 'that was because, he despises people and sees them only as more or less as docile instruments, and with his so obvious taste for Jesuitical dictatorship, he cannot imagine an organisation in which nobody commands, and nobody obeys.' Bakunin himself commented that few if any members of the General Council knew the facts. 'Look through the list of 47' persons who signed it, he wrote, 'and you will find barely seven or eight who might have *some* knowledge of the cause.' Most signatories, wrote Bakunin, were accommodating and blind instruments for 'Marxian' politics and anger.[189] It amounted to 'a pile of shit'. This and other libels amounted to political warfare, with abusive and *smashing* intent – something that will be explored further below.

Earlier it was remarked that the press of one language *might* travel abroad. The criticism just mentioned was not available in the English-language press. Likewise, the editors of the Jura *Bulletin* feared that lies told in the *Volksstaat* were believed, because German readers could not obtain alternative IWMA viewpoints. Key figures (Bakunin, Engels, and Marx) were adept in several languages, but few others had similar skills.[190] Few English speakers on the London Council would have been able to understand polemics in other languages. Even those with language skills were prevented from forming an informed opinion, they were refused access to the press of the continental IWMA and could not read all sides of an argument. John Hales, the General Secretary of the IWMA, who did have some knowledge of French, was unable to get even the addresses of IWMA federations and their journals.[191] Access to the IWMA press was jealously guarded by members of the sub-committee of the London Council. So, it should also be said that, for various reasons, communications and accountability were somewhat limited, from one language community to another. Hales worked on developing contacts with other IWMA organisations. At the British IWMA congress, held in Nottingham in July 1872, he proposed that

> the British Federal Council should place themselves in communication with all other federal councils, and exchange organs of information, with a view to greater solidity. One part of their aims, he remarked, was to prevent the capitalists from making use of the labour supply of one country to prevent the success of a strike in another country. (Hear, hear.) For this purpose, information must be circulated, and the federal councils were the best machinery for the purpose. Citizen CLARKE, representing Dundee, supported the proposal, quoting the case of the agricultural strike in Warwickshire, where an attempt was made to bring labour from Ireland. The correspondence in that case had to be conducted through the General Council, and it might happen that the General Council might be in America. To conduct a correspondence relating to a matter on the other side of the Channel via America was absurd. (Hear, hear.) Citizen DUPONT, of Manchester, moved, as an amendment, that things should remain as at present – that communication between the federal councils should be conducted only through the General Council. The CHAIRMAN said the other plan would be tantamount to doing away with the General Council altogether. (Hear, hear.) On a vote being taken, the motion authorizing direct communication[192] between Federal Councils was adopted.[193]

Hales saw improved communication when the British federal council established international contacts. Meetings of the federalist British Council in March and April 1873 recorded ten to twelve papers being received each week: *L'Internationale*, *Le Mirabeau* and *De Werker* from Belgium; *La Federacíon*, *La Revista Social* and the official *Boletin* from Spain; the *Bulletin* and *L'Egalité* from Switzerland; *Volksstaat* from Germany; *La Voce del Operario* from Rome; the *International Monthly* from Australia and *Le Socialiste* and *Woodhull & Clafflin's Weekly* from New York. Thus, the federation was 'in a better position than ever to carry out the real work of the Association'. Hales said copies of the *Eastern Post* and congress reports were sent in exchange. The policy of the British federation 'was to co-operate with all bona-fide Labour and Democratic movements that tended in the direction of the International platform …' – such as the honest Land and

Labour League. These meetings noted letters received from Bath, Brighton, Burton-on-Trent, Coventry, Derby, Liverpool, Ledbury, Manchester and Middlesbrough. There was correspondence with France, Spain, Portugal and five other federations. New branches were being formed in London (Limehouse and Stratford). They heard of a meeting of tailors in Brussels to discuss a project for a tailors' trade International,* of disputes in Germany and in the jewellery trade in Geneva – with demands for a nine-hour-day.** It was resolved to write to express support, and to raise the matter 'before the Trades of London'.

The scattered press of 'Latin' European IWMA associations facilitated organising and propaganda, discussion of priorities, and diverse viewpoints. A collective leadership for the continental IWMA existed, beyond the control of would-be managers in London, and mostly critical towards the London General Council.[194] James Guillaume remarked that many French, Italian and Spanish-language IWMA journals countered the line taken by the General Council: there were the Brussels journals *L'Internationale* and *La Liberté* (*** 1873); *Science Populaire* and *Le Mirabeau* (*** 1873) of Verviers; the Swiss journals *La Révolution Sociale* (*** 1872) and *Le Bulletin de la Fédération jurassienne* (*** 1878); *La Federacíon* (*** 1874) of Barcelona, *La Razon* of Seville, *La Justicia* of Malaga. *Le Boletín de la Asociacíon de Trabajadores* of Ferrol; *Il Proletario* of Turin, *Martello* and *Il Gazzettino Rosa* (*** 1873) of Milan, *Fascio operaio* of Bologna and *La Campana* of Naples.***

The line of the General Council was generally supported in the German language labour press: in *Tagwacht* (1879) of Zurich, *Der Volksstaat* of Leipzig, replaced by *Vorwärts* in 1876, and *Volkswille* of Vienna;[195] and by IWMA journals: *La Emancipación* (1873) of Madrid, subsidised by Engels; *L'Égalité* of Geneva (1872); and *Der Vorbote* a monthly published by Becker in Geneva, (1871). *Der Vorbote* had been a very important means of networking among German-readers and had readers in North America. The new New York *Arbeiter Zeitung* of 8 February 1873 announced that its goal was to organise and centralise American workers, in a language incomprehensible to most Americans.

General Council perspectives were also published in non-IWMA journals such as the pro-Mazzini journal *La Roma del Popolo* and in London's *International Herald* (*** 1873). The editor of the latter, William Riley, once told Marx: '7 in 8 of the readers of the *Herald* are as little interested

* Attended mainly by Belgians and some Hollanders.
** The *Eastern Post* (18 April 1873) reported success in 22 out of 32 workshops.
*** The year in parenthesis is when a journal ceased publication.

in Jurassians – Hague – Sorge – Alliance – federation – resolutions – &c. as they are in cosmogony or metaphysics';[196] and had the *Herald* been more of a Society [IWMA] affair, 'it would soon cease to exist from lack of support – customers'. In its final year, the *Herald* favoured co-operative progress and republicanism.

Editors played an important and political role. Max Nettlau commented on the Spanish IWMA: members there were shy of having a daily paper after a bad experience with *La Emancipación*;[197] 'a militant daily would be drawn into setting out position on the issues of the day immediately, through editors' personal opinions etc, and sections would be faced therefore with accomplished deeds; such things were inevitable in the role of organisations' so-called official daily papers'.[198] *La Federación* (Barcelona) often focused on the activities of trade and local federations, carrying several dozen reports in each edition, reporting on congresses, meetings and funds received. It might also report on *ateneos* (centres of educational and social activities) and carry articles on philosophical and political themes. News of international events might be given in a few columns.

In the USA, Victoria Woodhull had become a member of the Spring Street Federal Council and was an editor of the *Woodhull & Claflin's Weekly*. To outsiders, it may have appeared that the IWMA was associated with ideas that it had never discussed, and which were entirely unrelated to its agenda. The issue of how discussions might be shaped or how associations with others might be drawn was a touchy matter in any sort of organisation. *Woodhull & Claflin's Weekly* carried IWMA notices and was edited by a member but it was not, and did not claim to be, a paper of the IWMA. However, one meeting of the American Federal Council held on 29 October 1871, thanked the two sister editors of the *Weekly* for services rendered to the IWMA. Sorge and two colleagues had sought to restrict discussion of IWMA matters and requested that the *Weekly* should carry only official IWMA documents – rules, resolutions, congress proceedings, declarations.[199]

Volksstaat, the Social-Democratic paper of Bebel and Liebknecht[200] closest to Marx and Engels, usually dedicated its front page to a 'Political Overview' or a polemic. For example, readers were told that the 'secret' Bakuninist Alliance was moving 'heaven and earth' to substitute itself for the Congress majority at The Hague, while critics of Marx in Britain, when they held a congress in January 1873, 'represented only themselves'. It spread the view that things were bad in the Jura – the federation had, so it was reported, met a 'fatal day' at the Swiss Labour congress in Olten on 1 and 2 June, and five Jura 'preachers' had withdrawn. Followers of Lassalle, it wrote were 'teaming up' with these people.[201] The Jura Federation highlighted an odious and ridiculous amalgam alleging that they wanted a Bonapartist revolution.[202] 'The *Volksstaat* knows that it lies,' replied the Jura *Bulletin*, 'but German workers believe its every word, and by virtue of its dirty manoeuvres, which are veritable crimes against the cause of Labour, the chasm between the proletariat of Germany, and that of other countries gets ever more extreme.' 'The issue is not this or that isolated passage, it is a matter of a continuous system characterised by perseverance and unparalleled rancour.'[203] Such lies incited a hatred towards socialist critics (enemies).

The Jura *Bulletin* tried to maintain a factual tone. When it concurred with material in left-wing journals it might quote from them. For example, it reproduced comments from the centralist journal *Tagwacht* on how news of strikes was knowingly distorted in the bourgeois press and commented that the circulation of the socialist press had to be increased to obstruct such poison.[204] It even recommended that subscribers should read *Volksstaat*. The content and tone of papers such as these helped shape disparate political discourses.

Some papers presented diverse views: for example, *La Campana* received the Jura *Bulletin* and published texts sent from Perret in Geneva and Hales in London. The Brussels paper *L'Internationale* (6 October 1872) carried both comments that expulsions from the IWMA had been carried out in a Prussian-military manner, and the report of the London General Council on the congress at The Hague. *O Pensamento Social* of Lisbon was a centralist paper and carried reports on their congress, and notes on the congress of 'autonomists'. It had notices of events and of various federalist sections, and deplored bourgeois papers' libels about events in Alcoy. Also, it printed a text from Francisco Tomás presenting federalist perspectives.[205] The revolutionary socialist weekly *L'Ami du Peuple* of Liège mentioned papers taking different perspectives, on the one hand *Volkswille* and *Tagwacht*, on the other hand the Jura *Bulletin* and *Le Mirabeau*. *L'Ami du Peuple* was inspired by Jean-Paul Marat, by the great French revolution of the 1790s, and by the Commune of 1871; it was very hostile to the Catholic church, which it saw as a centre of reaction. *La Plebe*, a paper based initially in Lodi and later in Milan, took an evolutionary line; it published texts from the resolutely libertarian Italian Federation as well as those from the General Council.[206] *Vpered!* edited by Peter Lavrov, carried populist, Marxist and Bakuninist viewpoints.

In French-speaking Switzerland a series of papers were published over the entire life of the IWMA, with little state interference, except on a few occasions (e.g., one journal was closed when it solicited support for revolt in France after the fall of Napoleon III). 'More than any other international journal in these times the *Bulletin de la Fédération jurassienne* informed, translated and commentated, hence most likely – to a large extent – its popularity.' A print run of 600 was circulated with great regularity between 1872 and 1878, half of them going abroad and making it widely influential.[207] The *Bulletin* and the press of Belgian federalists circulated in France after the IWMA was banned there. Serraillier, the London-based plenipotentiary for France, reported that he had no journal to explain the line of the General Council. An announcement that he had been given plenipotentiary powers over the IWMA in France by New York council had to be published in Germany.[208]

In 1873, most of the press of the continental IWMA rejected the far away General Council and the proceedings at The Hague. *La Federación* (organ of Spanish Federation, 11 January 1873) wrote: 'The International Working Men's Association is not the General Council or the Congress of The Hague but rather what it has essentially always been: a pact of solidarity and of mutual defence between all workers in the world against the old pact of solidarity between the bourgeois.'[209] Two weeks later it printed a letter from Sorge demanding that the FRE recognise the congress at The Hague – it then explained why it was rejecting these demands.* The Spanish IWMA federation (FRE) wrote to New York, in February 1873 to say, 'be sure that despite its decree of suspension fulminated against the Jura Federation, the latter will continue to be recognised by the immense majority of the world's internationalists'.[210] The American Spring Street federation commented: 'It was reported that the so called General Council, appointed by the Hague Congress, had excommunicated their constituents for repudiating the action of the Congress, and the "Bull" of excommunication, as published in the *International Herald* of March 29, was read to the Council, but it merely elicited a smile and was unanimously laid upon the table.'[211] *Volksstaat*, (25 June 1873), carried the New York council's announcement (dated 30 May) that various federations 'had placed themselves outside the International' – or, in the case of Italy, had never joined. Seven federations ignored all this and carried on regardless.

Printshops and libraries in Geneva, Neuchâtel and Zurich facilitated publishing projects, printed leaflets, books, newspapers and pamphlets, and served as meeting places for rebels. The Jura Federation took on other publishing tasks, besides the *Bulletin*. It published a 400-page documentary

---

*   The journalism of the *Bulletin* and of *La Federación* contrasted with the style of the *Volksstaat*: the former allowed readers to read arguments that it rejected; the latter did not and set out a political 'line' often insulting persons with other views.

history of the IWMA: *Mémoire Présenté par la fédération jurassienne de l'Association Internationale des Travailleurs à toutes les fédérations de l'Internationale* in April 1873. It explained why the Jura federation had come to reject electoral politics and provided chapter and verse to show how the London General Council had abused trust. It showed how texts had been edited and mistranslated texts to suit partisan ends.

The IWMA had some capacity to raise funds, print and publish. The ongoing IWMA (or perhaps the 'federalist' wing of the IWMA) retained this strength; it was built up from hundreds of sections, mostly 'resistance societies', formed in a workplace or trade, or across several mixed trades, but with a few seeking to promote discussion, education and propaganda, organised in one locality. These organisations communicated directly by letter, and indirectly through journals.[212] For the most part they continued the activity of workplace organising that had been the regular stuff of IWMA activity. For example, the agenda of the fourth quarterly congress of the Liège federation of the IWMA, meeting on the 7 September 1873, and published in *L'Ami du Peuple* (9 July 1873), was: 1. Monetary report; 2. On partial strikes and the general strike; 3. On organising resistance; 4. Revision of an article concerning affiliation.[213]

Money

Regional and central financial records, expenditures and receipts throw light on what support the IWMA had. Membership dues were set at a penny per member. Accounts presented to the Cordoba congress of the Spanish IWMA for the period April to 2 December 1872 show spending of 6,656.21 pesetas (2,293.74 on administration and propaganda, printing 709.20; correspondence and postage 709.20, paper 99.40, and 2097.87 for costs of delegations and dues paid to the General Council).[214]

A communication from Marx to Gustav Kwasniewski records that at the [London] Conference, of 1871, 'Germany was not represented either by delegates or by reports, and no financial contributions have been received since September 1869'.

Notes on financial administration for the year to September 1872 show 'Actual income of General Council for 1871/1872' as £194 14s 1½d. The largest recorded receipts from societies were from English Basket-makers (£17 6s), Spain (£12), France (£7 15s 7d), Belgium (£4 8s), and American Federal Council for two years (£4 8s); there were also two individual contributions amounting to exactly £80.[215]

An expenditure of £2 18s 4d on printing IWMA rules in German was shown, and the same amount was shown in the income column – in other words zero income had been received from Germany, but the expenditure on printing German-language rules was counted as a receipt and as a balancing item. This was the *only* such balancing item; it appears that an embarrassing absence of funds from Germany was being covered up and that special measures were put in place to conceal it. (Non-payers might be refused the right to vote in IWMA congresses.)[216]

IWMA members had no easy access to financial records, but some were well aware that there was a gross imbalance between the level of dues paid and the national affiliations of persons making decisions through the London council. Financial records indicate the substantial weight of the federations that would go on to support the ongoing federalist IWMA, and the lack of income from German-speaking areas.

Congress preparations

Seven federations settled the agenda of the federalist IWMA congress and circulated it some two months in advance, restoring respectful procedures, allowing matters to be discussed in sections and federations,[217] and giving sections and federations an opportunity to mandate delegates.[218] Views on electoral politics varied among the federalists, but they had all experienced the workings of the London General Council and had concluded that authority, where it was centralised, hardened and congealed, would become poisonous.

The centralist New York council (1 July 1873) called for a general congress to meet on the morning of the 8 September 1873, in Geneva. Its agenda was to be: 1. Revision of the statutes, 2. Organisation of international labour associations, 3. Organisation of the working class on an international scale, 4. the Political position of organised labour and, 5. Labour statistics.

On 18 July, the General Council named a provisional commission to organise that congress: Johann Philipp Becker, Theodor Duval and Henri Perret. Engels, Marx and the General Council had asked organisers to exclude 'Bakuninists'.[219] The council sent out a list of people who might vet 'legitimate' delegates from particular countries: Farkas for Hungary, Walery Wróblewski for Poland, Marx for Russians, Engels for Italians, and Serraillier or Larroque for the French. Also, to be welcomed, were people in good standing with *Volkstimme* (edited by Oberwinder in Vienna) and the German Social-Democratic Workers Party. Engels, or his appointees, were nominated as financial agents.[220] Excepting Oberwinder, these plenipotentiaries were unable to get even themselves to Geneva.

Federalists had no intention of attending the centralist event. British federalists preparing the regional IWMA congress on 26 January 1873, thought it absurd that the General Council had demanded that the IWMA should get involved in a movement only after New York had been consulted. They commented: 'In other words sections are forbidden to do anything without the permission of the General Council.' *La Federación*, the IWMA journal of Barcelona, thought the General Council 'shows no signs of life' (14 June 1873). Workers in Montevideo condemned proceedings at The Hague and contacted the federalist IWMA.[221]

Burckhardt, the German Social-Democratic delegate to the 1873 centralist Geneva congress, remarked that at the recent party congress in Eisenach, 71 delegates and three officials had attended, but he said that lack of funds prevented delegates coming to such a 'distant location' as Geneva – special pleading since Geneva was not that far from southern Germany.* Perhaps the party feared prosecution.[222] In 1872 six delegates from Germany had gone to The Hague, but the party was disappointed by its results and the relocation of the General Council to New York had produced a 'frightful impression'.[223] Clearly, a party having 74 persons at a congress in Eisenach could have afforded to have more than one in Geneva, had it so wished.[224]

As regards General Council presence in congresses, the difference between 1872 and 1873 was spectacular. Twenty-one London council members had attended the congress at The Hague, but no one came from New York a year later. Money was a key factor. Engels, after he retired from managing business interests in Manchester, had funded travel costs to The Hague.[225]

The New York council was in theory accountable to members but, lacking funds, it could only send written reports.[226] No one was present at the centralists' congress to answer questions. Its handwritten confidential report noted that for five months, from January to May, it had been unable even to buy postage stamps. Its income, from October 1872 to August 1873, was reported as \$379.79 and its outgoings as \$367.87 (about £76).[227] Its poverty demonstrated just how little support it had. Engels noted that 'on our side everyone is going to sleep' or was 'apathetic'. He did not provide further travel subsidies for the Geneva congress, and his change of heart made plain that the majority constructed a year earlier had depended on his subsidies (and artificial or blank mandates).

The New York council wrote very detailed confidential instructions – covering thirty points – concerning arrangements for the 1873 congress – but found it difficult to have them implemented. It sought to have a rule that at least two-thirds of each section should be composed of 'wage laborers'. Congresses were to now meet every two years. It wanted the General Council relocated in Europe.[228] Engels refused to travel to Geneva. Serraillier was

* Many delegates to the federalist congress had to take far longer journeys to Geneva.

nominated instead, but refused, unhappy to convey instructions which might have further increased the powers of a General Council.[229] English centralists also declined to travel or support the congress. No Hungarian, Polish, Russian, or Italian delegates attended. The reports below show that in these things and in much besides, the congress did not run according to plan.

Force and Counter Force

Centralists were determined to work as much as possible within legal constraints. Many Social-Democratic newspaper editors were convicted for legal infringements, so too were many editors of other stripes. Social-Democratic parties sought electoral legitimacy by respecting the law. Respect for national legal constraints could not be squared with support for an illegal international organisation; also support for strikes, often declared illegal, and other activity by the International might easily cost votes. Neither of the two German parties were prepared to break the law and join the IWMA.

Compulsory military service, lasting two, three or five years, was a widely resented grievance in the lives of many young men throughout continental Europe. The IWMA congress of 1868 had recommended that workers should stop work in the event of war.[230] When the Franco-Prussian war broke out many thousand union members were conscripted, and union organisations were disrupted. The IWMA press and other labour journals opposed the war, presenting it as a dynastic conflict. Followers of Lassalle and Social-Democrats both opposed the annexation of Alsace-Lorraine by the new German Empire. Johann Most was imprisoned from September 1872 to October 1873 because he had disparaged the celebration of the victory at Sedan.[231] August Bebel and Wilhelm Liebknecht were sentenced to two-year prison terms in March 1872 for abetting 'treason' – opposing state policy, although they had asserted that their commitment to the International was limited to legal action and rejected the use of force to establish a people's state. At their trial they said they would not *make* a revolution but would wait for things to develop; revolution might come as social forces 'matured'.[232] *Der Volksstaat* deplored the possibility of a new war between Germany and France and remarked on recruit absenteeism.[233] On 10 October 1873 it demanded the replacement of the standing army by a popular armed forces (a *Volkswehr*). Chancellor Bismarck and General Moltke dreamed of inculcating military values into the school system;[234] they worked to eradicate socialist and dissident thinking from the barracks, shaping soldiers as a corps of loyal and obedient officials.

Here and elsewhere, desertion or emigration to avoid conscription was not uncommon. 'Strikes of workmen and wholesale emigration to escape the onerous military service are reported from every province,' commented the London weekly *The Graphic* (4 January 1873).

In Spain, over 25,000 workmen had been conscripted to support Spanish rule in Cuba. Military service was unpopular and hopes that a republic would end conscription were disappointed. One IWMA journal wrote that *los hijos del trabajo* (the children of labour) had no country of their own; patriotic talk was something invented by the wealthy to defend property.[235] Libertarians called on soldiers to fight not for their regiments, but for ending exploitation and reported on soldiers' rebelling.[236] The *Neuer Social-Demokrat*, (a Lassalle journal, 10 September 1873) noted that Spanish generals were ready to impose the death penalty on soldiers who refused to shoot their brothers.

In Switzerland, especially in times of industrial or social conflict, workers might be recalled to the militia and used to break strikes under military discipline. Workers might lose jobs while on Swiss military service (up to 45 days a year).

In Belgium strikers were treated as hostiles, to be beaten into submission; so too were army recruits demonstrating against military service. One IWMA paper remarked on soldiers being ordered to serve on the railways to replace strikers: '… these soldiers were almost all workers, their sympathies were with the workers, and they were forced to act against their feelings or disobey discipline! What an excellent measure to induce love for military service.'[237] It also remarked: 'Soldiers and gendarmes become ferocious beasts once let off the leash and dressed up in uniform; in consequence, freedom in any land, whatever its degree of civilisation, will be compromised so long as it has an army. There are no intelligent bayonets. And one should count even less on the officers' intelligence. These unhappy persons, brutalised by indolence and consequent vice, are incapable of any honest feeling.'[238]

The wealthier classes found ways to evade military service. Belgian soldiers were recruited by lottery and the rich were able to escape by paying someone else to replace them. In France similar circumstances obtained, and university students were given privileges. The Paris Commune had erupted when soldiers refused General Lecomte's orders to fire on protesters. When the French government regained control of Paris, the army had inflicted terror: some in public and some away from prying eyes in the Bois de Boulogne – so much so that even conservative commentators were revolted. This state-sponsored savagery was remembered in annual dinners and commemorations. Returnees from penal colonies reported on the whippings, thumbscrews and arrogance inflicted by the French army overseas. *Corps disciplinaires* were organised for persons suspected of disaffection, abuses later defined as *biribi*.

Progressive labour had welcomed the defeat of the Confederates in the American Civil War. That defeat had been facilitated by African Americans fighting for the north and by demoralisation in the south, where some soldiers realised that it was a rich man's war and a poor man's fight. One report, printed many years later, recalled sentiments in the Confederate Army: 'It seems to us that this war is all about negroes and property. Now, we don't own no niggers and as to property, we've got but mighty little of that, and so, as we told you sir in the beginnin', we don't see nothin' in it for us, and we're thinkin' we'll quit'. Such thought spread like wildfire and desertions ran into the thousands.[239]

Anecdotal comments such as these helped shape awareness of military immorality. Some IWMA members had begun to think about how the military could be subverted and how loyalties could be realigned and respect for working people prioritised. Bakunin went further in reflecting on how any rebellion might organise; he urged friends in Spain to build a solid but discrete understanding among themselves, to be prepared to support the people when they were ready to revolt, to find leaders who could co-ordinate and command, selfless men without ambition or self-interest.[240] Bakunin had written in a similar vein, in his 1870 text *K oficeram russkoj armii*, addressed to dissident Russian army officers.[241] In that text he had called for counter-plots – against the ongoing conspiracy of the rich and powerful – and the construction of a popular revolution for land and liberty. He looked to a programme of common principles to help unify the secret work of some hundreds, led by a committee of persons based in Russia, and ready to sacrifice all, committed not to personal power, but rather to facilitating popular power. He did not ask for members to stop thinking, or to renounce their passions, but did ask that anyone who freely and deliberately joined the ranks of counter-plotters should renounce individual action, knowing also that they might never 'exit' those ranks, because if they did so, that could endanger every other member. Casual discussion would be avoided: iron discipline would prevail. A radical programme would be well known even if committee-persons were 'unknown'. Such ideas were shaped by concerns to build a solid secret body able to resist Russia's security forces.*

---

* Whether such conspiratorial tactics were appropriate elsewhere, or in mass organisations in other lands, was another matter, one which Bakunin did not address systematically. He and other IWMA activists might have hoped for mass revolts, but only occasionally did these hopes prove well-founded.

Solidarity?

Centralists argued that a centralised organisation in the IWMA was more efficient and more capable of waging a war against reaction, but critics might have asked: who was to control this authority, and how would that power be used? The General Council was in no position to wage war against capitalism; its authority, such as it was, was limited to IWMA members. Critics pointed to the experience of the New York council's agents. These agents, wrote Eccarius, were invested with powers to expel individuals and dissolve sections – without even a hearing.[242] Jules Guesde wrote that D'Entraygues (alias Swarm), appointed by the General Council as its agent in Toulouse, a delegate to The Hague congress, had facilitated the arrest of forty IWMA activists. Guesde wrote: 'What indeed permitted D'Entraygues to deliver IWMA organisers in the South of France to the rural police was the leadership function in the IWMA allocated by The Hague congress to a central authority.'[243] Another agent, Van Heddeghem (alias Walter), also a supporter of Marx at The Hague, later the delegate for the General Council to Paris, declared when brought before the judiciary that he had become a bitter adversary of the IWMA. So, the General Council was experienced not so much as an authority of Labour, but rather as an authority over Labour. Laurent Verrycken, a baker and veteran in the Belgian IWMA (one of the most solid and experienced IWMA organisations), took a dim view of centralism, 'being in the habit of doing what seemed best to them without consulting the London Council, [they] had, after the triste results of The Hague, come to the conclusion that they could do without it'.[244]

In the spring of 1873 the New York Council, prodded by Marx and Engels from London, chose to derecognise the bulk of IWMA members.[245] The council said that members were refusing to abide by the rulings of the congress at The Hague and that these dissenters had 'placed themselves outside the IWMA'.[246] The bulk of the IWMA denied the legitimacy of the packed 1872 congress, its resolutions and the General Council in New York.[247] For federalists, these were fake, manipulated rulings, by fake, unrepresentative rulers.[248] They rejected their methods, especially trashing[249] and slander: distorted practices which made honest dialogue impossible. In the view of federalists, the IWMA was not the possession of a few unaccountable leaders, rather it was a commonwealth, where diverse viewpoints had been and should be respected, and where members practiced solidarity.

Marx had stressed 'solidarity', and 'moral authority' in a speech in Amsterdam late in 1872, but his determination to press on with mass expulsions contradicted these affirmations. Many groups were called 'riff-raff'. The term appears again and again in Marx's writings, targeting French refugees in Geneva and London, critics in the London German Workers' Educational Society, the 'unknown' in New York wrongly accepted into the IWMA, the Jura Federation, the secessionist federations in Spain, Italy, Belgium and England, the arrogant sectarians who 'attached themselves' to the International after the Commune, and, when they criticised the General Council, Henri Perret and his allies in Geneva. These and others were subjected to disparagement.[250]

The poverty of the New York General Council was a clear indication of how few people supported it or felt any solidarity towards it. It was a 'head' with little income, lacking a press and mass membership. It struggled to publish and make its views known. Centralists had claimed support in Britain, Denmark, Ireland, Poland,[251] but this support proved uncommunicative. Eccarius noted that correspondence from Germany was being directed to London and declared, 'Karl Marx is still the ruler of the International and that the Council in New York is only a servant … virtually the autocrat of the organization'.[252]

Federalists did not expect universal agreement in the realm of ideas, but they did stress solidarity where it was most natural – in workplace organising. In Geneva, in 1873, the federalist congress unanimously passed a resolution supporting solidarity – irrespective of any political loyalties and affiliations – with all workers in workplace struggles. In their view, working people should co-operate to improve their economic situation, whatever their differences on other issues; this everyday workplace solidarity was a fundamental task, albeit not the only one.

James Guillaume challenged both the methods used by centralists and the goals they prioritised. He defined proletarian politics as: 'Demolition of all existing political institutions and their replacement by economic institutions. Destruction of the centralised state, and its replacement by a federation of autonomous communes.'[253] Exploitation and oppression were shaped by hierarchical structures, in the world of work and beyond. Social change might be facilitated through organisation in workplaces and through devolved administration, where decision-making was drawn closer to working people. Libertarians criticised electoral-political mechanisms: for them remote electoral politics – even in 'democratic' republics like Switzerland – implied passivity, reliance on legislators, placing trust in legislation (often ineffective), and subordination to a state hierarchy. Adhémar Schwitzguébel set out a critique of 'state socialism'.[254] He looked not for a new form of a state, but for a federated network of non-hierarchical, accountable communes. For him, it was not enough for the state to decree wage rises, or shorter hours, what was needed was the triumph, in the economic domain, of Labour over Capital. Other tactics, he thought, would serve only to make some official 'noise' around the social question without resolving anything.

A labour association that did not own directly that Capital would be obliged to demand support from the state, through the intermediary of those managers and officials, fashioning the latter into fund-givers of public wealth. It is suggested that these functionaries will be elected by the people and that they would, in consequence only deliver the will of the people, but today, in the Swiss republics, governments are already elected by the people, and are held to work only for the will of the people, and yet, as everyone knows, they do only what *they want*. This is what authoritarian communism promises, this is what the political action of the proletariat in the state will lead to.

We are criticised for confusing the form of the current state with the form of a socialist state. But look at the authoritarian socialist programs in different lands – everywhere what is maintained is the centralised state; the development of centralised universal suffrage, the National Bank supporting labour associations, the expropriation by legal means, for the profit of the state, of railways, canals, mining rights, forests, and finally of land and manufacturing. Agriculture, the various branches of industry, commerce, in sum all human activity would become objects of state Ministries, and in this militarily organised administrative machine, in these industrial armies, *farewell the freedom of organised labour.*[255]

The Jura *Bulletin* (17 August 1873), reported on an assembly of the Jura federation at Undervelier and five resolutions on current perspectives:

1. Complete rupture with all bourgeois political parties without exception.
2. Absolute condemnation of any transactions at all with any bourgeois political organisation.
3. The *Union démocratique Jurassienne* which, under the pretext of serving popular interests works to have labour societies adopt the path of bourgeoise and authoritarian politics, will be considered by Sections as an enemy political party.
4. Sections recognise no politics other than revolutionary and internationalist politics, having as their goal the destruction of States and the creation (constitution) of free Communes and their free federation.

5.   They will not confine themselves to the propagation of revolutionary ideas alone, as formulated above; they will work to prepare to apply them, shaping the entire action of labour societies with sentiments entirely hostile to the current state of things and strengthening their organisation in such a way that they become a truly revolutionary force. They [the sections of the Bernese Jura] recognise the proletariat of Paris, in its rising of 18th March 1871 and its demand for communal autonomy. Today the fighting Spanish proletariat has the same ideas and has opened the only political path that can lead the proletariat to its emancipation from domination and from the exploitation of the bourgeois world.

The federation looked for mechanisms that might socialise authority. In a military crisis, an authority might be needed, but even then, measures should be in place to ensure that it was directed against external foes rather than internal critics, and should be limited, responsible and temporary. The Paris Commune revolution had indicated how difficult change might be, but it had been more than 'the most authoritarian thing there is'. It had facilitated new systems of mass democracy, accountability and federalism through local meetings, co-operatives, canteens, and clubs (sometimes using churches). In previous Paris revolutions the people had thrown out the old administration and had then left the stage; in 1871 it had 'refused to give up, and for two months administered, governed, and led the city's fight'.[256] It allowed women a space to make their own demands, something that will be discussed further below. Women appearing in uniform challenged conservative lifestyles. Elie Reclus noted in his diary that the harder the struggle became, the more women took part: 'Many of them gathered the rifle of their dead husband, brother, or lover. Some girls are disguised as men, and fight in the avant-gardes.'[257]

The Paris Commune had not been the creature of just one party, and had sought not Jacobin centralisation, but a co-ordinated federalist system, working with autonomous communes all over France.[258] The working people in Paris had drawn inspiration from many sources – perhaps Bakunin and Marx, but more likely the Jacobins of the 1790s, Considerant,[259] or Proudhon.[260]

Kith and Kin

All sorts of radicals opposed slavery – in the southern USA and elsewhere. The Frenchman Joseph Déjacque (1821-1865) had lived for a time in New Orleans; he is remembered for proposing a toast for 'the liberation of all men, blacks and whites', and for publishing a journal *Le Libertaire* commentating on American politics and opposing slavery.[261] Adolph Doaui (1819-1888) a German exiled after 1848, supported the abolition of slavery in Texas, and later in the north. The comings and goings of migrants such as these helped spread some awareness of conditions in different parts of the world. In 1864, Karl Marx wrote to Abraham Lincoln, to congratulate him on his re-election,

> *While the workingmen, the true political powers of the North*, allowed slavery to defile their own republic, while before the Negro, mastered and sold without his concurrence, they boasted it the highest prerogative of the white-skinned labourer to sell himself and choose his own master, they were unable to attain the true freedom of labour, or to support their European brethren in their struggle for emancipation; but *this barrier to progress has been swept off* by the red sea of civil war.[262]

Marx focused on the growth of industry in the north, especially on the development of an industrial settler-proletariat, very largely the white proletarians in the North, forming unions and pushing political progress. Marx thought former slaves, if they were squatters or smallholders, were not a great force for progress. A focus on the role of proletarians in the economic systems would detract from a broader focus addressing issues of post-war race relations and the sundered future of whites and non-whites.

Bakunin saw slavery arising from compulsion.[263] He was little aware of the situation of African peoples in the southern USA but was more familiar with ethnic tensions in Europe east of the Elbe, where Slav and German peoples came together.[264] Bakunin advocated land grants for former slaves, which he called a measure of practical socialism.[265]

Many working people believed that industrial capitalism was somewhat progressive and might assume that some countries and peoples were more advanced and others backwards. Such thinking might foster tolerance towards imperialist wars, if it were assumed that there was some progressive momentum in modern, industrial capitalism breaking up conservative, pre-industrial backwardness.

Imperialism and settler colonialism were at work on a world scale in these times and were throwing up complex reactions. The IWMA developed branches in Europe and the Americas, and ephemeral sections in Martinique, Guadeloupe and Algiers.[266] Some indigenous North Africans fought in the Franco-Prussian war, and a few joined in the defence of the Paris Commune; Mohammed ben Ali served as a lieutenant-colonel.[267] On 28 March, four Algerians signed a declaration asserting their complete solidarity with the Commune, noting also forty years of oppression in the colony. The Commune drew support from nationals from many lands. Towards the latter half of the 1870s Italians and others founded IWMA networks in cities of the Ottoman Empire (Alexandria, Cairo, Istanbul, etc.)

In Algeria, tensions were excited by the war with Prussia, by news of the defeat of Napoleon III and the weakness of the French state. French army units were withdrawn, and some locally recruited soldiers resisted being sent off to fight in Europe. Although a section of the International had been organised, there was little mingling between indigenous and European peoples. A large-scale revolt of Kabyle (Berber) people, led by Mohamed al Mokrani erupted in March, but it appears to have attracted little attention in the press of the IWMA, and the short-lived IWMA section there appears to have come and gone without making much impact on the wider International. The French state took reprisals: tens of thousands of indigenous peoples were killed, and some 2,000 were deported to New Caledonia.[268] Deportees from the Paris Commune, among them Louise Michel, met Kabyle rebels there; Michel warmed to them and promised to visit Algeria, a promise that she kept 1904.

In Western Europe there were some tensions between the peoples, and a rising tide of nationalism. Many German radicals feared the impact of the reactionary Russian Empire, and/or despised backward and illiterate Slavs. The antagonism between Bakunin and Marx was acerbated by conflicting perspectives concerning the radical potential of Slav peoples. For Marx's colleague Engels, some peoples were viewed as progressive, others as inherently reactionary. These tensions were felt in several IWMA congresses. In 1873, the London *Times* correspondent described one public evening session of the 'centralist' congress in these terms: 'the room was well filled by an audience belonging to the best paid class of artisans, the German element, judging by the cheers, predominating.' He summarised the views of one Austrian delegate, (Oberwinder) as follows:

> The sum and substance of his arguments was that it is the interest of the working classes in every country to lift the Radical bourgeoisie into power to become the ruling power of the State, and he quoted passages from Dr Marx's writings to fortify his opinion.[269] Reverting to the state of the labour movement, he said that, in view of this fact of Austria being composed of three-fourths of an alien race, yet living *de facto*, if not *de jure*, under feudal conditions – a race who could neither read nor write – the German workmen of Austria had very naturally looked out for

kindred spirits and allies. They had found them in the German working class outside of Austria and resolved to make common cause.[270]

The Times also carried comments by Nicholas Joukovsky,[271] a Russian teacher and federalist IWMA member:

> The majority of the Geneva workmen cared only to send a man or two of their own into the Great Council [local government]; they cared nothing about the social question, they were well paid. It was the badly-paid and hard-worked Savoyards* and Germans that the International must appeal to. Henri Perret, the old secretary, wanted but peaceable trade societies; no socialistic revolutionists.[272]

There is a striking difference of perspective between these two anecdotes. While Joukovsky saw the need to organise and support the great number of non-citizens working in Geneva, the Austrian delegate focused on race, and on allies chosen for their ethnicity, seeing the Slav race as *aliens* and illiterates.** The beginnings of a libertarian tradition owed something to a recognition of conflicting attitudes in the IWMA towards migrants and non-citizens.[273] Evidently, there were tensions between those who had empathy, who were open to working with outsiders (Slavs, and others as yet not much present in the IWMA), as against those, like Oberwinder, who embraced the progress of German insiders, with little regard for illiterates. In 1869, at the Basle IWMA congress, Neumayer (a delegate from Austria-Hungary) and Bakunin had both appealed for an alliance between Czechs, Germans, and Slavs.[274] Bakunin was angered by repeated allegations that he advocated Pan-Slavism and wrote that nationalisms should be drowned in common humanity. When he came to draft a programme for the Slav section of the IWMA in Zurich, in August 1872, he set out that it should:

> struggle with equal energy against all manifestations of pan-Slavism, that is to say the so-called deliverance of Slav peoples through the power of the Russian Empire, and also against pan-Germanism, that is to say a so-called emancipation through political action as imposed by bourgeois German civilisation, which today is seeking to organise itself as a great and so-called popular state.[275]

---

* Savoy had formed part of the territory of the King of Piedmont but had been transferred recently to France.
** At the founding congress of the Eisenacher party, Andreas Scheu had asked that, to facilitate sales to Czechs and others, the sub-title of its journal should omit the word 'German'.

Racism was present in the IWMA and in the wider world of labour, and most clearly in the USA. But some rebels were beginning to look for multiracial, transnational change and realised that progress depended on action against multiple vectors of oppression. Such matters have often been neglected in historiographical texts.

John Hales' report on the Nottingham IWMA congress (*International Herald*, 27 July 1872) noted that 'the fullest political liberty can avail nothing so long as the greatest part of the human race is steeped in ignorance, want and destitution'. There was for example, an undeclared international among seamen, but one in which non-whites (Chinese, Indians, Lascars, etc.) might be harshly treated, receive unequal pay, and were denied skilled on-board responsibilities. A Strangers' Home for Asiatics, Africans and South Sea Islanders was open in Limehouse (London), able to accommodate 200 sailors. Authorities were attempting to manage the presence of non-white peoples settling around seaports. Some Brazilian labour associations were supporting enslaved workers, saving funds to secure their release; efforts that elites regarded as dangerous. Although enslaved workers in Brazil went on strike, slavery would endure for another fifteen years. In the Spanish Empire, slavery was only abolished in 1886.

IWMA congress statutes declared a commitment to 'morality, justice, and truth as the basis of their conduct toward all men, without distinction of nationality, creed, or colour' – but this might amount to a certain blindness: some historical, social, cultural, racial and gender inequalities were not identified, or were passed over. There was perhaps a 'Jacobin' respect for 'equality', in the IWMA, as if all waged-workmen and unwaged-workers enjoyed equal wealth, health, and legal respect. This mindset was myopic, overlooking that there was economic exploitation and oppression through culture, race, and/or gender. A meeting of the London General Council (9 July 1872) had considered the scope of action of the IWMA. Maltman Barry argued that 'the International ought to embrace all mankind. None should be excluded.' Engels had replied that such sentiments might turn the IWMA into a philanthropic society like those inaugurated by the middle class: 'Modern society is the society in which capital rules and labourers are used as instruments. It was absurd to imagine that the slaves of Cuba and Brazil, or the population of China and India, could be at once developed in associative labourers, they must first be made free labourers before they could be emancipated.' The majority on the General Council rejected Barry's proposition,[276] leaving non-proletarians to the tender care of 'middle-class philanthropy', until such time that they might become 'free labourers'.

Obviously, there were differences between various layers of working men and women. A male typesetter, or a citizen-artisan in Buenos Aires, Geneva, Leipzig or New York, with some personal wealth, comfortable lodgings, working with skill in a luxury trade and not easily replaced, had a very different life to an agricultural labourer, a slave, former-slave, or a precarious lumpen-proletarian living in crowded, unhealthy conditions and lacking both status and a secure income. Skilled and privileged working-men – and insiders – might seek to restrict entry into their trades, feeling antagonism rather than solidarity towards the unskilled and the outsider, (perhaps of another ethnic group or of the opposite sex) who might dilute and reduce the value of their labour. Groups with strong social ties might shape specific forms of gendered, narrowly ethnic cohesion against outsiders,[277] claiming to represent workers' interests in general, and striving 'for the realization of socialist principles',[278] but failing to grasp that the concerns of some might obstruct the interests of others.

Just how a dozen men on the General Council voted in a closed room, unknown to members of the IWMA. or the wider world mattered little; what was of some consequence was the attitude of communities, unions, or parts of the IWMA to others, especially where various peoples mixed and where ethnic issues were pressing. When the demonstration of 17 December 1871 took place in New York, there was a confrontation about who was to lead the parade. The Chief Marshall, Theodore Banks of the Spring Street Federation came over to insist that the Skidmore guards should be near the front. He was reported as telling the Hawkins Zouave musical band that the (Black) Skidmore guards were 'every bit as good as they were'. Racism still flourished, and just because slavery had been abolished it did not follow that an era of brotherly love had commenced. Frederick Douglass once wrote: 'Opposing slavery and hating its victims has become a very common form of abolitionism'.[279]

One African American had viewed the civil war as a fight between two 'dogs', i.e., the authorities North and South who wanted power in their particular social and political systems.[280] Most African Americans saw progress in emancipation and in the victory of the North; they demanded the right to fight, and over 150,000 fought and formed an important part of the Union army. Black peoples in Haiti had abolished slavery seventy years earlier and created their own nation, but that was not the outcome of the American Civil War. There were no Black Generals, no distinct Black army, and no generalised and enduring land redistribution. Race and racism remained embedded as a key chasm in North American society. Perhaps in the immediate aftermath of the civil war there may have been some hope that unions would integrate all races, but this was not to be. Organised

African American workers in northern states were mostly in segregated trade unions. Sorge and his colleagues followed this trend and turned their backs on African American workers.[281]

African American soldiers in the Civil War, had sung a verse to *John Brown's body*: 'They will have to pay us wages, the wages of their sin / They will have to bow their foreheads to their colored kith and kin / They will have to give us house-room, or the roof will tumble in / As we go marching on.'[282] Their bravery earned them respect, and some white soldiers abandoned prejudices, but others, especially in the American South, were not at all ready to 'bow'. As regards the southern states, the following overview is telling:

> The race element was emphasized in order that property-holders could get the support of the majority of white laborers and make it more possible to exploit Negro labor. But the *race philosophy* came as a new and terrible thing to make labor unity or labor class-consciousness impossible. So long as the Southern white laborers could be induced to prefer poverty to equality with the Negro, just so long was a labor movement in the South made impossible.

New forms and mechanisms of oppression emerged in the South, such as share-cropping and debt bondage; African Americans faced the White League, Ku Klux Klan and similar terrorist organisations organising 'aggression upon the Negroes'.[283] The post-war situation of African Americans deteriorated drastically. 'The slave went free, stood a brief moment in the sun, then moved back toward slavery.' A war was waged to put down African Americans, and to prevent them having political influence.[284] New laws were enacted to enforce segregation (akin to Apartheid): racial privilege, separate schooling, a ban on mixed marriages, separate facilities in travel and entertainment, etc. Such laws were the public trappings of a racist economy. Some African Americans seized land, but African American communities had little potential to protect themselves. African American forces were disarmed, but white armed forces were not. White terrorism proceeded through a sequence of lynching and mass killings beyond the law. One notorious event occurred on 13 April 1873, when around over 150 Black people, including ex-soldiers, were killed in a conflict at Grant Parish, Colfax, Louisiana — most after they had surrendered. The killings were reported in terms of 'riot' or 'trouble' in Britain[285] and France, obscuring their significance. The *New York Herald*, (16 April 1873), headed its report with the words 'Civil War'. *The Spirit of Democracy*, (Woodsfield, Ohio, 22

April 1873), had 'War of Races'. The *New National Era* (Washington, DC, 24 April 1873), in an edition published over a week after the event, targeted the liberal *New York Tribune,* which had painted, 'the negro as hopelessly ignorant and degraded'. The *New National Era* commented:

> How base is the attempt of the *Tribune* to lead the people of the country into a belief that the Republican party in the late Presidential campaign in Louisiana were careful to array the negroes against the white population. There is not a particle of truth in the assertion, and that claim cannot be used to justify the wholesale slaughter of colored men at Colfax. [it concluded that these murders were encouraged by the belief that] support of Northern Liberals will be extended to them in their murderous warfare against the negroes; and in this belief they are strengthened by the *New York Tribune* and journals of less influence.

A year later, President Grant condemned such things as 'blood-thirstiness and barbarity ... hardly surpassed by any acts of savage warfare'.[286] The perpetrators went unpunished.

White terrorism also targeted radical whites: some were killed, and others fled. Among them were Albert and Lucy Parsons, forced to leave Texas in 1873. In 1886 they became famous at Haymarket, Chicago. Radicals and internationalists in northern states had only to pick up the *New National Era* to read how racism was gaining ground in the South. African Americans looked to the Republican Party and government for protection. Whoever controlled political administrations was able to appoint supporters to parish, county, state and federal offices. 'During the whole of the Reconstruction period our people throughout the South looked to the Federal Government for everything, very much as a child looks to its mother. This was not unnatural. The central government gave them freedom.'[287]

In California, Chinese people suffered greatly, receiving unequal pay and hostility from white labour.[288] Some plantation owners in the southern states briefly used Chinese workers instead of former slaves. The National Labour Union went so far as to make a call: 'That the presence in our country of Chinese labourers, imported by capitalists in large number for servile use, is an evil entailing want and its attendant train of misery and crime on all classes of the American people, and should be prohibited by legislation.'[289] There was little Chinese migration to Canada, but already there was a perception of a Chinese menace.[290]

Friedrich Sorge, had commented, at the congress of The Hague: 'The working class in America consists in the first place of Irishmen, then of

Germans, then of Negroes, and in the fourth place of American-borns, since the Americans prefer to speculate, lounge about in offices, etc.'[291] It was telling that there was no IWMA's official journal in English and that the man who was to be general secretary of the IWMA despised American-borns.

One of the reasons advanced by Marx for relocating the General Council to New York was that the International was bound to strike strong roots in struggles there, that many (white) settler-workers were migrating there, and that America was, as he put it, the 'workers' continent par excellence'.[292] This view did not grasp the situation of non-white and non-settler labour. Some (white) trade union locals did work to overcome racial divides, but most maintained racial segregation. White labour might fear non-white labour being used to break strikes, but that fear was often exaggerated and facilitated 'white' solidarity rather than multi-racial labour solidarity. It was generally much more difficult for unskilled labour to strike. Sorge focused on supporting northern trade unionism at a time when impediments were in place that discriminated against African Americans and other precarious workers, namely racist exclusion policies, unequal pay rates, unaffordable costs of joining a union (initiation fees), and restricted and discriminatory apprenticeship practices.[293] Where coloured unions were formed, they often ran as parallel sections, alongside white sections.[294] Sorge and his allies did not prioritise building a broad alliance against racism.

Victoria Woodhull, stood as the presidential candidate of the Equal Rights Party in the 1872 election. As was noted above, two sets of IWMA supporters split apart: some with narrow perspectives, focusing on the wages of organised, skilled workmen (especially German immigrants), others with a broader agenda.[295] Neither wing of the IWMA 'successfully reached large numbers of the Irish or any blacks';[296] both were largely based in northern cities.

In the matter of race-relations and gender, the centralist American IWMA had little to offer. In any case there was little or no feedback from the Americas to Europe at this time, and the issue of building a multinational and multiracial movements of women and men were not advanced by insights from the USA. No representatives of the American Spring Street network, or of the New York General Council travelled to Geneva. Their written reports did not touch on issues of migration, racial oppression, or gender.

Capitalism was often viewed rather simply, as the creator of universal wage slavery. However, discrimination and disparities of pay, and gender and ethnic conflicts were also deployed. They were very evident when incomers from the Bahamas, Canada, China and Cuba came to the USA. Hindsight shows that in a white or settler lens, labour migration was perceived commonly in terms of the movement of Europeans moving to open 'new' worlds, while non-white peoples were perceived – when they impacted and undermined the earnings of white labour – as aliens, even as uncivilised savages. Terms such as 'civilised countries' and 'civilised peoples', were widely used. Evidently much was lacking in such perspectives, and other lenses were needed. The discourse of 'civilisation' chimed with a view that white labour should protect its privileges. Cultural differences, white racism and gender issues coloured relations between working peoples.[297]

A discussion among IWMA members in Britain is also of interest. There were occasions when the condition of wage slaves in England was seen as being as bad, or worse than that of chattel slaves. Citizen Clarke, representing Dundee at the first congress of the British IWMA in July 1872 noted that England was the richest country in the world, but 'He had seen the slaves in the United States, and also in the Brazils, and he considered that they had better dwellings and more comforts than crowds of the working men of England, especially the agricultural labourers'.[298] Such thoughts may have astonished listeners brought up to believe that civilised Britons were particularly blessed.[299] There was, one might surmise, a racist twist here: white Britons were 'naturally' privileged, while Black and other communities were damned by 'Providence'. The term 'white slave' signified resistance to wage slavery and might also proceed from the thought that *white* people should not be slaves – so, as regards uncivilised, non-whites, there might be a lack of empathy and solidarity.

In December 1869, the Colored National Labor Convention called for more lots of 40 acres of public lands to be given to landless African Americans.[300] The law that might have facilitated this – the Southern Homestead Act of 1866 – was repealed ten years later. Radical republicans looked towards the formation of freedmen co-operatives. *Woodhull & Claflin's Weekly* (20 September 1873), reported on 'Communism' in Colleton County, South Carolina: 'colored people own, and are successfully conducting, some of the largest plantations; doing better together than individual smallholders.'[301] Disputes were resolved within their association – and they were becoming heavy taxpayers. Rare reports such as this might go a little way to counter racism, but such developments were perhaps as drops in the ocean besides the racist counter-revolution sweeping through and gathering pace in US society. The Spring Street federation made some efforts to form new sections of African Americans in Virginia and other southern states, and to support land redistribution of plantation land. However, the focal point for the African American community organisation in the South was more often the school or church rather than the trade union. In the era of 'Reconstruction', African Americans* in southern states supported schools and colleges and sought education, seen as the path towards a better future. Ku Klux Klan mobs attacked and burnt such schools. In the field of cultural identity and other fields, African Americans fought on,[302] but a carnival of reaction prevailed.

Progress, if it was complex and holistic, might have depended on economic, social, cultural, gender and community cohesion. Exploitation, or force – working through one or more vectors of cultural, race, gender, and/or class oppression – would often override formal and universal 'rights'. It might be asserted that the gaining of legal rights was key: 'With freedom of the press and the right of assembly and association it [the proletariat] will win universal suffrage, and with universal, direct suffrage, in conjunction with the above tools of agitation, it will win everything else.'[303] But experience showed that this confidence might be short-sighted and misplaced.

The differences in circumstances between various countries impacted on the International. Objectives adjusted towards progress in one country might appear excessively ambitious or utopian, or excessively limited and conservative in another. Long-term objectives which appeared essential might be viewed as utopian; current goals might be so attenuated as seeming to betray future ambitions. Any attempt to impose one set of priorities – adjusted to prospects at one time and in one location – might easily be seen as inappropriate elsewhere at another time. Policies and perspectives might be preserved and applied where they were not applicable. Furthermore, profound differences of perspective did exist and were beginning to shape conflicting projects.

Gender

Anecdotes aired in the European IWMA press give some idea of gender relations at this time. Sexist behaviour was challenged in the Belgian journal *Le Mirabeau*, with a woman contributor noting that fingers were pointed when a young woman was seduced by a young man, while the man faced few consequences.[304] A discussion of women and work was on the agenda of an IWMA section.[305] A view of popular feelings in a relatively progressive part of Switzerland was published in the Jura *Bulletin* (20 July 1873): the events in Paris had passed by with indifference and without making waves: 'There is practically no respect for women, she is considered as an inferior being,

* Cubans also organised an interracial school, in Key West.

good for cooking soup and washing clothes, but in no way a moral being with whom one shows solidarity. Those among us who affirm the social and moral rights of women are regarded as immoral utopians preaching the destruction of family life.'

A report taken from the journal *Die Gleicheit* (a Vienna-based paper critical of Oberwinder) reported that there were some 20,000 prostitutes in Vienna (in a population of a million). Most were unregistered, but 6,424 had medical and police documents; of the latter 5,312 were single, 902 were widows and 210 were married. They ranged from 15 to 47 years of age. Hunger drove women – even waged women workers – to sell themselves. The paper commented that no socialist could imagine a worse indictment against a bourgeois state.[306]

Many IWMA men believed that the place of women was in the home.[307] There were widespread demands that women and children should be kept out of factory work – to protect them, to prevent cheap labour, or perhaps to defend the 'family wage'. The *Volksstaat*, (25 July 1873) blamed the bourgeoisie and capitalism for destroying family life, when both men and women went out to work. It asserted that every setback for workmen had effects on womenfolk. In this perspective restrictions should be placed on the work of women and children – a perspective that restricted women.

At the time of the Paris Commune, radical women had challenged conservative gender relations and had formed the *Union des femmes pour la défense de Paris et les soins aux blesses* affiliated to the IWMA.[308] It took over some abandoned workshops, supported co-ops, and pressed for women to be on the frontline, either in arms or helping the wounded. André Léo (alias Léodile Béra-Champseix), a radical woman journalist wrote that no revolution could be made without us; women had suffered most; food was expensive and work scarce. It was time for something new, a revolution in which privileges – of race or sex – were put aside. A new society should serve all and should recognise the contribution of women.[309] Another active figure, Louise Michel, was beginning to rough out libertarian-socialist-feminist thinking, seeking financial and social independence for working women.[310] These two women and members of the Reclus family had founded the *Société de révendication des droits de la femme* (League to Demand Women's Rights) in Paris, some two years earlier.[311] Nathalie Duval (Le Mel), one of the founders of the *Union des femmes* was deported with Louise Michel, and they shared a cabin together.

Temma Kaplan, in her work on Andalucía, wrote that anarchism might soon have been destroyed had it not been for women and the work of their sections, libraries and co-operatives.[312] Women helped maintain IWMA structures and worked beyond the church to create new spaces for new values. Popular cafés might host important occasions: funerals, marriages, and naming ceremonies (e.g., naming a girl Electra after the Greek princess who defied the state).

In the USA, many German speakers in the IWMA believed that 'the gaining of the vote by women is not in the best interests of the workers'. In this view women's suffrage was a diversion – what was needed was the emancipation of workmen first, and after that gender equality might follow.[313] When the Social-Democratic party of North America was founded, point eight in the list of its current demands was for [general] restrictions on women working, and a ban on women working in areas (occupations) where men worked.[314] Here and elsewhere, the concept of a family wage had implications: men should earn more, women should not undermine the value of male labour; female waged work should be restricted (perhaps eliminated); women should do unwaged work.

As was noted above, conservatives were working to prevent the discussion of sex and fertility, but even so there were dissidents and experiments with alternative lifestyles. One of these was Perfectionist communities in Oneida (New York state), where the idea of an exclusive love of one man for one woman was challenged; the community promoted male continence.[315] The discussion of gender and sex in *Woodhull & Claflin's Weekly* was not taken up by IWA editors in Europe.

Several working women's organisations were emerging. There were *Arbeiterinnen Bildungsverein* (Women-workers educational organisation) in Vienna and Munich; the latter was deemed to be a 'political association' by the police and closed in June 1873,[316] and in Berlin an *Arbeiterfrauen – und Mädchenverein* had been founded in February. An active women's section (*Société libre de secours mutuels des femmes*) was formed in the Vesdre valley in Belgium; it had over 200 members (perhaps 300) and survived for many years. Among its members was Hubertine Ruwette and Marie Mineur. Mineur had begun work in a textile factory at the age of eight. She worked for labour, rationalist and lay organisations and women's emancipation, writing regularly for *Le Mirabeau* between 1872 and 1879 and attending the congresses of Verviers and Ghent in 1877.[317] IWMA sections and unions formed largely by women (often textile workers, occasionally in tobacco industries) came together, firstly in Lyon, Liège, Geneva[318] and Basle, and later in Aquilla,[319] Bologna,[320] Carrara, Imola, Perugia, Prato and Florence.

Maria Luisa Minguzzi (1852-1911) promoted an internationalist women's section in Florence (with some fifty members many of them in the tobacco sector), and a 'Louise Michel' women's anarchist circle in

Ravenna in 1873-4. She wrote a manifesto for *La Plebe* (Milan, 6 October 1876): defending the dignity of women and calling for support for the International – perhaps the first text for a socialist women's movement.[321] There were sections of women in the Jura[322] and in Spanish federation. Other organisations of women workers were formed: for example, in New York, a union of women typographers. A strike of lady boot-makers broke out there in May 1873.

Women were often confined to relatively unskilled sectors, with a pay gap vis-à-vis male worker. Pay differentials might impact on union membership if the lower paid were excluded, or if initiation fees were demanded. There were two parallel unions in the *Fédération ouvrière du Vallon* in the Saint Imier area: apparently one for men another for women, perhaps reflecting gender-defined divisions in the work process. Often women were confined to polishing or lower paid jobs. Pay differentials were considerable, with men earning 5 to 10 francs, while women earned 2 to 3 francs.[323] The Swiss labour congress that met in Olten in June 1873 had recognised that women workers needed to be present in labour organising and in all struggles for reform.[324] Where women did join unions in numbers, union leaders were often men; demands that women might have made – for nurseries, or equal pay for equal work – may not have been taken up.

In Spain, the second congress of the IWMA's *Federación Regional Española* (FRE) at Zaragoza (1872) had resolved, that women should have freedom: 'if we relegate women exclusively to domestic functions, we subject her as she has hitherto been subjected to dependence on men, therefore depriving her of freedom.' The family was an institution, but it was not one set in stone, it evolved, and women were not to be confined to a domestic life. Waged work might facilitate independence and freedom.[325] The old and despotic and anti-social family should give way to one based on freedom, love, and equality.[326]

Seven women attended the extraordinary IWMA congress of Saint-Imier (14 September 1872), albeit not as delegates. Members of the same group, including Vera Figner, attended public sessions of the federalist congress in the following year.[327] Some three hundred students from Russia and eastern Europe were living in Zurich, Bern, and Geneva. For these young women, travel offered freedom, access to new ideas, and escape from supervision and arranged marriages. At the time only Swiss universities allowed women to obtain medical degrees (which the Russian government chose not to recognise). Many were from wealthy families but helped each other and shared cheap accommodation. One group of fourteen young Russian women was named the 'Fritschi' (after the name of their landlady). They promoted gender equality and sought to encourage women to participate in radical networks through holding occasional women-only meetings. One story tells of them attending a meeting of the IWMA section in Neuchâtel, beginning sometime after 8 p.m. Naturally enough, the meeting finished late, and they took some time to walk back to their accommodation, only to face a torrent of reproach for their late return – decent girls were not out at such an hour.[328] In the face of such disapproval, these young Russians developed strong ties among themselves.

Learning, especially in sciences and medicine, was seen as something that might help radical young women prepare for social activism. The Russian imperial government feared as much, and ordered its women students in Zurich to leave, accusing them of immorality and of performing abortions. *Volksstaat,* (6 July 1873) reproduced this discourse, setting multiple exclamation marks as it disparaged these women who adopted the communist theory (!) of free love (!). Some, it wrote, 'had fallen so low' that they were making a special study of a part of the midwifery course [abortion] that all decent people condemned and that was prosecuted in all countries (!!!).[329]

In the first appendix to his *Statism and Anarchy* (published in 1873) Bakunin presented the Russian village *mir* as a body that might have some radical liberating potential – if its loyalties to tsarism and patriarchy could be broken. At the time he was working with a Zurich Slav section which, in 1873, sent 50 francs to the Jura federation.[330] Personal conflicts broke out in Zurich over the summer, and these may have prevented the section meeting and sending a delegate to Geneva; it expired later in the year. It did leave some legacy, however. Florian Eitel has written that that experiences and insights from the Congress of Saint-Imier were transferred to Russia.[331] So too were texts by Becker, Léo and Liebknecht and others. Among them was a text by André Léo, *Au Travailleur des campagnes,* signed by the 'Workers of Paris', and printed in April 1871 as an appeal to peasants to support the rebels of the Paris Commune.[332]

Armand Ross (Michail Sazin) wrote: 'Bakunin, after living some two months among women students in Zurich, accorded a great importance to the participation in our revolutionary activity of the female element.'[333] Bakunin drafted the section's programme including a call for the complete equality of rights and duties for women and men. In contrast, the German *Sozialdemokratische Arbeiterpartei,* only demanded limits to the working day to protect women and children. Several Russian-language texts were published in Zurich and Geneva, e.g., *Ausgaben der Sozialrevolutionären Partei* (Tasks of the Social-Revolutionary Party), *Istoritscheskie Rasvitie*

Internacionala (The Historical Development of the International).[334] 'Fritschi' women worked with Peter Lavrov, preparing the journal *Vpered!* (Forward), and later supported Joukovsky, Ralli and others in publishing the journal *Rabotnik* in Geneva. Russian exiles – women and men – supported reading rooms and printshops in Paris, Geneva, and Zurich. Several 'Fritschi' members met up in Moscow towards the end of 1874. Ralli published *Sytye i golodnye* (The Affluent and the Hungry) in 1875, a book looking at the position of working people and the International. These publications were intended for a popular readership and were smuggled into Russia. Some Fritschi attempted to spread propaganda; several of them were arrested but were supported by comrades. (A Pan-Russian Social-Revolutionary organisation was formed, in which some members advocated celibacy;[335] its programme was derived from the Jura federation and the Zurich Slav section.)[336] By 1877 there were several socialist circles in larger industrial centres involving factory workers and students.[337] Hundreds of young radicals were detained, and some died in prison. Vera Figner was one of the assassins of Alexander II, in 1881.

Speakers at the two 1873 congresses referred to *ouvriers* (male workers), but not to *ouvrières* (women workers). Some work was out-sourced rather than concentrated in factories.[338] The federalists noted that some workers did not produce for exchange but were nevertheless exploited. Production was perhaps mediated through the family and often women did not do the selling. There appears to have been little or no discussion of gender issues at either 1873 congress.[339] Two women delegates, Sattler and Boulanger, both seamstresses, represented the central section of working women in Geneva and attended the centralist congress, but there are no records of their contributions.[340] Neither wing of the IWMA defined itself as an organisation for both women and men.[341]

Part 2

The Official Report of the Sixth Congress,
1-6 September 1873

[James Guillaume noted that the federalist congress, 'decided that the Jura Federation should be responsible for publishing the *Official Report* of the congress's deliberations, as a brochure, in French, and that this should consist of an in-extenso report of public sessions, and a simple extract of administrative sessions.' Guillaume edited the *Official Report* following these guidelines.[342] The *Report* was printed in July of 1874 and sold at 60 centimes a copy.[343]]

[Introduction]

The general congress held in Geneva from the first to sixth September 1873, marked the beginning of a new era in the International. After the congress of The Hague, where a malleable artificial majority, obeying the orders an authoritarian clique smothered the voices of the delegates of the IWMA federations, the entire International gave voice to indignant protests. The regional federations refused to recognise the General Council, which the majority at The Hague had located in New York, and, while they waited for a further general congress, which would allow them to annul the work of the authoritarians, they concluded among themselves a special pact for mutual defence and solidarity.

Every federation disavowed the resolutions of The Hague and, with the General Council having been declared deposed, a question arose: how should one proceed to organise the general congress for 1873? Only one answer to this question was possible: it was up to the federations to take the initiative freely, to propose and adopt whatever measures they thought necessary.

At its congress of 26-27th April 1873, the Jura Federation, voted for the following resolution:

Considering, that in line with the general statutes [which set out that] 'as of right the general congress of the International should assemble each year, without there being any need for a call from Council General', the Jura Federation suggests to all the Federations of the International, to assemble in a General Congress on Monday 1st September 1873, in a Swiss city.

Some weeks later the Belgian Federal Council proposed, in a circular addressed to every regional federation, that the Jura Federation should take responsibility for organising the General Congress of 1873. In consequence, the Jura Federation chose Geneva to be the location for the congress; and, through a circular dated 8 July 1873, the Federal Committee based in Le Locle invited delegates of the regional Federations to assemble in Geneva, on Sunday 31 August at the Brasserie Schiess, (in the Pâquis area), for the Sixth General Congress of the International to open on the next day, 1 September. The Congress agenda adopted by the Federations, was to be as follows:

- The ratification of the pact of solidarity between the free federations of the International, and the revision of the general statutes of the Association.
- The General Strike.
- The universal organisation of resistance and the thorough completion of labour statistics.

On Sunday 31 August the delegates who had arrived in Geneva, held a preparatory meeting in the offices of the local Propaganda Section. There they were informed that the New York General Council had called a meeting of its followers which was to be held in Geneva on 8 September.

The sessions of the General Congress opened on the following day, Monday 1 September.

*LIST OF DELEGATES**
To the General Congress held in Geneva, 1 September 1873

Belgium

VERRYCKEN, Laurent, baker, delegate of the Belgian Federation, elected by the Antwerp regional congress.
CORNET, Fidèle, mechanic, delegate of the Central Federation.

---

* Countries were listed in alphabetical order in the French text, so *Espagne* came earlier; here it appears later.

VAN DEN ABEELE, Henri, merchant, delegate of the Antwerp Federation.

MANGUETTE, Laurent, weaver, delegate of the Vesdre Valley Federation.

DAVE, Victor, journalist, delegate of Verviers mechanics' section.

England

HALES, John: weaver, delegate of the English Federal Council and of the Liverpool section.

ECCARIUS, [Johann] George, tailor, delegate of the English Federal Council.

Italy

COSTA, Andrea, commercial employee, delegate of the federations of Umbria and the Marches, of the socialist propaganda circles of Tarento and Palermo, of the sections of Venice, Poggibonsi, Sienna, Imola, Faenza, Pisa and Menfi.

BERT, Cesare, mechanic, delegate of the 'Proletarian Emancipation' society, and of the International section of Turin.

MATTEI, Francesco, delegate of the Aquila (Abruzzi) section.

CYRILLE, Victor, employee, delegate of four sections of Florence and of sections of Livorno, Pomarance, Cortona and Burolo.

France*

(delegates of the various French sections)

PINDY, [Jean-] Louis, engraver (also named below).

PERRARE, [Antoine] metal worker (also named below).

BROUSSE, Paul, chemist (also named below).

MONTELS, Jules, commercial employee.

ALERINI, Ch[arles]., chemist, (also named below).

Jura

PINDY, Louis, engraver, (already named), delegate of the Jura Federal Committee, of the section of Porrentruy and of one section in Alsace.

SPICHIGER, Auguste, engraver, delegate engravers' and ornamentalists' section of Le Locle.

ANDRIÉ, Alfred, box maker, delegate of the Sonvilier and Saint Imier social study circles and of the engravers' and ornamentalists' section of the Courtelary district.

---

* To avoid providing evidence for the French authorities, some names of delegates (Henri Boriasse, Camille Camet, and others). and sections, were not published.

GUILLAUME, James, professor, delegate of the Neuchâtel section.
CLARIS, A[ristide], journalist and JOUKOVSKY, N[icholas]., professor, delegates of the Revolutionary Socialist Propaganda and Action Section of Geneva.
ANDIGNOUX [Édouard], tailor, OSTYN [Charles], copper turner, PERRARE [Antoine], metal worker (already named), DUMARTHERAY [François], lamp-maker, delegates of the *Avenir* section of Geneva.

The Netherlands

VAN DEN ABEELE, Henri, merchant (already named) delegate of the Dutch Federation, elected by the Amsterdam regional congress.

Spain

FARGA PELLICER, Raphaël, typesetter, delegate of the Spanish Regional Federation and delegate of the Barcelona local federation.
GARCIA VIÑAS, José, medical student, delegate of the Spanish Regional Federation.
ALERINI, Charles, chemist, delegate of the Spanish Regional Federation, and of the French language section of Barcelona. (already named)
MARQUET, José, sheath-maker, delegate of the Spanish Regional Federation.
BROUSSE, Paul, chemist, delegate of the Spanish Regional Federation. (already named)

MONDAY 1 SEPTEMBER – FIRST SESSION (ADMINISTRATIVE)

The provisional congress panel, charged with preparing the material organisation of the congress, and nominated by the Revolutionary Socialist Propaganda and Action Section of Geneva, comprises comrades Fuliquet, president engraver; Monin, Noro, assessors; Joukovsky, Claris, secretaries. The session was opened at 9 a.m. by comrade Fuliquet welcoming delegates, remarking on the importance of the congress, and hoping that personal matters would not enter into its deliberations.

A commission to verify credentials was immediately nominated, as suggested by Guillaume, i.e., with one member for each Regional Federation. It was formed by comrades: Costa, for Italy; Guillaume, for the Jura; Verrycken, for Belgium; Van den Abeele, for the Netherlands; and Hales, for Britain. It was agreed to reserve a place on this commission for a member to be nominated by the Spanish delegates, as and when they arrived. To allow the commission to accomplish this check a two-hour suspension of the session was proposed, put to the vote, and unanimously adopted.

At 11.30 a.m., the session reconvened. Van den Abeele reported for the credentials' verification commission approving the admission of the following delegates:

Bert, Mattei, Costa, Cyrille, for Italy.
Eccarius, Hales, for Britain.
Van den Abeele for the Netherlands.
Cornet, Dave, Manguette, Van den Abeele, Verrycken for Belgium.
Andrié, Guillaume, Spichiger, Pindy, Claris, Joukovsky, Andignoux, Ostyn, Perrare, Dumartheray, for the Jura.

The reporter noted that the Socialist Propaganda and Action Section of Geneva was represented by two delegates, comrades Claris and Joukovsky; and that the same applied to the Avenir section of Geneva, represented by four comrades, Andignoux, Ostyn, Perrare, Dumartheray; given that each section was entitled to only one delegate, it therefore proposed that at any one time the role of delegate for these sections should be rotated.

These initial conclusions of the report were unanimously adopted.

The reporter then announced that citizen [Carlo] Terzaghi[344] of Turin, had placed in the hands of the commission three papers, by virtue of which he requested admission to the congress as a delegate. These three papers are 1) a credential emanating from a group entitled the Intransigent Section of Turin, 2) a credential emanating from a group entitled the Intransigent Section of Treia, and 3) a credential delivered by the Society for Mutual Aid of butchers of Catane. The latter society does not belong to the International and so may not send a delegate to the congress; as for the groups entitled Intransigent Section of Turin and Treia, the commission, having taken the advice of the Italian delegates, has been unable to consider these groups as International sections. Consequently, the commission proposes that the congress should adopt the following resolution:

Considering that the credentials of citizen Terzaghi arise not from sections of the International but from sections entitling themselves *Intransigentes*, a word which has no significance for the congress, congress rejects the credentials of the *Intransigent Sections of Turin* and *Treia*, as well as that of the *Society for Mutual Aid of butchers of Catane* an association which does not form a part of the International.

Terzaghi replied that his presence was proof that the said sections do indeed belong to the international; and that if they do not belong to the Italian federation, that is so because that federation contains followers of the Garibaldi and Mazzini movements, representing authoritarian principles that he and his friends reject. It is for this reason that they thought it sensible to adopt the name of Intransigents.

Guillaume observed that the Italian Federation was not the issue, rather the entire matter came down to knowing if the Intransigent Sections really existed and whether these sections were part of the International.

Bert, in the name of the Turin internationalists that he represented, declared that he did not wish to engage Terzaghi in discussion, because he would then be forced to take the matter onto the personal level, something that he wanted to avoid.

Costa said that the so-called *Intransigent* sections were only created to fight against the Italian Federation of the IWMA for the benefit of the government. As for Terzaghi's assertion that the federation was composed of followers of Garibaldi and Mazzini, that was such an absurd fable, that it wasn't worth the trouble of refuting.

The Spanish delegates arrived at that moment, and the session was suspended to allow their credentials to be checked. One of the Spanish delegates, comrade Farga Pellicer, joined the commission to verify credentials,

When the session resumed, the reporter proposed the validation of the Spanish credentials. This proposal was accepted unanimously and comrades Farga, Viñas, Alerini, Marquet and Brousse were admitted as delegates.

Discussion of the Terzaghi matter then resumed. *Joukovsky* said that the groups calling themselves intransigent sections did not belong to the International. The proof, he said, was to be found in Terzaghi's inability to produce their statutes when these were requested. Therefore, he concurred in the rejection of Terzaghi's credentials.

Terzaghi replied he could not show these statutes because they had not yet been printed. He added that he had appraised the Jura federation that he had been delegated to participate in the congress and that no response had been made to his letter, addressed to comrade Guillaume.

Guillaume replied that he had received a letter from citizen Terzaghi, advising that he would be coming as a delegate to the congress, but that this letter did not prove that the intransigent sections existed. He called on citizen Terzaghi to declare that he was not a paid employee of the Italian government.

Terzaghi admitted that he was employed in the administration of the lottery.

Dave was astounded that the editor of a journal as violent as *Discussione* could publish intransigent articles without being disturbed and without losing his job.

Terzaghi replied that he was not directly employed by the government, he was only a lottery subcontractor, and his job did not have an official character. He admitted, when a delegate called on him to do so, that he had used the bourgeois courts in his disputes with adversaries.

As no one wanted to speak further, the commission's proposal was put to the vote and adopted unanimously excepting the vote of the delegate of the Avenir section. The president then invited citizen Terzaghi to withdraw as the congress was in an administrative session.* The session rose half an hour after midday.

MONDAY 1 SEPTEMBER – SECOND SESSION (PUBLIC)

A roll-call was called when the session began; with that formality done, *Fuliquet*, president of the provisional panel, invited congress to form a definitive congress panel.

Van den Abeele proposed a congress panel formed by each regional federation electing one member, leaving it to the panel to choose a president from among their number. That suggestion was adopted, and comrades Eccarius (Britain), Verrycken (Belgium), Viñas (Spain), Van den Abeele (Netherlands), Costa (Italy) and Pindy (Jura) were chosen, each by their respective federations to seat themselves as the congress panel. They elected Comrade Verrycken as president. The panel then co-opted as secretaries for the sessions, non-delegate comrades Desesquelles, Nora and Monin (all three members the Socialist Propaganda and Action Section of Geneva).

Van den Abeele asked congress kindly to approve giving priority on the agenda to the matter of voting by Regional Federation; he said he and other delegates, had an imperative mandate on this point.

Congress decided to begin with the reading of reports, as proposed by Guillaume.

Van den Abeele asked that his request be noted in the congress report. The congress moved on to the reading of each federation's reports. *Brousse* translated the written report of the Spanish Regional Federation, set out as follows.

---

* Public sessions were open, administrative sessions were for members only.

INTERNATIONAL WORKING MEN'S ASSOCIATION
Spanish Regional Federation
REPORT of the Federal Commission presented to the 6th General Congress of the International Workers' Association meeting at Geneva.*

Comrade delegates,

It is a pleasure for our Federal commission to inform you of the key facts relating to our regional federation since the Saint Imier International Congress. Both before and since the meetings of the congresses of The Hague and Saint Imier, the individuals who formed the so-called 'New Madrid Federation'** worked ceaselessly, using defamation and slanders, to divide and disorganise our regional federation. Despite all their efforts these disorganisers failed. When our delegates reported back to the Barcelona federation on the decrees and resolutions of these two general congresses, every section of the federation called for a third regional congress to meet without delay, with the goal of deciding what approach the Spanish Federation should take regarding the proceedings of these two congresses. Consequently, the Federal Council published the proposals of the section of Barcelona, along with reports of these congresses. When the local federations had been consulted, the majority of Internationalists decided that the third Spanish Regional Congress should meet in Cordoba on 25 December 1872. 20,402 internationalists were represented through 42 local federations, based on 236 sections. Next, 28 local federations which had unable to have themselves represented declared in favour of anarchist and collectivist principles and five other federations sent their congratulations to this congress, such that a total of 331 sections, composed of 23,601 internationalists refused to approve the authoritarian decisions of the congress of The Hague.

The congress of Cordoba,[345] composed of 50 delegates, representing, as can be seen, the immense majority of Spanish internationalists, rejected unanimously the decisions of the congress of The Hague, and refused to recognise its authoritarian decisions. It also expressed its approval of the Saint Imier Congress supporting the 'Pact of Friendship, Solidarity and Mutual Defence' proposed there. Every decision of the Congress of Cordoba was approved by the very great majority of Spanish internationalists who took part in the vote, and [only] very small numbers rejected a few decisions.***

---

*   See also a report on developments in Spain in *Woodhull & Claflin's Weekly* (New York, 27 September 1873).
**   A small group, allies of Marx and Engels, publishing *La Emancipación*.
***   A short congress report in the *Bulletin de la Fédération Jurassienne*, 15 January 1873. (translator's notes).

Those who acted for the authoritarians in our region, when confronted by solemn protests against their working, resolved, on 2 February, to constitute a sham Federal Council of the Spanish Regional in Valencia, and strove for two months to found a new Regional Federation, something which achieved nothing, since (as those who took part admitted) the sham Federal council could obtain only the payment of 40 dues from various places, proving just how few of these authoritarians were here among us. The members of this sham Federal Council soon came to understand that their efforts helped only the bourgeois cause, and, in contrast, how urgent it was to work to develop and defend the real Regional Federation. They then announced the dissolution of their Federal Council, and all those who had separated themselves from the Valencia federation returned and reunited with their brothers in that city.[346]

With the dissolution of the pseudo-Federal Council and with the death of the authoritarian organ *La Emancipación*, one may consider finished the campaign of Karl Marx's agents in Spain. It had only led to an utter fiasco.

The condition of our Regional Federation, as shown below, will allow you to judge how considerable is its development and the number of strikes that have been won.

We have been very active in spreading (verbal and written) propaganda. Many commissions have criss-crossed various communities and regions, promoting the principles of revolutionary socialism among workers; this mission has produced excellent results for the great cause of social revolution. New journals defending collectivism and anarchy have appeared: *La Solidarité Révolutionnaire* of Barcelona (a paper produced by French exiles), *El Orden* of Cordoba, *El Obrero* of Grenada, and *La Internacional* of Malaga. They have, moreover successfully complimented the work of *La Federación* of Barcelona, *El Condenado* of Madrid and *La Revista social* of Gracia, spreading the federalist principles that are accepted enthusiastically by Spanish internationalists.

The proclamation of the Republic on 11 February of this year, having in no way changed the exploitation which the bourgeoisie imposes on working people, produced as a natural consequence a great movement of support for the International, showing the correctness of our propaganda, which always consists of advising the proletariat that its radical and complete emancipation has to be the work of the working class itself, and nothing should be expected either from the bourgeoisie, or from governments. The tyranny of the bourgeoisie and of the agents of the republican government, who viewed with displeasure the developing International and the repeated success of organised labour, soon made itself felt.

The International in Spain did not have to suffer such numerous persecutions, so many slanders, so many terrible things, in the era of monarchical domination when the likes of Sagasta and Candau[347] made our association illegal, as regards bourgeois law, as it has had to suffer since the proclamation of the Republic. We must outline briefly the most remarkable facts so that our brothers in the labour movement can understand what is to be expected from bourgeois parties, however radical or democratic they may pretend to be. At Paradas the mass of the people, after a successful strike, joined the International. The town council (*Ayuntamiento*), fearing a loss of popularity, demanded a levy from the bourgeoisie in order to influence the governor so that he might order the closure of the local of our federation. That local was attacked, and furniture was broken or destroyed along with the documents contained.

At *Carmona*, workers of every trade, 800 in number, obtained success after a very brief strike. The town council and the bourgeoisie, always ready to revenge themselves on workers, sought labourers from other places, and, while a police group arrested the commission that had been elected by the people to inform rural labourers of what was happening, another group of henchmen headed by the *alcade* (municipal magistrate), broke down the door of the federation local, pillaged furniture and documents, seized the money they found, and after this pillage, destroyed the stored goods, which were the collective property of the Internationalists. A similar act of vandalism provoked a conflict, followed by an exchange of gunfire of some four hours between the people and the agents of authority. There can be no doubt that if the latter had not received the help of 2,000 men returning from Seville, they would have had to pay for their infamous provocation. The result of this conflict was that forty of our own were imprisoned and other comrades exiled.

At *Seville* the authorities, using internal struggles in the Republican Party as a pretext, arrested and persecuted workers of the International who were in no way involved in their squabbles.

At *Valencia*, the commission responsible for the administration of a strike was arrested, and its members were abused. Labour meetings, which had at first been authorised, were now banned, and on this occasion, some of the militia was converted into secret police; and lastly the homes of many federation members were violated.

At *Loja*, 108 Internationalists were expelled without reason from the locality; they were attacked as if they were wild beasts, and people called for their heads. [The secrecy of] Written correspondence, something sacred, was cynically violated, and read in public, a dishonour to bourgeois democracy and a great disgrace for the so-called Republican government.

At *Barcelona*, an atrocious crusade was launched against the International. A few workers supported the bourgeoisie and its slanderous rage, and this hatred turned out arrest warrants against several comrades, and others were seized shamelessly and indecently; mouths full of lies accused them of being the editors of the socialist journal *La Solidarité révolutionnaire*, of being organised by Carlists, and on this account arrest warrants were issued against them.

At *Palma de Majorca*, the *alcade* impeded freedom of speech and prevented comrades from speaking at a public meeting, on the pretext that their ideas were not to his liking and were certainly intended to incite conflict. At *Malaga*, the dictator, Solier, finding himself defeated in elections for the Committee of Public Safety, ordered his agents to seize some of our comrades and to send them off to Africa. His acts provoked a fratricidal struggle which for seven hours flooded the city streets with blood. At *Valladolid*, vile and cowardly slanders were thrown at Internationalists; republican volunteers went so far as to attempt to assassinate a comrade, and he was forced to leave the area. Not wishing to allow a propaganda of ideas the governor of *Leon* prohibited the entry into the city of delegates of the Federal Commission. Not content with this authoritarian act, he sent a telegraph to his colleagues in *Valencia*, and, when our comrades arrived, they were thrown into a dungeon, left there for thirty hours, and then released, without ever being told what the grounds might have been for their unjust and arbitrary detention.

At *Jerez*, after several acts of persecution, the judge and his agents pillaged the locals of the bakers and agricultural workers' sections, broke up their furniture and carried off their documents. The indignant people organised a demonstration, and the town council, terrified by possible consequences, resigned and was replaced by another composed of internationalists and intransigent workers. But, some weeks later that new council was forcibly dissolved, and the bourgeoisie again took possession of the administration and interests of the commune.

In the town of *Sanlúcar de Barrameda* [province of Cadiz], sometime after the proclamation of the Republic, a bourgeois by the name of Manjon summoned the republican militia and ordered them to fire on the front of the federation local, just as its members were meeting for a general assembly. When the volunteers heard the officer's orders, they threw down their arms and that particular bourgeois [official] himself threw his sword away. The arms were taken by the internationalists and returned to the authorities. A little later, the *alcade* and the judge prepared an attack on the federation.

They ordered the carabineers (custom guards) and civil guards to form up; and when these troops were set, ready to assassinate a defenceless people, the judge and the *alcade* ordered the closure of the federation local. But the people of Sanlúcar composed almost entirely of internationalists* promptly demanded their violated rights and dissolved the town council, making the local council of the federation responsible for the administration of the municipality. Various revolutionary measures were put in place, such as the demolition of churches and convents; a tax of 15,000 *duros* (125,000 francs) imposed on the bourgeoisie, also the latter were obliged to provide work for the unemployed.[348]

Lastly, in *Alcoy*, workers of all trades held a general strike to obtain a wage rise and a reduction in working hours. The *alcade*, being perfectly aware of the reasons for the strike, gave his assurances that he would remain neutral, so that workers and managers might freely come to some agreement. The same day, following a meeting with [the management of the] manufacturers, he published a poster insulting and slandering the strikers, all of them workers in the town and numbering 10,000. Alcoy's workers, surprised by such a brusque and unspeakable change, chose among themselves a commission to inform the town council that if it was not ready to observe complete neutrality as it had declared and promised, it was necessary to avoid conflict, that they should announce their resignation, its incomprehensible conduct having aroused very natural reaction, and very considerable agitation.

The reasoning and explanations of the commission were unavailing, and when they left the council buildings they were met by a volley of fire from the *alcade* and his agents, murdering several workers peacefully walking in the Square of the Republic, and wounding others. The provocateurs, having taken control of the strategic points of this public place, continued their murderous fire on unarmed people, and the latter, being forced to respond to force with force, ran to seize arms to counter their brutality. The fighting lasted twenty hours; four or five workers were killed, and many were wounded defending 'rights' that were so disrespected and violated by these gentlemen of the Federal Republic. On the side of the aggressors there were three dead and just a few wounded. Except in the fighting and only in those places where defenders were attacked, was the least insult offered against those who had raised their weapons against the people. Extreme measures were used against five or six buildings but only because they served as shelters for persons directing a murderous fire against workers.**

---

* The local federation had 612 members in January 1873. Max Nettlau, *La première Internationale en Espagne*, op. cit., p. 191
** Presumably, these buildings were set on fire.

Human blood spilt from balconies, priests being hung from lamp-posts, men soaked in petrol baths and killed by gunfire, heads cut off, Civil Guards paraded in streets, the premeditated burning of buildings, burnings of factories and of the town hall, houses pillaged, the rape of innocent young girls – all such horrors are abominable slanders, fit only for the tongues of middle-class ministers and the bourgeois press, who doubtless feel capable of such things themselves. Signed affidavits, set out without any kind of pressure by those who at the time were most involved in the acts of the authorities, and who alone were responsible for all the events of 9 and 10 July, (along with all we have said) clearly prove that the movement was provoked by the town council and that the people were in no way responsible what happened there.

Given that the Alcoy internationalists knew that any isolated revolutionary movement was more injurious than useful for the future of the social revolution, they went home with their arms as soon as they were sure that they would not be prosecuted, and that they would obtain their strike demands. They understood that they would achieve nothing by resisting the forces of General Vélarde. The results of the Alcoy movement were very favourable to working people. On the 10-11-12th all those who had taken up arms received 2 pesetas (2 francs) a day, and a pound of bread. Then on Saturday 12th the strikers, both men and women – in all some 10,000 – received their weekly pay. Thereafter every trade (with a few exceptions) obtained satisfaction for their demands. All this helped to implant good ideas in the Alcoy federation; all members are more than ever ready to continue the great work of social liquidation.[349]

The *intransigent* federal republicans took up arms against the *benevolent* or *platonic* federal republicans who took power after the events in Alcoy. The *intransigents* intended to set up through revolution, the Cantons or States of the Spanish Republic. Cartagena, Murcia, Cadiz, San Fernando, Seville, Grenada, Valencia, Salamanca, and other cities of lesser importance – with the agreement of the majority of the fleet – supported the cantonal movement. The government of the bourgeois revolution was in a difficult position with these people on one side, and the Carlist insurrection on the other. To supress the Cantonal uprising, it sought foreign intervention and threw itself into the hands of conservative and monarchic reaction. The government withdrew the troops fighting the savage hordes of Carlism, to send them off to against those who sought the establishment of political federalism.

The squads of Carlists, who had set fire to the stations and railways, burnt many houses, in many places looted from the people, and having once committed these acts of vandalism, went on to kill women and children. So long as the Cantonal insurrection lasted they were not disturbed by the troops of the Republic. The latter were directed for the most part to crush the intransigent federalists and the internationalists. Such things demonstrate that the bourgeoisie prefers to embrace the most rabid reaction rather than taking even a single step on behalf of the revolution.

The Cantonal movement was stronger at sea than on land. So it had to confront intervention from several foreign powers, especially Prussia, which first seized a steamship, and then the two best frigates that might have protected Cantonalist areas – the government being unable to deploy any ships against them. It is certain that, had the movement succeeded on the dry land, foreign forces would have disembarked – as was attempted in Cadiz. Setting up obstacles in the way of revolutionary movements is how bourgeois solidarity always operates.

Two powerful [army] divisions were organised to fight the rebels seeking to establish a political federation from *bottom to top* – as against from *top to bottom* as desired by the 'benevolent' federalists. One was directed against Seville, where there were 3,000 volunteers (of these 2,000 were of the 'benevolent' party). From the very first it was foreseen that the latter would not march against the troops of Pavía.[350] So, only a thousand men were ready to fight, encircling the town with cannons and barricades. When Pavia's vanguard began to attack Seville, the number of defenders had fallen to just 300, nevertheless the attacks were repelled, and the army needed three days to take the city. Seville's 300 defenders fought like heroes, fighting both army troops, and, at the same time, the gunfire of bourgeois ladies and gentlemen who, from behind shutters, traitorously fired on them. And, when caught in the act, this bourgeois riff-raff, was simply taken off to prison, without the least insult. The army troops behaved very differently, they took few prisoners, showing thereby that they were only obeying secret government orders. Furthermore, it was no surprise that these frantic soldiers and officers [who so] worthily took up profession of executioner, should shoot without mercy anyone unlucky enough to fall into their hands.

The bourgeois press vomited the most odious slanders against Seville's defenders, even though the latter burnt only houses from which gunfire had been directed onto them, or those that had to be demolished to protect a retreat, which was necessary because the bourgeois friends of 'Order' were even more implacable towards them than the army of Pavía. These *thieves*, these *assassins*, these *incendiaries*,[351] as they were called by the bourgeoisie, fought for three days without officers and without receiving a penny. And, despite it all, they stole not a farthing. But what about the Soldiers of 'Order', the valiant defenders of the bourgeoise! they behaved quite differently! They pillaged a great many private houses, and assassinated defenceless persons who had taken no part in the events.

If in Seville all workers had fought as the 300 did, these 300 who we have described, then it is certain that neither Pavía, nor his army division would ever have taken the city. The 300 men who fought with such great courage were or had been members of the International. So, it is not surprising that our comrades should be so cruelly persecuted, precisely by those who owe them their lives and who now demand their heads. Thus, it is obvious that those intransigents, the initiators of the movement, did not want to fight – and the only ones who did fight were those who had the least to gain from the fighting. One can say, without fear of contradiction, that Seville's internationalists – who, there and elsewhere, were the soul of the movement – fought not for the political federalism, but rather for rights that were being trodden underfoot by bourgeois republicanism.

After Seville was taken, Cadiz, a city of importance, was surrendered to the government through the treachery of a small number of men and through the cowardice of the intransigent republicans who led the movement. The consuls of the powerful provided many workers with safe-conduct passes, and these served only to have them arrested by the army of the central power, and they were taken back to Cadiz, as criminals, chained together two-by-two, through two files of bayonets, and locked up in dungeons. These shameful acts will arouse much comment and working people should not forget them.

When Cadiz and Seville were back under the power of the central government, it ordered Pavía's army division to divide itself into several columns and to spread across the various towns of lower Andalucía, to disarm any volunteers who had supported the Cantonal movement as well as those who had just sympathised with it. The entire population of these provinces is under the heal of this, most depraved, reaction. Most of our local federations have been dissolved, and those who do meet are threatened with prison. Many persecutions took place in Jerez. In Sanlúcar, more than 150 internationalists have been arrested – and we are not speaking of the persons pursued like wild beasts by the cavalry, almost all whom perished, victims of the defenders of bourgeois order and their savagery. The persecutions and slanders that have been suffered by our brothers, and that still afflict them – in Seville, Cadiz, Carmona, Sanlúcar, Malaga, Paradas, Lebrija, Chiplona, Arabal, Jerez, Puerto de Santa Maria, Grenada, and other towns besides – can only be compared with those that victimised our brothers of the Paris Commune.

The second division of the army of 'Order' commanded by General Martinez Campos was ordered to take Valencia, a city defended in the first instance by 10,000 men. Many days of bombardment and siege were needed to overwhelm the city's defenders, forcing some to abandon their arms, while others withdrew into the mountains where they continued to defend their sworn principles. After the entry of the army of 'Order' into Valencia and the seizure of Grenada and Murcia, the Cantonalist uprising was reduced to the occupation of the arsenal and centre of Cartagena. As we write these lines, the central power is preparing to bombard this last Cantonalist refuge, and as soon as their supplies and resources run out, they will be forced to abandon their arms.[352]

To conclude this account of the Cantonalist movement one should say that its leaders, from the beginning, showed as much ambition as their former co-religionists of central power, a complete lack of a revolutionary planning, and unparalleled cowardice. While pretending to be revolutionaries they set themselves up by their own volition as a provisional government. Although powerful at sea, like timid lambs, they allowed two armoured frigates to be taken by just one Prussian naval frigate* and although they had the ability to defeat the army divisions of Pavía and Martinez Campos, they allowed themselves to be defeated [separately and] in detail. Certainly, this movement had the sympathies of many internationalists, but it is also obvious that a victory would have been followed by their betrayal because, had they been victorious, Cantonalists would have continued with persecutions, just like any other bourgeois government which has to depend on conservative and reactionary classes.

This movement has brought only disappointment, persecution, and victimisation to the working class. For our part we hope this will be a salutary lesson for all sincere revolutionaries, for everyone who loves and desires social revolution. They should understand that it is necessary to work ceaselessly, not at all for a political federation, but rather for the establishment of an economic federation, which means complete autonomy for free communes and municipalities, and the complete and radical emancipation of the working class. Something that our brother workers must understand moreover, and that is a certainty, is that any successful local or national movement will be crushed without pity by foreign intervention, unless a large section of workers in other nations comes to its support. The solidarity that exists between the various governments and the bourgeoisie

---

* Much of the Spanish fleet fell into rebel hands. The Spanish central government named the rebel fleet 'pirates'; the British and German Navies and other foreign powers threatened port facilities and joined in operations against these so-called 'pirates'.

can be rooted out only through solidarity in the revolutionary action of workers of the most civilised countries, through the path of an international socialist revolution.

From our viewpoint, this is the work undertaken by the regional federations, which form the IWMA, and this task may be accomplished when a section of workers is convinced that destroying this infamous society, based on monopoly and injustice, is a necessity, and that it must be destroyed to establish a new world of free producers, a free federation of industrial and agricultural associations, controlling every source of life, and gathering the integral product of its labour.

* * *

This is the situation of the Spanish Regional Federation: on 20 August 1872, the Spanish Regional Federation numbered 65 constituted local federations, based on 224 resistance sections, 49 mixed all-trades sections, with individual members in eleven other towns. On 20 August 1873, the Spanish Regional Federation counted 162 locally constituted federations, encompassing together 454 trade or resistance sections, and 77 mixed trades sections.

If we add federations-in-formation to the regularly constituted local federations, the following summary totals arise: the Spanish Regional Federation had, on 20 August 1872, 204 federations (constituted or in-formation), with a total of 371 trade or resistance sections, 114 mixed all-trades sections, and eleven locations with individual members. On 20 August 1873, the Spanish Regional Federation had 270 local federations (constituted or in-formation), comprising a total of 557 trade or resistance sections, and 117 mixed trade sections.

Organisations of Resistance

The Spanish Federation has the following regional trades' unions and trades' federations.

Union of manufacturing workers

This union is composed of 33 sections of day-workers or assistants, 33 of machine spinners, 33 of machine weavers, 3 of woolworkers, 1 cylinder worker, 1 finisher, 83 of hand weavers, 3 of silk or linen, 10 of rope-makers, 6 of shoe-makers, 11 of dyers, 1 hand-painter, 1 mechanics and factory drivers, 1 chemical worker, 3 of sock makers, 2 of ribbon makers. A total of 233 resistance sections.

This union* has the following federations: Federation of day-workers, machine weavers and spinners; Federation of hand weavers; Federation of dyers and allied trades; Federation of shoe-makers; Federation of knitwear workers.

2 Union of Hide workers
Composed of 13 resistance societies.

3 Union of shoemakers
Composed of 31 resistance societies.

4 Union of Iron workers
Composed of 21 resistance societies.

5 Union of Agricultural workers
Composed of 44 resistance societies.

6 Union of wood workers and furniture workers
Composed of 14 resistance societies.

7 Federation of hat makers
Composed of 13 resistance societies.

8 Federation of printers and allied workers
Composed of 25 resistance societies.

9 Union of cooper workers
Composed of 21 resistance societies.

10 Union of building workers
Composed of 58 resistance societies.

11 Federation of Bakers
Composed of 12 resistance societies.

In summary 11 trade unions and federations with a total of 477 resistance sections.

*Strikes***

From 1 September 1872 to 10 August 1873 the following strikes were successful:

Arbas 1***; Arenys de Mar; Alcoy 2; Anna; Arahall; Barcelona 14; Badalona;

---

* A 'union' defined in this way might perhaps be termed a confederation of allied trades. (Guillaume, *L'Internationale*, op. cit., part 5, chapter 5, p. 133n.)

** See also the discussion on General Strikes in Appendix 3.

*** In most places only one strike is reported, where more than one strike a total is indicated.

Balgaren; Benillloba, Cortz de Sarria; Carmona ; Cadiz 9; Cornella; Cordoba; Cambras; Cocentayna; Esplugas; Enguera 2; Gerona; Grenada; Gracia 3; Horia; Hospitalet 2; Martorell; Malgrat; Mières del Camino; Murcia; Malaga; Manresa; Mataro; Molins de Rey; Prat de Llobregat; Palma de Mallorca 2; Puerto Santa Maria; Puerto real; Papiol 2; Paradas; Reus; Sans 4; Seville 4; San Boy de Llobregat; Sarria; San Just des Bern; Sanlúcar de Barramea 2; San Feliu de Guixols; San Andrès de Palomar 3; San Martin de provensais 4; Sama de Langreo 2; San Juan Despi; San Feliu de Llobregat; Tarragona 2; Terredembarra; Tarrasa; Tharsis 2; Valls 2; Vendrebt; Villanueva; Villafranca; Vinaron y Cadaques; Valencia 7; Vich 2 and Jerez.

In general, the strike demands of each trade were for higher pay and shorter working days. Many strikes were spontaneous, and these were supported by the trades which had declared them. Most were successful. It is difficult to estimate the costs of these strikes, but it is certain that they occasioned a total expenditure of at least 400,000 pesetas (around 400,000 francs).

Comrade delegates, the facts highlighted in this memorandum allow you to gather some idea of the progress made by collectivist and anarchic ideas among the workers of Spain; of the considerable development of our organisation from 20 August 1872 until today, of the successes won in continual struggles against exploitation and capital; of the unjust persecutions inflicted by delegates of the republican and federal authorities, of the struggle or revolutionary socialist movement that took place in Alcoy, following the provocation of the town council, with results that profited the workers of that city; of the Cantonal movement, a political movement, which had no happy results, but which on the contrary brought the brutal dissolution of a great number of our federations.

So, as you may understand, our regional federation, is facing persecution from the government in the South and from the Carlists;* it is encountering many obstacles which are impeding its current development, and it is indispensable that this state of things should cease, so that new federations may be created, and so that federations now dissolved should be reorganised.

Despite everything, the International in Spain is supported more than anything by the loyalty of thousands of workers and by a multitude of revolutionaries who have placed all their hopes in the organisation. Be certain then that the Spanish federation has not been defeated, for the very simple reason that it has not engaged in squabbles; today, as before, internationalists throughout the world can count on the moral and materiel

* Carlists were a reactionary movement named after a candidate for the Spanish throne.

support of their brothers of the Spanish region who proudly affirm the great principle of *solidarity*.

Comrades, we wish great success to your deliberations, and we leave you with our acclamations: Long live the IWMA! Long live anarchy, collectivism, and the social revolution!

Greetings and solidarity, Madrid, 19 August 1873. The Spanish Federal Commission. Address: *Miguel Pino*, Caballero de Gracia, No. 8 – lower, Madrid.

With this communication finished *Costa* reminded the Congress that, at the time of the events that occurred in the Paris area in 1871, the entire IWMA declared its solidarity with the acts of the Paris workers. He requested that today, through a similar declaration that [**congress**] **should accept and declare its solidarity with the struggle and sufferings of Spanish workers.**

That proposal was voted by acclamation.*

Pindy then read the written report of the Jura Federation, as follows:

REPORT presented by the Jura Federal Committee
to the General Congress of 1873

We believe we should present to Congress a succinct exposé of the situation of the Jura Federation and of its activities over the past year. In the first place we shall say a few words on the relations between our federation and the federations of other countries.

After the congress of The Hague, at which a few intransigents sought to transform the International, from a free federation of autonomous groups, into an association subjected to a despotic authority of a centre, the delegates of the various regional federations met in Saint Imier on the 15 September 1872, to examine the situation of the International as it was made by the coup d'état of the fictitious majority at The Hague. Our federation took part in this new congress and gave its full support to the resolutions taken there, among them the Pact of Friendship, Solidarity and Mutual Defence to be established between the federations who wished to safeguard their autonomy against the pretensions of the authoritarian party. The Jura Federal Committee, residing then in Sonvilier, was given the particular responsibility of drawing the proposals of the Saint Imier congress to the attention of every regional federation, and receiving their answers.

These replies were not long in coming. The congresses of the Spanish Federation and of the Belgian Federation, held one after another, last December on Christmas Day, voted their support for the Saint Imier pact.

---

* This resolution was published in the FRE journal *La Federación* on 6 September.

The Italians had expressed their opinion in advance, in their congress at Rimini on 4 August 1872. The Jura federation declared 'the General Council is not the International, and if we have broken with it, we for our part also once again affirm our economic solidarity with the workers of the world.'[353] The English, in their regional congress of 26 January 1873, declared that they recognised neither the congress of The Hague, nor the General Council of New York. The American Regional Council, in its meeting of 19 January 1873 gave its agreement to the propositions of the Saint Imier congress. Lastly, the Dutch federation, in turn, declared that it approved the conduct of the minority at the congress of The Hague. As for the Jurassians, they had adopted the propositions of Saint Imier at the special congress of 15 September.

Thus, seven federations, the only ones that are seriously organised in the International, had declared that they did not recognise the decisions of the congress of The Hague, and showed their determination not to allow a pretended General Council to dictate the law to the International. Besides these seven federations, France, through the organs of its [ongoing] constituted sections, with which we had established regular relations, also pronounced themselves for the preservation of the principle of autonomy.*

Among the countries where the International exists, only three did not take part in this general movement of protest, i.e. Germany, Denmark and Portugal.[354] We cannot speak of Germany, since for a year we have had no direct relations with Internationalists of this area, but we do believe that no regular [IWMA] organisation exists there, and perhaps, if a congress had been able to meet there as in Belgium and England, the voice of the German proletariat, which we have never heard directly, might not have been quite what it is pretended to be, by those who currently serve it as its dominant intermediaries.[355] In Denmark, whatever organisation might supposedly and really have existed, has been destroyed by government persecutions. Lastly, in Portugal, the intrigues of certain personalities for a time did manage to conceal the truth, but a salutary crisis has occurred recently, and the Portuguese federation,[356] released from the domination of agents of the authoritarian clique, now seems disposed to offer its hand to the other free federations.

However, as regards the Jura Federation, which the men of New York chose as the scapegoat and target for their grudges, it was not long before

---

* There were also sections in other countries e.g., a French-language section in Argentina, sections perhaps unknown at this point to the Jura federation. Max Nettlau, 'La Internacional en Buenos Aires en 1872 y en 1873', La Protesta: (Supplement, Buenos Aires, 15 November 1926.)

it received the penalty for its rebellion against the authority elected at The Hague. By letter dated 8 November 1872, Mr Sorge [General Secretary of the New York General Council] summoned Jura Federation to annul the resolution voted at its congress of 15 September, the resolution in which the federation declared that it did not recognise the acts of the congress of The Hague. The letter of Mr Sorge having failed to produce the effect intended, he announced to the universe, in a document dated 5 January 1873, that it was his great pleasure to suspend the Jura Federation. The universe was in no way troubled, and the Jura sections carried on no less nicely, which must have greatly astonished the author of this transatlantic communication.

Here we should note expressions of solidarity and sympathy for ourselves, received at this time from various federations, and must thank them cordially, noting simultaneously that we have maintained throughout the entire year the most fraternal relations with the federations attending this congress.

As for the internal affairs of our federation, our report will be very short. Our annual regional congress took place in Neuchâtel, from 27 to 28th of last April.[357] The Federal committee based in Sonvilier and having had to support the weight of a long struggle with the authoritarians, now resigned its responsibilities, and was replaced by a new committee chosen from the section of Le Locle. In a spirit of conciliation, we invited the International sections belonging to the Romande* Federation and a German speaking Swiss group to this congress; some replied with sympathetic letters, but, sadly, we had to note that the greater number was completely indifferent to [our attempt to affect] a rapprochement with the different fractions of internationalists in Switzerland.[358]

Proceeding with that same spirit of conciliation our federation sent delegates to the congress that was convened in Olten on 1 June, with the aim of creating a Swiss Labour League [the *Schweizerische Arbeiterbund*]. As regards any attempt to increase unity between proletarians, we were very ready to extend the hand of friendship, and we presented to the Olten congress a proposal for organisation based on federalist principles (which are those of the International); we were sad to see our proposals rejected; the great majority of the congress pronounced itself in favour of centralisation and for tasking a Central Committee with the direction of Swiss workers' affairs. Being unable to give our support to an organisation

* In 1870 the Romande (French-speaking Swiss) federation split. The majority refused to support electoral priorities. That majority later decided to adopt a new name, as the Jura (Mountain) Federation. The minority kept the name of the Romande federation. See René Berthier, *Social-democracy and Anarchism in the International Workers' Association*, 1864-1877, Talgarth: Merlin Press, 2015, pp. 70-71

which is exactly like to the one we have fought against in the IWMA, we have had to renounce taking part in a Swiss Labour League constituted on such foundations, all the while assuring the societies which constituted it of our complete solidarity in economic struggles.[359]

Our official organ, the *Bulletin de la Fédération Jurassienne*, has become a weekly since 1 July last, and we rely on it as an efficient means of propaganda among working peoples.

All that is left is to speak of the convening of this current congress. In its regional congress of 27-28 April, our federation decided and proposed to all federations to convene the next general congress in a town in Switzerland on 1 September. For its part, the Belgian federation proposed to all federations that the Jura federation should take on the responsibility for organising the next general congress. In consequence the Jura Federal Committee wrote to all the federations of our IWMA to ask them if they would agree to the congress being convened on 1 September in Geneva. In reply to this circular, the Jura Federal Committee received much agreement, and the presence of delegates here present proves that our proposal received a favourable welcome everywhere.

Let this congress, convened by the free will of the federations, work seriously to reorganise our great Association. Long live the IWMA!

Locle, 29 August 1873.

The Federal Committee: Pindy, Adolphe Roos, F. Floquet,
Auguste Spichiger, Alexandre Chatelain.

* * *

[Britain and the Netherlands]

With this reading finished, Hales delivered a verbal sketch of the IWMA's situation in England.* If he had observed some indifference among English Internationalists, the cause he said, should be sought in the intrigues and slanders of the Marxist clique; nevertheless 21 sections protested against the resolutions of the congress of The Hague. He hoped that this present congress through the reverberations that it may occasion and cause, and the sympathies that it may awaken in the working class, might exert a welcome influence on English workers, and reawaken their sympathy for the International.

In his oral report, *Van den Abeele*, observed that in the Netherlands, as in England, the congress of The Hague had vexatious consequences. However, thanks to the firm stance taken by the free federations, the damage had been

---

* There is some ambiguity in French terms, since 'England' is frequently used when Britain, or Britain and Ireland might be more appropriate.

repaired and one section even, that of Utrecht, which had thought it needful to maintain relations with the General Council and to separate itself from the Dutch Federation, had latterly reconsidered and rallied to the federation at the congress of Amsterdam of 10 August last. He finished by stating that he was mandated to take his place at the Congress of the authoritarians on 8 September, to demand firmly of those that might take part, to return to more conciliatory ways. If he was not successful in this attempt, the Dutch IWMA would break all relations with the General Council.

[Belgium]

Comrade *Verrycken* spoke to advise the congress of the situation in the Belgian Federation. After the congress of The Hague, the Belgian Federation had remained undecided for a certain time, before approving the decisions taken in Saint Imier. Once this support was given, the federation considered it appropriate to make certain modifications to its internal organisation. It was decided that henceforth, each federation would give an imperative mandate to a delegate, to represent it at the Regional Council, which would meet monthly; furthermore, to facilitate the development of an exchange of social ideas, four regional congresses should be held each year.

Few strikes have broken out in Belgium other than those concerning the Federation of the Centre, and all of them were successful. The great strike of Charleroi did not achieve an immediate victory, but happier consequences were not long delayed. The management, being terrified by the workers who entered the fray, were forced to make important concessions, and soon agreed to concede a wage rise that was much higher than that which had been demanded. A very serious strike took place in Alost. Weavers earned only 12 francs a day, and were obliged, to beg the bread they needed for their subsistence from one farm to another. In Flanders in general, workers are in a highly miserable condition; on Sundays they are forced to attend mass, they are also obliged to take part in musical societies and to join in small religious festivals – all under threat that the little work that they have, might be withdrawn.

The general situation of the IWMA in Belgium is satisfactory, however. In the Federation of the Centre there was, in the past, just one section, now there is one for each trade. In Verviers, the situation is the same. Due to the dishonesty and the notorious incapacity of the bourgeoisie, the workers of this river-basin area are going through an appalling crisis. A thousand workers are unemployed. Instead of having to produce one piece per week as they had to previously, barely one a month is all they are having to produce now. The Belgian Federation had resolved to provide monetary support to their brothers in the valley of the Vesdre, but the latter refused the subsidies that they were offered and expressed the desire that the funds that had been offered to them should be used to prepare the social revolution, the only remedy for their ills. Two new sections were created in Antwerp, despite all its misery, and despite the efforts of two – unhappily still very powerful – parties: the Catholic Party and the doctrinaire Liberal Party. In the Borinage area the sections founded in 1868 keep going. However, there too the pressure of the bourgeoisie makes itself cruelly felt, so much so that, in order not to displease the authorities, an owner of a hall rented for a popular meeting was forced to withdraw. Much progress has been made in the federation of Liège, and a new organ, *L'Ami du people*, has appeared (it survived up to 1876). The International has encountered rather powerful enemies, among two organisations which attempt to impede its development: these are, in Brussels the General Labour Association, and throughout Belgium, Catholic societies for mutual aid. The former receives its inspiration from liberal doctrines, the latter makes its propaganda in the home, through the means of its clerics. However, the efforts of the General Labour Association to create a federation in Brussels have failed, and the alms-giving of societies for mutual aid attracts few workers.*

---

*   The *Leeds Mercury*, 6 September 1873, included the following comments: In the Vallée du Centre they had for years tried to organise the trades, but in vain; no one would unite with the other. It was all piecework; people were never fully employed, and there were always so many out of work that nothing whatever could be done. In the Vallée de la Vesdre every trade was organised, and the trades were federalised. They had subscribed some money to organise the Centre. In the Flemish provinces of Belgium, the misery of the workpeople was extreme. They had to work day and night for the merest pittance, and every attempt at organising them for the improvement of their condition was counteracted by the Catholics, who were very strong there. In the colliery districts of Charleroi. they had lately gained advances of wages without strikes which formerly no strike could have obtained. In consequence of being well organised, the colliers had in a short time raised their wages from 5f[rancs] to 9f. a day –an amount which they could not have dreamt of before the foundation of the International. In the Borinage there was much room for improvement. The Sections already in existence there had some money, and they were going to extend their organisation, but they met with opposition at every step. They had lately resolved to hold a public meeting in favour of the Centre, and engaged a hall, but as soon it become known the Municipality threatened the proprietress of the place to withdraw her license if she allowed the meeting to be held. They had then been obliged to resort to an open-air meeting, which had been as complete success. There were now five local Federations in full working order in Belgium, well organised and prepared for any emergency which might arise. – there were also comments on Italy: Costa said the bourgeoisie of Italy and the Government and the Mazzinists had so denounced and vilified the workpeople of Paris in their recent struggle that the workpeople of Italy had become indignant and had entered upon a regular struggle to oppose the Government. On account of the persecutions and maltreatment of the workpeople, riots had been provoked in

Cornet asked to speak to complete this report. He mentioned the international trades' unions which have established themselves among tailors, rope-workers, woodworkers, and stonemasons.

[Italy]

Costa made an oral report in the name of the Italian Federation.[360] It might be said that the IWMA did not exist in Italy before the Paris Commune. It was only really founded when Mazzini insulted the workers of Paris.[361] From then on immense progress has been made, due in part to governmental persecutions. A first congress had been held in Rimini in 1872; it was attended by only 25 delegates;[362] at the congress held in Bologna, meeting a year later, 60 could be counted. Our association had not been spared persecution. If there were no Marxists in Italy, there were, other than *intransigents*, followers of both Garibaldi and Mazzini. So lively was the struggle that bloody tussles have taken place. Revolutionary action was needed in Italy if one wants the IWMA to make progress.[363] Italian workers are very little concerned by theory – what they want is struggle. As regards strikes, successes were half and half, there were many, with some victories, and some defeats.

[Geneva]

Joukovsky spoke, reporting on the situation in Geneva. After the Congress of The Hague the bourgeoisie was celebrating the death of the IWMA, but quite the contrary, it had grown more than ever, and the disruption produced by the General Council was diminishing, because workers have been taking the principle of autonomy as the basis of their organisation. The decree of the New York General Council, suspending an entire federation, had opened the eyes of everyone; the Romande sections of Geneva, in a regional congress held in August, had decided unanimously to reduce the functions of the [General] Council to that of a simple correspondence bureau. What is, as yet, unknown, is whether they will agree with the congress in relation

---

various places, but the good sense Of the bulk of the people had prevented any particular mischief being done. At the Congress of Bologna, a coterie of Marxists had tried to impede all progress, but in vain, They had also had some strikes to support. They had to contend against the Garibaldians as well as against the Marxists. The Garibaldians had been well enough in their day, for a national revolution, but they were altogether out of place for a social revolution. They knew nothing, either of theory or science; all they could understand fight! fight! fight! The Mazzinists were out of sorts with the International because they would not recognise any authority. The propaganda of the social movement required theorists and debaters, not fighting men. They had to sustain a very hard struggle against the fighting revolutionists of the school.

to the matter of the political attitude of workers.

After these reports were heard *Pindy* read a letter of an American section of New York, entitled the Socialist Revolutionary Group (former No. 2 section)* which extends its support and its regrets for not being able to send a delegate.

Verrycken read the following letter addressed to the congress by the Federal Council of the North American sections (Spring Street).**

American Federal Council [letter] to the IWMA congress meeting in
Geneva (Switzerland)

Comrades,

We are happy to acknowledge receipt of the communication of *L. Pindy* corresponding secretary of the Jura Federal Committee, dated the 8th of last month. We are happy to learn of the measures being made to receive delegates but, as yet we are unsure if one of our sections might be able to have itself represented by a member attending the congress in person. The costs of a journey to Europe, and back to America, can only be heavy, and in relation to your aforementioned communication, it is very improbable that we will be able to obtain representation otherwise than by the letter now in your hands.

L. Pindy submits certain proposals to us, placed on the agenda by the congress of Saint Imier of 15th and 16th September 1872, with a view to knowing our opinion on the future of the IWMA.

The particular propositions concern:

1. the constitution of a Pact of Solidarity between the various federations belonging to the Association.
2. the revision of the General Statutes of the IWMA.
3. the General Strike.
4. a universal resistance commission and complete statistical tables for labour.

Also, the corresponding secretary wishes to know if we will be represented at the congress and [if so] by how many members.

Believing that you may be meeting in May, as we were told, we sent you

---

* Francophone internationalists had promoted the demonstration of 17 December 1871; including supporters of Blanqui; Michel Cordillot, 'Les Blanquistes à New-York (1871-1880)', *Revue d'Histoire du XIXe siècle*, No. 6, 1990, pp. 81-82.
** See letters published in *Bulletin de la Fédération Jurassienne*, on 1 April and 20 July 1873, 32 out of 43 sections in the USA were with the Spring Street Federal Council on 11 February 1872; and on 5 May that year, 40 out of 50 were with Spring Street.

an address, directed to the bureau of the congress Saint Imier, wishing you to forward it onwards. In this address, the Council expressed its opinion frankly on general principles and goals of the IWMA, also concerning the means, through which these principles and goals might be attained in each nation. In this envelope we are sending you copies of this address. But recent facts, in Italy, Spain, France and Belgium, along with the resolutions of the Congress of Saint Imier, lead us to make certain additions, to facilitate a better understanding of the rest.

We wholeheartedly approve propositions of universal solidarity, and for the reconstitution of our Association in conformity with this principle. Certainly, workers of every federation supporting the IWMA must help workers of every other federation needing assistance, in whatever manner those federations may ask for help. Circumstances vary from one federation to another, which implies that the remedies to be applied cannot be the same everywhere, so each federation must judge for itself, what is most desirable, and practical. This recognition of human solidarity, which guarantees help for each federation in need, is the first duty of IWMA members in every country throughout the world.

We also approve the revision of the General Statutes; the statutes should guarantee the right to take initiatives – for each member of each section, for every section, and for every federation; they must also recognise progressive methods of action. Tomorrow's necessities may demand the use of different methods, rather than those that appear to be applicable today; and the statutes should be such that each member of the IWMA should be left perfectly free, to propose and choose the measures that seem best to them, and the most appropriate moment to apply them.

It must be clearly understood, however, that the responsibility for taking an initiative should be confined to the individual, to the section or to the federation, from which it emanates, so that while guaranteeing the autonomy of each individual, of each section and each federation, the publication of a proposition, if not approved at some later point, should not be made in the name of the entire IWMA but rather in the name of its author – be it an individual, section or federation.

Naturally, we support the proposal which intends to limit the functions of general and federal councils to purely administrative functions. Experience has shown that representative and legislative bodies are always inclined to substitute their own will in the place of those who have given them a mandate, also to usurp and appropriate powers which have never been delegated to them.

On the matter of the General Strike, we have only one word to say – it is for you to decide. If the social and political conditions of a people are such that a strike is the only practical means of improving practical conditions, the people concerned are the ones to judge that necessity. Neighbouring peoples, linked to them by solidarity, have just one responsibility, to respect their judgement, and to help it succeed by every means possible. In America experience has shown that strikes generally result in a loss of resources, without corresponding benefits except that workers are educated in matters of organisation. All the same, if workers affiliated to the IWMA came to determine a particular day for a *general strike*, not just to obtain a reduction of hours and a reduction of salaries,* but to find a way of living in co-operative workshops, through groups and colonies, we could not prevent ourselves from offering assistance, and we make an appeal to members of all nations, to give material and moral support.

The necessity of naming resistance commissions, and above all of completing statistical tables for labour – all this – we fully recognise, and in this matter we will follow any instructions that the congress may give our delegates.

In short, on this point, we approve the resolutions of the Belgian congress held on 1st and 2nd June of this year, such as we can find them, in the *Bulletin de la Fédération Jurassienne*, of 6th June.[364]

Now, may we be allowed to suggest an idea concerning the workings of the congress. This idea concerns an economical method of international communication, through the post, through correspondence cards, such as those used in America, England, and certain European states. There can be no reason to limit such correspondence within state frontiers alone. Congress should therefore approve the efforts now being made for this purpose. A Postal Congress is about to take place in Switzerland on 9th September next, postal relations between nations attending are on the agenda of this congress; you might make an appeal on this point to this International Postal Congress.

Lastly, comrades, we salute you – defenders and propagators of social revolution! Once again in the history of the IWMA, a history so rich in events, you are coming together freely, to discuss the means by which the last vestiges of despotism – as much military, theocratic and capitalist – can be made to disappear, to be replaced by a permanent and stable social republic, means of organising labour, finding [ways to] convert workers who are now oppressed into free citizens of the greater social collective, with capacity, education and the means for directing the proletariat's thinking, feelings and activities, towards the emancipation of the human race. Above

---

* Perhaps an error – the editor probably intended to write an *improvement* in salaries.

all a great, and noble task! May love and wisdom direct your councils!

Long Live the Social Revolution! Long Live the International!

Receive our fraternal greetings,

B. Hubert, General Secretary for correspondence.[365]

T. Kinget, Corresponding Secretary for England.

Wm. West, Secretary-treasurer

Hugh McGregor, B. Hubert, Wm. West: members of the Committee.

[Methods of voting]

With the reading of reports concluded, a discussion opened on what method of voting should be used in the Congress's deliberations.

Van den Abeele expanded on his proposal that voting should be by federation.

Hales proposed that the question should be adjourned, until the revision of statutes – which, logically, included this issue.

Brousse observed that mandates still had to be validated, and in his view, it would be unacceptable to allow any difference in the way mandates were validated. He proposed that the congress should go into an administrative session, to proceed to this validation, and that a commission be named to study the matter of voting methods.

Guillaume agreed with this, with the modification that the commission when elected should also discuss the revision of the statutes.

After a short discussion, in which *Van den Abeele, Farga, Claris, Hales, Eccarius* and *Verrycken* took part, the proposition was adopted unanimously.

The congress decided that it would reconvene in a public session at 8 p.m.

Verrycken read the names of members chosen by the delegates of the various federations to take part in the commission to revise the statutes. These were: *Bert* (Italy), *Farga Pellicer* (Spain), *Van den Abeele* (The Netherlands), *Manguette* (Belgium), Guillaume (Jura), *Hales* (England). The session was adjourned.

MONDAY 1st SEPTEMBER – THIRD SESSION (ADMINISTRATIVE)

The session was opened at 8.30 p,m. The president *Verrycken* read a roll-call of delegates. *Hales* and *Eccarius* were absent.

The agenda called for the verification of the mandates of delegates of the French sections and a discussion on their admission.

A point of order from *Pindy* was agreed – requesting that a member of the Geneva sections should be at the door and be responsible for checking that persons entering [the hall] are indeed carrying IWMA membership cards.

Van den Abeele, reporting for the commission verifying mandates, said that in the meeting of this commission, it had been decided to wait, until just after the official constitution of the congress. That done, the commission went on to present its review of two mandates which the congress had requested.

Guillaume, a member of the commission corrected this report in this sense, that, according to him, the commission had decided not simply to propose to the congress the validation or the information about the French mandates, but [also] firstly, to raise a preliminary question for discussion, i.e., should the congress admit delegates from French sections, that is to say, from delegates whose mandates cannot be made public.

Claris proposed the postponement of this question, until after the revision of the General Statutes, which should establish a definite rule on this point.

Van den Abeele, replying to Guillaume agreed that certain reservations had been expressed in the commission regarding the French mandates; but nevertheless, he understood that the congress should consider their validation, in the evening session.

Verrycken, a member of the verification commission said that Guillaume had correctly reiterated the general thinking of the commission.

Claris expanded on his proposal. The section that he presented thought that the congress should allow the French delegates only a consultative voice, and that French sections that wanted to send a delegate to the congress should be required to make their existence know to neighbouring federations at least three months before the opening of a congress.

Pindy believed this was not the moment to have a discussion of Claris's proposal as regards the mandates of the French. Congress should first deal with two questions? Should French mandates be accepted? And secondly, if yes, how should the [French] sections be represented, and their representatives, designated?

Manguette proposed that the mandates of the French sections should not be accepted – on two accounts – firstly, either these mandates are serious, and so we might compromise our friends, or these mandates are the products of fantasy and then we would fall back into the same abuses that were produced by the Congress of The Hague.

Guillaume thought that the mandates of the French should not be rejected absolutely; the absolute exclusion of delegates from France would produce a bad impression on devoted men, who in that country work courageously for socialist propaganda. His view was that the congress should check the authenticity of the mandates, consulting the federations that have relations with them as to the real existence of these sections, and if these mandates appear to us to have sufficient guarantees of authenticity, if the mandating bodies find respondents for admitting them to the congress, it should admit these French delegates, but allow them a consultative voice only.

Claris maintained his proposal to reserve the matter of principle until the discussion of the General Statutes; and as for the French mandates, which the commission was reviewing, he thought they could not be accepted, these mandates were irregular, if only on this account – that they could not be known by [normal] regulation.

Pindy requested permission to read the various texts addressed by several French sections to the Jura Federal Commission, texts which would show the congress the principles and aspirations of these sections. This was agreed and Pindy read some passages from official documents emanating from French sections.

Brousse thought that French delegates should be admitted once the authenticity of their mandates had been properly checked. He spoke of the devotion and courage of the French sections; we cannot exclude by a stroke of the pen sections which it is true have to remain secret, but which in the crisis that now exists in France, do their duty. One should keep in mind that at the congress of the authoritarians, due on 8 September, French mandates will be accepted with alacrity and from the first moment; we therefore run the risk of pushing the French sections into the arms of the Authoritarian Party.

Guillaume reiterated his proposal, to seek to find and present a guarantor for the authenticity of each French mandate, and to consult the congress on the value of these guarantees.

The president announced that the Jura Federal Committee was ready to guarantee the mandates of many of the French sections and that these [mandates] nominated Pindy as the delegate of these sections. He asked the congress the following question: 'Does the congress consider that the guarantee of the Jura Federal Committee establishes sufficiently the authenticity of the French mandate which Pindy bares?' Congress replied unanimously in favour. The president then put for discussion the second part of Guillaume's proposition: 'The French mandate of Pindy being recognised as authentic, should the delegate be admitted with a consultative voice only?'

Viñas said that once the authenticity of the mandate was accepted there was no reason not to allow the mandatory a deliberative* voice – equal to

* The congress distinguished between consultative and deliberative voting rights.

that of other delegates – because his situation is the same as delegates of sections from other countries.

Guillaume was of the opinion that things were not just so, we have only been able to express a vote of confidence on the French mandate, whereas delegates from other countries have passed through a public process, so it cannot be said that the situation of a French delegate is exactly the same as those of delegates of other regions; and in his view, it would be best to reserve a deliberative voice for delegates of countries where the IWMA functions in public.

Brousse said that, above all, one should try to recognise the real existence of French sections that wish to be represented – even if the latter are secret. If their real existence is assured, their delegates cannot be given a status inferior to that of delegates of other countries, above all considering the dangers that they were exposed to attending the congress.

Bert said this was a vital question for the International. Indeed, if all monarchical regimes take the position of wishing to prohibit the IWMA, then our association will be forced into secrecy almost everywhere, and then the delegates of most countries would be deprived of having a deliberative voice in General Congresses on the pretext that sections that are represented have no public existence. The speaker found, on the contrary, that things should be easiest in respect of countries where the IWMA is persecuted, and it would be highly unjust to refuse a deliberative voice to their delegates.

Brousse proposed, to finish the discussion, that the position of French delegates be decided when the General Statues were revised, and until then French delegates should be satisfied with a simple validation of their mandates.

Manguette asked, what rights were being given to the French delegates, with the validation of their mandates? in that case, he saw none.

Andignoux made the same comment.

Dave said that in France effective propaganda for socialist ideas should be encouraged, but such results will not be obtained by accepting the mandates presented here. The sections that really exist should connect with neighbouring federations; that is what we should demand.

Verrycken said that, acting in line with an imperative mandate, he would vote for the admission of French delegates without restriction once their mandates had been authenticated.

Pindy warned that the French delegate, carrying a second mandate, whose authenticity the congress would have to determine, requested that in place of his name there should be substituted the name of comrade Perrare,

Decisions were made only by the votes of delegates with deliberative rights.

to whom he would relinquish his mandate.

The President then asked the following question: 'Does the congress consider that the guarantee of Comrade Brousse establishes sufficiently the authenticity of the French mandate, which the holder has transferred to comrade Perrare?'

The congress expressed itself unanimously in favour.

Viñas requested that the congress should decide immediately on the holders of the two French mandates and how their status should be defined.

Van den Abeele formulated the following proposition: 'The French delegates should be admitted as equals of the others until such time as the General Statutes are revised.'

Viñas did not accept the qualifying words: 'until such time as the General Statutes are revised.' If, when the statutes are revised, the congress was to agree the principle of non-admission in respect of delegates in countries where the IWMA cannot be a public body, that decision should only be applied for the next congress; it is indeed acknowledged, even by our adversaries, that laws should never be applied retrospectively.

Van den Abeele, withdrew his proposition, in view of the observations of Viñas, and replaced it with the following: 'The French delegates are admitted'.

Guillaume observed that the new draft text of Van den Abeele was not clear, because it does not specify in what capacity the French delegates should be admitted. To avoid equivocation the proposition should be expressed as: 'The French delegates are admitted in the same capacity as other delegates.'

The president put to the vote the proposition of Van den Abeele as follows:

The French delegates are admitted in the same capacity as other delegates.

This proposition was adopted by every federation. A Belgian delegate and a Jura delegate voted against. Pindy and Perrare who had been taking part already, in their capacity as delegates of the Jura, were therefore recognised as French delegates.

At the request of a member, the president read the names of delegates designated in the public session to form the commission to revise the General Statutes: comrades Bert, Farga, Van de Abeele, Manguette, Guillaume and Hales.

Bert observed that the French delegates were not represented on this commission. The aptness of this observation was shown by the addition of comrade Pindy to this commission. At the same time the congress decided that there was no reason to add to the bureau a new member for France, and that Pindy who was a member in his capacity as a delegate of the Jura, could also at the same time represent the French sections.

Guillaume proposed that there should be no congress sessions on Tuesday morning, so that commissions could do their work. At the same time, he proposed that a commission for the matter of statistics should be nominated and another for the question of the General Strike, and that the question of the pact of solidarity should be attributed to the commission reviewing the general Statutes. These propositions were adopted.

On the observation of *Van de Abeele* and *Dave* it was decided that every delegate had the right to take part in the sessions of every commission with the right to speak.

Having consulted other Belgian delegates, *Manguette,* requested that he should be placed in the commission on the General Strike rather than on that for the revision of the Statutes, for which he had been designated in the public session. The congress agreed to this request and Cornet was designated to replace Manguette on the commission revising the statutes.

The commission on the general strike was composed of the following: Manguette, Costa, Brousse, Perrare, Andrié, Hales, Joukovsky.

Andignoux requested that he should be added to the commission on the General Strike, to which he might bring some updates. This request was agreed.

The commission for statistics was composed of the following delegates: *Verrycken, Dave, Cyrille, Viñas, Spichiger, Pindy.* The congress agreed that there should be no session on Tuesday morning to allow commissions time to meet.

Claris requested that the congress should fix a regular schedule for its sessions. If an administrative session should be again necessary, he proposed that it should take place only in the mornings and that the rest of the day be allocated to public sessions.

Dave asked, what would be the use of further administrative sessions since the agenda for them seemed to him to have been more or less exhausted. What was most needed in the congress, was public sessions. He proposed that the hours of public sessions should be announced to Geneva's workers through posters and notices.

Andignoux said that if the four questions on the congress agenda were to be treated in public sessions then, in his view, further administrative sessions seemed superfluous.

Pindy thought that the four questions on the agenda should be discussed in public sessions; however, he insisted that there should be at least one more administrative session on Tuesday, as we still must come to an understanding on several points which can only be discussed in an administrative session.

Van den Abeele proposed that there should be an administrative session at 3 p.m. on Tuesday. This proposal was adopted.

Guillaume recalled an idea arising from the informal meeting of Sunday; the Propaganda Section of Geneva had announced a wish to take charge of organising a meeting in which congress delegates would have an opportunity to explain IWMA principles to the public of Geneva. He asked if the section had taken on this project.

Claris on behalf of the Propaganda Section of Geneva replied that nothing had yet been formally decided on this matter by the section, because it wished to consult the congress on the timing of the meeting and on the terms that might be used to announce it.

After a short discussion, the congress unanimously adopted the following project:

International Working Men's Association

On the occasion of the General Congress of the International all workers of Geneva are fraternally invited to take part in a popular meeting which will take place on Thursday night at 8 p.m., at the brasserie Schiess, (Pâquis area), Agenda: The International, its aim, and its means of action. The federative principle.

The session ended at 11 p.m.

TUESDAY 2 SEPTEMBER – FOURTH SESSION (ADMINISTRATIVE)

The session was opened with a roll-call, at 3.15 p.m. Hales and Eccarius were absent.

The reporter for the commission verifying mandates announced that a new French mandate had arrived, appointing Montels as a delegate, and a further mandate also from a French section, nominating Pindy as their representative. These mandates were accepted, under the guarantee of the Jura Federal Committee, and Montels was admitted and seated as a French delegate.

After a short discussion, congress adopted the following propositions, as proposed by the bureau:

Each speaker should only speak twice on the same point, after which, they should not be allowed to speak, unless they had a special authorisation from the congress.

Guillaume, reporting for the commission revising the General Statutes, spoke on the matter of the voting method that might be adopted by congress, a question that the commission had been asked to review. The commission, said the reporter, first asked itself the following preliminary question: 'Should the method of voting currently employed by the congress, be reviewed?' All members of the commission expressed their agreement, except Hales, who thought that the question of the method of voting was somewhat immaterial, and that its importance could no longer be as it had been at the congress of The Hague. The commission then considered the Spanish proposal, consisting of counting, in votes, not the number of delegates, but the number of Internationalists represented by those delegates.

The imperative mandate on this point, given to the Spanish delegates, already dates back to [the time of] the congress of The Hague, and the Spanish member of the commission, Farga, explained that the Spanish Federation had not had an opportunity since the congress of The Hague,[366] to reconsider this matter, and perhaps, if the question was looked at again, the Spanish Internationalists might have come over to the idea of a vote by federation.

The Spanish proposal was rejected by most of the commission, with Farga and Bert being the only votes in favour.

The Dutch and Belgian delegates had an imperative mandate to request voting by regional federation and had expounded this proposal within the commission. Hales asked what was meant by 'voting by federation'. The commission had not wanted to provide a formula, which would have been very difficult; it limited itself to observing facts as they were: the IWMA can now count on eight regional federations, whose names no one can contest, these are the following: America, Belgium, England, France, Italy, Jura, the Netherlands and Spain. Each of these eight federations would have a right to a vote in General Congresses.

After this explanation, the commission concluded with the following proposition, adopted unanimously, less the vote of Farga who abstained, and Bert who voted against:

The vote should be by federation, with each regional federation having one vote.

The discussion on the commission's proposition was opened.

Costa expressed his support for the proposition.

Brousse said that, as regards the current congress, there would be no difficulty in the absence of a definition of what was meant by 'regional federations'; but for the future, it would be necessary to decide on one, as a situation might arise in which delegates from a fictitious federation, composed of a few members only, might arrive at a future congress.

Joukovsky said that the Jura Federation had typical features for a regional federation, it was in fact composed of sections in Switzerland, France, and the Alsace,* with identical economic interests, united irrespective of political or territorial divisions. In eastern parts of France, workers' interests were inducing them, as they acquired capacity to organise themselves, to become a part of the Jura Federation rather than a federation based in the north or south of France. So, a regional federation might be constituted by virtue of geographical and economic interests, and not in conformity with national and political frontiers. The speaker then recalled the abuse that resulted from a vote by head, as at the Congress of The Hague. He also criticised the voting method proposed by the Spanish delegates, because if it were adopted, just one country with numerous sections might, with its votes, crush other federations where organisation was not equally advanced and where prospects were difficult.

Cornet replied to the objection of Brousse saying that if a case arose of a fictitious federation wishing to send a delegate, Congress would be able to examine the existence – real or not so real – of that federation.

The reporter of the commission said he thought it was not possible to arrive at an entirely satisfactory definition of a regional federation.

---

* The Swiss Jura shared a border with France and Germany; Alsace was annexed by the new German Reich after the Franco-Prussian war. Most, but not all, members of the Jura federation were primarily French speakers.

He thought it best to proceed as the commission proposed, to deal with things as they were, and to say that the regional federations each having a vote in the congress, were the eight regional federations now in existence. Later, if a new federation presents itself, asking to be admitted sharing in the International Pact as a regional federation, a future congress will have to decide on its admission, without having to define some more or less arbitrary abstract model for a regional federation.

Andignoux thought that the method of voting by federation would annihilate the autonomy of the section, and to avoid one evil, one was falling into another – he requested keeping [the practice of] voting by a head count of delegates.

Viñas remarked that if the method of voting proposed by the Spanish is criticised for the inconvenience that one federation alone might overwhelm all other federations through the number of its voters; the opposite criticism also might be addressed with equal justice, against the method proposed by the commission, i.e., the vote of a federation with many members might be overwhelmed by the voting of many smaller federations.

The *reporter* for the commission replied to Viñas that there are other arguments to be considered as against the Spanish delegates' proposals: i.e., that the method of voting that they advocate would be, in practice, unachievable and it could not be subjected to any serious verification. Furthermore, it would be unjust to judge the importance of a federation uniquely by the number of its active members; there are countries where the organisation has not yet taken off greatly, but the small number of workers who are organised there may be considered as representative of the whole of the proletariat of their country, and that later, our propaganda will lead them to join. In summary, none of the methods proposed is perfect, but voting by federation is the method that seems to present the fewest inconveniences; and, to attenuate any deficiencies, there is a means – to vote as little as possible. Moreover, congress decisions are only notices, and in the last resort it will be up to sections to vote. Furthermore, to safeguard the free expression of sections' opinions, it is clearly understood that the delegates of sections who disagree with the majority of a federation to which they belong, may always record their opinion in the minutes.

The proposition of the commission resolving **that the method of voting should be by regional federation,** was put to the vote:

In favour: Pindy, Guillaume, Mattei, Cyrille, Costa, Spichiger, Andrié, Dave, Van den Abeele, Cornet, Manguette, Verrycken, Joukovsky, Montels. Total 14.

Against: Bert, Farga, Brousse, Viñas. Total 4.

Abstentions: Alerini, Andignoux, Total 2.

The proposition was therefore adopted by 14 voters out of 20.

Cornet asked if the three French delegates would have three votes, or would they be considered as belonging to just one regional federation, having just one vote.

Viñas proposed that the French delegates should be attributed one vote, determined by the majority of their voters, as is the practice for every other regional federation. This proposition was adopted.

Joukovsky said that the section of propaganda of Geneva had mandated him, as their delegate, to request that the discussion of the question of the general strike should take place in an administrative session. He explained the reasons for this proposal, and after a short discussion, this was agreed.

Congress then decided that as a rule, administrative sessions should take place in the morning from 8 a.m. to noon, and in the afternoon from 2 to 6 p.m., and public sessions should be in the evening from 8 to 11 p.m.

The session was terminated at 7 p.m.

TUESDAY 2 SEPTEMBER – FIFTH SESSION (PUBLIC)

The session was opened at 8 p.m. with a reading of the minutes, which were adopted unanimously. The first matter on the agenda was the *revision of the General Statutes of the IWMA*.

Guillaume, (reporter of the commission for the revision of the statutes) [said]: The commission has not yet finished its work, but it thinks that already it is possible to call to the attention of the congress, that part of the task that has been accomplished. We began by discussing the general principles of organisation which should be at the base of the statutes, and first, we have had to come to an opinion on the institution of a General Council. The commission examined two questions, one after the other: 1) Should the General Council be maintained in its present form? 2) Should the General Council be preserved with some modification of its remit? The commission decided unanimously, to propose to the congress a negative resolution on both points; and, to put it another way, the commission is unanimous in proposing the complete abolition of the General Council.

Having decided that, there remained [the matter of] considering if a new institution should be created to replace the General Council. On this point different opinions were evident.

The English delegates proposed the establishment of a Central Federal Commission, denuded of any power, its role being limited to the execution of decisions taken in General Congresses. The Belgian and Jura delegates agreed, seeking the creation of three different commissions for general services, commissions that should be left to the care of three different federations. One of these commissions would be tasked with the preparation of the next general congress and the elaboration of its agenda; a second should be charged with a centralisation of all information on strikes and would transfer these to every federation and the last one would accumulate all statistical documents. However, it was observed that the workings of these last two commissions would have a great number of interlocking points, and it would be possible to merge them into just the one.

The Italian delegates observed that each year, each congress would be tasked with choosing a federation and with the allocation of various mandates and responsibilities. They saw a great danger in the creation of a central commission; the latter might come to usurp the powers vested previously in the General Council, and in that way, beneath the shadow of a new designation, come to replace it.

The commission had decided to put the entire matter before the congress, to have it consider how it would be best to discuss it all, and then decide.

Hales, I, like the commission, wish to see the General Council abolished, however, while I see the guilt and abuse of power of the latter, I do not see a sufficient reason there to oppose the creation of a central commission. If, a year since, the English IWMA found itself paralysed, if the events which have taken place in Spain were not understood by workers in England, if they were recast and distorted by the bourgeoisie, all of that arises from the absence of a central information point. It has been proposed to establish several commissions to avoid that inconvenience. One central commission seems preferable to me. It would ease work and be economical. One wishes to prevent a commission usurping power? It is easy to find guarantees against such a danger. Let it have no power, let it be a commission responsible for limited activities. There is little logic in foregoing the benefit that an institution might bring in the future, because bad things have been done in the past. And for the rest, I do not fear the non-acceptance of this English proposal, because were it to be rejected this year, it is certain that congress will have to reconsider that decision next year and accept it.

Brousse asked to speak on a point of order. He would like to see the debate defined more exactly. Is it the abolition of the General Council that is being discussed, or the English proposition?

Guillaume, the reporter, read the first of the propositions that the commission was submitting to the congress: **Does the congress wish to maintain the General Council in its current form?**

Joukovsky: When our Association was founded regional federations had not been organised and while workers were organised only in scattered sections, then one had to have a General Council. Such an institution was absolutely necessary. At first then, the General Council had its utility. Moreover, it presented few dangers. Up to the congress of Basle, it had neither rights, nor powers. It served only for the goal for which it was intended, for isolated sections it clarified a path when the latter asked for advice, it structured a link of solidarity among them.

But the General Council obtained powers at the congress of Basle, powers that it then exceeded. Manifestos were sent out, sections suspended, and all that in the name of the International. Where did the General Council find the right to act in the name of our Association? What allowed it to co-opt individuals without a mandate, some of them not even affiliates or members. I come to the congress of The Hague. The [delegates of] sections were a minority, almost only the General Council was represented there. Those of our comrades [Bakunin and Guillaume] who did not toe the line behind Karl Marx were thrown out, by means of a fictitious majority. By means of this majority, the right to suspend an entire federation was usurped. The newly elected General Council, now located in New York, as the faithful – but perhaps unintelligent – executor of Marx's orders, suspended the Jura Federation. Immediately the Internationalists of England, Italy, Belgium, Spain ceased to correspond with the Council. It kept its title as General, but it remained a General without soldiers. Is it possible to allow such authoritarianism to subsist among us? Evidently no. So, I conclude, the General Council must be abolished.

Perrare: In my view, the discussion that we have begun is not needed. All of us are against the institution of a General Council in its current form and I do not believe that any of us here have a mandate to protect its existence.

Costa: I agree with comrade Perrare, I request an immediate vote on the first point.

A roll call was taken, and the vote – **that the General Council in its current form should be abolished** – was unanimous (Prolonged applause in the auditorium).

Costa: I request a vote by acclamation on the second question.

Cyrille: I, on the contrary, request a vote by roll call.

Joukovsky: I agree with Cyrille's proposal.

A roll call vote was then agreed, and the second question was read out: **Should the institution of a General Council be completely abolished?** There was a unanimous and affirmative vote for that proposition. (Raucous and long applause in the auditorium).

The discussion on the third question was then opened:

Is there some reason to replace the institution of a General Council by some new administrative mechanism?

Ostyn: I reject the institution of a central committee as proposed by the English, and on this matter, I request the congress to vote on that prior question.

Van den Abeele: Comrade Ostyn's views are not the same as mine, the English proposal does not imply the organisation of power, but only of an executive committee, responsible for receiving and fulfilling orders.

Brousse: I request permission to ask congress a question. The abolition of a General Council has been voted and three propositions have been tabled. Some request – as a replacement – the creation of one single commission; others prefer three commissions; and others would like to give one federation the responsibility of taking on the International's administration. Before opening a discussion of these three questions, might not the congress find it useful to allow those of us to speak who reject all of these ideas? I find myself among the latter, and if it is allowed, I would reject all three. The vote just taken clearly shows that every delegate opposes the authoritarian principle. Is it logical to retreat, and to re-establish this principle in the shadows, under a new name? I think not. A central commission – even without powers – one with duties but no rights, does not seem to me to be [something] with no danger. It will have its creatures, its official propaganda, its official statistics, its pretensions. It will take advantage of every possible opportunity to establish its authority, to become a government. It will succeed. Soon, the General Council that we have just abolished will in effect be re-established in another form. Should three commissions be established instead of one? The danger would be even greater. Should one believe then in a division of labour? One would have only a multiplicity of powers. Instead of one government, we would have three. I vote against.

If one entrusts the administration of general services to a special federation, one re-establishes a government in a new form, and the worst of governments, a national government. One might no longer have to put up with the authority of a General Council, or a Central Committee, or three commissions, but one would establish one federation as the Queen of the International. I vote against. As for me, I do not wish to put anything else in place, instead of the power that has just fallen. And indeed, there is no need of anything. Did the International ever find itself, will it ever find itself, in a more critical position than the one it has been in recently? Without a central point, it had to face up to a force that was strongly organised and used to being obeyed. It survived not only without its government, but despite it, and what is more, it beat it. And if it can do as much in a time of war, can it not do as much in a time of peace? To ask the question is to resolve it. [If] you wish to abolish the structure of authoritarianism, then your programme is anarchy, and [yet] you appear to want to retreat from the consequences of your work? Do not hesitate. Your axe has struck – let it strike again, twice, thrice, and let the whole edifice perish.

Dave: I agree completely with what Brousse has just said.

Van den Abeele: Much as I am a partisan of anarchy, it seems to me that we are not yet strongly enough organised to make this become something real. A central power is a problem – that much has been proved. Well, comrades, we in the Netherlands are partisans of experimental practices. Temperaments are calmer in our country than among comrades of the South. I recommend experimentation, and having tried central power, we should try something else, three commissions for example. We cannot yet do without a correspondence centre, above all because of strikes. And take note of what has happened with affairs in Spain. Events in Alcoy only became well known long after the event, because there was no information centre. So, we need some organisation, and in this I am expressing more the opinion of those who gave me a mandate, rather than my own views, and I support the Jura proposition. We should not throw ourselves into the unknown from one day to the next.

Costa: I entirely share the opinion of comrade Brousse. Like him, I will vote against the three propositions. I will be fulfilling the mandate I received in doing so. We have just destroyed the General Council, if instead we designate one or more commissions, we will not have changed our institutions. The word would no longer exist, but the substance would remain. If we really want to abolish the authoritarian structures, we must uproot their very foundations. If we vote to establish a commission, we might see it almost without powers at first, but it will usurp them little by little, then it will make itself the master of every line of action, as the General Council did. Furthermore, it isn't easy to organise a good correspondence commission. Where will we find members with a knowledge of every language who can dedicate their every moment to the accomplishment of these tasks, which, if they are centralised, will become a crushing burden. Conforming to my mandate, I reject these three propositions.

Hales: Brousse and Costa, among the opponents of the English proposition, are the only comrades who have shown that they are being logical. It is between a central commission and anarchy that the discussion should really be confined. I reject anarchy because the word and its meaning are synonymous with dissolution. Anarchy means individualism, and individualism is the basis of the current social situation which we wish to destroy. Anarchy is incompatible with collectivism. Suppose there is a strike. Can one hope to win with an anarchic organisation? Everyone being their own master in that system, might do as they please, stopping or restarting work. General interests will be sacrificed to individual caprice. A true application of the anarchic principle would amount to the dissolution of the International, and the goal of this congress has its re-organisation, the precise opposite.

Authority and organisation should not be confused. We are not authoritarians, but we should remain organisers.[367] Far from voting for anarchy, which is the current social condition, we should combat it by the creation of a central commission and through the organisation of collectivism. Anarchy is the law of death; collectivism is the law of life.

Ostyn: Comrades, I did not expect to see this matter discussed in this way, and above all, I did not expect that it should be given the character attributed to it by the English Federation. For me, anarchy is a powerful means to achieve the goal that we want to obtain, and when one says that current society has an anarchist principle, one might appear to have the semblance of logic but, in reality, one commits a comprehensive error. Society takes children in the cradle, and never allows them to exercise free will; from the cradle to the grave it imposes its will, never permitting any free expression or free will. To break these fetters what should we demand? The method of anarchy. We seek one goal – the achievement of human fraternity – but we seek to obtain it through voluntary discipline, and not at all through the discipline that current society seeks to impose on us – the discipline of the soldier, or the discipline of religion.

What is needed to break this discipline? The means of anarchy. Whenever you delegate authority to someone, even with the guarantee of an imperative mandate, you alienate your every initiative, your every liberty. We should not accept any dictator, because no dictator is faithful, not even the one that Marat might have dreamt of. The Parisians were criticised because in their 72 days of struggle they did not find a man who was fully up to dealing with events. Consider then that we have just finished having to put up with twenty years of Imperial [Napoleonic] authoritarianism. When the Commune movement broke out, we gathered just what we had sown; we had grown used to that old [Napoleonic] discipline, and individual initiative was lacking. I will vote against any authoritarian centre. Each federation can take care of its concerns, congress will serve to maintain relations between the federations as they exist.

Guillaume: I do not intend to continue the discussion on its current lines. That would be to go too far. The International's press has addressed the matter from a theoretical viewpoint; here, it would be more useful to study things from the point of view of practical means. Let us consider our experience and the things it has taught us. I am indifferent if experience is considered one way or another, it doesn't bother me. We know the danger we run into with a single central commission. We might remove all its powers, but by virtue of its privileged position, it would keep them in practice. So, on this point, experience has taught us, and taught us well. Also, it is certain that we will have a congress next year; a federation will take on responsibility for organising it. We can already agree on that point. As for the matter of commissions on statistics and strikes, we might try one or other of the proposed combinations; if or when we might find that an institution was damaging, we might replace it by another, and, in turn, test that.

Perrare: We are facing two propositions, one seeks to replace the General Council, now abolished, with one or more commissions, the other seeks to avoid putting anything else in its place. When we came to abolishing the General Council, did we desire to kill off a word or particular men? Evidently, neither the one, nor the other. It was the very principle of authority that we wanted to kill off. If we create one or more commission, we are retreating on ourselves, we are returning to institutions that we thought it sensible to destroy. One may divide up power more and more, but it will still exist. So, I support the proposition that we should not create any commissions.

Van den Abeele: I recognise what has just been dispensed with was evil, and to be logical, we should therefore try out a form of organisation that is its antithesis. Certainly, representatives always seek to increase their powers. But since a General Council has been so easily destroyed, is there really some danger in trying out a few scattered commissions? I see none. Let us try these methods, which we can easily abandon if they become damaging.

Costa: I request a vote.

Brousse: I think we shouldn't close the discussion.

Viñas: So far, we have discussed words, rather than substance in depth. The definition of anarchy given by comrade Hales is as bad as that of comrade Ostyn. I think it would be useful to establish a statistical and correspondence commission, provided we give it no powers. The danger of a similar institution has been discussed, a danger to be seen in a possible moral ascendency over our Association. Moral ascendency may be collective or individual. Certainly, it will be exercised by those whose intelligence will promote our Association. If I prefer one commission to many, that is because work that is centralised in that way will be easier. If it is contended that the institution of a similar commission is contrary to principles, we should press on, and abolish committees in our sections and federations.

Returning to the definition of the word *anarchy*. That which comrade Hales calls anarchy is individualism: anarchy on the contrary, signifies the negation of authority. Bourgeois society has understood perfectly that anarchic principles were making immense progress among the masses and to stop that progress, it made anarchy the synonym of disorder. Anarchy means organisation of an economic order, and the negation of political authority.*

Brousse: Hales has given the word anarchy a particular definition, one that I cannot let pass without a protest. Anarchy does not mean disorder; it is nothing other than the complete and absolute negation of all material authority. It is the abolition of governmental regimes, it is the introduction of a regime of contracts: contracts engaged between workers, between communes, between corporate bodies. In all this I see nothing contrary to collectivist organisation. As for the practical side of the question, I am also in favour of an experimental practice. But we have experience already. We have seen the inconvenience of an international power; in the struggle which just now has reversed it, we have seen the advantages and the absence of all authority. Logic would therefore indicate that we should remain faithful to the anarchic organisation that has enabled our victory. If we organise any power at all, we will, without doubt, be repeating bourgeois history. We abolished the dictatorship of a General Council just as absolute monarchy was abolished; your three commissions correspond to the constitutional governments of the liberal bourgeoisie. It is fitting for internationalists to do without governments now.

Van den Abeele: I persist in supporting the proposition of Belgium and the Jura. You have been told that experience has condemned the General Council and any possible commission; so just one thing remains – for us, to try dispensing with any central organisation at all. Following that logic, one would not stop there, one would forgo every organisation throughout the International and one would order the abolition of all IWMA commissions including those of sections and federations. I do not think that there is any danger, as has been said, in entrusting a federation with the responsibility of constituting a central bureau. No parallel should be established between such a bureau and the ex-General Council. We propose the creation of

---

* *The Times*, 6 September, has this wording: "The present state of society knew of no other than political organization. What was required was the social and industrial organization of society.'

commissions – for statistics, strikes and correspondence. It matters little if two or three commissions are agreed. We might even come to agree – with comrade Viñas – on creating a single commission. But we are told, such entities are full of danger: the men who would compose them would exert a moral ascendency and the consequences would be damaging? Never, say I, can such an ascendency be destroyed, and moreover, it is not dangerous. Did it impede the General Council's destruction? It will be even more impotent in the service of a simple commission. Belgium has had the benefit of experience with this institution. Our regional council delivers great service, and given that it receives orders, but never issues them, it remains a faithful servant.* We suggest you extend to our entire Association our very successful experience.

(Many delegates requested the termination of the discussion.)

Pindy: To me, it seems impossible to delay the question until tomorrow evening, given the other work which remains. I request that the next session should be used to resolve it.

Joukovsky: Given the importance of the subject, I, on the contrary request that it should be addressed in a public session.

Dave: submitted the following proposition:

The IWMA congress, in line with aspirations demonstrated often in different circumstances by the proletariat in favour of the principle of anarchy, a synonym of organised order, declares, that this principle should find its first, real and effective application in the making of revised general statutes, refusing – either from the point of view of propaganda, or from the point of view of labour statistics – to create one or more central commissions responsible for official business.

Verrycken, president: I cannot allow the opening of a discussion on the proposition just submitted to the bureau at this moment. First, one must decide if the matter should be taken on into a public session.

The congress voted to remit it to the next public session.

The session was ended.

---

* *The Times*, 6 September quoted him saying: 'We have our Federal Council for Belgium, and the men composing it have by their moral ascendency rendered an immense service, but they have no authority, and do not exercise any power. Authority is the absence of the absence of well-defined laws. Where these exist, things are regulated according to law, and then no authority is required to exact obedience.'

WEDNESDAY 3 SEPTEMBER – SIXTH SESSION (ADMINISTRATIVE)

The session was opened at 3 p.m. with a roll call. Perrare was absent.

A preliminary discussion was opened concerning which of the points on the agenda should be given priority. The congress decided to address first the question of congress costs, and how they should be shared.

Joukovsky suggested that the costs should be divided equally among the federations participating in the congress.

Pindy announced that the American section, by virtue of the letter it had written, had requested to share in the costs of the congress.[368] However, it would be best not to ask anything from the French sections, he thought.

Montels said that the French section which he represented was ready to pay its share.

Brousse said he too was sure that France would want to contribute its quota, and he would oppose it being exempted, because no one should be able to use this exception later as an argument to reduce the rights of the French sections

Joukovsky thought that it would be better that the French section retained all their resources for the needs of propaganda in their country, and he proposed that in future, and as a general rule with respect to countries where the IWMA was banned, that they should be excused from contributing their share of congress costs.

Cornet supported Joukovsky and, like him, thought that it would be more useful for French sections to allocate their funds to propaganda.

Congress decided that regional federations should share equally the congress costs,* but that France should not be included, or pay a share. The question of printing [a report on] the workings of the Congress was discussed next.

Congress decided that the report on its deliberations should be entrusted to the Jura Federation and printed in the French language, and that it should comprise an extract of the administrative sessions, and the stenographic report of public sessions. The costs of printing should be covered, in the first place by the selling of the brochure, and if a deficit was left, it should be divided up and shared in equal parts by the regional federations.

The next question on the agenda was the General Strike. Having heard Joukovsky, the commission reporter on the matter, delegates Manguette, Verrycken, Alerini, Guillaume, Costa, Brousse, Bert, Viñas, Ostyn, Spichiger and Hales spoke in order.

---

*   These amounted to 158.20 Francs, so 22.60 per federation. James Guillaume, *L'Internationale: documents et souvenirs 1864-78*, part 5, chapter 5, p. 117.

The continuation of that discussion was postponed to the administrative session of the following day. The session was ended at 7 p.m.

WEDNESDAY 3 SEPTEMBER – SEVENTH SESSION (PUBLIC)

The session was opened at 8 p.m., presided over by Verrycken. The roll call showed that every delegate was present. The president read a telegram of congratulations sent to the congress from a meeting of 6,000 workers in Berlin. This was the sense of the message in the original.[369]

Berlin, 3 September, 1.20 p.m.
– to the *International Congress*, Geneva, Switzerland, Brasserie Schiess, Pâquis.

The popular assembly, meeting in Berlin on 2 September, 6,000 persons strong, confronting the ruling classes' rejoicing and their celebration of bloody battles and annexations,* believes it is duty bound to freely and frankly declare: We, workers, condemn all national hatred and desire the fraternity of peoples, so that the working class of every nation should free itself from the yoke of reaction and the power of capital; consequently we offer the hand of fraternity to those who fight with us, on the terrain of socialism in every country.

By order of the assembly, the bureau: Hasenclever, Hasselmann, Winter, Ecks, Derossi.

Dresdenerstrasse, 63.

---

* This is a reference to the inauguration ceremony for a victory column celebrating victories in recent wars, held in Berlin, in September 1873. Wilhelm Hasenclever and Wilhelm Hasselmann were editors of the paper *Der Neuer Sozial-Demokrat*, the journal of the Lassalle organisation, the *Allgemeiner Deutscher Arbeiterverein* (German General Labour Union, ADAV). On the 3 September it commented that this *Sedanfeier* and celebration of past and future bloodshed came as a danger to peace. On the 7th it defined war as an attack by 'furies'. *Der Volksstaat*, (journal of the Social-Democratic Workers' Party), also carried reports on the *Sedanfeier* on 10 September. *Der Neuer Sozial-Demokrat* carried further reports on the federalist congress on the 12 and 17 September. On the 12th it noted that the intrigues of Herr Marx and his comrades would be prevented in future by the abolition of the General Council; henceforth, some co-ordination would be in the hands of the federation hosting the next congress; it also noted that the IWMA's Spanish membership was between 35,000 and 50,000. The edition of the 5th had commented on the IWMA: '… lies have been told that the ADAV was an enemy of the IWMA. When it was attacked, it fought only against the clique of Marxists.' On the 17th it noted that the various federations that refused to place themselves in subjection to the General Council were now free of it. The Jura Federation exchanged publications and had cordial, but not close relations with the ADAV.

A round of applause greeted this reading.* The bureau proposed that the congress should reply to the Berlin workers' greetings, and send a telegram in these terms:

Brasserie Schiess, Geneva, 3 September 1873
The delegates of the autonomous international congress, meeting in Geneva, thank the workers of Berlin for their fraternal greetings. They are happy that German workers, defying government persecutions and authoritarian intrigues, declare their solidarity with the internationalist brothers in the struggle against capital.
The bureau: Verrycken, Costa, Van den Abeele, Viñas, Eccarius, Pindy.

This reply was adopted unanimously. The minutes of the public session of the previous day were read and adopted. The agenda called for the continuation of the discussion on the revision of the general statutes.

Brousse: I think we should review the proposition put by Dave at the end of yesterday's public session and I request that it be read out.

The president read Dave's proposition.

Guillaume, reporter of the commission: The commission has already considered this proposition. After last night's discussion we became aware that we were not so far from an understanding and, indeed, the commission came to agree, unanimously, on a draft text which appears to us, to reconcile all the propositions that have been tabled. The commission hopes that the proposition that it is about to propose may also reconcile every opinion in the congress, just as it has among the commission itself. I request authorisation to read out the commission's entire draft text.

Dave: I am opposed to the entire proposal being read just now, and request that congress discusses my proposal.

Perrare: I request that congress first considers Dave's proposal before considering the substance the commission's proposal.

Manguette: I support comrade Perrare.

Van den Abeele: I do not think that Dave's proposition should be discussed at all. The discussion in yesterday's session showed that although we here may all be anarchists, our constituents are not all so. So, I think that it is not useful to discuss that proposition, and I request that we return to the agenda.

---

* *La Federación*, 20 September 1873, commented that it had been pretended that there was unanimous support in that region for authoritarian and centralist opinions; the telegram indicated that this was not so, and where communication was direct from workers to workers, things were very different. The exchange of telegrams was published in *Der Neuer Social-Demokrat*, 5 September. *Der Volksstaat* (1 October 1873), commented that they were the true partners of this international and comic Lassalleans were chasing the 'phantom of respectability'.

Dave: I do not oppose returning to the agenda; but I cannot let what Van den Abeele said pass without a protest. I must declare that the mechanics of Verviers gave me a mandate to defend anarchy, and that all the worker mechanics who made me their delegate to this congress are anarchists.

[Draft Statutes]

The congress decided to hear a reading of the commission's draft statutes.[370]

Guillaume, reporter: this is the draft text.

Considering,

That the emancipation of workers should be the accomplishment of workers themselves; that workers' efforts to win freedom should not allow the development of new privilege but should establish the same rights and the same duties for all.

That workers' subjection to capital is the fount of all servitude – material, moral and political.

That, for this reason, the economic emancipation of workers is the great goal to which every political movement ought to be subordinated.

That hitherto all struggles have failed, for want of solidarity between workers of various trades within each country, and for the lack of fraternal unity between the workers of different regions.

That the emancipation of labour is not a problem that is simply local or national, and that on the contrary it concerns all civilised nations, and its solution necessarily depends on their practical and theoretical co-operation.

That the movement now coming to fruition among workers of the most industrious countries of the whole world, in raising new hopes, calls for the combination of efforts that are, as yet, isolated and gives a solemn warning against falling back into old errors.

For these reasons:

The Congress of the *International Working Men's Association*, held in Geneva on 3 September 1866, declares that this Association, and every individual or society joining it, will recognise *morality, justice,* and *truth* as the basis of their conduct toward to all men, without distinction of nationality, creed, or colour.

Congress considers it a duty is to reclaim the rights of man and of citizens not only for members of the Association, but also for whoever accomplishes its duties. *No duties without rights; no rights without duties.*

The Regional Federations represented at the International Congress meeting in Geneva on 1 September 1873, inspired by the above declaration of principles, have revised the general statutes of the IWMA, and have adopted them in the following form:

[Articles]

1. The International Working Men's Association has the goal of bringing about the unity of workers of all countries on the terrain of solidarity in the struggle of Labour against Capital, a struggle that must achieve the complete emancipation of Labour.

2. Whoever adopts and defends the principles of the Association may become a member, subject to the responsibility of the section that admits them.

3. Sections and Federations forming the Association preserve their complete autonomy, which is to say their right to organise themselves as they see fit, to administer their own affairs, without any outside interference and to choose for themselves the path they intend to take, to achieve Labour's freedom.

4. A General Congress of the Association shall meet each year, on the first Monday in September.

5. Each section, whatever the number of its members, has the right to send a delegate to the General Congress.

6. The Congress has, as its mission, to provide a place for workers of various countries to present their aspirations, and through discussion to bring them into harmony. At the opening of congress each Regional Federation shall present a report on the development of the Association in the past year. Except for matters of administration, there will be no recourse to voting; questions of principle cannot be objects for a vote. General Congress decisions are mandatory only for those Federations that accept them.

7. Voting at a General Congress will be by Federation, each Regional Federation having one vote.

8. For the countries where the International Association is banned, sections or federations wishing to be represented at the congress should be take care to advise a neighbouring federation, three months in advance, and they will gather information necessary to check that these sections and federations do exist. Their delegates will be admitted to the congress only where there is a guarantee from the federation which has made these checks and will have only a deliberative voice.

9. Each year Congress will name a regional federation to take charge of

the organisation of the next congress. The federation having received this mandate will serve as the Federal Bureau for the Association; and questions that the various federations or sections that would like to have placed on the congress agenda should be sent, at least three months in advance of the event, to that federation, which should then bring them to the attention of every regional federation. The Federal Bureau may also serve as an intermediary on matters of strikes, statistics, and correspondence in general, between the federations which may so address them.

10. The congress will itself designate the city where the next congress should be held. On the date appointed for Congress delegates will come together in regular fashion on the day and in the place appointed without there being a need for any special notification.

11. Over a year, at the initiative of a section or federation, a vote of regional federations may change the place or date of a General Congress or convene an Extraordinary Congress, in the light of events.

12. Whenever a new regional federation seeks to become a member of the Association, it should announce that intention at least three months before the General Congress, to whatever federation is acting as the Federal Bureau. The latter will make this known to all regional federations and these will have to decide whether to accept the new federation, and accordingly they will mandate their delegates to the General Congress, which in the last instance will decide.

I should remark that the text of the preamble, up to the words *No duties without rights; no rights without duties* is a reproduction of the text of the old preamble, as it can be found heading the official statutes in French, as adopted at the Congress of Geneva in 1866. The commission has simply replaced, in the sixth clause, the words 'in the most industrialised countries *of Europe*' with 'in the most industrialised countries *of the whole world*'. I should also advise congress, that, regarding article 8 of the draft, that the commission was divided; and that some members wished to give delegates from a country where the IWMA was banned only a consultative voice; and others wishing them to have a deliberative voice.

The discussion on the preamble to the General Statues was then opened.

Bert: I insist that nothing should be modified or added to the old preamble, because it is a historic monument that should be respected. In 1866, the international movement was limited to Europe; let us therefore leave in the preamble a recognition of that fact; workers will know, without it being written into the statutes, that today the great movement is spreading over the whole world.

Ostyn: I do not demand any changes to the preamble that has been suggested by the commission; I would like an explanation of this clause: 'That the emancipation of workers should be the accomplishment of workers themselves.' It would be good to define what is meant by *worker*, because it is the touchstone which determines who may be admitted into the IWMA. If what is meant by this expression is the entire world of labour then the International must open its arms to everyone; if on the other hand the term 'workers' is intended to mean only manual workers then [in the considering clause] the preamble should use something more precise, which would indicate the path to be followed for admitting members of the Association. This is a question asked everywhere, so without any change to the preamble, I request that the meaning of the word *worker* should be very clearly defined.

Claris: I do not share the viewpoint of Bert, and I believe that in clause 6 of the preamble it is necessary to replace the words *of Europe*, with the words *of the entire world*, and on this point, I rely on what Bert himself has just said: i.e., that the International is not limited to Europe and has spread to the entire world. As for the point raised by Ostyn, it is addressed in draft article 2, in which it is said that any individual who adopts and defends the principles of the International may be received as a member, so in consequence I believe that there is no reason to engage in a discussion of that matter as it relates to the preamble.

Dave: comrade Ostyn requests that the word 'worker' should be defined. Well, when the International was founded its founders did not call it the International Association of Manual Workers (In French *ouvriers*), but International Association of Workers (In French *travailleurs*); so they saw a difference between the word 'worker' and the words 'manual worker'. I believe we should keep the original wording which says 'workers' and not 'manual workers', and this term 'workers' should comprehend at the same time both those who are called 'thinking workers' and 'manual workers'. It is not possible to carry out the least task of manual work without employing intelligence, just as it is impossible to do the least intellectual work without muscular effort playing a part. Moreover, thinking workers like manual workers are waged workers. In my view there is both justice and reason to comprehend, under the term 'worker', all those who live from the product of their labour, without creating distinctions which would serve only to divide the forces of socialism.

Perrare: As against comrade Claris, I request that there should be a very serious discussion of what is meant by the word 'worker' (*travailleur*). If the

International is only to admit manual workers, draft article 2 which Claris mentioned, should be suppressed. The word 'worker' (*travailleur*) should be properly defined, so that it is known if the founders of the International erred by allowing in people who brought divisions with them. We should not allow in people who might say they are salaried – such as lawyers, journalists, and others.

Bert: Again, I insist that the 1866 preamble should be preserved without any modification. As for defining the word 'worker', I see no need.

Costa: It seems to me there is some confusion: one person has requested to speak on the first clause of the preamble, another on the last clause. We should come to an understanding on the point being discussed. Also, it was agreed that a delegate should speak only twice on the same subject, and I request that this rule should be applied.

Eccarius: I would like to observe that the meaning of the word 'worker' (*travailleur*) is defined by the sense of the English equivalent of this expression. The English text of the statutes has 'working man' where the French text has *travailleur*, and 'working man' signifies manual worker (*ouvrier manuel*).

Dave: In that case the matter should be settled at once. Since the English text has 'working man' and since the term 'working man' signifies *ouvrier manuel* (manual worker) one must know if the English text is the only official text of the statutes, and under what conditions the French translation was made.

Guillaume reporter: There was no translation into French of the statutes, rather there was a *French official text*, which was adopted by the Geneva Congress in 1866, and which is to be found in the report of that congress. One cannot appeal to the English text as an original text, therefore.

Dave: If that is the case, I maintain what I said in the first place. It is not manual workers alone but all workers who should be able to take part in the International. Also, I must reply to Perrare, that it was not those called thinking workers most especially who brought divisions into the International (which moreover will [soon] be ended), there were also intransigents among manual workers. As for thinking workers, Perrare thinks that as regards them, there is cause for much apprehension, for the influence that they may acquire, however, but there is little to be feared in that influence, because the number of thinking workers will always be small in number and will never obtain a majority. As for the rest, I do not understand all these chicanes and quibbles as regards the word 'worker' – it is moreover very simple – one calls a worker everyone who uses his physical or intellectual faculties to create or work on socially useful objects – and all workers without distinction should be allowed to join the International.

Viñas: For me, Dave's definition does not appear sufficient. I consider as workers everyone who is exploited in current society, and anyone who is exploited has a right to join up, to end the exploitation of man by man. Therefore, I recognise that every man has a right to fight in our ranks, and I prefer that the current wording of the preamble should be kept, with the reservation that later, some exceptions may have to be made, if needs arise.*

Verrycken, president, read the Bert proposition requesting that the preamble – as set out in 1866 – should be kept entirely unchanged.

Van den Abeele: We have discussed the matter of knowing how, and to whom, the term 'worker' should be applied. Like comrade Viñas, I am little concerned with the difference that might be established between manual and other workers. The International is a revolutionary association, it wants to end the exploitation of man by man. So, to me, any man who sincerely wants revolution is fit to become part of the International. I would ask manual workers if, on the day of the revolution when the time for discussion was left behind, when one was on the streets, and when one entered the domain of facts, would they repel thinking workers who came to fight on their side? I would ask, have thinking workers not shown their worth, and are they not struggling already today with manual workers, side by side for the triumph of the revolution? Also, I cannot understand the spirit of exclusivism that would shut the doors of the International on them.

Hales: The founders of the International were members of *Trades Unions*, supported by some workers from Paris. When it began, the Association had no goal other than a struggle for wages; also, that idea, in the mind of the founders, was applicable only to manual workers. It was only later, in replacing the English word workingmen by the vague expression worker (*travailleur*) that the doors were opened to the bourgeois, and they brought about the discussion that has [since] divided us; those divisions are the work of the bourgeois whom we allowed to join the International on the pretext that they were thinking workers.

Ostyn: I do not want in any way to make this a matter of persons, and I am addressing only the question of principles. I request [a definition of] what is meant by the phrase: 'The emancipation of workers should be the accomplishment of workers themselves'. Because, if one wants to interpret things in a certain way, everyone is a worker – the Marshals of France work, the Pope himself, each works in his own way. Well, when I look at this phrase, so plain, so precise: 'The emancipation of workers should be the

* *The Times*, 8 September: 'All who subsisted by their own labour were to be admitted, and those who lived by the profit of other people's labour were to be excluded.'

accomplishment of workers themselves', I wonder what the founders of the International wished to say, what did they have in mind. I recognise perfectly that the little teaching we have comes from philosophers, from the learned people, from journalists, who are thinking workers, and are consequently bourgeois.* But, let us get the root of the matter, we see popular classes seeking allies among their oppressors; but always they have been deceived by them, because the latter act in their own interest – witness Mirabeau, La Fayette and others. And it is quite simple: these men come among us, they are educated, we are not; naturally, things work out in such a way that they take over things, and it is we ourselves who give them the means. Look at what happens in congresses – sections and federations almost always have bourgeois delegates. Well, we, we have our suspicions concerning bourgeois people, and we believe that if proletarians alone were in the International, they would not go out to seek helpers who, taking charge, would make them lazy, because they are more educated, for the tasks that need doing, which should be workers' affairs. From a theoretical point of view, I recognise all men as brothers, but in practice when someone does something good for me, I ask, in what interest, and in what way, do they work for me? I support Hales's observations; and without requesting any change in the first considering clause, I request that meanings be defined.

Pindy: Ostyn has just said that he doesn't want to change anything in the first considering clause; and since he alone raised an objection, I think that the discussion might be closed.

Perrare: I oppose the termination of the discussion, and if comrade Ostyn wants to end discussion on this point, I would like to continue.

Cyrille: I do not wish to reply to everything that Ostyn has said. I would just like to say that all workers have the right to be admitted into the International, as equals, and I propose the following definition of the word 'worker': 'A worker is a citizen who dedicates his physical or intellectual faculties to create or improve objects that are useful to society.'

Many voices: Close!

Perrare: I oppose a closure.

Costa: I would like to say just this to our manual worker comrades: I believe that one would enormously limit and restrict revolutionary forces by wishing to eliminate those who are called thinking workers; no force should be rejected when one wants to make revolution. And I add, that if you refuse to accept any and every revolutionary force, you will be taking the

---

* *La Liberté* (Paris, 6 September) reported that of the thirty delegates, 25 were thinking workers. The notes on delegates quoted in the *Official Report* above, suggest that around half of the federalist delegates were manual workers.

risk that at a certain moment you may see the forces you rejected, turning back against you.

Brousse: I request we should not create further dilemmas, and that we should vote on the considering clauses just as they are. We can easily agree on the sense of the word 'worker'; an excellent definition has been given by comrades Dave and Cyrille. But I believe that one should make the following distinction, that those whose productivity depends on a capital acquired through exploitation cannot be considered as true workers.

Guillaume, reporter: It seems to me that this is not the place where that sort of question should be discussed. The considering clauses do not seek to define the qualities required for membership of the IWMA. It would be better to wait for the moment when we will discuss the second article.

Montels: I think that if we agreed the restrictions that Ostyn and Perrare suggest, we would be placing ourselves in contradiction with the principles of truth and justice written in our statutes. In particular, a restriction of this sort would drive away from the International a class of exploited people: I speak of employees. Do you believe that an employee paid 100 or 120 francs monthly is not exploited as much or more than many workers, even if his position obliges him to wear an overcoat? Any person who is exploited has a right to join the International, and we should only exclude exploiters.

Claris: There has been a reply to Ostyn and Perrare, giving the true definition of the word 'worker', but there has been no response to Hales, who suggested that the original text of the statutes has been altered because the French version replaced the words English word 'workingman' with the word 'worker' (*travailleur*). No credence should be allowed for this historical error. There is no original English text: given that the only official statutes of the International were adopted at the congress in Geneva [in 1866], given that they were discussed and adopted in French, such that the word *travailleur* of the French version is quite as original as the English word 'workingman', and the word 'worker' is not an unfaithful translation created after the event. Ostyn tells us that never has there been a bourgeois who has worked with disinterest for the popular cause: but [what about] Proudhon, but [what about] Buonarotti, but [what about] Grachus Babeuf, but [what about] Anacharis Cloots[371] – were they manual workers then? And would you have shut the door of the International on them?

Hales: I think that on this subject the discussion would be more useful as regards the second article.

With Perrare no longer requesting time to speak, the president put the first five considering clauses to the vote and they were adopted unanimously.

Guillaume, reporter read the sixth considering clause. He recalled that in the draft the commission had replaced the words 'of Europe' in the old text, with the words of 'the entire world'.

Bert: I request that nothing in the old text should be changed.

Hales: On the contrary, I propose that the clause should be entirely supressed.

Cyrille: I propose the following text: **Considering that the movement that is developing among workers of the most industrialised countries, in giving birth to new hopes, offers a solemn warning to not fall back into old errors, and that, to avoid paralysing its advance the working class of all countries must combine all its efforts to achieve enfranchisement simultaneously.**

Guillaume: As the reporter for the commission, I must reject Hales's proposition. The preamble to the statutes is a historical monument of sorts, it is a programme that in few lines defines the aspirations of the modern proletariat. It should be left to subsist as it is, it cannot be changed without being spoilt. There is another reason for leaving the preamble intact which should persuade this congress, and that is that it is the work of the old General Council. When adversaries do something good, one should recognise that; let us not allow others say of us, that we mutilated the preamble of the statutes for the puerile pleasure of undoing the work of others.

Cornet: I request that the clause be put to the vote.

Bert: I claim priority for my proposition: I proposed that that the current text of the sixth considering clause should be preserved as it is.

The president: I will first put to the vote the most radical proposition, from Hales, which requests the complete deletion of this clause.

The Hales proposition was rejected – 17 voted *no*; against 3 voting *yes*.

The president: The congress should now decide on the Bert proposition.

Manguette: the commission proposes only a small change in the text; taking into account that the International should also embrace workers in America, it would replace the words 'of Europe', with the words 'of the entire world'. Bert on the other hand wants to keep the words 'of Europe'. I agree that we should not mutilate the preamble of the statutes, but neither should we fall into fetishism conserving every word as if it was a relic; I would vote for proposal of the commission.

Cyrille: I have proposed a new wording for the sixth clause, and I note that I deliberately introduced the word 'simultaneous', because we have all recognised that a social revolution cannot take place in an isolated fashion; it is important that we introduce that word into the considering preamble so that proletarians of the entire world know that they must revolt in simultaneous fashion.

Guillaume, reporter: I must also reject Cyrille's proposition. It is not because we have put the word 'simultaneous' into the statutes, that workers will adopt it entirely for their revolutionary movement. A new version of the clause might become the subject of endless discussions on the interpretation that should be given to this text. Also, in all respects, I think it best to keep to the proposition of the commission.

Cyrille: I do not want to provoke tiresome discussion, and in face of these objections, I withdraw my amendment.

Hales: In that case I take up Cyrille's proposition because I believe that the movement must be accomplished by all workers at the same time. I propose this text: **Considering that the movement must be accomplished through the cooperation of all workers in civilised countries.**

Perrare: I would like to know what is meant by workers of 'civilised' countries, and if [we think] exploitation should continue to exist for workers in countries designated as non-civilised.

Hales: I withdraw the word 'civilised'.

The Hales amendment was put to the vote and rejected.

Guillaume, reporter, announces that the commission has adopted the proposition that consists of deleting the words 'of Europe' without replacing them with the words 'of the entire world'.

That proposal was adopted unanimously, less the votes of the English delegates.

Guillaume, reporter, read that part of the preamble to the statutes up to the words 'No duties without rights, no rights without duties'.

The discussion was opened.

Alerini: I do not want to prolong debate, but in the text just read out there is a word that shocks me – the word 'moral'. The definition of this word is so vague, so elastic, that really it has no positive meaning; in reality, there are so many different moralities, that anyone ends up with his own. As the word cannot be defined in a scientific way, I believe there would be nothing untoward in deleting it.

Costa: I support Alerini's view. At a congress of sections in Romagna, there has already been talk of suppressing this word – and correctly so. There are many 'moralities' in the world – one has the morality of priests, of the bourgeoisie, of soldiers, and of workers, perhaps there is a morality of robbers too. One must then, in any case, give this word a clear meaning in saying 'revolutionary morality'.

Guillaume, reporter, it seems to me that the objections just heard are rather metaphysical in nature, and do not take reality into account. One should keep in mind that the statutes of the International are addressed to workers, and to them only; philosophical subtlety does not exist; and to be understood, one must use the most ordinary expressions very simply. Remain calm, workers will not mistake the sense of the word 'morality'; they know perfectly well that the morality at issue is not that of priests or that of the bourgeoisie.

Perrare: I agree with Guillaume's reasoning and add that if one wanted to delete the word 'morality' because its meaning is badly defined, one would also have to cut the word 'justice', which might carry the same objection, because there are many ways of understanding justice.

Brousse: in my view the words 'justice' and 'morality' duplicate meaning, and if we keep the word 'justice', there is no reason to keep the word 'morality'.

Hales: Certainly, the bourgeoisie understands the words 'truth', 'morality' and 'justice' differently than us; so, there is no reason to dispute one of these words more than another and such a discussion would be very lengthy. I think it would be simpler to maintain the three words 'truth', 'morality' and 'justice' and to go on to something else.

Alerini: the reasons given haven't resolved my objections to the word 'morality', but so as not to lose time I withdraw my request for it being deleted.

Hales: I propose that the words 'The Congress of the IWMA, held in Geneva on 3 September 1866' should be cut from the preamble. I think that it is not necessary to say that a congress was held in Geneva in 1866 in our statutes.

Guillaume, reporter: the commission on the contrary thinks that this reference should be kept in the statutes, because it is a reminder of the most important date of our century, the foundation of the International.

Brousse: I share Hales's opinion, if the phrase in question is maintained, the revision that we are about to make will appear to emanate from the 1866 congress.

Guillaume, reporter: I note that after the old preamble, the commission has inserted a new clause, which does not allow any misunderstanding on this point; it is set out thus:

The regional federations represented at the International Congress meeting in Geneva on 1st September 1873, inspired by this declaration of principles, have revised the General Statutes of the IWMA and have adopted them in the following form.

Viñas: I support Hales's amendment, because for me, the reasons just given do not seem conclusive. If the date of the first IWMA congress is memorable, it can be preserved somewhere else, other than in the statutes.

Hales: The preamble does not need to be more sacred than the text of the statutes; if it is useful, let it be changed, we should change it without allowing ourselves to falter on account of a date or terms. Furthermore, I will restrain myself, but come back later to propose something else – changing the title of our Association. Indeed, the current form of the Association is no longer the same as it was when founded in 1866; it is therefore logical to give it a new name, and I propose this: *International Labour Federation*. But that discussion will come later; for the moment I propose only the deletion of the words that I indicated in the preamble.

The president put Hales's proposition to the vote, and it was rejected.

The last part of the preamble to the statutes, as drafted by the commission was then adopted.

The president announced that the next public session would be held on Thursday 4 September at 2 p.m.

The session was ended.

THURSDAY 4 SEPTEMBER – EIGHTH SESSION (ADMINISTRATIVE)

The session was opened at 9 a.m. with a roll call.

Van den Abeele read a letter from France wishing the federalist congress good luck.

Congress then returned to the discussion of the question of the general strike.

After a discussion in which various delegates took part – Joukovsky, Manguette, Van den Abeele, Cyrille, Verrycken, Hales, Guillaume, Alerini, Bert, Farga and Costa – the congress unanimously adopted the following resolution, proposed by the commission: **Congress, considers that in the current state of the organisation of the International no complete solution can be given to the question of a general strike, it urgently recommends workers to organise international unions of each trade, as well as active socialist propaganda.**[372]

The reporter of the commission for the revision of the General Statutes requested that, with the question of the general strike now completed, congress should resume the discussion of the General Statutes.

Brousse supported the proposition of the reporter, but as congress has decided that the continuation of the discussion on the statutes should be held in a public session, he thought that congress should conclude its administrative session and should declare itself in a public session.

Joukovsky believed, since the administrative sessions are open to all members of the IWMA, congress could very well continue the discussion of statutes in an administrative session. Therefore, he supported the proposition of the reporter.

Van den Abeele believed he must comment that, if the question of statutes was resumed, the discussion on the word *travailleur* (worker), which is most important, would resume, and as this discussion began in public, he thought it was necessary that it should continue in a public session, so that it could not be said that such a serious discussion was hidden away.

The reporter maintained his proposition and, on the contrary, thought that one should avoid making it public, given the tediousness of discussion on particular words.

Dumartheray supported Van den Abeele and requested that there should be an adjournment until the afternoon public session.

Costa supported the reporter's proposal.

Dave thought it would be better if the discussion of the statutes should take place in a public session, but there were, in his view, in the work of the commission for revision, certain things which, without inconvenience, might be discussed in an administrative session.

Hales said that the articles of the statutes that relate to general questions should be discussed in a public session, but he thought that the articles dealing with administrative matters might, without inconvenience, be treated in an administrative session.

Joukovsky rejected Van den Abeele's suggestion that the public might say that that we wanted to engage in jiggery-pokery. The public has nothing to do with our business, and since every federation is represented here, we are discussing things in front of them, it is to them that we must render accounts, and not to the public.

The proposition to continue immediately with the discussion of the statutes, and to transform the administrative session into a public session was put to a vote and adopted.

The congress declared that it was in public session.

THURSDAY 4 SEPTEMBER – NINTH SESSION (PUBLIC)

The session opened at 10 a.m. The agenda called for a discussion on the revision of the statutes.

Guillaume, reporter of the commission, read the new clause that was proposed by the commission to be inserted after the old preamble mentioning the revision of the statutes.

Hales: before congress goes on to discuss this clause, I would like to put the proposition that I mentioned yesterday. I request a change of the name for the IWMA. In England, there are actually two Internationals fighting each other, and fighting between them for an alliance with the Trade Unions, and the latter understand nothing about this division, and do not know who they should listen to. Perhaps someone might reply and tell me that it should be up to our adversaries of the authoritarian party to renounce the title of the International, but I think we would be the wiser if we renounced it first. What do names matter if we have the substance and the reality!

Guillaume, reporter: if the situation was the same in every federation as in England, Hales's proposition might be considered, but quite the contrary, things are not like that. In Spain, in Italy, in France, Belgium, the Netherlands and the Jura, there is only one International – our own. We cannot renounce our flag and abandon a name which belongs to us.

Verrycken: A moment such as this is not the time to consider abandoning our flag – one which has braved so many storms. Moreover, if tomorrow you were to baptise our association with another name, the slanders of the bourgeoisie would be redirected against the new name, just as much as against the old one. Since its foundation, it is always the same men in Belgium who make war against us, and those who fight for the rights of the proletariat are the same men: names might change, but the situation would still stay the same. It has been said that there were two Internationals, but the party of Marx and his General Council exist only in a phantom state, and nobody takes seriously the congress that those people will hold, here, on 8 September. We should continue our work without concerning ourselves with sterile intrigues of ambitious and disappointed people, and we should keep our name, because there is no other International, beyond the one of the labour federations represented here.

Costa: Hales has said we have the reality, and that the name matters little. On the contrary, the name matters a great deal. The International is a formidable power; the bourgeoisie doesn't know for sure what it is, but they are afraid of it, and among the workers there are many who come to us drawn only by the prestige of the name of our Association. Abandoning our name, a name that constitutes a part of our strength, would be an abdication.

Hales: I did not request a change of an entire name – the word International would still figure in the name we propose.

Guillaume, reporter: whether we limited ourselves to modifying only a part of the name of our Association, or if we had changed the whole name, the effect produced would be the same – we would be just one Labour Association among many, the first labour federation on the scene – we would be no longer the International that made the old society tremble, and which is the incarnation of modern revolution. And, do you know what they would say? It would be said that we did not dare accept responsibility for the acts which 'public opinion' calls 'the acts of the International'; that we sought to reject responsibility for the Paris Commune and the events of Alcoy – and only yesterday congress declared its solidarity with those events.

Spichiger: in reply to Hales I would add that there is no great evil in propaganda, if two opposing bodies dispute the organisation of the popular masses. It would be a good thing if the people were to learn from the workings of these two currents and see that the one wants freedom, and the other the negation of freedom, which is to say the principle of authority.

Joukovsky: There is, as has been said, power in the very name of the International. If you change that name, the mass of the membership will go towards those who have kept it.

Manguette: I would like to ask if, while keeping the current name of the International, we might add words which would clearly designate to which fraction of the International we belong.

Guillaume, reporter: If we were to adopt a sub-title, as Manguette suggests, that would be a recognition that there are two Internationals, whereas for us, only one exists. We have nothing to fear, manifestos emanating from the authoritarian party cannot be confused with our own, the contents alone will serve to make recognition sufficiently clear, and workers will not confuse them.

Costa: If we changed the name of the International, we would be like sons who deny their mothers.

Hales: I speak as a delegate from the Liverpool section which gave me an imperative mandate to present this proposal. I must add that I believe that in next week's congress, the authoritarians will transfer their General Council from New York to London.

Many voices: Let us close!

Closure was announced.

Hales: Given the unanimity of opinions voiced here, I withdraw my proposal.

Verrycken, president: There remains then, that we should vote on the clause proposed by the commission. I put it to the vote.

The clause is adopted unanimously.

Guillaume, reporter: With the discussion of the preamble finished, we have come to the discussion of the articles. The first article of the commission's draft has the following wording: **The IWMA has the goal of bringing about the unity of workers of all countries on the terrain of solidarity in the struggle of Labour against Capital, a struggle that must result in the complete emancipation of Labour.**

The first article was adopted unanimously without discussion.

The reporter: This is the draft second article: **Whoever adopts and defends the principles of the Association may become a member, subject to the responsibility of the section that admits them.**

Alerini: I request that the discussion of this article should be delayed until this evening. I know that one delegate, who is now absent, should be able to speak against it, and it should not be said that congress took advantage of his absence to vote on this article without discussion.

Guillaume, reporter: I do not share Alerini's opinion. It is the duty of the delegate in question to be here. We cannot enter into emotional matters; it is not possible to go to those who have sent us as delegates to this congress and say: 'We have not done the particular work you entrusted to us, because a particular comrade was absent, and the congress thought it would be acting indelicately, to go on working without him.' I propose that the discussion of the second article takes place now.

Dumartheray: Yesterday we announced that the discussion of the statutes would restart only this afternoon, and the comrade in question went to work this morning to have his afternoon free to come here.

Van den Abeele: Given that this article consists of a distinct matter, and that other articles might be discussed independently of it, I think it would not be inconvenient to delay discussion of article 2 until later.

Costa: I really do not understand the reservations of certain delegates. The congress has very limited time, I propose that the discussion of the articles should take place in the normal order, without being interrupted by secondary issues.

Verrycken, president: I put to the vote delaying the discussion of article 2. That delay was voted through by 4 federations against 3.

The reporter: Draft Article 3: **Sections and Federations forming the Association preserve their complete autonomy, which is to say their right to organise themselves as they see fit, to administer their own affairs, without any outside interference and to choose for themselves the path they intend to take, to achieve Labour's freedom.**

Article 3 was adopted by acclamation, without discussion.

The reporter: [Draft] Article 4: **A General Congress of the Association shall meet each year, on the first Monday in September.**

Article 4 was adopted unanimously without discussion.

The reporter: Article 5: **Each section, whatever the number of its members, has the right to send a delegate to the General Congress.**

Article 5 was adopted unanimously without discussion.

The reporter: Article 6: **The Congress has, as its mission, to provide a place for workers of various countries to present their aspirations, and through discussion to bring them into harmony. At the opening of congress each Regional Federation shall present a report on the development of the Association in the past year. Except for matters of administration, there will be no recourse to voting; questions of principle cannot be objects for a vote. General Congress decisions are mandatory only for those federations that accept them.**

The president: I put to the vote the first clause of article 6.

The first clause was adopted unanimously without discussion.

Joukovsky: With respect of the second clause, I would like it to be understood that if a regional federation cannot present its report through the medium of a delegation, it should be sent in writing.

Pindy: I believe that the reports of every federation should be sent in writing, and I request that after the words 'every regional federation should present their report' there should be added the words *in writing*.

Pindy's amendment was put to the vote and rejected.

The second clause of article 6 was then adopted unanimously.

Manguette: I would like to speak on the third clause. The Vesdre valley federation has voted against the idea set out in these words.

Costa: the clause says that questions of principle will not be voted on, and I find that correct. As regards theories, we can only discuss and seek to persuade each other, but we cannot impose through a vote, for example a certain programme on the English Federation. We have protested against the Congress of The Hague; we should not act as it did.

Hales: I, too, cannot accept that every federation or section should be obliged to accept the same theoretical principles; but I believe one should add that each federation is responsible for the principles that it promotes.

Alerini: Proclaiming compulsory dogmas is something we should avoid. Each federation should bring its opinions to congress, congress will discuss, and generally the questions which are not agreed at first will end up being clarified and understood everywhere, but we should not impose an official opinion. We have general principles inscribed on the frontispiece of our statutes; it is up to each member of the International to draw out the logical consequences for himself.

Viñas: I agree with the spirit of the clause, but not with its wording. It is always useful to have statistics on opinions within our Association, and the only means to have these is voting. But the vote will not commit and engage anyone, and it will not be an obligatory decision; it will only note the different opinions that exist.

Eccarius: I too think that one should not renounce voting on matters of principle, however, it should be understood that voting has as its goal only a measurement of statistics, and not the force of law. If there is no voting, one will not know what, in reality, was the opinion of the congress on the matters that were discussed.

Guillaume, reporter: That is precisely what we have been fighting against; there must no official Congress opinion on this or that matter of principle. And, as for taking note of the diverse opinions that may be found in congress, the minutes allow that, and all the various opinion are registered there.

Eccarius: There is no obligation in voting in the fashion that I propose – it is simply an English custom, which affirms the opinions of each person on matters under discussion.

Brousse: I am opposed to voting and to me it does not seem a true way of making known each person's opinion. Voting simply divides an assembly up, into majority and minority; so, it is not the exact image of the diversity of opinions, in a question that is a little complex, there may be more than two, different points of view at hand; there might be as many viewpoints as persons. To make an accurate assessment of opinion the only truly practical means is to consign them to the minutes without voting.

Van den Abeele: I too find that observations in the minutes are sufficient to make known opinions, and I am opposed to the procedure of voting.

Joukovsky: Voting creates a majority and expresses the opinion of a majority and so to say, it always ends in creating some species of law. Well, we should not legislate on matters of principle. I, therefore, am in favour of the commission's wording.

Hales: I propose that it should say: 'There should be no voting-with-obligation on matters of principle.' I am in favour of voting, on condition that there should be nothing obligatory about it. Furthermore, congress has already voted on a matter of principle – the issue of strikes.

Guillaume, reporter: The vote that was agreed on the issue of the general strike did not decide a matter of principle; what was on the agenda was only a matter of organisation and not a theoretical question.

Viñas: I would be opposed to voting if voting had the force of law; but I think it is useful, in the form indicated; minutes are not sufficient to register opinions, because to do so would require every delegate to inscribe his own views in the minutes; and it would be simpler to count opinions through the means of voting.

Guillaume, reporter: It seems to me there is nothing simpler than making a count without recourse to a formal vote. It would be enough for the president to call a roll call and to ask each delegate to set out an opinion on the matter under discussion. It would not be a vote in an ordinary sense, because what constitutes voting is the making of a majority and an official doctrine thereafter.

The amendment of Hales was put to the vote and rejected.

The third clause of article 6 was then adopted, by 5 federations against 2.

Discussion of the last clause of article 6 was allocated for the afternoon session. The session was ended at 12.30 p.m.

THURSDAY 4 SEPTEMBER – TENTH SESSION (PUBLIC)

The session was opened at 2 p.m. under the presidency of Verrycken. The agenda called for discussion of the 4th clause of article 6 of the draft statutes.

Verrycken: I approve completely the principles set out in this clause. One must clearly distinguish between a law and a contract: a contract is an engagement which links only the contracting parties; law is the will of a few, imposing itself on all. Moreover, the federations of the International may well commit to establishing reciprocal contracts between themselves, but will not have congresses to establish laws over themselves. Furthermore, it should be well understood that federations should not be held to account by the delegates who attend congress for them, and that they reserve the right to support, or not support propositions that may be discussed by General Congresses. Thus, those who have given their support will be committed by their freely given consent, those who have not given their support will not take on any obligations.

Guillaume, reporter: To clarify the meaning of the clause under discussion, I would add that congress is to be considered not as a body delivering decrees, but as only discussing draft resolutions, resolutions that become definitive only when they are ratified by the various federations. But, they might say: if a federation does not accept a decision that may have been accepted everywhere else, and if a refusal by this federation has a severe impact on the common cause, will you not take some action to coerce those who are recalcitrant? I would reply no: we would take no such action, and first of all, for a very simple reason, because we would not have the means to force a federation to execute a decision that they might reject: the very force of things makes the principle of free contacts an essential feature of our organisation, by virtue of which nobody does anything more than that which they have consented to do. Congress resolutions have as their only force the impetus given them by the voluntary support of federations; and if that support is lacking there, no reglementary prescription that we might imagine could remedy that deficit. The only measure, both equitable and practical, that might be taken against a federation that refuses to join in a resolution that is recognised as essential by other federations, would be to declare that its attitude is considered as an injury against solidarity, and that in consequence the federations which have been hurt by this attitude, would retaliate, suspending solidarity with it, until a friendly entente has smoothed things over.

Manguette: It is in conformity with our principles that federations are not committed by congress decisions and that the decisions are reserved for those federations. But we must foresee the possibility that a federation, even after ratifying a decision, might default on its commitments. In such a case the penal sanction would be to say to that federation: if you do not follow through on the commitment you made, you will have no right to participate in the congress's deliberations.

Perrare: I have the same opinion as Guillaume, and I agree that it is up to federations to ratify congress decisions.

Dave: I share this opinion, and I would like to draw the attention of the congress to a precedent – at the Congress of The Hague, the delegates of the minority agreed resolutions, known under the name of *Declaration of the Minority*. These resolutions were to have been submitted to the federations for ratification, but the federations did not ratify them and substituted other resolutions, more radical ones instead. As can be seen, ratification or non-ratification is not a new matter, and experience shows us that the procedure entailed by this course of action is neither too protracted, nor too difficult.

Pindy: Indeed, I must recall that on this point the Jura Federation denied and negated the decision of its delegates and did not accept the propositions that they had underwritten, considering them insufficiently energetic.

The fourth clause of article 6 was put to a vote and adopted unanimously.

Guillaume, reporter: This is article 7 of the commission's draft. **Voting in General Congresses should be federation, with one vote per federation.**

I should point out that this article only ratifies a principle that is already in practice in the congress.

Article 7 is adopted unanimously without discussion.

The reporter: Article 8 of the draft.

As regards countries where the International Association is prohibited, at least three months before congress, sections and federations wishing to be represented at that congresses should be obliged to inform a neighbouring federation and it will seek out information needed to verify the reality of these sections or federations. The delegates of the latter will only be admitted to the congress under the guarantee of the federation that has carried out these checks, and they will not have a deliberative voice.

I have to say that the commission was divided over the second part of the article: some of its members wished to allow a deliberative voice to delegates where the International is banned, while others thought the opposite.

Brousse: In article 8 there is one good thing, which I support: as regards countries where the International is banned I would like not only that sections should make known their existence three months before a congress, but also that an ongoing correspondence should prove that they really exist, and that, in the eventuality that it might be impossible to establish a federation in the proper country, that they should be recommended to join a neighbouring federation. But would you, once the existence of sections was properly recognised, wish to remove a deliberative voice from their delegates? And if they are running the greater risks, would you then deprive them of their rights? No – that cannot be. Congress, once it has taken the precautions needed to be sure that these are serious delegates, should allow these delegates a deliberative voice. I therefore request the deletion of the last line of the article.

Montels: I support what Brousse has just said. I understand well enough the motivation that inspired the restriction – the desire to prevent a fictional majority, something which we reject – but this danger is countered already by the provisions of article 7, with voting by federation. At this moment there are only two countries, France and Germany, which fit the case foreseen by article 8. So, I ask that the countries where the International is banned should have a deliberative voice like others, and this is the wording that Brousse and I propose for article 8.

Sections formed in places where the International is banned, should advise their closest neighbour as soon as they are formed, and the latter will advise other federations. These sections may have themselves represented in congress when, at least three months before a congress, they have advised [others] of their existence.

Eccarius: I wish to recall that in earlier congresses, delegates from Paris and Germany contributed to having the International take on financial commitments, but later, when it came to paying, the societies which sent these delegates replied that they could not do so, because the legal obstacles that they faced in their countries obstructed them from making regular payments.

Guillaume: If we refuse a deliberative voice to the delegates of sections where the International is banned, the Jura Federation would find itself in a rather strange situation. It is indeed composed of sections based in three different countries, and in two of them the International is banned. Thus, within the Jura Federation there would be sections which had no voting rights in a General Congress and others which would have rights, yet our sections in France and Alsace are regular sections, which belong to the Jura Federation on the same basis as those of Switzerland. One might perhaps say this through article 8: 'Sections of countries where the International is banned, may have a deliberative voice when they are part of a neighbouring federation where the International has a public existence.'

Joukovsky: I ask what is meant by the guarantee that one regional federation might give to a section existing in a country where the International is banned? Would this mean that all the all the members of a regional federation, each one – personally and conjointly – would provide a guarantee for a section? Evidently not. The guarantee then, is given by the Federal Council of the federation. So that is precisely what should be said. Next, would this be a real guarantee? Would the committees of regional federations be able to exercise a real check on sections which came to them for this reason? I do not think so. Also, my view is that one should allow delegates of sections where the International is banned only a consultative voice. I have a mandate to propose for the Propaganda Section of Geneva, the following wording for article 8:

As regards countries where the International is banned those groups wishing to be represented at congress should advise the federation most near to them, at least three months before a congress, so that it might call for requisite information. They should have the choice of having representation through a member of a particular federation, but in any case, the delegates of these countries will have a consultative and not a deliberative voice.

There is a disposition with just this meaning in the draft general statutes presented to the last Belgian congress in Antwerp.

Verrycken: As a Belgian, I must reply to Joukovsky that the Belgian Federation refused to establish a difference between delegates of each country. And my mandate obliges me to claim the same rights for every delegate. We might surround ourselves with any number of guarantees, we might exert severe control on the existence of sections, but once that existence is recognised, we should accept those delegates on an equal basis with others. To exclude delegates from countries where a government has deprived workers of rights of association would be to associate ourselves with the iniquity of those governments. I request the deletion of the last words of the article.

Pindy: Three amendments are tabled: that of Montels, that of Verrycken and that of Joukovsky: I believe it would be best to divide the article to facilitate the discussion.

Dave: In my name, and for Cyrille and Mattei I submit the following proposition: **the undersigned request the pure and simple deletion of Article 8 of the draft statutes.**

Brousse: I agree that there are guarantees to be obtained, and they should be obtained. But once a section is admitted, a delegate should be given the same rights as others. With the opposite system and to annihilate the International, governments would only have to ban it in every land – then delegates of every section would have lost the right to deliberate. You can see just what the logical consequences are of the proposition I reject. As for the idea of obliging sections of a country where the International is forbidden to belong to a federation of a neighbouring country, I must comment that you would be gravely wounding French sections if you were to deny them the free right to organise themselves as a federation among themselves. Lastly, as for financial arrangements alluded to by a speaker, and which might not be paid up, I can affirm that once you set the French sections to have the same rights, they will pay like the others.

Alerini: I reject the proposition that the article should be deleted. Guarantees are needed against fictitious sections; we have seen too many examples of all sorts of abuse.[373] But to wish to deprive the voting rights of sections located in a country where the International is banned is to disregard a natural right.

Costa: We need to come to an agreement on one point: are sections that exist in a country where the International is banned to be considered as forming the regional federation of that country? If yes, then they can be given a collective voice. But if they were to present themselves as isolated sections, with each of them claiming a voice, what would we do?

Dave: If we are asking for the deletion of the article, it is not because we want to do without guarantees – quite the opposite, rather we think that the article cannot foresee and specify every possibility, that these dispositions will necessarily be incomplete, and in consequence futile. Through the deletion of the article, sections based in a country where the International is banned, will be placed on an equal footing.

Guillaume: Given the difficulties presented in having to seek guarantees, rules-based determinations and having a path to follow in this case, I would vote for the deletion of the article. It seems to me that it would be better to leave to each congress the duty of evaluating if the guarantees offered by the delegates are sufficient. This is what we have done this time as regards the mandates of Terzaghi and the French sections. As for Costa's observation, asking if sections of a country where the International is banned are to be considered as forming a regional federation, congress has already replied with a practical solution: we have agreed that delegates of French sections should have a collective voice, just as much as regional federations constituted by regular processes.

Verrycken: I am against deleting the article, because if we do not take out guarantees, we risk seeing delegates arrive who are not serious.

There was a demand to move to a vote and the president read out the various proposals that had been drafted.

First, a vote was taken on the proposal of Dave, Cyrille and Mattei, requesting the pure and simple deletion of draft article 8. The Italian, Spanish, French and Jura federations voted *yes*. The Belgian and English federations abstained. The delegate of the Dutch federation was temporarily absent.

The deletion of draft article 8 was therefore adopted.

Guillaume, reporter: here is draft article 9 of the statutes, which has now become article 8, given the deletion that you have just voted through.

Each year Congress will name a regional federation to take charge of the organisation of next congress. The federation having received this mandate will serve as the Federal Bureau for the Association; and questions that the various federations or sections would like to be placed on the congress agenda should be sent, at least three months in advance of the event, to that federation, which should then bring them to the attention of every regional federation. The Federal Bureau may also serve as an intermediary on matters of strikes, statistics, and correspondence in general, between the federations which may so address them.

The reporter added that, for the commission, this article seemed to have brought together the diverse ideas raised in the discussion on the General

Congress, and it was unanimous in presenting it to the congress.

Dave: Those of the delegates who, along with me, signed the declaration demanding the retention of the principle of anarchy, in the public session of 2 September, wish to explain why they have come around to supporting the draft of the commission, and I have been requested to read the following declaration:

Considering that the new commissions draft says, at the end of article 9 that: 'The Federal Bureau may serve as an intermediary between federations,' which implies that federations – if they so desire – may not make use of this intermediary; [considering] that the Federal Bureau has no longer a duty for making official propaganda, or for official statistics; [considering] that in consequence the draft of the commission respects the anarchist ideas defended by the undersigned; the undersigned declare that they are rallying to support the draft of the commission, and request that their support should be recorded in the minutes in the form set out above. Geneva: 4th September 1873. Signed: Dave, Brousse, Montels, Perrare, Dumartheray, Joukovsky, Cyrille, Mattei, Costa.

Verrycken: Having been given an imperative mandate to request three distinct commissions, I cannot accept the draft of article 9. Allocating the whole responsibility to just one federation fulfilling the office of a Federal Bureau would give it too much work. We want decentralisation – and allocating just one federation all the work and all the responsibility does not do that.

Cyrille: At first, I shared the opinion of the Belgian delegates, but [now] I am moved to support the proposal for a Federal Bureau. What would hinder a federation charged with this responsibility from dividing up the work of a Federal Bureau between three commissions, if it turns out that there is too much work for one? That is a simple matter for internal regulation.

Eccarius: If you create, as the Belgians demand, three distinct commissions in three different federations – one for strikes, one for statistics, [and] a third for congress organisation – you will greatly increase the weight and costs of correspondence. Like Cyrille, I believe it should be left to the Federal Bureau to be responsible for naming one, two or three commissions, as needs be, and I am rallying to the support of the commission's draft of the statutes.

Joukovsky: After having at first supported the Belgians' draft project, we have had to acknowledge the practical difficulties that would be presented by having a multiplicity of correspondence, and I too will vote for the commission's draft.

The reporter: Before a vote is called for on this article, the commission believes that the minutes should note that it should be clear that the choice of a Federal Bureau need not imply as a necessary consequence, that the same federation should be chosen as the meeting place for a General Congress; and on the contrary, if the Federal Bureau might be placed for example in Spain, the congress might take place in Belgium or Switzerland.

Verrycken, president: I will put article 9 to the vote, while observing that, given their mandate, the Belgians cannot vote for the draft of the commission.

Draft Article 9 (having become article 8 of the statutes as adopted) is voted unanimously less the vote of the Belgian federation.

The reporter: Draft article 10 (article 9 of the statutes as adopted): **The congress will itself designate the city where the next congress should be held. On the date appointed for Congress delegates will come together in regular fashion on the day and in the place appointed without there being a need for any special notification.**

The article was adopted unanimously without discussion.

The reporter: Draft article 11, (article 10 of the statutes as adopted): **Over a year, at the initiative of a section or federation, a vote of regional federations may change the place or date of a General Congress or convene an Extraordinary Congress, in the light of events.**

The article was adopted unanimously without discussion.

The reporter: Article 12 and last of the draft (article 11 of the statutes as adopted):

Whenever a new Regional Federation seeks to become a member of the Association, it should announce that intention to whatever Federation is acting as the Federal Bureau at least three months before the General Congress. The latter will make this known to all regional federations and these will have to decide whether to accept the new federation, and accordingly it will mandate its delegates to the General Congress, which in the final instance, will decide.

The article was adopted unanimously without discussion.

The agenda called for the continuation of the discussion on article 2, postponed to the end.

The reporter: this is the draft text. **Whoever adopts and defends the principles of the Association may become a member, subject to the responsibility of the section that admits them.**

Costa: From the moment that we agreed to the autonomy and the independence of each section and each federation, it was for them alone to decide which persons they may wish to join them, on their own responsibility. So, the whole matter is there – do we, yes or no – recognise the autonomy of sessions? If yes, the discussion is finished, if not, we are reneging on all the principles just now adopted.

Dumartheray: If we accept the responsibility of sections and federations as a sufficient guarantee for their members, the article becomes unnecessary, and I propose that it should be supressed.

Alerini: I believe the article is needed, for it is in stipulating that sections are responsible as regards their members, and thus that it is for them to judge, that we will prevent a return of scandals like those of the expulsions announced by the fictitious majority of the Congress at The Hague.

Dumartheray: It seems to me there is a confusion between article 2 and the 'considering' preamble to the statutes.

The reporter: I request Dumartheray to be so good as to formulate a clear proposition in respect of article 2, so that we can recognise just what he is wanting.

Dumartheray: I propose that article 2 should be worded in the following fashion: 'Manual workers only will be part of the International.'

Manguette: For my part I do not propose to close the door of the International [and allow in] only manual workers, but I propose that journalists, professors, etc, should have to form distinct sections.

Verrycken: I must reject energetically the proposition of Dumartheray and that of Manguette. We in Belgium have sections with men who are not manual workers, men who belong to the bourgeoisie, and who are revolutionaries no less than manual workers. These men have rendered us eminent services: it is they who have taught us what we know, and where would we be today without them? It is natural that we should not admit them into our trade and resistance sections – and none of them has ever had the pretence to join them; but to repel them completely, or to oblige them to organise in distinct sections, would be disastrous, and the results would be deplorable.

Guillaume, reporter: Manguette proposes that non-manual workers should constitute distinct sections. But a distinction needs to be made because there are two sorts of sections. Is it a matter of trade [French *corporative*] bodies? in that respect it makes perfect sense to exclude not just non-manual workers, but also all those who have another trade – a shoemaker is not right for a society of mechanics, and neither is a schoolmaster.* On

* Guillaume himself had been a schoolmaster.

that point we agree. But, along with trade sections there are mixed sections, bodies which we call social studies circles, which admit workers of every profession; and we are of the opinion that to close the door of these mixed sections to workers who do not have a manual profession would be both unjust and dangerous. We are told that non-manual workers may acquire a certain influence in manual workers groups, but it would be much worse if you were to set up these men in distinct sections. On the contrary, one should seek to draw manual workers as a close as possible to those who are called thinking workers; they should be encouraged to know each other better, to come together in their sections day by day, living a communal life, such that men leaving the bourgeoisie, who come to acquire morality and to develop in revolutionary ways in contact with manual workers, have the opportunity to shed entirely their caste prejudices, and become real internationalists.

Costa: The goal of the International is the abolition of classes and the establishment of human brotherhood. Would it be fitting with our goal to sanctify within our own Association the class distinctions that we want to annihilate? How could one want bourgeois people to learn to sympathise with manual workers, and to share their aspirations, if those workers push them away. In my view there are two categories of men – those who want revolution, and those who don't, and what's more – there are some bourgeois who want revolution with a great deal more energy and serious intent than certain manual workers.

Perrare: I admit that it is difficult to define what is meant by *workers*, who are to be admitted into the Association. If, in the International, you leave both bourgeois and workers next to each other, it will only be to the detriment of the latter, because the bourgeois – being better educated – will obtain a certain influence which will always be bad for manual workers. The man who is not born working, who does not know what an overseer is like, what a boss is like, cannot understand the aspirations that experience has shaped for such people; the bourgeois will always come along to prove that manual workers are in the wrong. I cannot say to thinking-workers: 'You are pariahs', but I do say that their admission causes ruin in the International; already our Association has ceased to scare the bourgeoisie, and they might take over the International.

What happened in the Romande Federation[374] in Geneva? It had trade sections and a mixed or central section. In that central section all and sundry were accepted, and just so, men entered, who through their education came to impose the arguments they possessed; and the working class who did not hear the discussions that went on in the central section, accepted all that without discussion. No discussions were heard in the trade sections, to hear discussions one had to go to the central section; but as it became a habit not to go there, they heard nothing [of such things] and let themselves be taken in hand by the reasoning of those who worked to ensure that the arguments of the central section should prevail. The trade sections ended up adopting whatever came from there, and the central section ended up directing the Romande Federation entirely, and from then on, it belonged to certain individuals. You can still see those men governing the federation today.[375] So, given what we have seen, I just want to say this to you: we have just proposed, not the banning of thinking workers from society, but to say to them: 'Go organise yourselves on your own, we will hold a hand out to you, but so that the International should not deviate from its goals and so as not to be subordinated to your influence – and to avoid these mistakes we do not want to be with you.' Let us not discuss further the word *worker*. What we don't need is men who know too much, men who misdirect us through their pretty words.

Guillaume: The argument that we have just heard may be reduced to this: it is not so much the bourgeois that we push away, but educated and capable men, wherever they come from. Perrare is simply indicting intelligence; what he fears is not the so-called thinking worker, but intelligent and capable workers wherever they might come from. To satisfy him, one would have to proscribe all workers who have attained a certain degree of intellectual development, and already among manual workers, there are many who have cultivated their intelligence, and who in consequence have become dangerous in the eyes of Perrare. Without looking very far, in the Jura Federation we know of many manual workers who are much better educated than many who have a seat in bourgeois parliaments; and do you know how these manual workers have acquired their education? It is through stubborn and solitary work, passing their night in study, in skimping on necessities to obtain means to learn. Well, if Perrare's theory was followed, once one of these men had come to know as much, or more than a bourgeois, one would have to show him the door of the International.

As for those who degraded the central section of Geneva, those who directed every intrigue that Perrare mentioned, were they bourgeois? Doubtless a few of them were, but for the most part they were manual workers: engravers, box-makers, carpenters, etc.[376] I don't need to name them, you know them well, and you know that it was they who did the most harm. You say bourgeois persons should be excluded because they don't know what a boss is like, and yet, is it that we see? Among the declassed bourgeois who joined the International almost all have had to obtain their bread by manual work; and many among them, lacking a trade, have had to make do as unskilled labourers. There are some among us who are in that position, there are others who, if they do not do manual work today, who have had to try it, and others who will have to try it tomorrow. And [yet] you have said that these men don't know what misery is like, or exploitation, that they cannot understand the aspirations of the world of labour? But no, on the contrary, nobody has a more immediate and direct interest in revolution than they.

This spirit of intolerance – I will call it petty jealousy – do you know where it may lead? I will cite an example which many of you will be aware of. There was, in one section, a man who belonged to the bourgeoisie by birth and education, he had been a schoolmaster; having entered the International he sought to learn a manual trade, but as he edited a socialist journal he was always seen as a man of letters rather than as a manual worker; and that provoked concerns of the sort which you have heard just now. Moreover, in consequence of him hearing it repeated that he was not a real worker, that he belonged to a privileged class, that he should be treated with some suspicion, and the like, the poor man ended up losing his bearings, and, wanting to keep persons from opening their mouths to slander him he took peremptory action – he left his section and his journal behind, and went off to a nearby town and made himself into a café waiter. Is this the sort of result that Perrare would want to achieve? And as for those amongst us who write for journals, who give lectures and who work on propaganda – should one not believe that they render better services for the International, than they might be rendered, if they imitated the hopeless course of the comrade I have just mentioned?

Lastly, if one wanted to examine seriously where the bourgeois are in the International, isn't it rather among the ranks of certain manual workers that they are to be found. There are manual workers who earn 10 to 15 francs a day, who dress in black with silk hats, who live within the bourgeois world and share their prejudices, but they are manual workers and on this account Perrare would have the doors of the International held wide open for them. And on the other hand, there are commercial employees who earn 100 francs a month, and precarious professors who sometimes barely earn 3 francs a day; they depend on their work, like manual workers they are exploited, but they do not handle tools, thus, according to Perrare they are bourgeois. Yet the latter will be devoted and serious revolutionaries, while the silk-hatted manual worker is an out and out reactionary. To me, there is a clear conclusion, I vote for keeping article 2, in the form drafted by the commission.

Manguette: I would like to explain my proposition. I have not spoken in in favour of anyone being excluded. It is said that I have wanted to confine the bourgeois in distinct sections, but if one does not want to accept that idea, if regulation is rejected, it would be better to cut out the article entirely, leaving each section free to do as it wished. Much good has been done by the bourgeois in the International, but as much has been done that is bad, so I believe that each section should reflect carefully before allowing them in, and it would be best to say nothing [on this score] in the statutes.

Alerini: As yet, it has not been possible to define exactly what a worker is. A manual worker who works on his own account is not someone exploited, whereas there are some bourgeois who are exploited much more than most workers, and the dividing lines are so difficult to fix that – until we have succeeded – I request that we leave the article just as it is. Let sections submit bourgeois people to quite special checks – that would be natural; thus, in Spanish sections, they are asked to declare their principles – any number of guarantees may be sought, and I understand every reservation, but to say that the category of non-manual workers cannot belong to the International, that would not be just. Also, the article does not say: 'so and so *must* be a part of the International', only that they '*may* be a part'. Therefore, the right of sections to make a judgement in the last resort is reserved.

Viñas: In Spain, this question has been controversial – it was on the agenda at three consecutive congresses, but one has had to abandon the matter because of the difficulty experienced in defining the words *worker* and *manual worker*. Every definition that was proposed excluded this or that category of exploited persons who were not be included in a definition. If we want to achieve the liberation of all exploited people, we need the help of every exploited person. There are today [many] classes of exploited people who are not included among those understood ordinarily as being *workers*, such people as grooms, domestic workers, the Swiss who do not create exchangeable products but who are yet exploited. We cannot accept the support of the bourgeoisie as a class, but if some individuals who are convinced of our cause come over to us, let us not reject them. Let us take precautions and exercise care regarding them, that is possible; let us keep an eye on them, that much is necessary, but let us leave sections the right to appreciate whether a particular individual who presents himself is worthy or not of being admitted.

Spichiger: I would like to say a word as a manual worker on the matter under discussion. I do not think that manual workers would be right to repel those who are called thinking workers. Consider indeed the current economic situation and the causes that have brought it about. Under the modern regime of business and industrial freedom, it was at first a rat race for the bourgeoisie seeking their fortune, at first it went well; with education and [hard] work everyone might make believe that they had a chance. But the centralisation of capital has come about, and with it the hopes of the petit-bourgeoisie have been ruined: the result is that the petit-bourgeoisie is opening its eyes, recognising that the cause of its ruin is the evil organisation of current society, and that this is an organisation that should be destroyed. Those people are therefore forced, by lethal economic forces, to come to us. Compared to manual workers they are revolutionaries, as much or more, and being better educated they can help our cause and render it great services. True, one might fear that they might acquire too great an influence among us, but it is up to workers to know how to combat that influence, and whatever might be bad in it, and to neutralise it. Moreover, each section will remain free to admit those bourgeois only within the limits they judge appropriate. It would be very irritating if the socialist party was divided into two bodies – the only result would be an antagonism that would be fatal for workers. However, if all manual workers were united and ready to resolve social problems, I might admit that they might wish to walk alone and rely on their own strengths, but sadly we are not there, we are only a minority, and we should not divide our forces. In consequence I will vote for article 2.

Van den Abeele: Creating an association alongside the International, designed especially for the bourgeois would be a serious danger. The Versailles government* member Franclieu, once said that the only way to fight the International was to organise the bourgeoise and all its strength. Far from repelling bourgeois persons who are socialist, the International should keep them close among them, fearing otherwise that they might increase other organisations which might someday become an obstacle to the revolution.

With no one else wanting to speak, the debate on article 2 was closed.

The president put to the vote the amendment of Dumartheray. Perrare and Dumartheray voted *For*. Eccarius, Hales, Manguette, Cornet, Cyrille and Viñas *abstained*. All other delegates voted *Against*. The result: the amendment of Dumartheray was rejected by six federations with the English federation abstaining.

The president then put to the vote the amendment of Manguette. Manguette and Cornet voted *For*. Eccarius, Hales, Cyrille, Dumartheray and Perrare *abstained*. All other delegates voted *Against*. The result: the

---

*   The French republican state that emerged in 1871, and that directed the repression of the Paris Commune was at first based in Versailles.

amendment of Manguette was rejected by six federations with the English federation abstaining.

The president put to the vote the draft of article 2 from the commission, Dumartheray, Perrare, Cornet and Manguette voted *Against*. Eccarius and Cyrille *abstained*. All other delegates voted *For*. Thus article 2 was accepted by unanimity of the federations.

The president: With the discussion of the articles concluded there remains to vote on the draft as a whole. Congress has adopted the articles, and I now put to the vote the new revised statutes as a whole, Voting *For* were: Farga, Viñas, Alerini, Marquet, Manguette, Verrycken, Cornet, Dave, Van den Abeele, Spichiger, Andrié, Guillaume, Pindy, Joukovsky, Montels, Brousse, Costa, Mattei, Bert, Cyrille, Eccarius and Hales. There were no votes *against*. Dumartheray and Perrare abstained. The whole draft statutes were therefore unanimously adopted by the federations.

The agenda called next for the report of the commission on statistics. The report was read, and the discussion postponed to the next day's session. The session was closed at 7 p.m.

* * *

On 4 September at 8 p.m. a grand meeting took place in the congress hall, seeking to set out the principles of the International before the labour public of Geneva. The hall was full. The speakers were Lefrançais, Dave, Verrycken, Costa, Van den Abeele, Farga, Eccarius, Guillaume and Joukovsky. The meeting lasted till 11 p.m. Given that the present report must limit itself to the official congress sessions, those seeking information on this public session are directed to the press of the International.*

FRIDAY 5 SEPTEMBER – ELEVENTH SESSION (ADMINISTRATIVE)

The session opened at 9 a.m. under the presidency of Verrycken. Perrare was absent.

Guillaume requested through a motion of order, that the translation of the general statutes into various languages should be prepared by the delegates of the various federations, while the congress was in session, and submitted for congress approval, so that in each of the six languages –

---

* See Appendix two. *La Federación* (20 September 1873), remarked that the meeting heard speeches in French, and in German, Italian, Spanish and English, the latter were translated into French. Only one German spoke to contradict Eccarius; 'his arguments were pulverised, and he was utterly bested.' The meeting had to finish at 11 p.m., although many other wanted to speak; Swiss federal law prohibited meetings going on after 11. Printed announcements advertising a meeting also had to be lodged with the police.

French, English, German, Spanish, Italian and Dutch – there should be an authentic and official text of the statutes.

That proposition was adopted.

Pindy made known a letter from America, announcing that the American Federation had sent funds to help cover the congress's costs. He proposed that these costs should be shared equally between the regional federations. The proposition was adopted.

A short discussion took place on the report presented by the commission on statistics; after several comments by Italian delegates and others, the first part of the report was adopted.

The president then asked for propositions concerning the country where the next general congress should be held. Cyrille proposed Switzerland; Costa and Guillaume, Belgium: Montels and Alerini, Spain.

Viñas spoke against the choice of Spain – in a year's time Spain would be either in social revolution or in full reaction.

The federations designated Belgium unanimously. The Belgian delegates then proposed that the congress should meet in the city of Brussels and that proposition was adopted.

The agenda called for a choice as to which federation should take on the functions of Federal Bureau. The Jura delegates proposed the Belgian Federation. The Belgian Federation was designated unanimously as the Federal Bureau of the International for the year 1873-1874.

The congress also decided that the general dues levy of 10 centimes a year should be abolished. The balance of costs for correspondence and for the organisation of the congress, which might burden the Federal Bureau in future, were to be advanced by the federation which hosted the Federal Bureau; and then, at the time of the congress, these costs should be divided up between the regional federations.

Farga raised the question of attitude to be adopted to the congress of the authoritarian party, which was to meet in Geneva on 8 September. He thought that one should not abandon all hope for conciliation and thought that congress should vote for a declaration expressing its solidarity with all workers, whatever organisation they might belong to.

Van den Abeele declared that he had received a mandate from the Dutch Federation to be present at the authoritarian congress, and he would attend, to place an ultimatum before them: we shall then see, he said, if anything can be done with those people, and if there are some among them who know how to place the cause of revolution before personal disputes.

After a short discussion congress decided that a commission formed of one member per federation should draft a resolution concerning universal workers' solidarity, as practiced and understood by the International.

The session was closed at noon.

FRIDAY 5 SEPTEMBER – TWELTH SESSION (PUBLIC)

The session opened at 2 p.m., under the presidency of Verrycken.

Costa, reporter for the commission on the general strike presented his report. Congress decided to discuss the report in an administrative session. The agenda called for a discussion of the report on the commission on statistics.

Cyrille proposed the following proposition: **Given that the question of work statistics does not enter the agenda of revolutionary debate – either because it is almost impossible to assess labour statistics completely, or because limited practice has not demonstrated its general usefulness – congress moves on to next business.**

Pindy made another proposition: **Given the difficulties, or even impossibilities that may arise gathering the information demanded in the report on statistics, [I propose:] that the report of the commission be adopted, and every federation should be enjoined to carry out studies and to bring responses to the next congress on those matters that they have been able to research.**

The proposition of Cyrille was put to the vote and rejected unanimously by those who voted, less the vote of its author. The proposition of Pindy was adopted by a unanimity of federations.

Farga: I propose that the congress should vote for a resolution recommending the organisation of trades' federations, such as exist in Spain. We began by creating centralised organisations, then we recognised that this was a retrograde system, and we decentralised, forming separately the different branches of each industry, based on federalism. Thus, all manufacturing workers were previously grouped in just one union; experience has shown us the inconvenience of such centralisation, the union of manufacturing workers subdivided itself into several branch federations. – This is the resolution that I recommend that congress should adopt:

The IWMA congress held in Geneva on 1st September 1873, considering that it is indispensable to accomplish labour organisation that labour associations should organise by trade bodies that are federated from a federal and international viewpoint; Further, considering that to sustain the struggle against capital and to affirm solidarity between all workers, to

get to know conditions of production in its diverse aspects and relations scientifically, it is no less useful to organise trades' unions; Congress recommends to all sections organising through trade bodies and by international and regional federations, as well creating unions of trades. It calls attention to Spanish experiences, experiences that have proved the necessity of taking as the base of the unions, not the centralised system, but rather the autonomy of trades' federations that join in the same branch of production, united among themselves through a pact of solidarity and mutual defence. Lastly, congress invites those federations and Unions that are already formed to facilitate this organisation through publishing in the organs of the IWMA all news and information and noteworthy experience to facilitate the prompt action of these federations and trades' unions.

Guillaume: I support Farga's proposition. It is not enough to proclaim the principle of federation and autonomy in theory, we should seek to achieve them in labour organisation now. Besides, in Switzerland most trades' federations are constituted on this principle; and even those which pretend to go along with the authoritarians, practice federalism in reality, if unknowingly. To prevent the confusion that our adversaries seek to sow for their own benefit, it is good to clearly establish this fact: that the outcome of labour organisation as it is practiced today in Spain, Belgium and Switzerland has arisen from the principle of federation and autonomy, which are our principles; whereas the logical consequence of the authoritarian principle is strongly centralised organisation, which stands condemned by experience.

The proposition of Farga was put to the vote and adopted unanimously.

Van den Abeele: The Antwerp Federation, which I represent, has tasked me with proposing as an agenda item for the next congress, the following: 'The Labour movement in its relations with political movements.' I request that congress should take a view and decide if this matter should feature on the agenda of the 1874 congress.

Guillaume: The general statutes indicate the path to be taken to place an item on the congress agenda: the matter should be addressed to the Federal Bureau, and the latter will inform all regional federations, at least three months before a congress. To me, it seems that the Antwerp Federation should abide by the regular path.

Van den Abeele: having been given the task of presenting this request by my federation, I had to fulfil my mandate, but I recognise the correctness of the observation just made, and I will engage the Antwerp Federation to write to the Federal Bureau on this matter, that it wishes to see placed on the agenda of the next congress.

The president: Congress needs to decide on the proposition of the American Federation relative to an approach to the Postal Congress of governments which is due to meet in Bern soon, in order to obtain a reduction in the costs of sending letters.

On this proposition a request was made and adopted, to [move on] purely and simply to the next item on the agenda.

The president: Another proposition has been submitted by a London section composed of French refugees. This group requests that committees of sections and federations should be composed only of manual workers. It seems to me that it is not up to congresses to prescribe rules for the election of committees to sections, and they should be left entirely free to choose those men who enjoy their confidence; also, I believe that we do not have to discuss this proposition.

A request was made to [move on] to the pure and simple agenda of the day.*

Guillaume: I propose an order of the day – in the following terms: **Considering that it is not appropriate for congress to prescribe what should be the mode of election for committees, for sections or federations, the congress moves on to the [next item on the] agenda.**

That proposition was adopted unanimously.

The commission nominated that morning in the administrative session, to draft a resolution concerning universal solidarity between workers – as the International intends it should be practiced – presented the following draft:

The congress of the IWMA meeting in Geneva on 1st September 1873, believes it is its duty to declare that this Association intends to practice solidarity towards all workers of the world, in the struggle against capital to achieve the liberation of labour, whatever organisation they may adopt.

A unanimous vote adopted that resolution.

Congress decided to hold a final administrative session on Saturday morning, to resolve some financial details.

Verrycken, president: We will shortly be closing our public sessions having run through the congress agenda. But as we complete our deliberations it is important, to identify clearly the significance of this congress. Two ideas, federalism, and authoritarianism, were in conflict after the Congress of The

---

* Or, in other words, move on to next business.

Hague. It is the first of these ideas that won through within every federation of the International and we were sent here as delegates to reorganise the International on a federalist basis. The congress of Geneva of 1866 had concluded the first pact of union among workers; thereafter the intrigue of a few ambitious persons made the International turn away from the path which it had first set itself. The congress of Geneva of 1873 has reset our Association on its true path; working people have had enough of chiefs and bosses, they want to take the management of their affairs into their own hands.

You have decided that the next general congress will take place in Brussels. As a Belgian, I can assure you that you will be readily received there, with that same cordiality that we received here. We count on the attendance of the greatest possible number of delegates, and hope that the congress of 1874 will be a fitting sequel to that of 1873.

I thank all delegates who have made my task of presiding easy, and I declare closed the public sessions of the sixth General Congress of the International. Long live the International Working Men's Association! Long live the Social Revolution!

(Applause and cheers from the delegates and the public).

The session finished at 6 p.m.

That same evening delegates and many workers of Geneva met in the congress hall for a banquet. The festivity was enlivened by speeches and singing, and a spirit of true fraternity was enjoyed, it was a fitting ending to the working of the 1873 congress.

SATURDAY 6 SEPTEMBER – THIRTEENTH AND LAST SESSION (ADMINISTRATIVE)

The session opened at 9 a.m. under the presidency of Verrycken.

Secretaries read those minutes that had not, yet, been read.

The congress decided that the Jura Federation should be entrusted with the printing of the report, as a brochure which should cost no more than 50 centimes.

Viñas requested a clarification of certain words of article 10 of the general statutes: 'may change the place or date of a General Congress'. Should one understand from this that one might change only one of these two things, either the date or the place? However, there might be circumstances that require us to have the ability to change both the date and the location of the congress.

Brousse proposed that in this wording the word *or* be replaced by the word *and*, to easily allow a change in both date and place for the congress. The article would then be reworded as follows: **Over a year, at the initiative of a section or federation, a vote of Regional Federations may change the place and date of a General Congress or convene an Extraordinary Congress, in the light of events.**

This proposal was adopted.

The president announced the bill for congress costs. These costs were to be shared between the regional federations, amounting to 22.60 francs per federation. The sum of 36 francs, arising from a discount obtained regarding the location of the congress hall is allocated to the secretaries on account of an indemnity.

A vote of thanks was given to the Propaganda Section of Geneva, which had been entrusted with congress preparations.

The session was then ended, at 11 a.m.

General statutes of the International Working Men's Association

Considering,
That the emancipation of workers should be the accomplishment of workers themselves; that workers' efforts to win freedom should not allow the development of new privilege but should establish the same rights and the same duties for all.

That workers' subjection to capital is the fount of all servitude – material, moral and political.

That, for this reason, the economic emancipation of workers is the great goal to which every political movement ought to be subordinated.

That hitherto all struggles have failed, for want of solidarity between workers of various trades within each country, and for the lack of fraternal unity between the workers of different regions.

That the emancipation of labour is not a problem that is simply local or national, and that on the contrary it concerns all civilised nations, and its solution necessarily depends on their practical and theoretical co-operation.

That the movement now coming to fruition among workers of the most industrious countries, in raising new hopes, calls for the combination of efforts that are, as yet, isolated and gives a solemn warning against falling back into old errors.

For these reasons:

The Congress of the International Working Men's Association, held in Geneva on 3 September 1866, declares that this Association, and every individual or society joining it, will recognise *morality*, *justice*, and *truth* as the basis of their conduct toward to all men, without distinction of nationality, creed, or colour.

Congress considers that it is a duty is to reclaim the rights of man and of citizens not only for members of the Association, but also for whoever accomplishes its duties. *No duties without rights; no rights without duties.*

The Regional Federations represented at the International Congress assembled in Geneva on 1 September 1873, inspired by the above declaration of principles, have revised the general statutes of the IWMA, and have adopted them in the following form:

1.   The IWMA has the goal of bringing about the unity of workers of all countries on the terrain of solidarity in the struggle of Labour against Capital, a struggle that must achieve the complete emancipation of Labour.

2.   Whoever adopts and defends the principles of the Association may become a member, subject to the responsibility of the section that admits them.

3.   Sections and Federations forming the Association preserve their complete autonomy, which is to say their right to organise themselves as they see fit, to administer their own affairs, without any outside interference and to choose for themselves the path they intend to take, to achieve Labour's freedom.

4.   A General Congress of the Association shall meet each year, on the first Monday in September.

5.   Every section, whatever the number of its members, has the right to send a delegate to the General Congress.

6.   The role of Congress is to be a meeting place for workers of various countries to present their aspirations, and through discussion to bring them into harmony. At the opening of congress each Regional Federation shall present a report on the development of the Association in the past year. Except for matters of administration, there will be no recourse to voting; questions of principle cannot be subjected to a vote. General

Congress decisions are mandatory only for those Federations that accept them.

7.   Voting at a General Congress will be by Federation, each Regional Federation having one vote.

8.   Each year Congress will give the responsibility for the organisation of the following year's Congress to a regional federation. The federation so mandated will serve as the Federal Bureau of the Association. Any section or federation wishing matters to be placed on the agenda of Congress should address these to it three months in advance so that all regional federations are made aware of them. Moreover, the Federal Bureau may serve as an intermediary between federations for matters brought to its attention [such as] statistics, strikes or general correspondence.

9.   Congress will itself designate the city where the next congress is to be held. On the date appointed for Congress delegates will come together in regular fashion on the day and place appointed without there being a need for any special notification.

10.   Over a year, at the initiative of a section or federation, a vote of regional federations may change the place and date of a General Congress or convene an Extraordinary Congress, in the light of events.

11.   Whenever a new regional federation seeks to become a member of the Association, it should announce that intention to whichever federation is acting as the Federal Bureau, at least three months before the General Congress. The latter will make this known to all regional federations and these will have to decide whether to accept the new federation, and accordingly it will mandate its delegates to the General Congress, which in the last instance will decide.

Part 3

The Congress convened by the General Council, Geneva, 7-13 September – newspaper reports

[Reports on this congress were sent to the New York General Council but were not published, however the newspaper reports below give a fair idea of its public discussions. Many articles were published two or three days after the events they describe. The first report below concerns an open evening meeting, held in the Hotel de la Navigation, attended by a diverse audience. The congress participants included: Austria-Hungary: Vienna – Heinrich Oberwinder (alias Schwarz, journalist). Germany: Stuttgart – Burckhardt. Netherlands: Henri van den Abeele (left the congress on the 12th, merchant). Switzerland: Basle – Gustav? Rathenau; Geneva – Gustave Bazin (jewellery worker), Johann Philipp Becker (cigar maker, journalist, sales representative), Bontauger (seamstress), J Coutés (Courtis, Courtés, mason), Duparc (jewellery worker), Theodor Duval (joiner), Bruno Gutsmann (carpenter), M. Josseron (cultivator, watch-case maker), Henri Perret (engraver), Sattier (seamstress), Savoyal, Wolff (tailor?); Haserer – German educational unions; Burand Saranat – Jura; Rossetti – Ticino; Wilhelm – Zurich.]

La Liberté, report dated Monday 8 September, published in Paris Thursday 11 September.

[Notes on the public meeting in the evening of the 7th. Young women circulated with glasses and water, very much needed in stifling heat. The strangest odours were being exhaled from that cosmopolitan gathering. A large blond man – a jewellery worker we believe – presided at the meeting. the congress proper was only to open on the following day to discuss its agenda.]

In the hall, a few Russians, but on the other hand the entire personnel of the *other* congress without Guillaume certainly, but [including] Ostyn, Claris,

Van den Abeele, Chalain,* Eccarius, Weryken [Verrycken], Dave, etc., are in the first row; behind them the authoritarians, Beck [Becker?], Perret, Duval and the others who had organised the meeting. As delegates, a few German-Swiss, the Austrians and the Berliners have only just arrived, and one awaits the Americans [later] that night.

The president, who expresses himself rather badly in French, declares that despite being called an authoritarian, he would allow everyone who wanted to, to speak. Fulfilling that promise, after a few Marxist speeches, the Jura activists mounted the rostrum, and the indefatigable citizen Lefrançais taking issue with some earlier speeches and with some insults towards 'his party', he declared that given such facts and the partiality of the president, their opinion was being forbidden. The president replied to the accusation, that at the moment these accusations were made from the rostrum, he was not in the hall.

After that incident, citizen Duval launched an all-out attack on the dissidents. He went back to the first deluge, forgive me the beginnings of the International; he spoke in inadmissible French; but besides that, he shouted very loudly and at length. The assembly, visibly wearied by it all, applauded vigorously when this honourable representative of the manual workers gave way to a former member of the Commune, Chalain, one of those recently expelled from Vienna.

On this occasion there was a confession: the speaker began with a *mea culpa*, 'I was one of the greatest authoritarians in the Commune, he said, [but] on the General Council I was, on the contrary, part of the minority'. Why this change? The speaker was mute on this point, only, he returned to past events, which are not without a certain interest. 'When the members of the Commune arrived in London, after May 1871, although they had always been strangers and even hostile to the Association, they were accepted that very evening, both as members of the IWMA and as members of the General Council.'

He added that he was never able to speak out in the Council sessions, the members of the majority prevented it, making an infernal racket with the rulers on their desks. He finished with a sentence that he uttered in a faithful and inspired tone: 'Partisan as I am of authority as a means, but not as an end, if I had in front of me a squad of Versailles [soldiers], I would be even more authoritarian than ever.'

At that moment, citizen Perret one of the leaders of the Romande

---

* Like Pindy, Louis Chalain had been sentenced to death in absentia and became a member of the Jura Federation. There are no reports that he was a delegate to the Geneva congress in 1873.

federation mounted the tribune. His entire speech was an accusation against the Jura activist and the Communards. He accused the latter of being authors of every evil, and further challenged them for something even worse – of being nothing but bourgeois who, whilst the people were being killed, busied themselves with seeking passports and packing their cases.

From that moment on, it was war. The Jura activists shouted and blew; the Communards rushed forward; fists raised towards the bureau; a collision was imminent. The president prevented it by allowing citizen Lefrançais to speak. Calmly, coldly, seriously the ex-professor spoke an *apology* for Delescluze, Rossel, Ferré, Vermorel, etc.* 'All bourgeois! he shouted; and I am one too!'

That blow visibly disconcerted the pontiff of liberal communism [Perret?], and after a few showy tirades, he descended the rostrum – amid cries, whistles, and some rather timid applause. Tomorrow will be the first session of the congress.

* * *

The Times (London), report dated Monday 8 September, published Friday 12 September.

We have now arrived at the second stage of the Congress.

What is the International? Anyone passing the Hotel de Navigation yesterday and seeing the revolutionary red placard announcing the opening of the Sixth Annual Congress of the IWMA might have been led astray by the belief that the representatives of the proletariat of the world were about to assemble, as on all previous occasions, but the delusion would have been dispelled on ascending the stairs and going inside the very spacious hall in which the Congress meets. There was to be a preliminary meeting, at which all the world might take part. The schismatics mustered in force; they had stayed for the purpose of seeing the goblin that had frightened them.

At 8 o'clock [on Sunday 7th September] M. Josseron (a watch-case maker), the local president, ascended the tribune, and announced the happy event that was about to transpire in the morning, and that for the evening any one was free to speak, and the schismatics were invited to let the meeting hear what they had to say for themselves. A caution was given to both sides not to be personal. Things went on smoothly enough throughout the evening until the president himself transgressed. The Geneva workmen who spoke had but one tale to tell – that the workmen would be united enough and manage their own affairs were it not for heterogeneous elements which divided them. One spoke rather plainly,

---

* Persons who lost their lives in the fight for the Commune.

proclaiming himself to be a free-thinker, but objecting to making Atheism the creed of the International, which had driven the bulk of the Geneva trade societies out of the International. All this was meant for Backounine and his friends, but no names were mentioned. It is a fact that about two-thirds of the trade societies, after gaining their strikes by the assistance of the International, have turned their backs against it, and those who remain charge Backounine with being the cause. Gutsmann, a rather intelligent German cabinet maker launched out, in German, against the insidious slanderers who said the International was dead. It was flourishing in Denmark, the Social-Democratic party in Germany was stronger than ever, and the Austrian Government had shown its fear of it by expelling certain Frenchman who had visited the Exhibition [in Vienna], and he wanted to know how the workpeople could overthrow despotism without exposing it by a centralised organization. The other side boasted of their freedom and talked of the beauty of anarchy, an International in which everybody could do as he liked. When the hour of winding up arrived, the president in his closing speech stated that the whole of the mischief had been done by men who had come to Geneva without passports. This expression was unanimously and rather boisterously resented by the audience. Le Français [Lefrançais] took it up, as being aimed at the Communist refugees. I was too far out of the crowd to understand what he said, but his arms went like a wind-mill, and there was tremendous cheering. When quiet was restored the president apologised, saying that he did not mean the Communal refugees, but other persons he knew. This finished the preliminary meeting.

* * *

Journal des débats politiques et littéraires (Paris), Thursday 11 September

[Letter dated Tuesday 9th, the writer began with a report on a meeting of the League for Justice and Peace, which was also taking place in Geneva.]

… Now, let us deal with the International, whose meetings, though they may serve to express opinions which are more or less strange, at least demonstrate some great vitality. These people may die a violent death, but they are certainly not anaemic.

Yesterday, Sunday [7th], a public meeting took place in the great hall of the café de la Navigation, to inaugurate the Congress of the 'authoritarians'. That label – authoritarian – one moreover that they do not dare deny or reject in public, seems to offend the orthodox fraction of the International. Be that as it may, on opening the session on Sunday, Josserand [Josseron] declared that, although he might be authoritarian, he would allow anyone who wanted to, to speak. There would be just one condition, that there should be no personal comments. The restriction was observed for the first few speeches, but soon a German speaker, an authoritarian, declared that idiots or traitors had produced the dissent in the International, and the discussion warmed up. The anarchists reproached the authoritarians for their working with the Peace Congress and the authoritarians replied by recalling what had occurred at the Basle Congress, where the Bakuninists were the first to do everything that they reproached the Marxists for doing thereafter.

What is most remarkable is what both sides said: it was the bourgeois who divided the Association. Only, the accusation was directed at Karl Marx, Desgnettes [?] and his friends for some, and for others at Bakunin and his supporters.

You might say perhaps there is a sensible middle course, one which might consist of sending the two enemies – the German and the Russian – to face off against each other. Certain symptoms make me believe that things might sort themselves out so. At the Sunday meeting several Geneva authoritarians expressed the idea: We have had enough of all your theories and of all your social transformations: we will not examine whether they are right or wrong in themselves; we will not blame those who concern themselves with such things, but what we need is regular progress, beginning right now. 'It's a question of the stomach,' said one of the speakers, Mr. Perret, rather prosaically.

Another issue touched on was the political issue. We should not concern ourselves with politics, said many of the same men, not because we reject it, on the contrary, we encourage all workers to do their duty as citizens, but to do politics, they should work through political associations. These men suggest that the means should consist of a re-organising of the International, based on unions of trades, like those that exist in England. They do not reject the non-manual person, but they do not want to admit them except in associations, such as those of organised professions.

The session ended with violent scenes, provoked by M. Perret, who accused the 'bourgeois' of the Commune of having sent the people into battle while cautiously avoiding endangering themselves. According to him, that was the common tactic of bourgeois ultra-revolutionaries. A veritable storm resulted from this frank declaration, members of the Commune and other refugees being very numerous in the auditorium. M. Lefrançais protested, and cited the names of Vermorel and Delescluze, who were bourgeois. He was outraged by these words: And you?*

* Gustave Lefrançais, went on to write that the federalists 'regenerated' the IWMA.

Yesterday the first public session of the congress took place, but it had no interest; I will speak about it along with other matters in my next letter.

* * *

London Evening Standard
[Extracts from a very substantial report dated the 8th, and reporting on the open meeting of the 7th, published on 12 September 1873. The journalist commented on the split in the IWMA: '... a kind of dictatorship was affected which savoured too much of Imperialism for the views of the great bulk of the rank and file. Increased privileges were appropriated, wider powers usurped by the governing body, until at the last congress, those who desired that a system of federation should be the guiding principle of the International Society refused any longer to obey the behests of the governing body ...' He then wrote on the open meeting of Sunday 7th as follows.]

On the whole, the sense of the meeting was in favour of conciliation, without, however, abating any of the powers of the [General] council. Just before the meeting concluded the president, M. Josseron, of Geneva, brought a hornet's nest about his years [sic] by an unfortunate expression. He supported the policy of admitting into the association only those who earned their bread by manual labour and objected to the introduction of the brain-workers, the *travailleurs de pensée*. He added that he objected still more to the introduction of men who came across the frontier without passports in their pockets. As this was supposed to be a reference to the Communists [of the Paris Commune], there was immediately raised a storm of hisses, and wild scenes ensued. About a dozen members were trying to speak together, and the president in vain attempted to give an explanation. The friends of the Communists protested against the observation, and the president having eventually explained that he referred only to one or two individuals who had brought disunion into their midst, calm was restored, and the meeting shortly afterwards terminated.

* * *

The Times, report dated 8 September (Monday), published Friday 12 September.

This morning 28 delegates presented themselves with credentials from various places, but there are hardly half-a-dozen who reside outside Geneva.

République et Révolution: De l'attitude à prendre par le prolétariat français en présence des partis politiques, Geneva, 1873/4?, pp. 31-32. In the *Almanach du peuple* (1874), he defended 'communalism' the necessity of constructing a polity founded in communes, administered by working people, as against centralised states.

A committee of delegates speaking the various languages was appointed to examine the credentials, which were all found to be in order. There is a novelty which deserves mention. There are two lady delegates representing the central section of the working women of Geneva. They are both seamstresses, of middle age, neatly dressed, and intelligent looking. The one *citoyenne* (Sattier) is German, the other *citoyenne* (Bontauger) is French Swiss. The credentials having been verified, and the delegates having voted themselves all rights, it was resolved that the public proceedings should begin at 3 o'clock in the afternoon, and that the utmost facility should be given to admit the public to witness the deliberations of the Congress at this important juncture.

At 3 o'clock Josseron took the chair and read the decree of the General Council convoking the Sixth General Congress of the IWMA. The space reserved for the delegates is large enough to seat delegates from all the world, but as it is the Congress looks rather attenuated, the seats that ought to be filled by the wayward brothers being vacant. Like a family party from which the most important members are absent, the delegates do not look happy. An army with a general and staff, in whom the rank and file have confidence, is nothing without its general and staff, but neither is here. The General Council of New York has, no doubt for very good reasons delegated its right to be represented at the Congress to the London staff, and the London staff has sent what it has to say by post. There is but one consolation, and that is a telegram from Portugal, appointing August Serraillier (a resident of some year's standing in London and the French Secretary of the New York Council) as its delegate, but regretting that he will not be able to be here before the 12th of September.* Arrangement have just been made for the winding-up banquet on the evening of the 12th, so that Serraillier may just arrive in time to be too late, unless it be that he simply comes to receive instructions from the Congress about the General Council for the ensuing year.

The first thing that engaged the attention of the Congress was a proposition by Savoyal, [of] Geneva, for each federation to appoint one of its number to constitute a committee on the credentials that might yet arrive. The chairman announced that six had arrived from Germany since the morning, and that the case was urgent. After some remarks by various delegates, the committee appointed in the morning was commissioned to take charge of the matter. The members at once withdrew, and on their return announced that the six German credentials were all in order. They came from Stuttgart and the surrounding districts and were all for one

---

* Serraillier did not attend.

delegate, who took his seat.

Then came the question as to the constitution and composition of the Bureau. Savoyal again proposed one from each federation. It could not be irony, for he is too old and serious a man for that, and a man who seems to take a great deal of trouble, and not without success, to make himself useful. He has the statistics and main facts of the Trade Union movement in England and other countries almost at his fingers' ends; it could only be childish simplicity and ignorance, for there is no federation besides the few Genevese trade societies represented. He found no supporters, and it was resolved that a Bureau of five should be elected by ballot. That done, it was resolved that the Bureau itself should distribute the various official functions among its members. The Bureau retired, and on its return Van den Abeele announced that Duparc, Geneva, had been elected president, himself one vice-president, Josseron the other; Gutsmann, German secretary, and Savoyal, French secretary. It was then resolved that each secretary should have an assistant, and the two who had the next highest number of votes in the ballot for the Bureau should be the chosen. Hofferer, a German resident of Geneva, was the German assistant, who also acts as interpreter, and Basin [Gustave Bazin][377] the French assistant.

The ubiquitous Van den Abeele has obtained credentials from the Hague section, which has remained faithful to the General Council. It consists for the most part of German mechanics residing at The Hague. Never backward, he has planted himself to the right of the chair to be the first vice-president.[378] The president, on taking the chair, said that, considering the importance of the business for the transaction of which they had met, he hoped no one would speak without having really something to say on the question before the Congress. It was then proposed that no one should speak more than twice on the same subject.

Henri Perret, the Secretary of the French Swiss Federation, believed that everybody could express his opinions in fifteen minutes, and to rectify, or reply to, anything that might be said five minutes ought to be allowed. Van der Abeele would hear of no limitation. He moved and carried the order of the day, relegating the question to a private sitting. Telegrams were read from Wiener-Neustadt – Vienna Newtown – urging the Congress to wield the sword of the mind against State-craft, priest-craft, capitalists' craft, craft of every kind. Similar ebullitions of enthusiasm came by telegraph from the tailors of Winterthur, from the sections of Zurich, Herisau in Appenzell, and other places. Basin [Bazin] proposed a fraternal response to all of them by telegraph, but Gutsmann thought desirable as it might be, it would cost too much, and Basin, [Bazin] seeing the weight of the argument, would content himself with a reply by letter.

Wilhelm, of Zurich, attending a congress for the first time, said it had never been done before, and if the telegrams were entered on the minutes that was all that was required. The Chair, perhaps, if it was thought advisable, might reply to them in the *Tagwacht* of Zurich by a general letter. As the Portuguese did not read the *Tagwacht*, Basin [Bazin] thought they were entitled to a special reply. Schwartz, representing Austria, and who has lived long enough outside the Fatherland to speak French very fluently and with a French accent too, moved the simple *ordre du jour*, [next business] which was carried.

Then came the traditional address of the General Council, which was anything but an account of the present state of the orthodox side of the Association; it was more a statement of the doings of the Governments, and utterly silent about the state of the International at the head-quarters of New York in particular, and the United States in general. The address began by a statement that the Association had gained great influence in Great Britain, that the efforts of the men of the political *demi-monde* there, who had been bent upon sowing dissension and division, had failed, and that the Manchester Congress at Whitsuntide had been completely successful; that English working-men, particularly in the north, were becoming more and more conscious of their own interests, and that the gulf which had hitherto separated the English from the Irish labourer was being bridged over.

En passant, it may be news to some of the readers of *The Times* who do not file the reports of the International Congresses that at Basle, where Backounine proposed the abolition of the right to inheritance. the London Council opposed it as nonsensical, and it was got rid of by a combination of English and German "noes" and French Proudhonist abstentions, which in the aggregate amounted to more than the collective "ayes." At Manchester (*vide* the reports in *The Times*) it was Mr. Maltman Barry, Dr Marx's protégé, at the Hague, who proposed the same thing, and it was carried unanimously.[379]

The address then goes on to say that slaughtering the Communists has not saved M. Thiers, and that before long the workpeople of France will re-conquer France for the people of France. At Olten near Basle, a Swiss Working Men's Congress was called some time since to amalgamate the Swiss trade societies, and the address boasts that the orthodox have eliminated the peace-disturbers – the Backounists. Well, the French-Swiss hold aloof. The Backounists wanted societies* first, and an executive emanating from the constituency. The orthodox created a central council and threw upon

---

* i.e., resistance societies (workplace organisation, unions, syndicates).

it the burden of finding and creating a constituency. The Backounists say it is a failure; their opponents say that they have 5,000 members adhering already. I shall leave it as I found it, simply remarking that if it should come to anything it must be outside the International, and the men at the helm are conscious of it. Spain and Belgium are touched with velvet paws. The erring brothers, both in Belgium and Spain, to punish whose waywardness the powers of anathema, expulsion and dissolution were voted at the Hague, will discover their errors before long, and return to the shelter and fatherly direction of the General Council or a General Council. There were some allusions about the Spanish Republic mowing the workpeople down, about the German Empire playing the part of policeman of the Party of Order, and about the reactionary Governments throughout the world, which previous to the disaster of Sedan seemed to be the special business of Napoleon III. All that is said about America is that the great republic beats kingdoms and empires in the greed for gain; that public morality is "get money, never mind by what means," and that culprits have been acquitted and made honourable by votes of Congress. Further that General Oliver, who really did tell the truth about the condition of the factory workers and all other workers in Massachusetts, has been dismissed as chief deputy of the Massachusetts Bureau of Labour Statistics.[380] In conclusion, the members are advised to eliminate pretended friends – a very wholesome piece of advice – and to trust to themselves and centralize their power. All these bickerings and innuendoes convey a very great deal of truth, and if those who see the splinter in the eyes of others would only take the beam out of their own, all would be right. When the reading of the report was completed it was a quarter to 6, and at 6 o'clock the hall had to be vacated for somebody else. To enter upon the discussion of the report was hardly worthwhile, and the question was, "should it be discussed in a public or a private sitting." The Genevese said the workmen ought to have a chance of being present at the meetings, and they could not come in the daytime. Van den Abeele proposed that all administrative business be disposed of in the daytime and the rest at night. He proposed administrative sittings from 9 to 12 a.m. and from 2 to 6 p.m., and public from 8 to 11 p.m.

Josseron objected that it was too much for simple working-men, who were not in the habit of thinking so much, to have three meetings a day. They would become exhausted, and the work would be done slovenly. People who made it their business to travel about visiting Congresses might be able to get through it. He was against it. Gutsmann could not see why men who could work with their hands fourteen hours should not once in a way be able to work an equal length of time with their heads.

The matter was finally arranged to the satisfaction of all – that to-morrow morning an administrative sitting should be held at 9 o'clock, a public sitting at 2 o'clock, and that in the meantime inquiries should be made whether the hall was engaged every night after 6, and if so another place must be found for evening meetings.

The local committee stated that there was no other place to meet in, and they had been glad to accept it on any conditions. In conclusion it was announced from the Chair that whoever could show that he was a member of the International, no matter on which side of the controversy, should be admitted to the private meetings as a visitor.

That finished the first day's proceeding as of the second half of the sixth International Working Men's Congress.

∗ ∗ ∗

The World, (New York) dated 10 September, published 11 September 1873.*

THE INTERNATIONAL: ADDRESS AND ANNUAL REPORT
OF THE GENERAL COUNCIL

CONDITION OF THE ORDER – AN APPEAL FOR UNITED ACTION

The sixth General Congress of the International Working-men's Association was appointed to meet yesterday, in Geneva, Switzerland. The following address and report were prepared for presentation by the General Council. FELLOW-WORKING-MEN: Our organization is rapidly gaining strength and influence in Great Britain. The plot of some vain men to change the line of action of the International Working-men's Association has failed. Some honest working-men resisted successfully the plans of the new Decembrists and carried our ship to port. The late congress at Manchester was a complete success, and the English working classes – industrial and agricultural – move in immense bodies to put into practice the declaration of the Hague congress: "To conquer the political power is the first duty of the working class". Irish working-men begin to feel the necessity of co-operating with their fellow-sufferers across the channel, and a mutual understanding between the British and Irish Labourers is soon to be hailed. The persecutions and trials of the of the International Working-Men's Association in France – the "captatio benevolentiae" [rhetoric designed to win over an audience] thrown out to the incurables of Versailles – have not prevented the ignominious downfall of the hangmen of the "Commune". His successors are trying to force back history! French working-men, those untiring pioneers of social progress, will yet prove the futility of such

* Also printed in *Der Volksstaat*, 28 September 1873.

beginning, and they will reclaim France. The working-men of Southern and Northern Netherlands [Belgium and Holland] are shaking off old prejudices and joining hands for common action to the indescribable horror of their terror-stricken master. Danish working-men hold aloft the banner of Internationalism, and the "poison of socialism" is even penetrating to the patriarchal domain of the Bernadotte family [Sweden]. The German Empire is playing its role of universal chief of police and detective exceedingly well, to the delight of the "order" raving bourgeoisie of both hemispheres, and the introduction of laws for the "regulation" of popular rights of the press, of association, coalition, etc, at home is to serve as an "elixir d'amour" for some prudish maidens of medieval and trans terrestrial predilections. The organization of the German working-men has made great progress during the past year; just now they are very active and mustering their forces for the approaching general election. Strikes in Russia demonstrated the awakening of its oppressed classes. The fear of the Government is only equalled by its stupidity in looking for the origin of the disaffection everywhere but in the right direction – in the miserable position of the workers. Idle efforts are made by the "constitutional" Government of Hungary to suppress the labour movement. The formation of a working-men's party was prohibited, their executive imprisoned, and the printing establishment of their organ confiscated. The Austrian police authorities are dissolving the trades-societies, withholding the approval of their statutes (being obligatory in that enlightened country) for years, expelling the spokesmen of the working-men, and to crown all these heroic efforts they disperse committees of working-men formed for the purpose of providing cheap lodgings for such of their fellow-working-men as might come to visit the universal exhibition. What an exhibition! The Working-men's Congress, lately held at Olten, Switzerland, has done good work by constituting a centralized Swiss working-men's association[381] despite the opposition of a few professional disturbers, who were left out in the cold. Italy is paying so dearly for the "gallantries" of her "gallant" King, that an inversion of the old law of succession is not improbable – the father to follow his son (Amadeo). The early establishment of a national federation in Portugal is announced. Several strong sections at Buenos Ayres, South America, have sent in their adhesion. The excellent official report of the Bureau of Labor Statistics in Massachusetts, United States, have aroused the ire of the ruling class by the astounding and undeniable revelations of the crying evils of the capitalistic way of production. Unable to refute the damaging conclusions of these official labour reports and not courageous enough to attack the Bureau openly, the bourgeois authorities attempt to falsify the future reports and cripple the usefulness of the bureau by removing its honest and tried officers and supplanting them by servile creatures of the parties in power. The spirit of solidarity among the working-men has repeatedly given convincing proofs of its growth during the last year. We only point to the strikes of the Geneva jewellers, of the German typographers, of the Dutch tobacco-workers and cigar-makers, and to the cordial aid extended to our persecuted Italian brethren. The attempt to destroy our organization by playing secession has miserably failed in all the great industrial countries. The late Congress at Olten proved the insignificance of the Jurassian federation, this herd of the separatist plot. The Spanish working-men will certainly find out before long that something different from "anarchy" is wanted for grappling with the powers that be. And if our brethren in Belgium, the only country where secession was successful, will go through the same bitter ordeal of experiences, they surely can blame nobody but their own short-sightedness.

Workingmen, the modern capitalistic system of production being based on the exploitation of labor by the appropriators of the products of labor, the standard of public morality naturally conforms to the accepted morals of the official society. The amassing of wealth being their only aim, the manner of amassing it becomes utterly irrelevant; scruples about the means to be employed are ridiculed and rather obsolete, and the degree of respectability is measured by the absence of respect for other people's rights and property. Examples of this state of public morals are abundant in all "civilized" countries, whether they be called republics or empires or kingdoms. But it was left to this "free country," to this great "model republic" of the United States to show the utter depravity of public opinion and to demonstrate the complete shameless demoralization of present society by the cool fact that public receptions of honor were and are tendered to men – legislators and high functionaries – who have been officially and publicly proved guilty of venality and perjury.

Fellow-working-men, observe the growing dissolution of old society and – draw your ranks closer, perfect your organization to be ready for performing your historic mission of establishing the new society, based on labor! Six months ago, on the twenty-third day of February, the General Council warned the Spanish working-men against the establishment of a second republic Thiers, against the heroes of the parliamentary comedy. Behold today those artists of the tongue at the head of affairs in Madrid! Cowards in the struggle with the enemies of all human progress, they whistle up their courage against but too natural outbreaks of the down-trodden men of labor. Unable to get a decent force for chasing from the Spanish soil the puerile aspirants to feudal restoration, they have armies ready to crush every effort of the working-men to secure a human existence. Perfectly willing and ready to exchange prisoners and civilities with the Carlists, who pillage the country and desolate it for years, they cry "pirates" too, and are begging the assistance of all the reactionary powers of the world against the working people who seize the implements of war, created by their own toil, with the view of putting them once at last to their own justifiable use – to the defence and assertion of the rights of the working masses. The example set by the rurals of Versailles is followed so strictly by the senores of Madrid that even connoisseurs would be unable to distinguish between this second edition of the republic Thiers and its original.

Laboring men of the world, the emancipation of your class must be your own work. To effect it we must organize, we must combine, centralize our forces; for without centralization, we will never be ready to act, and all our isolated efforts will be crushed. Is there not blood enough shed to teach us this lesson? Must disaster and defeat decimate the ranks of the working classes of every nation before acting in accordance with that simple rule? Must every branch of the great human working family make the same sad experience instead of learning by the example of their brethren on the other side of a mountain range or a river? Awake, ye men of labor, to your duty dictated by your own interest! Banish the false prophets, cast off the pretending friends, close your ears to their shallow phrases, and return to your own deliberate judgement of things and measures, which will certainly lead you to a perfect understanding, to common irresistible action with the workers of the whole civilized world!

The General Council:
F[rancis]. J. BERTRAND, S[imon]. DEREURE, F[riedrich] BALTE [Bolte], C[arl].F[erdinand]. LAUREL, C[onrad]. CARL, F.A. SORGE, S[amuel]. C[K]AVANAGH, C[Karl]. SPEYER.

* * *

La Liberté, dated Tuesday 9th September published Paris, Thursday 11th September.
[Congress opened at 3pm with 25 delegates and a reading of the report of the General Council. 'It was a first-class funeral.' Delegates postponed until tomorrow the discussion of the conduct of the Council.] 'there is talk of it being indicted.' – the General Council report above was printed and was not available in Geneva.]

* * *

London Evening Standard, report dated the 10th, and published on 12 September 1873.

Yesterday the delegates of the International, sitting in Congress here, made very little progress with the business before them, for the morning and afternoon were occupied by a private discussion of the report of the general council in New York. Many of the matters touched on in that report, of which I have sent you a brief summary, have evoked a considerable amount of criticism, but the secrecy of the deliberations has been well maintained, and the report itself has not yet been made public. An open sitting was arranged for yesterday afternoon, but in order to give those of the working classes who desired to attend an opportunity of doing so the meeting was postponed and did not commence until eight o'clock. At that hour M. Duparc, the president of the Congress, took the chair, in the grand salle of the Hotel de la Navigation. Nearly all the delegates who appeared on the previous day were present, and the number of occupants of the deputies' benches was augmented by the arrival of some German and German-Swiss representatives. The body of the salle was well filled by the *ouvriers* of Geneva, and there were over a dozen females, generally young and well-dressed, among the audience. The latter were most attentive listeners, and in general tendered as much applause to the speakers as the sympathisers of the male sex, who, on the whole, were rather undemonstrative.

The proceedings were confined to the reception of reports from the different federations. The first report was by one of the German delegates who said a congress had been recently held at Eisenach, and 71 German sections were represented by their delegates. He had been deputed to represent the congress at Geneva, and, but for a want of funds, a number of others would also have been sent. The difficulties of the International had to contend with in Germany were serious, for there were 34 different States, and nearly as many codes of laws, and in many parts of the empire – Prussia among others – the very name of "'International'" was interdicted. To meet this a change of name was adopted, and the members of the International Society in the places he had alluded to styled themselves "Socialist Democrats". In Berlin the Socialist Democrats Society started an organ to aid in healing some dissensions in their midst and to promulgate their doctrines, but the Government managed to get the journal into its own hands, and it did more harm than good. They had, however, ten or twelve organs in different parts of the empire, and besides their assistance in disseminating the principles of the International, delegates from the large towns were continually forwarding the work throughout the country. The speaker gave no statistics but stated that the progress made during the past year was considerable.

The Swiss delegates next read their reports. The society in Switzerland is divided into two federations, one in the German-speaking portion of the country, and the other in the French cantons. The delegates from the former stated that the International society was not looked on with great favour in German Switzerland, but at a recent workmen's congress 10,000 workmen were represented. The *bourgeois* were striving hard to counteract their influence, and, if possible, to drive the International out of the country, and many sympathisers joined societies similar in object, but having a different name. The Geneva delegates said the local federation consisted of a number of different societies. They were not, however, in accord on all points with the International Society, for the opinion prevalent amongst the members was that political and religious matters should not find a place in their discussions, and that the movement should be confined to affairs connected with the interests of workmen.

The delegates from Austria said that in that country the name of the "International" was forbidden, but the working classes had joined under the banners of different societies. Before the Austro-Prussian war there was no possibility that liberty could find a foot hold in the country, but the political changes after [the battle of] Sadowa produced a better order of things, and the workmen commenced to organise themselves. In 1868 they joined the Eisenach Congress, and afterwards held a monster demonstration in Vienna, which got them an instalment of their demands. Since then, the workmen formed corporations. of which there were twenty in Vienna, and a great many others in different parts of Austria; but these were closely watched by the Government, and the newspapers which advocated their claims were in continual danger of suppression. In the manufacturing districts the men were hard worked and badly paid but were careless and uninterested in the movement; while in Hungary the state of education was very low, and the majority of the working men could not read. They were struggling manfully against all these depressing circumstances, but the general co-operation with their brethren elsewhere had been rendered impossible this year on account of the late financial crisis in Vienna, which threw out of employment 20,000 work-people.

The last report which was read was from a section in the Bernese Jura [Moutier], which can scarcely be described as a branch of the International. It appears that when disunion was caused in the ranks, this section formed an independent neutral body, and has since turned its organisation into use in more practical channels. It started co-operative stores, and the delegate stated that, by the assistance of a bakery, grocery, and butcher's shop, conducted on the principles of co-operation, the 800 members of the society were supplied with the necessities of life at 30 per cent under usual price, and there still remained a profit to divide.

This concluded the nights proceedings, and the Congress was adjourned until to-day.

* * *

La Liberté (Paris), Wednesday 10 September, published 13 September

There are 40 delegates (not 25). Agenda:

1.   Revision of the statutes.

2.   Organisation of international trade unions.

3.   Organisation of workers in general on an international basis.

4.   Political action of organised workers.

5.   General labour statistics.

The bureau comprises: President: Duparc (jewellery worker), Josseron (cultivator), Van den Abeele (who had attended the federalist congress). Van den Abeele read the[382] General Council report.

This document, completely silent about labour issues, is nothing but a long and diffuse set of phrases on revolutionary politics. It is the work of Karl Marx, they say, and an IWMA member assures us on this matter, that the so-called General Council in New York never existed that there was in that city only a letter box, and a Marxist agent, charged with returning correspondence arriving in the Americas to his master ...

* * *

The Times, report dated 10 September, published 13 September.

Last night the Congress, which, though in date of meeting Congress No. 2, assumes, it must be remembered, to be the only one which has any right to be described as the "Sixth International Working-Men's Congress," hold another sitting, and the attending audience were entertained with detailed reports about the German labour movement.

The room was well filled by an audience belonging to the best paid class of artisans, the German element, judging by the cheers, predominating. The sanctuary of the delegates is separated from the space where outsiders may put their feet by a deal table right across the hall, at one side of which sit the reporters, at the other side the Russian lady Nihilists, who mustered in considerable force. They are all young girls, who are going to devote their lives to the study of the problem of the Communistic regeneration of mankind and listen very attentively to everything that is said. The President took the chair at 8 o'clock and informed the audience that the programme of the evening was the reports of the Federations.

Burckhardt, of Stuttgart, was called upon to begin. He said as the only delegate from Germany he offered the good wishes of the whole of the German working class to the people assembled. Everyone knew that in Germany, as elsewhere, the labour movement was much impeded, and the working men, being poor, had not the means required to send delegates on long journeys. They had to support their trades' congresses, of which several had been held lately, and they had also held the Social Democratic Congress for the whole of Germany at Eisenach, at which 73 delegates had taken their seats, which would show that, in spite of obstacles, they had worked hard and made rapid progress in propagating the principles of the International. The opposition itself tended towards making their principles better known. The obstacles they had to contend with were Government persecutions, prohibitions and dissolutions of meetings, and imprisonment. There were also other opponents, the false friends of the working class, against whom they had to struggle. This opposition, however, had the advantage of bringing their principles to the cognizance of people who might otherwise never trouble themselves about them. Compared with England the movement was only in its infancy, but he thought they had done wonders. He then launched out into the habitual charges of the Social Democrats of his party against the Social Democrats of the other party, whose journal, *Der Neuer Social Demokrat* is published at Berlin, and supposed, to be subsidised by the Prussian Government. He had no doubt that they would soon beat the traitors out of the field, for wherever there was a fair field for discussion they always succeeded in drawing away the best elements, and in a short time they must draw away the mass and leave the Berlin leaders by themselves. Besides the official organ, the *Volksstaat*, they had ten political papers and a number of trades' papers advocating the principles of the International. The English trade societies were admirably organised, better than the German, he would admit, but the English workman had been led astray by the abstaining of the Unions from politics.* The French labour agitation was no good either.

* *Der Zeitgeist* (Munich), 18 September 1873, mentioned Burckhardt saying that party and union propaganda was carried through hand in hand – and that papers, brochures and leaflets reached into every village. Legal impediments meant there were no sections of the IWMA in Germany, but in spirit every party member was an IWMA member. Other reports were given: by Gutsmann of Geneva on the Swiss *Arbeiterbund*, Schwarz [Oberwinder, Vienna] on Austria and Hungary, van den Abeele on the Netherlands,

The French workmen confined themselves to the large centres of industry and left the country to take care of itself. The ways of his party were the best. They served the workman wherever he was to be found in town or country and supplied him with newspapers and pamphlets. He advised the French workmen to do the same. Some Frenchmen who had been at the Vienna Exhibition had acknowledged the superiority of this mode of proceeding. He then alluded to the fact that in United Germany there were still 34 States with 34 different codes of law. In Prussia political societies were forbidden to amalgamate, but in the smaller States they were free; and the difference was evident from the greater progress made where association was free than in Prussia. He could not understand how the Swiss, with their free laws, could halt behind the Germans; but he supposed they would now turn over a new leaf, and soon come up. His party had already made itself feared, and in a short time they must make head[way]. The next General Election would show what they were made of. In conclusion he declared that in spirit they were all with the International, but the difficulties of becoming real members were almost insurmountable.

Gutmann [Bruno Gutsmann] gave an account of what the International had been doing in Switzerland. He said the labour movement could not be forced into a particular groove. At the outset, national associations and attachments had prevented the Swiss from largely joining the International. Besides that, the middle-class press had been very busy to destroy the association, but a change had occurred place. They had held a labour congress at Olten a short time ago, where 82 delegates, representing 10,000 workpeople of all the different nations residing in Switzerland and native Swiss, had taken part, and they had all agreed on one thing – to unite, and, they had established the Swiss Labour Union. He might be reproached for not affiliating the Union at once to the International, but there were good reasons why that should not be done. They wanted the mass of the Swiss workpeople, and these were still intensely national, but if the matter was agitated properly and newspapers and pamphlets circulated, they would soon get over that, and then they would enter the association in their thousands. The *Grütli Verein*, a society of native German Swiss numbering 700 members, and the German *Arbeiter Bildung's Verein* [Swiss Labour Educational Union], with 600 members, had already joined, and in the Cantons of Glarus and Appenzell the union had taken root among the trade

Burand Saranat on the French Jura, Bazin on the *Arbeiterbund* in Francophone Switzerland, Courtis [Coutés?] on masons in Geneva, Wilhelm on the section in Zurich, Wolff on tailors in Geneva, Rathenau on the section in Basle and Haserer on German educational unions in Switzerland.

societies. The co-operative society of Zurich, which had a printing press of its own, was with them, and in a short time they would get up a movement the like of which had never been seen before.

Basin [Bazin] reported on behalf of the French-Swiss Federation that the old Federation had been dissolved, on account of the difficulty that had existed of knowing who belonged to it and who did not. Some sections had dwindled away, others had left, others again, had merely existed on paper. In consequence of this, it had been resolved to dissolve the old Federation and nominate a Committee of Reconstruction. They had issued a conciliatory appeal to all the societies, but the answers had not yet come to hand. He was convinced that, if they confined themselves to the social question, and did not allow themselves to drift into politics and doctrinary controversies, they could reconstitute themselves and go on. The workpeople must take their own affairs into their own hands.

One of the Austrian delegates gave a detailed account of the labour movement in Austria. He said after the victory of the reaction in 1849 Austria had been in a state of stagnation till after the battle of Sadowa, in 1866. The liberation of the serfs in 1848 had created a proletariat, and, consequently, laid the foundation for a labour movement; but, up to 1866, all agitation had been impossible. By the fall of the old despotism in 1860, a very limited right of association had been obtained, but it had been enough to begin an active propaganda. The *bourgeoisie* at first had made no use whatever of the new right; not being accustomed to meet to deliberate on public affairs, they had not known what to do with their new liberties. The workpeople, on the contrary, had received leaders and teachers from without; men who had been engaged for some time in the labour movement elsewhere, had taken up their abode in Austria and inaugurated the new era. At the beginning everybody flocked to their meetings they had been veritable monster meetings, and the Government and the *bourgeoisie*, not knowing what to think of, or do with the new phenomenon, had remained passive. The great advantage of that had been that the working classes of Austria had never contracted political friendships and alliances of any kind with middle class politicians, but he wished it to be distinctly understood, Austria, was not yet a modern State. To be a modern State required that the *bourgeoisie* should be the ruling power of the State, which was not yet the case in Austria. The feudal system was abolished in theory, but, with the exception of a few German Provinces, the condition of the people existed in practice, much the same as ever. The Austrian public functionaries were still the same as of yore, they had become petrified in the groove in which they had moved, and everything new disconcerted and frightened them; they could not adapt themselves to the new state of things, and, therefore, they created more disturbance and vexation then might otherwise be the case. The Constitutional Government of Austria was a farce! In all constitutional countries, even where constitutionalism was but a sham, the Lower House dictated the policy and furnished the *cadre* of the Ministries. In Austria Ministries were created over night without the knowledge or consent of the *bourgeoisie*, and he stoutly asserted that the struggle between the modern bourgeoisie on the one hand, and the old aristocracy and Clericalism on the other hand, was not yet fought out in Austria.

Reverting to the state of the labour movement, he said that, in view of the fact of Austria being composed of three-fourths of an alien race, yet living *de facto*, if not *dc jure*, under feudal conditions – a race who could neither read nor write – the German workmen of Austria had very naturally looked out for kindred spirits and allies. They had found them in the German working class outside of Austria and resolved to make common cause. They had sent delegates to the Nuremburg Congress in 1868, where the question had been decided whether the German working class should follow the lead of the Radical *bourgeoisie*, or make a stand of its own; in principle the programme of the International had been accepted by the great majority of the delegates present at Nuremberg, but it had not been until the following year, at the Social Democratic Congress at Eisenach, that the thing had assumed shape. The German working men of Austria had also sent delegates to Eisenach, but there had been traitors in the camp. At Eisenach one of the Austrian delegates had insisted upon proclaiming the Social Democratic Republic as the end and aim of the movement, and it had subsequently been extracted from his own mouth, in cross-examination, that he had been in the pay of the police. The Eisenach Congress, followed by the International Congress at Basle, had marked an epoch in the Austrian labour movement. Before that the *bourgeoisie*, functionaries of the Government, and the Government itself had looked quietly on, wondering what in the chapter of accidents might turn up next, but after that an unrelenting persecution had set in. At first the permission to hold meetings of their own had been refused to the working classes, and then they had assembled their hosts in public meetings of the Radical *bourgeoisie*, which had been allowed by the police. In these meetings a fair hearing had always been accorded to the foremost spokesmen of the workpeople to state their case, by which the intentions of the police had been frustrated. Then the authorities had determined upon making a clean sweep, once for all, of the labour movement, and had brought about the memorable December demonstration to show that it was not simply the imported demagogues, but the bulk of the Vienna proletariat, who were in opposition. That demonstration had the effect of inducing the Government to grant the right to combine for trade purposes; but the concession had been clogged with provisions making it penal for the tailors to combine with the shoemakers to assist each other in the same locality, or for the tailors and the shoemakers of various localities to combine for mutual protection, by which the concession had been rendered practically null. This had been a device to detach the mass of the workpeople from the leaders before seizing and imprisoning them. The spokesmen had been seized immediately upon that, imprisoned, and, after a course of prison discipline, put upon their trial. Instead of having the desired effect, these proceedings had given a new stimulus to the labour movement, and the result was known. The men put upon their trial had been sentenced to long terms of imprisonment, but shortly afterwards pardoned. Since then, dissensions had arisen within their own ranks as to the value of the contemplated electoral reform. The Ultramontane party had opposed it on one ground, and the Extreme Socialistic party on another ground, and between the two opposing powers it might have been shipwrecked. He had vindicated the side of gradual but sure progress, and for that he had been denounced by his former fellow-workers as a renegade. He was convinced that the Government of the State by the Liberal and Radical *bourgeoisie* was a necessary corollary of the success of the labour movement, and he who aided their advent to power propitiated the International. He admitted that the factory lords had very great influence in their own places, but in the affairs of State they were swamped by the Slavonian race, who could neither read nor write. The new electoral law was tending in the direction of making the factory *bourgeoisie* the ruling power of Austria, and it was not until that became the established policy of the Austrian Empire that the labour movement would yield any tangible results. Independent of all collateral circumstances, he put it to the meeting to tell him how the tailors of Vienna could obtain better working conditions without taking the shoemakers, who might only be separated by a wooden wall, into confidential relations. The sum and substance of his arguments was that it is the interest of the working classes in every country to lift the Radical bourgeoisie into power to become the ruling power of the State, and he quoted passages from Dr Marx's writings to fortify his opinion. Concerning the literature of labour, he had a sad tale to tell. Between the opposition of the Government and the ill-will of pretended friends, the *Volks Wille* – the Labour Paper of Vienna – had had to contend with a great deal, but it was still alive, and that implied a very hard struggle. In the factory districts of Bohemia and Silesia, where the Germans might be said to constitute the aristocracy of labour, the foolish treaty of the Austrian

Government with England had put the manufacturers to such straits that they had been obliged to discharge large numbers of their workpeople. Where formerly 500 copies of the *Volks Wille* had been subscribed for, in manufacturing villages, scarcely 50 copies were required now, and in Vienna the Government had prohibited its sale at the newspaper kiosks. To obtain it workmen must pay a quarter in advance or go without it. It was impossible to bring it home to the door of every workman who desired it. They lived in blocks of buildings which were a maze to strangers, and even if they subscribed quarterly to have the papers sent by post it would puzzle the postman to find them. The commercial crisis had thrown 20,000 men out of work in Vienna alone, all of them sympathetic to the International, but to make headway in Austria it would require gradual progress, step by step in a constitutional and legal manner, else the movement might be thrown back, and not recover its present position during years to come.

Savoyal, who has all the appearance of a man of independent means, without aping the gentleman, was called upon to state the case of the Montagnards in the Jura mountains belonging to the Canton of Berne. He said that since dissensions and divisions had arisen, his constituency, a very small one, had not endorsed the views of either side, but minded their own business. They researched the principles of the great associations and concluded that without some material and immediate benefit to the toiling millions all the hubbub of the International would be a vain effort to rally the working classes at large to its standard, and they had come to the conclusion that co-operation was the only thing. At Moutier (Bernese Jura) some 900 workmen were constantly engaged in the various branches of the manufacture of Geneva watches. On taking stock they had found, that out of their scanty earnings a good many people, employing others to do the work, made a very comfortable living, and that they might pocket those profits by employing people to do the same for them. A sum of 1,500 francs (60£) had been got to start in business three years ago, and they now had a grocery, a butchery, a bakery, and an eating establishment furnishing cheap and nutritious food for the single men and women engaged in the workshops. Since they had started in business, the grocers, bakers, butchers, &c., of the neighbouring districts of Courtelary, &c., had reduced their selling prices by 10 to 12 per cent. This, he considered, something palpable for workpeople to understand, and if the International would pay attention to such things as that, the mass of the people would support it. That wound up the business of the evening.

∗ ∗ ∗

La Liberté, 10 September evening, published Paris, 13 September.

This entire evening consisted of reports in German, and that these were abbreviated and poorly translated into French. In the Netherlands, the IWMA had 5,000 supporters, mostly in tobacco manufacturing. In Geneva stonemasons had recently won a six-week strike and had obtained a wage rise. In Basle small sections of ribbon workers and carpenters had approved the decisions of The Hague. The German delegate noted that it was possible to send only one delegate to Geneva because of the costs occasioned by a recent congress in Germany.

[This correspondent's report concluded that, in these different sessions the majority of delegates declared that the IWMA should maintain itself exclusively on the economic terrain and should entirely abandon political action.] What will the congress decide on this matter? The following session will probably inform us on the import of a return to the original doctrines of the Association.

* * *

Journal de Genève, Friday 12th September published 14 September and *Le Temps* (Paris), published 16 September.

The general feelings of the workers of Geneva were however expressed by Mr. Duparc, a jewellery worker and congress president: the worker [he said], once he has for the sake of form, paid homage to socialist theories, that worker has to come to an accommodation with the current situation, while at the same time making efforts to improve on it. The worker should not take the state aside to say to it: 'You should deliver my well-being'. In Switzerland we have the power to change peacefully the laws and institutions that inconvenience us ...

[Van de Abeele replied: We have had experience of Co-operative societies! and they have produced nothing. In England, there is one society that has developed into a millionaire, it employs workers, isn't this still the reign of capitalism?][383]

* * *

The Times, report dated 12th, published 16 September.

The subject of yesterday's public discussion was the march of the International. Opinion seems to be divided on the question of what the aims of the International are and ought to be. In the opinion of the seven trade societies whose spokesmen have signed the little pamphlet I cited yesterday it ought to be nothing but a federation of Trade Unions and should leave all other matters outside. They do not object to politics, but they do not want the Association, as such, to trouble about them. They are in favour of the Unions devoting their surplus funds to Co-operation, and they believe in the possibility of arriving some day at a state of things which will replace the wages system by a system which will make the labourer a participator in the results of his labour. Everything else is to be left to the volition of the people of the different countries in their capacity as citizens. In Switzerland, it is contended, the laws are such that the workpeople can work out their own emancipation by legal means, but they must do it their own way. They only want the International for trade purposes.

Van den Abeele scented too much of the bourgeois spirit in this. The true mission of the International was to organise and prepare for the Social Revolution. Co-operation would never emancipate the workpeople, nor would they achieve anything by dabbling in politics. This is, in a few words, the substance of the morning's debate.

Rossetti (Canton Tessin) opened the debate in the afternoon. He said at the beginning all the branches of Geneva had been paternally united, but that union had been disturbed by men who had endeavoured to foist doctrines upon the International which ought to be left outside. The same men who to-day fought against authority had first invoked its aid for their own purposes. The Jurassians had started with the object of forming a Latin Confederacy, and they had ended in splitting the Association in two – a Latin half and a German half. The proceedings at the Hague had not been the cause of the split, they had simply been the result of the Basle Congress. He was not for the exclusion of politics, but he did not want them to be made use of as they had been in France, where they had produced the Government of the 4th of September. He was for the suppression of authority within the Association. As to the head workers, that was a question which very much depended on the condition of the people with whom they had to deal. In Italy the workpeople were so ignorant that it would be impossible to go on without the aid of men of superior education. The first Section in Turin had been formed by a lawyer. The religious difficulty would disappear when people became more enlightened. Co-operation was a means of attaching men who could not participate in anything without the prospect of some material benefit. Co-operation was the practical part of the social question. He was for leaving each Federation free to make its own politics.

Van den Abeele was afraid he had been misunderstood. He was not against Co-operation, but he wanted corporations or groups of workmen to be organised for productive purposes, not the joint-stock Corporation with wage labour which was in vogue now. The first thing to enable workingmen to study social questions was a reduction of the hours of labour, to give them more time.

Henri Perret said an impression had been created that the Genevese were *bourgeois*, and that they were not revolutionary. They wanted to make their Social Revolution in a legal way, and that could only be accomplished by organizing trade societies. The Unions were the training-ground where the men fitted themselves for their political duties. It was the Unions which had resisted the Government when it had felt inclined to deliver up the Paris refugees. The organization of the masses would prevent a bloody revolution.

Bazin said the Social Revolution was not yet understood. A complete understanding of what was wanted was necessary. All revolutions had miscarried because they had only been local, and the movement had proceeded from some directing head downwards. He wanted the complete autonomy of every Federation and Section, which would give the most complete organization; individuals first, next Sections. then Federations, then a Federal agency. Thus, the movement would go upwards, and then it would succeed; from top to bottom would never do.

He had protested against the minority at the Hague revolting, because he was sure it was only certain persons who had quarrelled, and the affair might have been got over without a split. He was for a complete reconciliation. What to do with the head workers he hardly knew. The workmen had not time enough to study questions thoroughly. If all was left to those who had to get their living by manual labour, the movement would be greatly impeded. Journalists and other learned men had done good service in the past, but he had a doubt whether the harm done by their quarrels and polemics in the papers did not outweigh the good they had done. With religion the International had nothing whatever to do. He believed the result of this Congress would be to find a common ground for a complete reconciliation. No man of sense would lose sight of politics, but it was high time that working men should study their own dignity, and not elevate charlatans into power who would betray them on the morrow.

Wilhelm said Unionism brought home the benefits of combination to the door of everyone. Without the masses the International would be powerless, and the masses could only be drawn in by holding out some immediate benefit. The result of the Olten Congress proved this. He would admit that in Switzerland they had such complete liberty of association, press, &c., that they required no struggle, and could sit down to attend to their social affairs quietly, but in Germany those rights had yet to be gained by political agitations. They had to had to be constantly on the look-out. As to the head workers, if the work people were taken in it was their own fault. It was the business of the best educated workmen to look after them, but until the bulk of the manual labourers had better schooling than at present the concurrence of the head workers was a necessity. They were not necessarily rogues, though they might be so.

The Austrian delegate who reported on the state of Austria on Tuesday thought he was in duty bound to say a few words about the head workers. He could not see the drift of the Genevese argument that a doctor and a professor had caused the dissensions which had led to the split. If the workpeople were on their guard it would be impossible for such men to domineer over them. It the Geneva idea should prevail, that the head workers should be discarded after all the services they had rendered, it would produce disastrous results, because the workpeople could never again reckon on the assistance of men of brain. Nor was he convinced that the hand worker was more entitled to the confidence of his fellows than the head worker. His experience in Austria was that the [illegible] workers were the traitors. Polemics in the party papers were very necessary, because they cleared the air. Sometimes people who did not deserve it were getting too much influence. and they must be exposed. With workmen who had their wits about them dangerous characters would never become leaders. Phrasemongers wore themselves out very soon. If the spirit of the Geneva pamphlet was to be made the ruling spirit of the International, the society would become more intolerant than the priests.

The Chairman, thinking he had heard enough, proposed the closing of the discussion, which was carried. He then announced that there would be a "free and easy" in the evening, that the Commission on the revision of the rules would report early in the morning at an administrative sitting, and that at 10 o'clock a public sitting would be held to discuss the formation of the International Trades Unions.

When I arrived this morning at the Hotel de Navigation I was informed that obstacles had arisen in Committee, and that there would not be a public meeting till 8 o'clock to-night. There were several of my profession from Paris, Berlin, and New York. We were looking at each other, wondering what the chapter of accidents might have in store for us next, when one of those young lady devotees whom I have mentioned came joyfully into the room and told us to make haste, as the public performance was about to commence upstairs. Out of civility, the matter had been reconsidered, and the sanctuary was thrown open. Out of the 30 delegates who now compose the congress 18 were present. Scattered over a space which would seat the British House of Commons the Congress looked anything but imposing. The order of the day was "the establishment of International trades societies", and the definite proposals were those of the General Council. They were in print, but there was only one French and one German copy. Between open windows, an empty room, and the noise outside hardly anything could be understood, but as soon as the seven *considerants* had been read, J. Coutés, of the Geneva stonemasons, rose to protest. He said that the Congress had met to curb and diminish the power of the General Council, not to increase it. He was pacified by an explanation that though the General Council, might become the Central Agency which had been talked about, it would not be obligatory that it should be.

When the voting commenced the President had left the chair, the Vice-President was officiating, and there were only 12 delegates present, as the rest were attending to more important affairs.

The propositions of the General Council adopted by the twelve are, as near as I could catch:

1. All the trades of a country shall combine to establish an Executive for that country. (The Germans added, "as far as the law will permit").
2. These Executives shall be in constant communication with each other by the intermediation of a General Executive.
3. Special funds shall be established and controlled by these Executives to support indigent members of the Union in any country here they may require it, and to defray the expense of the General Executive.
4. In case of strikes the Unions are bound to assist those on strike if they are short of funds.
5. Every member of such a Union shall, in case of emigration, have equal rights with older members of the Union in the country to which he transfers his residence.
6. If a member is obliged to leave his country on account of political persecutions and prosecutions, he shall be entitled to the same benefits as he was entitled to where he lived.
7. The Union shall prevent the importation and exportation of workmen in case of strikes.

There was a motion that the sixth proposition should be rejected, but I cannot say what became of it.

The next question was the organization of the proletariat on an international basis. This implied a political organization, to which the Vice-President was the first to object. He declared that politics must be eliminated from the labour movement. The aim of the Association was the economical emancipation of the working classes. On that they could be united, but on politics they could not be. He had no objection to politics, but they must remain outside the International.

Wilhelm had instructions from the section of Zurich not to submit to any prescription or regulation on the question of politics, but to leave everybody at liberty to do as he like. This was unanimously carried, and the meeting adjourned till 8 o'clock tonight. Thus 12 delegates have undone in half an hour what 20 were sent to the Hague to establish.

The faithful have been thrown into a state of consternation by a communication from New York. The New York Council is aware of the heresy of the Genevese and is not prepared to put up with it. It will either maintain its powers unimpaired or die for its principles, and that is the reason why neither New York nor London had sent delegates. If Geneva should come out victorious, the faithful will not hear the last of it, and, if defeated, they will come to the very reasonable conclusion that for all the assistance the New York Council can afford them they may as well call themselves the Federalized Trades of Geneva and have a Trades Council as call themselves International. But there is worse. Some fire-brand has proposed the suppression of the General Council in Committee. The Congress looks as if it was pregnant with something, but conscious that its offspring will be an abortion.

* * *

The Times, report dated 11th, published on the 15th.

The Congress (No. 2), last night, did not present a very animated spectacle. To the left of the chair the seats were moderately well occupied by the Germans, but on the right there was a great void. On closer inspection I found that some partly acclimatized Germans, who generally sit among their French Swiss friends on the right, had gone over to the left, sitting on the inner benches, with their backs towards the chair and the audience. This with a few absentees, who otherwise would have taken their seats on the right, made that side look very desolate, while the other side looked more than usually serious. The sitting was to be opened at 8 o'clock, but it was a good deal later before anything was done; and when at last the Chairman's bell had announced that the performances were about to commence, there was another little delay. The business of the evening, which everybody expected to be the consideration of the report of the General Council as announced on the previous day, was the continuation of the reports from the Federations. Van de Abeele was called upon to relate what he had to say for the Dutch.

A smile ran along the reporters' table, participated in by our fair friends from Russia, who had been fortunate enough to get a seat alongside of us; but on the next bench it became a giggle, and one of the Schismatics, who has remained here since the close of Congress No. 1 to watch proceedings laughed just low enough to escape the ringing of the bell.

Van den Abeele seemed to appreciate his awkward position and did not answer to the call with his usual alacrity. What could he say? Had he not declared a few days before that all Holland was with the Schismatics except a few obdurate blockheads in Amsterdam?

All eyes were turned upon him, and after a few moments of suspense he rose. He told us what valiant fellows the Dutchman he represented were, how they had been the champions of civil and religious liberties ever since they had been a nation, and that they were surely not going to put up with capitalist oppression. Then he stated that 5,000 cigarmakers had the alternative put to them of leaving the International or submitting to a lock-out till they did. They had stood out six weeks, but owing to the spirit of solidarity prevailing in the International, the masters had not been able to get men either from England or Germany and had at last been obliged to give in. He stated inadvertently that the English cigar makers had paid the Dutch during the lock-out. The fact of the matter is that the cigarmakers of England, Belgium, Holland and Germany have had for several years past an International Trade Society, which has nothing whatever to do with *the* International. There was never any danger of English cigarmakers going to Holland to work for less than the Dutch; the troubles were in the opposite direction, and the London Society has made immense sacrifices to bring about the happy state of things of which Van den Abeele claimed the glory for the International.*

Like epidemics, the example of the General Council taking credit for things in which the International had no hand seems to be contagious. After Van den Abeele had finished, Wilhelm of Zurich made a statement. The section was not numerous but compensated in zeal for what it lacked in numbers. Before the war they had been stronger, but the dispute whether the French or the Germans were right has reduced them, although they had kept their ground. He then told the Congress what the wood trades, the metal trades, the shoemakers, and the tailors had done, which, however, for want of funds, had not all been successful. But the blacksmiths had made a stand. Formerly they had worked from 5 o'clock a.m. till 7 o'clock p.m., with only a short interval to take their dinner, and they lodged and boarded with their masters. Their wages had been reckoned at 3f[rancs] 50c[entimes] a day. Now they only worked 10 hours a day, could sleep

---

* *The Daily Telegraph* (London, 16 September 1873) carried extensive comments on cigar making and made clear that van den Abeele asserted that the strike was supported by an international trade body and not by the IWMA itself.

and dine where they liked, and the *minimum* wages were 4f[rancs] a day. These trades, he was bound to admit, did not belong to the International. Nevertheless, the Association had all the influence, because the leaders of those Societies belonged to the International, and he promised something handsome for the next year.

After that we had the praises of Basle sung by a German who is here on a visit and received credentials. Basle is an important place on account of its size, its manufacturing industry, and its geographical position. The mother section in this important place had 30 members, a riband weavers' society had 24 members, and a shoemakers' society as many more, all belonging to the International, and they severally declared by written documents that they were perfectly satisfied with the doings of the General Council. Then there had been a Sunday's excursion into Germany, in which 3,000 persons had taken part, and the section of Lorach, a factory place in Baden, had made great progress. He was aware that the membership of Basle was anything but worth boasting of, which, however, was compensated for by the fact that the whole of the workpeople of Basle belonged in spirit to the International.

Henri Perret, the delegate of the Carouge section, [Geneva] said that after hearing all the reports, it appeared to him that the International had lost much ground, and he thought that was the result of wasting its time with things that did not concern the working men. Instead of doing something practical, the time had been wasted in controversies and discussing theories which had cause dissension and divisions among workmen. If they would confine their attention to the economical question, and, above all, to the Trade Societies, they might in a short time count their members by millions.

The sitting closed a few minutes before 10 o'clock

A little pamphlet addressed to the Internationals and signed by seven Genevese belonging to as many different trades, of whom Henri Perret, engraver, is the first, has been freely distributed here, and deserves notice. It contains a summary of the troubles of the International, and asks: "Whence came the schism? At first it was a doctor and a professor* who fought for the preponderance in Switzerland, then came Backounine to make the International a vehicle for the propagation of Atheism."

The reply to this is to the effect that the workmen have no time for such speculations, that they are better left to lazy and debauched minds, to the imbeciles and the hypocrites. Out of the controversy between London and Backounine's Alliance it is stated the terms Marxists and Backounists had

---

* Perhaps a reference to Dr Coullery and to the Russian exile Alexander Serno-Solov'evich, active in the French-Swiss federation before the Basle congress of 1869.

come. The one had preached abstention from politics, the other the contrary under a direction of an authority which had produced disastrous results.

The remedy proposed is: "No more Marxists, no more Backounists, but the sincere alliance of the real working men. The cause of disunion has arisen from the successive changes introduced into the spirit of the first rules −1, Exuberant personalities; 2, philosophical, religious, or ideological doctrines substituted for aim of the Association; 3, the principles of authority and centralization."

The dangers of having head workers in the General Council, and of leaving it so many years in one place are dealt with at considerable length, and the remedy proposed is to make the General Council in reality nothing but a letter-box and a register-office for statistics, so that it cannot become either Pope or gendarme. Another remedy spoken of is that no member shall be re-eligible more than once. It concludes with some definite propositions for the reconstruction of the Society, preceded by a series of recitals, of which I shall give a part:

Considering that the representation of the sections at the different cantonal, federal, or general assemblies, ought to be real and not fictitious; that it has been found that sections of three or four persons reciprocally delegate themselves cannot have any other but a private interest; that if simplified every member who can read and write can perform the functions of a member of the Council, the undersigned propose to the Congress the following resolutions:

1. No one can become a member of the International Working Men's Association who cannot prove that he is a working man living by his own labour.
2. No section has a right to a delegate till it has a fixed number of members.
3. The rules are constantly open to revision. It shall suffice that one Federal Council, supported by a majority of its sections, shall demand a revision and discussion, and, to make it valid, the majority of the Federal Councils shall transmit their votes to the General Council.
4. The General Council shall be appointed by the Federal Councils, each Council appointing two members, one to sit at the General, the other at the Federal Council. The latter may, after consultation with the Federal Council have the power to annul any decision come to by his colleague at the General Council. The members of the General Council shall receive a salary equal to the highest wages they can earn at their trade.
5. The functions of the General Council shall be strictly used to prepare

the universal labour statistics and facilitate the exchange of useful information between all the sections. It is bound to transmit without comment all it may be ordered to transmit by a Federal Council with the approbation of its sections.

6. The seat of the General Council shall be in Europe but shall not be taken back to London before the lapse of two years.

'The undersigned, in proposing these resolutions, have but one aim, to stop the division which exists among the working men, not of their own making, but brought about by some persons who are strangers to their real interests. In returning to the simplicity of the primitive mission of the Association, discarding exuberant personalities, strangers to manual labour, making an end of all that may far or near have the semblance of despotism, we hope firmly that in future we may all unite, and that nothing will divide us. What divides us now are not questions of labour or labourers, but the questions raised by those who by the nature of their education and the diversity of their interests have led the working man astray.'

* * *

Journal des débats politiques et littéraires (Paris), report dated 12 September, published Monday 15th.

I believe I was right in expressing doubts as to the capacity of the internationalists who compose the authoritarian congress to engage with the issues expressed in their programme. For three days now the congress has been dragging through reports of federations and sections, all more and more insignificant. A matter maybe deserving some attention is being touched on – only today: that of international trade federations.

[The writer relates an argument in which van den Abeele, accused the Geneva delegates of being bourgeois and not revolutionaries – a red rag to a bull. He reported the congress president Duparc saying:]

'The workers, he said, once having offered a bow for form's sake to socialist theories, need, while trying to change circumstances, to adjust themselves to those circumstances. The workers should not challenge the State or say: you should provide for my well-being. In Switzerland we have the power to changes peacefully, both to laws, and to institutions that obstruct us, and we must understand that we do not have the right (although we have the greater numbers) to subordinate other social classes.'

These words struck me all the more, because they are, especially in the last part, the most absolute contradiction to that which was said by the representatives of the same group at the Congress of The Hague. 'The wealthy owning class should be subjugated by the might of the armed proletariat.' That was the manner in which Vaillant, ex-member of the Commune, (not a worker), summed up the doctrine of the International. The means for change indicted by M. Duparc and by those that spoke in his vein are improving wages, reducing the working day and establishing cooperatives. On all this Van den Abeele inveighed, and there was no one to reply to him. Wage rises! he said: but everyday necessities also rise [in price], and the real victims are workers in trades that are not organised, who see their gains unchanged. As for co-operatives, in England there were co-ops that have become millionaires employing workers, but isn't capitalism still dominant?

The first argument evidently merited discussion, as to the second van den Abeele feels no need to study the subjects he addresses. His objection against co-operation reduces itself, in the end, to the same [argument] formulated by General Cluseret towards the end of the Empire [of Napoleon III]. 'Through co-operation', he said, 'you are going to make workers into owners and conservatives; and then, who will be with us to make a revolution?' And no one in that assembly got up, to say to this Belgian-Dutch journalist: What is a social revolution? What is your understanding of that? What will you put in place, on the day that you would destroy what exists now? And for sure, whether the aim might be to push a nation forward to progress or backwards, good or bad in itself, a political revolution is self-explanatory, it has an aim, but is that the same for a social revolution? But I am forgetting my role as a *reporter* for that of a discussant; I shall stop.

The result of van den Abeele's sally was that the Geneva delegates had to declare that the societies they sought should be *co-operatives*, which is to say they should contain every worker in the trade, i.e., pure communism.

[Further comments concluded this article: on head and hand workers; the role of journalists, and a social evening.]

* * *

La Liberté (Paris), 12 September, published 15 September.

… Having come to Geneva with an agenda that was most interesting, and in facing these large social problems of the organisation of labour and of trade unions, they were able to prove only their profound incapacity and their complete ignorance of these matters. As for reconciliation, there was no question of that …

… Citizen Duparc, the congress president, said that the workers of the Fabrique* had been enthusiasts for the International from the first, but soon

---

* The Fabrique denoted a set of skilled and affluent citizen-workmen in luxury trades

two currents established themselves, with thinking-workers promoting them. One spoke of grand theories, hollow words, with proposals for abolishing inheritance, and collective property and soon wearied the workers of Geneva, who were more practical rather than theoretical. Duparc said that our action programme came down to four points: 'mutual education, resistance funds, legal opposition to management and trade associations'.

… Yesterday morning, the congress resumed its sessions, and at last touched on the agenda indicated on its programme.

The first item for discussion was the following: *the Organisation of International Trade Unions.* The president read the resolutions drafted on this question by the General Council of New York. They are in the form as follows and *in extenso,* after the congress lightly amended them, and voted through without discussion:

Considering

1. That the struggle of labour against capital is neither local, nor national, but rather a social problem embracing every country in which modern society exists.
2. That there is, among capitalists, an international entente for the exploitation and oppression of working people, and for that reason, the resistance efforts of the working class have failed, because of a lack of solidarity between workers of the various professions in each country and of fraternal unity between the working classes of the many lands.
3. That the principal of solidarity commands workers everywhere to help one another.
4. That the emigration or exportation of the forces of workers from one country to another necessarily increases competition between the workers of the latter country.

For these reasons, the General Council of the IWMA submits to the various resistance societies (*Trades Unions*) of every country the following plan to enlarge the prosperity and activity of the *Trades Unions* over every country (*sic*).

Article 1: Every trade association or resistance society in one country should come together to elect a central executive for their country.

Article 2: All the executive committees should establish regular

(jewellery, watch-making), living near the city centre. 'the privileged workers of the watch trade in Geneva … treated the mass of the factory hands with a sort of contempt and were in no haste to become martyrs to the socialist cause.' Peter Kropotkin, *Memoirs of a Revolutionist,* Boston: Houghton, Mifflin, 1889, p. 207.) 'hollow words' refers to the Geneva IWMA's proposals to the Basle congress of 1869.

communications between themselves through the intermediary of a *general executive council,* in order always to be informed of the correct state of trades and labour in every land – *conforming to the laws existing in the various countries.*

Article 3: Funds should be levied and controlled by *the executives* of the various countries to aid union members in case of need, *wherever that may be,* and to cover the costs of the *General Executive Council.*

Article 4: Every central executive of the various trades of each country will come together for mutual assistance *whenever* a particular trade, lacking means, is unable to continue a struggle against the exploiters.

Article 5: In the case of relocation or emigration, each member of an international union will enjoy in a new country such rights as those of older members in that country.

Article 6: Every member of any international, having to quit his country for political reasons will receive the *same support* in a new country, which was his due in the country that he left.

Article 7: These international unions, through their central executives, should as much as possible impede the importation or exportation of workforces under contracts concerning strikes, emigration, and immigration.

After a very short discussion on article 3 of the agenda (organisation of workers in general on an international basis) the congress named a commission to study the matter and addressed article 4 (the political action of organised workers). By eleven votes, against ten, and with many delegates abstaining, a resolution on this article was voted through. Henceforth federations will organise political action in their respective countries, *always in conformity with the law as established.*

The congress then addressed revision of the General Statutes: these are the only changes made to the former articles:

Article 3 (new). A general labour Congress composed of branch delegates of the whole Association is to take place every two years. Each congress will nominate a federation as the seat of the General Council.

Article 4 (new). The federation in which the General Council is based will choose its members from among its number, and they will not in any case co-opt new members.

Article 5. The Council may convene an extraordinary congress with the agreement of three quarters of the federations.

Article 15. (new) The congress declared the abrogation [annulment] of all previous statutes prior to this new revision.

Other matters on the agenda were to be addressed in a private session for tomorrow, Saturday. As for the question of the [location of the] General Council, we are told that the Geneva federation will be the one that, this year, is responsible for nominating the membership of that body.*

Should this transformation of the International be considered the last word? We do not think so. Once again it has proved the truth of our judgement: The IWMA is dead – Its debris is scattered all over the world!

London Evening Standard report dated the 12th, published on 16 September 1873.

THE INTERNATIONALIST CONGRESS. (FROM OUR OWN
CORRESPONDENT.) GENEVA, Sept. 16

The consideration of reports of purely local interest, and discussions on generalities, have occupied the Congress of the Internationalists for the last few days. In the eyes of the Swiss delegates the affairs of petty trade societies, numbering, perhaps, not more than a couple of hundred members, are considered of sufficient importance to merit discussion at the annual meeting of an organisation having such comprehensive aims as the International, and at the same time the apple of discord has been thrown into the council by some of the representatives.

The order of procedure for the past three days has been – in the morning the discussion of the report of the general council, which seems to have presented endless difficulties, for it has not yet been adopted, amended, or put into shape for presentation to the public, and in the evening public sittings to receive reports and discuss them. The morning assemblies are wild and stormy, and the differences of opinion on the policy of the New York central body are such as to threaten another serious division in the ranks; while even in the public seances delegates cannot always control their feelings, and imprudent expressions often lead to "scenes." On Wednesday night a delegate from Holland gave some idea of the progress of the International in that country, and it would appear that however sympathetic the working classes are with the International, their surroundings prevent an open adhesion to the body. The bourgeois give a strong opposition to the movement, and employers threaten with dismissal all *employés* who countenance the federation. The strength and organisation of the workmen were, however, shown, it was alleged, by some recent strikes, particularly that of the cigarmakers, who, with the assistance of substantial donations from their English and German brethren, were able to beat the masters. There

---

* See also a report in *Journal des débats politiques et littéraires,* dated 15 September, below.

was a thorough understanding among the working classes of Holland, the delegate affirmed, and they were determined not to submit to despotism of any kind. The representatives of some of the trades of Geneva, Zurich, and Bâle [Basle] described the efforts of the working classes in their respective towns to improve their condition as to wages and hours of labour; and the remainder of the sitting, which occupied several hours, was taken up by the details of the various strikes.

The long recital of reports, which, though perhaps very interesting to the parties concerned, had little to do with the International or its objects, came to an end yesterday;[384] and afterwards an old source of dissension got into the discussion, and, the topic being continued to-day, almost led to a rupture. Amongst the many societies affiliated to the International, the most pronounced in its peculiar views is The International Alliance of Socialistic Democracy, which must not be confounded with the German societies of a somewhat similar name. It was founded by Bakounine in 1868, and eschews religion and politics,[385] for its two primary rules are "The Alliance declares itself Atheist" and "The Alliance decides on absolute abstention in political matters". It sought incorporation with the International in 1869, and it was agreed to recognise it in the same way as any other section. At the International Congress at Basle its representatives demanded the adoption of resolutions committing the association to the opinion that there should be "the immediate abolition of the law of succession" [inheritance] and other departures from the regular programme.[386] They were outnumbered and have since been in a state of incessant warfare with the general body. Three or four of the delegates sitting in the present Congress are members of the Alliance, and this disturbing element showed itself in its true colours when the neutral ground of hearing reports was passed. To this must be added another cause of strife, for the delegates from the French Swiss federation demand that the general council shall be reduced in number, shall consist entirely of workmen, who shall serve one term only, and that it shall be removed to Europe. Not content with this, they desire to take away some of its functions, and it is easy to perceive that this section, while not going so far as the federalists, is in consonance with that body in many things, and that very little would induce it to secede from the central organisation. With all these fertile causes of discord, it is not surprising that the Congress can form no definite plan for the future, and that its secret sessions for the revision of its statutes have been without avail.

The delegate from the Hague, who is an adherent of the Alliance, condemned what he termed the narrow views of some of the Swiss representatives, who thought questions of wages and hours of labour were those only which concerned the working man. They were, he considered, not a radical cure for the workmen's wrongs, but an anodyne. They might be looked on, however, as a means to the end, for increase of wages made a man independent, and shortening his hours of work gave him time to study the questions which were allied with his interests, in which study, in the speaker's view, philosophy should have its share. The co-operative movement spoken of so exultingly by the Bernese Jura [Moutier] delegate did not seem to him matter of congratulation, for the co-operation in groups is opposed to the principles of the International. However, he would admit that co-operation to resist the power of capital was a different thing, and under circumstances absolutely necessary. Then he advocated a negative position in politics, and particularly entire abstention from bourgeois politics, for in his opinion the working men should confine themselves to those matters of politics which affected themselves. This led to that moot point, the definition of a working man, but without attempting the fine-drawn distinctions affected by some, he contented himself with a denunciation of those who favoured the admission of the *travailleurs de pensée*. And in fine, [sic] as the last and most important part of his programme, he propounded a scheme for the complete demolition of the social state, with a view to its ultimate reconstruction. Those views he wished to have embodied in any code of laws or resolutions issued for the guidance of the sections, and they may be looked on as the "platform" of the "Alliance and Socialistic Democracy."

The parent body, the real and original Internationalists, will scarcely adopt those ideas, believing, as they do, in the efficacy of intervening in all political movements, and conceiving partially the necessity of introducing brain-workers into their ranks; while the Swiss delegates to a man, including even the well-wishers of the Alliance, would never consent to a social revolution, with all its attendant horrors, while they are so contented with their present mode of government. In fact, the Swiss are Internationalists only in name, and while seeking the amelioration of themselves and their fellows, they would feel little difficulty in severing connection with a society which would ratify the prospectus of the Alliance. Many of the Swiss delegates defended a moderate line of action and joined issue with the Hague delegate in almost all his propositions. A Zurich representative, connected with the Alliance,[387] expressed the opinion that the workmen of German Switzerland would never permit themselves to be dragged into a social revolution in order to obtain for another country – Austria for instance – that which had already been granted them in Switzerland. The same delegate was in favour of a conditional admission of brain-workers, who should not be allowed to acquire too much-influence. Other delegates thought it would be impossible to eliminate the *travailleurs de pensée*, for their aid was indispensable; but, on the other hand, many contended that journalists and men of their class had already destroyed sections, and if they wished to adopt the principles of the body they should form a group apart, and carry forward outside it such measures as they wished. The discussion on this question was continued at considerable length, and the Congress seemed to be pretty evenly divided on it, the members of the opposition to the admission believing that there was sufficient brain-power amongst the working classes to enable them to carry out their ends, while their opponents considered the long working day fatal to concentrated study.

Next came up for discussion the advisability of abstention from interference in matters religious and political, and it was contended by a delegate that politics gave too much room for agitators, and plunged the workman into a labyrinth of perplexities which he could not understand, and that interposition in religious topics gave a force of opposition to their enemies which it was altogether unnecessary to raise. As feeling runs high in the Congress on this point, the President suggested that the sitting should be made private, which was unanimously agreed to. The Congress will continue for several days, but from present appearances the delegates will scarcely be able to agree on a manifesto or series of resolutions, and some people would not be surprised if a general disruption were the *finale*.

* * *

The Times, dated 13 September, published 17 September.

Last night the revision of the rules was proceeded with in the public sitting. What the young schismatics of Congress No. 1 refrained from doing last week the old ones have done this week in Congress No. 2. The preamble referring to the revival of the working classes in Europe ten years ago has been altered by substituting "the entire world" for "Europe," and it was carried unanimously. In the articles referring to the Congress "biennial" was substituted for "annual;" Van den Abeele and Courtés stood up for annual Congresses and Rossetti for triennial. The reasons urged for the change was that these Congresses were an expensive affair, which the working men could not afford every year. The counter-argument was that the frequency of such meetings tended to bring men of different countries more in harmony with one another by dispelling national prejudices. Van den Abeele urged, with all the seriousness imaginable, that it would kill the Association to have only one Congress every two years, and Courtés was afraid that two years would be too long a time to leave the General Council without giving an account of its doings. The last sentence in Article 3 – that "the Congress shall appoint the General Council" was struck out. In future the Congress will simply appoint the place where the General Council is to have its seat, and the regional Federation of the place is to elect from its number the members who are to form the General Council. It shall consist of working men; but the old proviso of men from the different countries represented in the International has been struck out, as well as the power of adding to the number of its members. Instead of the customary address, the General Council shall in future render an account of its stewardship to the Congress. The proviso that two-thirds of the delegates must be in favour of a revision of the rules before it can be undertaken has also been struck out, so that the article concerning it reads "The present rules may be revised by each Congress." Gutsmann defended the old proviso on the plea that it gave a certain stability to the Association, but Ph. Becker was of opinion that the present arrangement could not last long if the federations at present existing only on paper should become a living reality. The version of the rules in the hands of the Commission was the one published previous to the Hague Congress, and, consequently, did not contain the obnoxious resolutions of that Congress. To make everything clear and prevent mistakes, a special declaration has been appended that by the present revision all former editions of rules and regulations are annihilated and of no effect. This completed the business of the evening, and the President announced that the next public sitting would begin at 8 o'clock this morning.

At 8 o'clock this morning only the President and one secretary were present, and it was not till 9 o'clock that there was a muster of about 20 delegates. On declaring the sitting opened, the President proposed that the Congress should sit in permanence till its labours were completed, only taking a short interval at noon. This was agreed to. The administrative regulations were on the order of the day. Article 3 – "Each delegate has but one vote in the Congress" – was opposed by Van den Abeele. In some Congresses, he said, resolutions having the force of law had been passed by delegates representing but a minority. There was the whole of Germany with but one delegate, and Geneva had more than half the delegates of the Congress. There were also people residing at Geneva with credentials from other places. Those who came from a distance were outnumbered; it was might prevailing over right. He proposed that the vote should be by regional Federations, and that each Federation should have one vote.

Basin, [Bazin] as reporter, stated that the Committee had considered the matter, but had not come to any conclusion. Gutsmann said it was not a good proposition; it would leave the voting power as unsatisfactory as it was now. The Dutch Federation would count as much as the German or the Spanish, and that would not be fairer than now. The International was as yet in a nascent state. It might happen that small sections sent the best men, and they ought to have full play. The only just mode of voting was the referendum, and until that could be introduced things had better be left as they were.

After some further remarks by other speakers to the same effect the amendment was rejected, and the article as it stood adopted by a small majority, Van den Abeele abstaining. He claimed the right to explain his abstention by a speech, but the President ruled him out of order. He then stood up, put on his hat, and declared that he would not submit to such treatment, and left the vice-chair and the Congress.

On the article charging the General Council with the preparation of the Congress programme and order of the day, Courtés objected that it was re-affirming the authoritative attributes of the General Council. Basin [Bazin] could simply see an initiative conferred on the Council, and Duparc saw nothing in it, but the logical arrangement of the communications received by the Council. He did not want the Council reduced to a cipher. The articles referring to the details of the Congress were retained till it came to Article 12, providing that the General Council questions should take precedence before all the other questions. Henri Perret proposed the suppression of this article, and to substitute a declaration that each Congress should fix its own mode of proceeding. Carried.

In the second part, treating of the General Council and the admission of members, Articles 4 and 5 were remodelled. In future single sections may announce their adhesion either to the nearest Federation or to the General Council. The Council retains the powers of refusal and must make inquiries before it admits single sections. Federations can only be admitted by four-fifths of all the Federations voting in favour.

Article 6, giving the right of suspending sections, was proposed to be struck out. The reporter said the committee had had a very long discussion about it, and the majority had come to the conclusion to suppress it. The Austrian delegate could not see how the International could be kept in the right groove without the General Council having that power. He had rejoiced when the power was conferred. There were designing men who would form sections purposely to bring disgrace on the society. They would proclaim all manner of things, and the society would be charged with them. The minority had a proposal that if any section or Federation transgressed the General Council should demand explanations, and if not satisfactory send them to other Federations. Wilhelm said if there were rules, they must be observed, and transgressors must be put down by the central power, and if hampered with provisions that would make action so slow that it would not have any effect.

Gutsmann said the Association was held responsible by the middle class press for deeds it never dreamt of, and expulsion would not cure that. The General Council was not always well-informed, and if it played the part of a vigilance committee, and police, a suspended section would make all the more noise. Still, there ought to be a remedy; but the General Council must simply have to execute orders. The burden of suspension and expulsions must be thrown on the Association itself. How could, for instance, the Council of New York know what the members were doing in Switzerland? If any unruly characters turned up it would be for the Swiss to take the initiative. Josseron maintained that all the mischief had arisen from this power of suspension. The reporter suggested that they should suppress the article and substitute something to which all could agree. The German delegate wanted to know how transgressors were to be reached without the initiative of the Council in cases where no one cared to complain? The controversy resulted in the following: "When the General Council receives complaints about the attitude of a section or Federation towards the rules and programme of the Society, it shall appeal to all the Federations to decide upon the suspension till the next Congress. The result of the *plebiscite* must be published within six weeks from the date of forwarding the documents of both accusation and defence to the Federations. A simple majority shall decide." Suspended sections and Federations have the right of appeal to the next Congress.

At that stage, a pause of half-an-hour was made.

On resuming in the afternoon, it was agreed that all the editions of rules and regulations in the different languages should be submitted to the approbation of the General Council before publication. The question of contributions, which, in accordance with resolutions passed at the London Conference of 1871, have been levied by the sale of adhesive penny stamps, which were meant to be fixed to the rules of every member as his receipt, was stopped by the German delegate. It was out of question altogether to levy contributions in that way in Germany, and he insisted that the question should be postponed till the other business was disposed of and be dealt with in an administrative sitting. The proposition was agreed to.

The next stumbling-block was the advice, dating from 1869, to abolish the office of President in sections and Federations. Not comprehending the difference between a president of a section and the chairman of a meeting, a delegate asked how business could be transacted without someone keeping order. The recommendation was struck out.

The last article was "The addresses of the Offices of all International Committees and the General Council are to be published every three months in all the organs of the Association." This would not do in Germany, not only on account of the law and the police, but the very term "International" was injurious. Instead of attracting it repelled. Several trade societies having branches in various places had used the word "International" at first, but had been obliged to give it up, and since they had done so they had made rapid progress. The Congress left it to the discretion of the Germans to do as they thought best.

The question of statistics was not entertained, and the order of the day was voted on the appendix to the rules and regulations.

Basin [Bazin] desired that the Congress, composed of 27 handworkers, and three headworkers, should declare that the efforts of the International had been frustrated by want of union and by divisions among the old members, and that the General Council should be charged with circulating the revised rules in every country, to raise a sound structure and basis for the International. One of the three headworkers resented the distinction between head and handworkers and thought he could see malice in it. He demanded the relegation of the matter to a private sitting.

The President embraced the opportunity to inform the Congress and the public that they must leave the room, as it was shortly wanted for another purpose. He thanked the delegates for the facilities they had given him in the transaction of business and declared the public portion of the Congress at an end. There would be a private meeting to dispose of the rest.

The German secretary returned the compliment on behalf of the Delegates, and the Congress separated.

The spectators were taken by surprise at this sudden turn, they being anxious to know something of the whereabouts of the next Congress, and what Federation was to be trusted to furnish that half of the International with a central letter box. Everybody thought, of course, that question would be decided as soon as the rules were passed, but it was not so much as mentioned. There was time enough, as it was only a quarter to 4 o'clock, and the other business for which the room was wanted would not begin till 7. These meetings generally wind up with a little hilarity, but here everybody looked sombre, and, to say the least, it was a gloomy close to Congress No. 2.

* * *

Journal des débats politiques et littéraires, reports dated 13 and 14 September, and published on Tuesday 16 September.

[This edition carried a lengthy article on Bakunin, reproducing material from 'The Programme and purpose of the organisation of International Brothers'[388] and other texts of his; it also carried a text mentioned above: 'The Alliance of Socialist Democracy and the IWMA'.[389] There was also a report dated the 14th, saying that there was little of interest in the centralists' congress.]

The only important fact was agreement to the proposition of the General Council tending towards the establishment of national Trade Unions – in England called *Amalgamated Societies*, which would subsequently be linked together internationally. There was no interesting discussion to go with this vote; all that was done was to add, to one of the articles, that these Unions and their relations should be established only insofar as the law in different countries might permit. This organisation of Trade Unions is, on its own, much more serious than the International itself.

In the words of the considering clauses, this amounts to the potential to promote and sustain strikes, which might, if needs be, last for several years; that would be a means to increase wages without even going on strike, by simply reducing the number of persons on the market. What is it that Mr Arch and the other leaders of agricultural agitation are doing?[390] They are organising the emigration of agricultural labourers, being fully convinced that when farmers find labour scarce, they will be compelled to raise wages through the simple play of supply and demand.* One only has to reflect a short while to understand the enormous influence that such organisations might have on economic conditions. I do not know if the congress members were aware of what they were doing, in any case, they seemed unable to comment, since it took them only in ten minutes to vote through the project.

For the disinterested observer, the revision of the statutes was another cause for astonishment. These so-called authoritarians proceeded to enact exactly the same reforms as their rivals. They did not abolish the General Council, but they did enormously reduce its powers. Moreover, they confided a regional federation with the responsibility of naming that council.

---

* Arch was a popular liberal and National Agricultural Labourers' Union activist. (Joe Arch he raised his voice/ 'twas for the working men/ Then let us all rejoice and say/ We'll all be union men.) He travelled to Canada in 1873 to investigate the possibility of resettling agricultural labourers there. Migration, it was hoped, might provide better lives for migrants and, by reducing the supply of workers in England, would reduce the supply of labour and encourage higher wages for those who remained.

So, as one can see, exactly the same system as that adopted by the anti-authoritarians. Thus, henceforth there will be two Internationals organised in the same fashion. The directing centre of one, that of the anarchists, will be in Brussels, the city where the next congress will be held, while the other will be in Geneva, and it will only hold congresses every two years. Both will organise trade unions, and the only difference between them will be that the first will preach social revolution, letting them act and supporting strikes to maintain their influence, while the others, under the influence of these Geneva workers, will concern themselves more with smaller matters and through their programme will move sensibly closer to the English Trade Unions.

The question of workers' political action was discussed in a private session, open only to IWMA affiliates. I do not know what the text was, for the resolution voted through, but I do know that this act, rejected by the Genevans and promoted by the Germans, was nevertheless accepted by a majority of one. The private sessions closed yesterday at midnight.

An addendum noted the reaction of the *Journal de Genève*: in its view the two congresses aroused only very restrained interest. Further comments on the impact of the congresses were quoted: 'No! let us be properly understood. Geneva or to put it better in the whole of Switzerland feels the most profound antipathy for all the senseless doctrines that resulted in the horror of the Paris Commune.' It went on to say very few Swiss attended the centralists congress last Sunday for such reasons. The *Journal de Genève* referred to good sense in Britain and reiterated the recent decisions of Amalgamated Engineers to disassociate from the International. It concluded with quotations from *Landbote* of Winterthur, to the effect that that anti-authoritarians appeared to be insisting on the need to beat the authoritarians – such things were evidence of ongoing stupidity.[391]

* * *

The Times, published 18 September.

[The two congresses have come to an end. Both were 'dull and unprofitable', lacking common sense. In this view working men might 'be expected to behave better', forgo 'wild talk', and avoid becoming 'selfish and insensate Communists'.]

* * *

London Evening Standard, report dated the 14th, published on 18 September 1873.

THE INTERNATIONAL CONGRESS. (FROM OUR OWN CORRESPONDENT) GENEVA, Sept. 14.

The private meeting of the Congress for the purpose of discussing the disputed points mentioned in my last letter seems to have been of a conciliatory character, and by a policy of mutual concession the delegates were enabled to avoid the threatened rupture. The abstract propositions of the Hague delegate were talked over at considerable length, and ultimately declared outside the "order of the day" and the Congress then proceeded to the consideration of the recommendations and suggestions of the general council, and the revision of the statutes. There was, of course, a preliminary council held in private, when it was resolved that nearly all the suggestions and many of the rules whereon there was a great divergence of opinion should not be decided on in public by the representatives. The cause of many internal dissensions has been the introduction of politics into the organisation, and what seemed an insurmountable obstacle in the revision of the statutes was the question of permitting political interference. It came on indirectly when the report of the general council was taken into consideration, for one of the principal means proposed by that body for giving increased vitality to the International was the formation of trade unions in the different countries, and their alliance for concerted action in political matters. This, which was the only part of the report discussed in public, was compromised through the influence of the Swiss delegates, and it was resolved that each federation should be left the power of taking active part in politics or not as it chose, but that the International should not be mixed up with its line of action.

Then came the revision of the statutes. A committee had suggested some alterations and devised a new code, and the old rules with any correction were submitted paragraph by paragraph to the meeting. The original preamble was considerably altered by the committee, and, after much discussion, a preamble was adopted, setting forth, *inter alia,* "That the emancipation of the working classes must be achieved by the working classes themselves. That the struggle for the emancipation of the working classes means, not a struggle for class privileges and monopolies, but for equal rights and duties, and the abolition of all class rule. That the economical subjection of the man of labour to the monopoliser of the means of labour – that is, the sources of life – lies at the bottom of servitude in all its forms, of all social misery, mental degradation, and political dependence. That the economical emancipation of the working classes is, therefore, the great end to which every political movement ought to be subordinate as a means." There follows a flourish as to the necessity of the International and its prospects of achieving "the emancipation of the working classes," and then come the rules. The first rule deals with the governing body, and the constitution of the general council and its relation to the federation were, as might have been expected, matters for warm discussion. The supporters of the New York council were, however, overruled by their associates, and seemed inclined to abandon their claims of extended power for the council. One of the Geneva delegates demanded the entire suppression of the general council, but such a sweeping proposition, was at once negatived, and he contented himself with asking a limitation of its powers. The old regulations provided that the Congress should annually select the seat of the general council, but at the suggestion of the committee it was resolved to give it two years' tenure of office. The next rule provided that the federation where the Congress meets shall choose the general council from within its own members. This was also adopted, and then the functions of that body had to be decided on. Its primary duties were defined as the dissemination of reports, carrying out the decisions of the Congress, &c. At present the council has the power of suspending till the next meeting of Congress any branch of the International. The committee proposed the suppression of this rule, but a minority report was sent in proposing that after the suspension of a section the reasons for it should be submitted to the Congress, and its validity should be decided by a majority of the federations. It was resolved in the end that in case of complaint against any section, the federations should be called on by the general council to decide the question. Some other slight powers, such as establishing communication between the sections, were accorded to the general council, and all the power given it by the former regulations was then revoked. The new council thus, instead of being the ruling spirit of the body, has become a nonentity, and its functions are merely those of a secretary. The new mode of appointment puts an end, of course, to the rule of the Now York body, or, indeed, of any particular section, and, so far, is in accordance with the views of the federalists. Whether the latter body will accept the new code, and re-join their old collaborateurs [sic], remains to be seen, but it is probable they will hold aloof until the practicability of this experimental scheme is tested. The subject of the next meeting-place of the Congress was reserved for private discussion, but there was a conversation as to the advisability of holding the Congress only once in two years; no alteration, however, was made. The qualification of members, another element of strife, was settled in the same manner as the question of politics.

The expulsion of the *travailleurs de pensée* [thinking-workers], was again mooted, but the president expressed an opinion (with which there was a pretty general coincidence) that too much importance had been attached to the point. The compromise of the committee, "that each section shall be responsible for the integrity of the members it admits," was then accepted. The Congress then proceeded to revise the administrative rules; and the first one. which gives each delegate one vote in Congress, was opposed by the delegate from Holland, who considered that each federation alone should have a vote. The present arrangement, he held, was an unjust one, for the local representatives would always outnumber, and consequently outvote those from a distance, and, to put each section on an equality in the Congress, it was necessary that each federation should have a single vote. This was pretty generally opposed by the Swiss delegates, and the old rule was allowed to stand. After the sense of the meeting had been taken, the dissenting representative rose to explain, but was prevented by the president, who ruled that he was out of order, and he left the room in high dudgeon. The number of members empowered to send a delegate to the Congress was reduced from five hundred to three hundred, and after some slight alterations in unimportant rules, the remaining statutes were adopted, with the exception of three or four left for private discussion. A short address from the president terminated then the public proceedings of the Congress. The difficulties which presented themselves during its deliberations were many, and it required both tact and concessions to reconcile so many conflicting elements, but the marked differences of opinion which almost led to a split were met by ready compromises, and if no great advantage to the organisation results from the sixth Congress its attendants can well claim more success than their predecessors in steering clear of dissension and schisms.

* * *

Journal des débats politiques et littéraires, report dated 15 September, and published on the 17th.

From Bern we are told: This morning, before leaving Geneva, I posted off a letter to you. In that letter, I advised you, based on the best of information that I had, that Geneva had been designated as the seat of the future General Council of the authoritarian International. In fact, yesterday matters were pretty much resolved, the Germans had proposed Geneva and the Genevans were ready to accept. Just now, when we stopped in Fribourg, I saw descending from my train a delegate from Basle, a conscientious *reporter*, I asked him for news, and he told me that at the last moment the congress changed its mind and that the General Council is to be maintained in New York. The most important reason that worked in favour of Geneva – the ease of finding men speaking various languages – had then been turned against that town being chosen. That at least was the reason that I was given by the delegate from Basle.

However, between ourselves, I can tell you that I do not believe in this reason. The prophet of Germanic communism has remained, in reality, the director of the International, although he lives in London and although the seat of the General Council is, since the congress of The Hague, in New York. An occult [secret] committee is composed of three members: Karl Marx, correspondent for Germany where he still has a preponderant influence, and for Russia; Engels, the friend of Karl Marx, and like him a German proscribed in 1848, the correspondent for Spain; and Serraillier, ex-member of the Central Committee and of the Paris Commune, correspondent for France. In reality the dictatorship of Karl Marx. This committee was really the true General Council, because that of New York, is, in the words of Eccarius, former friend of Karl Marx, a delegate to the anti-authoritarian congress, and a *Times* correspondent, only a letter box.[392]

Well, Karl Marx does not want to abandon his post, which allows him authority without responsibility; furthermore, the feelings of the Genevans, which I have made known, and which were exposed in a small recently published brochure, have displeased Karl Marx, who fears to see the International ceasing to promote his communist ideas. He had, in consequence, given instructions to his German lieutenants, and they, following the same tactics of their master at The Hague, only showed their hand at the last moment.

I have to give you my opinion. I believe this vote will provoke the birth of a new schism – that of workers and practical men, at whose head will be the Genevans. As for the authoritarian group, whose council will be based in New York, it will lose the right to call itself an International, given that it will involve only Germanic elements.

Der Volksstaat (organ of the Social-Democratic Workers' Party), 19 and 24 September 1873

[*Der Volksstaat* of 19 September had a short paragraph on the congress, followed by comments taken from particular bourgeois journals (*Frankfurter Beobachter, Braunschweiger Volksfreund*). Comrade Burckhardt of Stuttgart had attended. The General Council would remain in New York, and the next congress would be held in Zurich. A paragraph reported on the most important decisions of the congress in Geneva. Extracts from the 'considering' clauses were quoted and amendments noted: the remit of the IWMA was to be the entire world, rather than Europe.

The edition of the 24th set out the plan of the General Council for a worldwide organisation of unions (quoted above: *La Liberté*, 12 September). It was noted that henceforth congresses would be held every two years. The IWMA congress would not designate the membership of the General Council but would only designate its location; the members of the federation so named would designate the General Council, and the latter was not to co-opt members. It noted the congress had resolved that the statutes might be revised at each congress. There was a congress recommendation to the Austrian labour movement that it should re-unite; there was also a resolution that Congress deplored the split within the IWMA and instructed the General Council to direct a Proclamation to workers of all lands, and to endeavour to reverse that split. Key points from the General Council's report were printed. There was one key resolution, which left political direction to each local decision-making. This edition also criticised reports in the *Beobachter* (Frankfurt, 19 September) and false comments made by the ADAV.]

As regards political organization, the proposal of Johann Philipp Becker proposal was accepted:

Congress, while recommending that the working class should participate in any politics which has as its aim their emancipation, leaves it to the members in the various countries to act according to the given circumstances.*

---

* 'Indem der Congress der Arbeiterklasse die Betheiligung an jeder Politik, welch ihre Emanzipation zum Ziele hat, empfiehlt, uberlasst er es den Bundgenossen der verschiedenen Lander nach der gegebenen Umständen zu handeln.'

Part 4

After the two congresses …

Further Press Reports

Many reports on the two congresses can be found in national and regional papers; some even made the front page. American, Australian, and regional British papers might reproduce near identical texts.[393] Similar patterns appeared through the Francophone and Hispanic press, for example texts from the *Journal des débats politiques et littéraires* (Paris), were quoted in French provincial papers, and even in the *Journal de Genève* – despite it having the congress on its doorstep.

The attitude of the journalists was quite variable: a few reports were factual, many were hostile and inaccurate, some added local colour. *La Liberté* of Paris carried reports on both the federalist and the General Council congress. Bakunin, it was alleged, had given the signal for absurd uprisings, most of these had ended only in incendiarism and slaughter; proof of which, it alleged, is to be found in recent events in Spain – as witnessed by 'a reliable source'. Bakunin, out of prudence it wrote, had stayed away but Russian 'nihilist' students from Zurich were there to applaud things on his behalf – a fan club of both sexes, with the women particularly grotesque – dressed in black, and smoking. They 'looked at new arrivals with an air of sovereign disdain'. (Back in Russia such looks might have signalled dissidence and might have occasioned arrest.) The congress hall was pretty full, it wrote, but local IWMA critics stayed away. The public evening session on the 3 September had considerably more visitors, but only a dozen manual workers.[394] *La Liberté* wrote that the federalist congress had failed to conclude anything useful on the issue of a general strike. The matter of statistics was not resolved and was remitted to the next congress. It reported that the ending the split in the IWMA was on the agenda (an untruth), that it had failed, and therefore the IWMA was dead (another untruth).[395] It remarked on the energy of the centralist event and commented although it had an interesting agenda, it showed itself unable to address issues of great social problems and labour and trade unions, showing only 'their profound incapacity and their complete ignorance concerning these questions'.

Many French journals, including *Le Figaro*, and *Le Petit Journal* (8, 10, 11, 13 and 16 September) had short or largely dismissive comments, 'a source of dangerous ideas, a centre of hideous hopes ...'[396] finishing without any significant act.[397]

Reports in the London *Daily News* (6 September), and *Morning Post* (10 September) were impressionistic. One 'special correspondent' began with a comment of delegates chatting away with each other: 'If the Congresses of the International do nothing else, they must give the delegates a greater knowledge of the habits and ideas of their fellows in other countries than they could ever acquire by reading.' Delegates were bent upon getting every possible information from each other. There were comments on Poles and Russians – the latter making a public hall, (a very good one), 'somewhat inconveniently crowded'. The Russians presented a very curious aspect to the stranger, most of the men wearing their hair very long, while the ladies had very short hair.* The Russian ladies, most of them young, appeared totally unlike anything that this English mind associated with feminine propriety. They puffed at cigarettes, wore green spectacles, made speeches, sang, and had 'hybrid' clothing, so that, when they were sitting, one could hardly tell to which sex they belonged! And they were nihilists!**

The *Daily News* reports published on the 5th, 6th, and 8th, noted that the federalist congress delegates were able to understand enough French to converse without translations, although some found French rather awkward. They addressed each other as 'companion' rather than 'citizen'. The *Süddeutscher Telegraph* (Munich, 13 September 1873) remarked that some Commune refugees in the thirty strong Revolutionary Propaganda section of Geneva were mostly with the 'secessionists'. The notorious General Cluseret was present.

The reports of a special or occasional *Times* correspondent in Geneva, (almost certainly Eccarius), were quite detailed. Several articles on the two congresses were published, up to 18 September and some supplement information published elsewhere. For example, *The Times* of 5 September 1873 noted Pindy quipping on behalf of the Jura Federation, and with a little good humour, that: 'Sorge, the Secretary of the New York Council, had anathematised them as schismatics, but the curse had produced no effect.'

---

*   A year later two such women were among twelve 'Bakunin adepts' tried before a Russian court of state security. Leaflets were seized, and there were further arrests of agents of the 'Bakuninist International'. *La Liberté*, Paris, 8 August. 26 October 1874.

**   A reference to the 'Fritschi' women's group of Zurich.

A report of an interesting speech by John Hales was also carried:

[He] was sorry to say that in England no progress had been made during the past year. Before the congress of The Hague, sections had been established in every large town in England, but after the Congress all progress had been impeded by the writings of the friends of Dr Marx. *The International Herald,* too, had been gained over to the Marx party, and in consequence of that, the opposition had been deprived of its means of communication.*
Out of the 26 Sections which had existed this time last year the majority had been for the present Congress, but everything which had been reported in England about the proceedings on the Continent had been contradicted by the Marxists, so that it was with great difficulty the Association had been kept together. They had, however accomplished one thing, and that was killing the other side. The present followers of Dr Marx in England had no influence whatever. They consisted of a few crotchet-mongers and an occasional contributor to the conservative press.

The Daily News (London, 5 September 1873), commented:

Though the International had not gained much headway, the labour movement had made rapid strides. In nearly all trades workmen had improved their position, and there were more trades' unionists than there had ever been before. The most remarkable progress had been made by the agricultural labourers, who had, so to speak, stepped out of serfdom into manly independence. They now had an organ which was most ably conducted, and they had shown that they fully understood the advantages of united action. The miners, too, had made rapid progress, and now stood in the foremost ranks of labour. Altogether there were great hopes for the future in England.

Both congresses were roundly condemned in the British conservative press with journalists lampooning impractical and utopian ideas. The paucity of numbers – of both wings – showed 'how little there is left of the terrible bugbear of Internationalism ...' A hostile report, (*Manchester Guardian,* 12 September, repeated in the *Morning Post* on the 13th and *New York Times* on the 28th) had it that only three members came to the London meeting that selected delegates and they appointed themselves. The *Daily News* of 18 August had reported on this meeting and noted it had been chaired by Jung but made no mention how many persons were present. Hales and Eccarius found newspapers to pay travel expenses, but Thomas Mottershead did not, and did not travel. Newspaper editors sympathetic to the claims of labour

---

* The *International Herald* ceased publication in October 1873.

took fright when aggressive action was contemplated. For example, the *South Wales Daily News,* (20 September 1873), commented:

> Self-assertion on the part of Labour is consequently not to be condemned, whether it be the lot of the worker to exercise his mental or physical powers for daily bread. But the sacred right of unity is prostituted by men who desire to subserve purposes and advance projects of a sinister kind; when in the name of Labour delegates seek to establish Communism in its worst form when, instead of passing laws for mutual protection, they aim at establishing a reign of terror, and, relinquishing a defensive attitude, assume a position of defiance, the sympathy of the respectable portion of every community will be withdrawn ...

The *Bee-Hive (People's paper and Organ of Industry,* 20 September 1873) disparaged proceedings in Geneva. It recommended arbitration when conflicts arose and condemned covert practices which sensible British trade unions now eschewed. 'In fact,' it declared, 'unionism amongst working men, is, even by employers, beginning to be regarded as the very best means of promoting a moral discipline amongst our workers of the highest use to themselves' – it only hoped that the blessings of such workplace relations should be felt on the continent. In its view the two British delegates to the federalist congress were wholly unrepresentative; it urged trade union leaders to repudiate 'ravings'.[398] In the same vein, *The Examiner* (6 September 1873) concluded: 'The best we can hope is that, when the present International Association, from which so much was expected, and which has actually done a great deal of good, has crumbled away, one or other of its fractions will become the nucleus of a really serviceable movement for the correction of social evils which are many and great enough to need correction.' Views such as this seemed to suggest that the British model of labour organising should be adopted elsewhere.

In Madrid, two papers, *La Epoca* and *La Discusion,* carried reports on the 13 and 14 September. *La Epoca* reported that citizen Farga had said that although members of the International may have joined in insurrections in Spain, the IWMA federation had not made that choice, rather it avoided efforts to replace one government with another, all governments being bad. Otherwise, the brief comments were similar; they named the Spanish citizens present in Geneva. They referred to the ongoing impact of the Paris Commune. A report in *La Imparcial* (Madrid) 15 September, repeated some of these points and quoted membership figures of over 50,000 for the federalists. *La Federación* (18 October 1873) carried a letter from the

American Spring Street federation approving the workings of the federalist congress in Geneva.

A report in the *Neue Freie Presse* of Vienna, commented on the centralists' congress. Henri Perret said that the International of deeds lived on, but the International of [idle] phrases was dead, and philosophers were now unwelcome. Duparc stressed that socialists should show high moral standards – a reference to Russian women who were everywhere smoking and stirring up enmity and scandal! The decision of the Basle congress against land inheritance was criticised, but the proposal for national trade-union organisation received general approval.[399]

The names and projects of various bodies might be deceptive. In Europe, book-binders and other unions taking in German-speakers[400] might be designated as 'internationals'– even where it was mainly or only German-speakers who were organised; unions of iron moulders, typographers, etc. were named as 'internationals' in the USA; some had branches in Canada, and bi-national might have been a more accurate designation. Exaggerated claims of support were present around both congresses.[401] Tens of thousands supported the ongoing, federalist IWMA, but not the millions that Joukovsky claimed. The *Bulletin* (21 and 29 June 1874) was more realistic, when it remarked that 'millions of workers and peasants were unorganised, and had not the least idea of organisation', and this was one reason, besides a lack of a common purpose and means (money), why strikes failed. Nevertheless, occasional demands, such as the shortening of the working day, were won.

Reports published after the congresses in *The Times*, *La Liberté* and elsewhere suggest that in certain sessions the centralist delegates asserted themselves against Becker. Proposals from the New York General Council had been criticised, and resolutions and rules adopted at The Hague were not reaffirmed. The centralists' line – as adopted at The Hague in 1872, and at the London conference of 1871 – had been for the prioritisation of electoral politics, and the New York General Council's draft text had reasserted: 'To conquer the political power is the first duty of the working class.' The centralists' 1873 congress resolution, that in matters of politics, sections could each choose their own path, had undermined that line.

The Geneva IWMA and their allies had voted through resolutions that might have circumscribed the influence of the New York General Council, had they been respected. A resolution that a congress should fix its own mode of proceeding implied that congress agendas might not be set by the General Council. This, and new rules on expulsions, seriously reduced New York's power to 'manage' the IWMA. Evidently, then, the 'authoritarian' congress had been split, many delegates were critical of New York, and some resolutions contradicted the line of The Hague. The report in the *Journal des débats politiques et littéraires*, dated 15 September, shows that Becker was able to have a resolution passed keeping the seat of the General Council in New York away from the hands of critics in Geneva, only at the end of the congress. No official report was issued.

Exaggeration

The recent Swiss labour congress at Olten in June 1873, had brought together 82 representatives from diverse labour organisations. The largest body present had been the *Grütli* association, full of nationalist spirit (700 members).[402] It had both managers and workers as members, and it excluded the non-Swiss, an afront to the IWMA as an *international*. There was also the educational *Arbeiter Bildungs Verein* (600 members), medical insurance networks and other German-Swiss labour and co-operative associations. An ephemeral *Schweizerischer Arbeiterbund* (Swiss Labour League) was set up, but without the Jura Federation. The *Arbeiterbund* had *Tagwacht* as its journal. Bruno Gutsmann[403] had apologised at a session of the centralist, General-Council congress, for not getting this league to affiliate to the International and said that Swiss workpeople were still intensely national. He had hoped that 'if the matter was agitated properly and newspapers and pamphlets circulated, they would soon get over that, and then they would enter the association in their thousands'. Becker was not so honest when he told the New York Council that the leading elements of the *Arbeiterbund* were tied exclusively to the (centralist) IWMA, and many sections sided with it.[404] Some 'support', for some projects might have been reasonably claimed, through some leaders close to the IWMA, but the mass of members were not internationalists. Gutsmann cited the IWMA in Denmark as being with the centralists, whereas the Danish organisation had been smashed, and the New York Council's confidential report had advised that it had received neither dues nor direct communications from them.

The New York Council's report said that the English working classes was moving in 'immense bodies'* to put into practice the declaration of the Hague congress – an untruth. The council's confidential report was more cautious, saying only that the British federation was 'on the road to fair success ...'[405] Most British trade-unionists knew little of The Hague congress resolutions. On 6 September 1873, *The Times* reported the Amalgamated Engineering Union had rejected participation in the IWMA because it had

---

* *Neue Freie Presse*, 11 September 1873 told readers that in the UK, the centralist IWMA had won 'influence and power'!

'degenerated into a political society'. A report in the *Volksstaat*, on 25 October 1873, told readers that the current leadership of the British trade union was drowning every truly revolutionary movement of the proletariat. In August 1874, in a letter to Sorge, Marx admitted: 'In England the International is as good as dead for the present.'[406] One historian described the congress in Manchester, mentioned in the New York Council's report, as 'a pathetic affair representing an organisation that had largely ceased to exist'.[407] The New York Council's report also asserted, but offered no evidence, for its statement that German labour organisations were making 'great progress'. Overall, this report concealed how many IWMA supporters had rejected the General Council, and claimed support which did not exist. It was deceitful.

Becker's *Volksstaat* report on the Geneva congress (appendix five) had further exaggerations and omissions. Becker could not acknowledge that the Spanish labour movement was a mass organisation. His report featured the oft-repeated distortion that anarchy meant disorganisation and that federalists were impractical utopians. As they collected funds for political prisoners and strikers, federalists showed how untrue these statements were. *La Federación* (8 and 29 November; *Bulletin de la Fédération Jurassienne*, 7 December 1873), reported how the Federal Council of the Central Region of Belgium raised funds to support a Belgian mechanics' strike, recording the following donations (in francs):

Resistance society of Haine-Mariemont miners	2,600
Resistance society of Besonrieux	43
Resistance society of Cernieres, miners	116
Resistance society of Haine-St-Pierre	126
Resistance society of Sars Lengcharups	400
Resistance society, Metals, de Croyére	157
Resistance society of Fait	75
Mutual aid Society of La Croyére	282
A comrade of the centre	1,000
Charcoal workers of Fait	30
Gouy-Lez-Pieton section	60
Comrades of Houssu	26
Comrades of Fayt	22
Hatmakers in a Jolimont workshop	16
Mechanics of Brussels	150
Mechanics of Liège	100
Stonemasons of Liège	30
Propaganda group of Ivoz-Ramet	10

Carpenters of Brussels	300
Painters of Brussels	25
Section of Gemmapes,	1000
Section of Gohyssar (USA)	25
Taylors of Brussels	150
Shoemakers of Brussels	50
Tanners of Brussels	500
Jewellery workers of Geneva	200
Propaganda section of Geneva	46
Jura Federation	75
Neuchâtel section	30
Amberes section	12
Belgian Council	100

And, for the following week:

Jura Federation,	50
Propaganda section of Geneva,	25
Neuchâtel section	33
English steelworkers (£25)	625
Stonemasons of Geneva	100
Carpenters of Geneva	100
Plasterers (?) of Geneva	500

So, a strike in Belgium was being reported in IWMA journals and support was forthcoming from local workers' organisations and from Alsace, England, Switzerland, and the USA. This everyday activity facilitated by the ongoing International organisation, exposed the lie in Becker's trope that federalism meant anarchy and disorganisation.

On 22 September 1873, Becker addressed a private letter to 'Dear Brother Sorge': he had been very unwell for the week of the congress, with pains and fever overnight. 'But what should I do? I took responsibility for the success of congress …' He wrote to say that after the news arrived of the disappointing absence of Serraillier and of the English Federation, he acted, 'to give the congress the appearance of a respectable number of participants, and *to ensure a correct direction of the majority*, I had *immediately to create thirteen delegates out of nothing*, and in the end things went well, and much as I had expected.'[408] The secret was soon revealed to federalists: once again blank mandates had been used to create a congress majority. Readers of the *Volksstaat* were led to believe that the more sensible Social-Democratic perspective had prevailed, while the truth – that Becker invented fake delegates – was concealed.

Difficulties

The following years were not easy ones; political and social difficulties increased; economic depression and political repression were accentuated and affected all sorts of radicals and socialists. Artisan production was under threat as machine and factory production increased.[409] This might undermine particular groups of workers, for example some Swiss workers producing timepieces were threatened by the development of new watchmaking processes in the USA. Such changes might undermine and weaken labour's bargaining position. The IWMA and other rebels were unable to roll back or reverse this tide.[410] In France local mutual aid organisations were legal but syndicates were not, and the public organisation of IWMA branches might result in activists being imprisoned. In Britain unions were partially legalised and some labour 'leaders' were being given – and were gratefully accepting – recognition as subaltern partners in the body politic. In Germany, Bismarck would attempt to limit workplace organisation to local apolitical networks, preferably supporting an entente between managers and employees; to be rewarded (after 1883) with some contributory state health insurance.

Migration might seem to offer an escape to a better life for some. Empires were expanding in the 1870s and after, opening new fields. Russia was reported as having sent off 121,948 deportees to Siberia in a year.[411] Large numbers of Indian and Chinese indentured labourers were recruited. Nationalist and racist ideology inhibited reflection on these movements, and their effects on countries shedding and receiving labour. The ideal of an International above creed, race and colour might be appealing, but it was undermined by a mindset that identified slavery and servitude with darker races and assumed the superiority of 'white labour'. Progress was often equated with industrious modernity but sometimes one nation's or one community's modernity might be injurious to another. It would be some time before older, non-white, communitarian models of living were given sympathetic consideration, and before the benefits and costs of industries were carefully assessed. IWMA congresses fed on an optimism and on a belief that labour should receive its due; in promising times these ideals made progress; in less promising times they did not, and radicals of all sorts confronted various reactionary forces. Both congresses recognised that the IWMA had spread beyond Europe. Some labour leaders took pride in being civilised and 'advanced', as against being 'backward', an attitude that might turn towards nationalism or racism. In relations between communities and peoples, federalism might signify a respect for diversity. Progress might be viewed, not as the spread of one modern, developed, industrious form of society, but rather through respect for different social forms, eschewing one-size-fits-all concepts. Below, there are notes on problems faced by labour in particular regions.

Spain

In 1873, Spain was nearing the end of a six-year liberal interlude. Liberal and secular culture had challenged tradition and the Catholic church; men and women had supported new associations. Despite being outlawed in January 1872, the *Federación Regional Español* (FRE, Spanish Federation of the IWMA) had grown, and had a peak membership around 60,000, and with a substantial implantation in Barcelona, Catalonia and Andalucía.[412] It developed strongly in areas where literacy was above average, and it supported modern, integral forms of education, as an alternative to church influence.[413] It raised various demands: for an eight-hour day, free lay schools, a ban on work for the under-12s, equal pay for men and women, cleanliness in workplaces, credit for workers' societies (co-ops) low rents, care for invalids, minimum wages and mixed juries of workers and management.[414] The FRE had its own co-op, the *Cooperativa Solidaria de consumes* in Barcelona but was not enthusiastic about co-operatives as a means of building socialism.[415]

The official FRE report referred to the short-lived Spanish Republic that emerged in February 1873, and which was beset by conflicts between centralisers and devolutionists. Ten members of the IWMA had been elected to the constituent assembly.[416] A Federal Republic was declared in July 1873 and passed some liberal legislation. *Woodhull & Claflin's Weekly*, (30 August 1873), noted that the new constitution spoke of '1. The right of life, and its protection. 2. The right of free expression of thought. 3. The right of diffusion of ideas. 4. The rights of labor and of commerce. 5. The right of holding meetings. 6. The rights of property without encumbrances or entail. 7. Equality before the law. 8. The right of trial by jury, the right of defense by counsel …'

The Spanish Federation (FRE) neither endorsed candidates in elections, nor placed any confidence in the new republic, thinking that it was not so different from the French Republic that had massacred rebel Paris. One report commented on circumstances in a southern section (Loja): 'The conduct of the republicans towards the Internationals here can only be qualified by the word horrible. The Internationals are hunted like wild beasts, and a cry goes aloft for their blood. Their letters are opened and read in the market-place.'[417] The FRE published journals in the various towns and cities where it had a presence, articulating the life of the federation and reporting on, and liaising with internationalists elsewhere. These internationalists sought to share their experience, stressing the need for decentralised and federalist organisations grouped through various trade branches. From time to time much of the FRE press (including *La Federación* and *El Condenado*) was banned or suspended. The listings in the Spanish regional report above show that the IWMA in Spain was generally a workplace-based organisation. It had a base in industries and manufacturing in several parts of Spain, and attracted rural day labourers, and peasants. It confronted forces of 'Order' dissolving rural federations in the south and, in the north, faced reactionary Carlist forces. Despite repression the IWMA retained 25,000 members and broad peripheral support.

On 14 July, the FRE federal commission sent out a circular referring to recent event and declaring that it had nothing in common with political parties.[418] Max Nettlau speculated that the FRE may have thought that they were not yet strong enough to make their own revolution, and therefore continued with their own projects. It sought: 'to go forward until the triumph of anarchism and collectivism, that is, with uprooting all authoritarian powers and class monopolies: no popes, no kings, no bourgeois, no priests, no soldiers, no lawyers, no judges, no notaries, no politicians; but a free universal federation of free agricultural and industrial associations.'[419]

Friedrich Engels wrote a polemic for the *Volksstaat* of Leipzig, published in October-November 1873 and telling readers that 'Bakuninists' had provided a lesson in how *not* to make a revolution. It was republished as a pamphlet *Bakunisten an der Arbeit* ('The Bakuninists at Work'). The FRE report reproduced above was written before Mr Engels' polemic was published, but a reading of it goes some way to answering the question of whether there was a revolutionary opportunity of some sort in 1873.

On 15 June 1873, the FRE's correspondence commission advised: 'Workers must distance themselves from bourgeois politics from its every farce and from every farce-maker, they must organise and prepare for proletarian revolutionary action, in order to destroy as soon as they can those privileges that sustain authoritarians' strength and power.' Legislation might 'ban' child labour and put in place some protection for women workers, but these laws remained dead letters. Organisers might conclude that labour should build its own strength and that could not trust the radical bourgeoisie. James Guillaume recalled that electoral abstention did not imply political inactivity:

Should one, if one had to abstain from the games played by enemies, also abstain from working in one's own interest, and for one's own cause? Certainly not. The moment had come for the Spanish International to be more energetic and active than ever. It should take advantage of the general effervescence of spirit to spread popular propaganda on a vast scale, to organise the proletariat wherever it is not yet organised, to get rid of the army, to arm the people, to create action committees and to ensure that these committees actively correspond with each other. It should take advantage of every government failing to enlighten all those who hold the dangerous illusion that the Republic means the emancipation of the people. To conclude, everyone should be awake, ready to confront whatever problems arise, and if the federation is not yet strong enough to make a revolution, it should be strong enough to impede the consolidation and everyday functioning of every sort of government.[420]

On 17 June, *La solidarité révolutionnaire*, an FRE journal produced by exiles from the Paris commune in Barcelona, drew distinctions between words and realities: going forwards required substantial autonomy: for the individual, the trade organisation and the commune.[421] The editors wrote of contracts for production and consumption – reciprocity with some give and take. Four days later a key FRE journal, *La Federación*, had this to say on its front page in an article entitled 'The Road to Revolution':

We are, so it seems in a Federal Republic. From the moment it became not just talk, but reality, every part of the social body – the individuals, trade organisations and Communes – should have entered into possession of themselves. Today, as ever, they have a right to their autonomy; their rights arise and are enjoyed from their own being. If things do not develop in that way, these times will be seen only as an unworthy farce, and in consequence, in the annals of the people they will be consigned as yet another mystification. … We entirely distrust them. Workers know what the word federalism means in the mouth of the bourgeoisie; they know how far the political exploiters of the masses are sheltering with hypocrisy behind the name *republic.*

Matters were complicated and confused as republican ranks split, and with the development of 'cantonalist' or regional administrations in Cádiz, Cartagena, Seville and elsewhere. Multiple conflicts surged all at once: between monarchists (with rival claimants to the throne), liberals and republicans, cantonalists (sometimes called federalists or intransigents) and the labour movement. The FRE had rejected collaboration with bourgeois republicans, and the latter had, on several occasions, sought to suppress them.[422] The IWMA internationalists and various bourgeois republican authorities soon came into conflict, and the Spanish Federation had to confront multiple enemies. There were popular movements in the rural south, supported by some IWMA members. 'The internationalists saw the cantonalists above all as local bourgeois politicians, and while some or many of them joined in immediate struggles, the International as a whole stood aside.'[423] Francisco Tomás a long-serving FRE bricklayer and sometime editor of *El Obrero* commented that some Italian comrades believed that the cantonalist movement was an 'International' movement, but it was in fact made by politicians who were not in touch with Internationalists.[424] Some canton administrations embarked on reforms: land redistribution, distributing arms, the confiscation of assets owned by the church, taxes on the wealthy. The *Daily News*, (London, 5 September 1873) noted: 'In Cadiz and Cartagena, the struggle was not commenced by the workmen, but by certain men who desired to obtain power. The working men were obliged to take part in self-defence, but it was against their will.' The Jura *Bulletin* (7 December 1873) reproduced the decree of the Cartagena junta issued on 1 November, concerning property: it was considered legitimate if it arose out of workers' labour, but illegitimate if it came from inheritance, royal decree, or was acquired at knock-down prices from government sales. A 'half-measure' thought the *Bulletin*.

Did these conflicts forebode a revolutionary crisis? Some thought so, writing that now was a time for action not theory: 'In the epoch in which we are living we are seeing the last moments of the bourgeoisie, and the agony of a world on the way out ...'[425] There was a certain ambiguity as between cantonalism and the FRE federalism: both looked forward to a decentralised Spain, but for the FRE also looked for workers' emancipation, empowerment and solidarity. Reworking a famous watchword, Barcelona's IWMA journal (*La Federación*, 14 June 1873) wrote: 'The *defence* of the workers should be the work of the workers themselves,' an army was needed to defend labour's interests and was to be based on labour principles. Earlier *La Federación* had asked soldiers to revolt. If yesterday they were mere weapons and slaves, today they should stand up, and become, 'legitimate sons of the people,' working to support the aspirations of the proletariat.[426] These texts supported the creation of IWMA defence groups. Some activists formed distinct detachments, others joined cantonalist bodies; they had some support from soldiers and sailors who mutinied and joined rebel forces. Supporters of the Paris Commune and other refugees also offered to form commandos, asking only that they should elect their own leaders. (A precedent for the international volunteers who supported the revolution after 1936.)[427]

Between 1868 and 1878, 180,000 soldiers had been recruited and shipped to fight in Cuba and other colonial wars. Many merchant seamen were fully conscripted, others were subjected to military discipline to help maintain overseas campaigns. Complaints about poor rations were enough to land them in prison.[428] Sailors in the Cartagena harbour rebelled and took control of several warships. Local prisoners, conscripts, and political dissidents among them, were released by the cantonalists and were disparaged as 'pirates' by both the Madrid government, and by Mr Engels.[429] In1868 leaders of rebels fighting for Cuban independence decreed the liberation of all slaves belonging to their enemies. Rebel forces mobilised diverse ethnicities, include some Chinese and Afro-Cubans. Some local tobacco workers and survivors of the Paris Commune joined the struggle for independence. Some Cuban exiles agitated in the USA, looking forward to a Universal Social Republic and exchanging greetings with the FRE.[430] Events in the Spanish Empire attracted little attention in Spain itself, but there was some opposition to waging war.[431] In Cuba, the ideas of Proudhon attracted a little attention, and in 1872 anarchist cigar-makers Enrique Roig San Martin and Enrique Messonier began publishing *El Obrero* and organising an education centre.[432] Often the press in Cuba was censored, and authorities worked to prevent the spread of rebel thinking. Some rights of association were allowed in May 1873.

Revolt?

Internationalists were prominent in upheavals in the southern towns of Sanlúcar de Barrameda and Alcoy.[433] Labour uprisings emerged, albeit briefly, alarming conservatives and raising fears of a Spanish Paris Commune. Sanlúcar had a substantial labour community, workers had a food co-op, a lay school and library. A revolt in February lasted five days: a revolutionary committee was formed; the police and other authorities were placed in prison and archives were burnt. A second revolt occurred in June. The authorities were removed, elections were held, and local anarchists became town councillors. The town was held for a month without any violence, until the army forced its way in. 500 people were then deported overseas.[434]

Alcoy (Alicante province) was a town of some 30,000 people, harbouring some 5 or 6,000 internationalists, many working in textile and paper trades.

It was also the seat of the Spanish regional IWMA federal commission. A local assembly was called to prepare for action, and a general strike was called, perhaps the first general strike in Spain.[435] Unarmed workers staged a public rally to present strike demands, for better pay and an eight-hour day, but were fired on by forces under orders from the local mayor. The indignation that resulted provoked in the burning of five or six houses used by those firing on people in the street. Several workers and the mayor were killed. A Commune type administration, or revolutionary junta, emerged briefly.[436] It took a form defined by libertarians in terms of: 'interim delegation, permanently revocable, defined by mandates which were clearly determined.'[437] The rebels had barely a thousand weapons, and few munitions, so had little capacity to resist when 6,000 well-armed state forces approached the town.[438]

The Times (18 July 1873), carried a report on events in Alcoy, writing of mobs, mutilations, blood, and petrol-burning-executions – although it had the sense to acknowledge that it was unsure if these stories were true. Such lurid tales were circulated in the Spanish capital and served to justify the brutal repression of so-called 'vandals, petrol-bombers, and assassins'. Conservatives cast events as a revolution of incendiaries and fanatics, ready to murder members of religious orders.[439] The FRE commission issued a statement on 14 July, to refute slanders.[440]

The shape of revolt and protest varied from place to place and between rural and urban areas (such as Barcelona with its growing textile industry). It was not a lack of courage that led some internationalists in the north to urge caution, while southern counterparts supported uprisings. The historian Miklós Molnár wrote:

> The real cleavages were to be found between urban centres which were more or less industrialised on the one side, and predominantly rural regions on the other. It is not an accident that IWMA groups in Andalucía and in the Levant [region] threw themselves into the revolutionary whirlpool, whereas workers in Barcelona abstained and leaders of the federation preached prudence and moderation. Different regions, different conditions, different mentality – in my view, it is in these directions that one should look for explanations, to grasp the duality of the International in Spain in the crucial moment of the revolution of 1873.[441]

Strikes were difficult in in the rural south, where casual and day-labour employment patterns were common and where there was a mass of unemployed labourers available to replace strikers. Labour relations were violent, and workers might turn to destruction and sabotage. Although FRE leaders and editors urged caution and distrust towards the canton authorities, much of the IWMA base lent them some support. Members of the International were prominent in Cadiz, Grenada, Jerez, Malaga, San Fernando, Seville, Valencia and elsewhere.[442] Some prominent IWMA members – Melendez in Cartagena, Rodriguez in Grenada, Mingoranza in Seville, Rosell in Valencia – joined local juntas, and many joined volunteer militias.[443] 'Everywhere the anarchists supported intransigent republicans.' They saw – or hoped to see – juntas as accountable and local communal administrations, as against some Jacobin centralised state.[444] Clara Lida has written that a bourgeois pattern prevailed in most Cantonalist risings:

> The sudden collaboration between workers of the federation, intransigent politicians and communalists from abroad cannot be understood as class solidarity, but rather as the union of several groups, glued together through the myth of insurrection and the Commune as a symbol of solidarity. In this context the predominance of the republican bourgeoisie within various committees and revolutionary juntas explains why the insurgents found it impossible to resolve the deep and general malaise through fundamental economic and social measures.[445]

(The reference to the Commune and its myth might be taken to refer to the diversity of rebel society and politics in Paris two years earlier – rebel Paris was largely a city of artisans and contained several radical viewpoints.) On 3 June 1873, a letter from three activists in Barcelona (Paul Brousse,[446] Charles Alerini[447] and Camille Camet)[448] urged:

> The Spanish International saw that the situation was very dangerous and formed within itself several groups tasked with preparing action. However, we can tell you that we did not feel the need to choose officers. Officers – what would you want with them? [...] be confident and prepare revolutionary forces and then the hour will come. Greetings, anarchy, collectivism and above all, *action.*

Fifty collectivists, among them Paul Brousse and José García Viñas,[449] occupied Barcelona's city hall on the night of the 19-20 June, hoping to proclaim a free Commune. The government was condemned for its attacks on working people, and for its inadequate response to the Carlists.[450] However, finding that they were not exciting much support, they left the building on the following day – without even arousing a reaction from the police. Local labour organisations wanted to avoid conflict with republicans and feared Carlists.[451] Calmer feelings may have prevailed in Barcelona afterwards. A reduction of working hours, down from twelve to ten, was obtained for a time. The Spanish Federation (FRE) attempted to promote labour interests without launching itself into desperate adventures.[452]

Friedrich Engels condemned the Spanish federation for failing to prioritise electoral work: 'it was *certain* that any candidate nominated and supported by the International would be brilliantly successful in the industrial districts ... and that a minority would be elected to the Cortes *large enough to decide the issue** whenever it came to a vote between the two wings of the Republicans.'[453] He also wrote: 'Spain is *such a backward country* industrially that there can be no question there of immediate complete emancipation of the working class. Spain will first have to pass through various preliminary stages of development.' He concluded: 'the Bakuninists in Spain have given us an unparalleled example of how a revolution should not be made.'[454] So, readers were told that Spain was too backward for complete emancipation, and yet Spanish 'Bakuninists' had failed to carry out the impossible.[455] Earlier *Der Volksstaat* (13 August 1873) had published another opinion: 'We know better than anyone, that the time has not yet come to realise our ideas and for that reason we held fast to our organisation and propaganda' (views taken from *La Federación* of 26 July).

The Jura *Bulletin* (9 November 1873) noted: 'Such is the violence of Mr Engels' all so personal spite on this subject, that he loses all his restraint and, it must be said, all his decency. ... He takes delight in recounting the victories of reaction and revolutionaries' defeat ... one has to read these incredible pages to understand how far *hatred and a spirit of vengeance* may lead a man into moral aberration.'[456] This was an inadequate grasp of the matter: what was at issue was not so much a one-off and personal reaction, but rather something promoted deliberately and systematically, just one action in the campaign of political warfare. Engels' polemic sought to motivate a priority for electoral politics and some sort of (loose) alliance of labour with the radical bourgeoisie against any rebellious movement. Many years later, Max Nettlau commented: 'the more one examines the documents of 1872-73, the more one comes to understand proportions and sees the really small extent of the Mesa-Lafargue-Engels intrigue and their powerlessness

---

* *Solidarité Revolutionnaire* (Barcelona, 14 August 1873), had published a different view: that the various factions of the bourgeoisie were all determined to persecute rebels. They agreed to revoke the parliamentary immunity of deputies suspected of radicalism. The FRE report (quoted above) remarked: 'the bourgeoisie prefers to embrace the most rabid reaction rather than taking even a single step on behalf of the revolution.'

in relation to the great mass of regional International sections; and further one also becomes indignant against the scandalous abuse of power through which this intrigue was supported by every voice of international Marxism …'[457]

Bakunin met with the Spanish delegates after the Geneva congress; he concluded that energy for revolution was insufficient, among working people and FRE leaders.[458] The FRE Federal Commission published circular No. 34 on 10 November 1873, denouncing government excesses.[459] The FRE set up funds to support workers in Alcoy and Sanlúcar.[460]

On 3 January 1874, General Pavía staged a coup d'état and the Cortes was dismissed; then, in December, the Spanish army staged a coup d'état, the monarchy was restored and the International banned.[461] The FRE maintained a half-public, half-secret life for the next six year. When it could it organised in open societies and federations, but when circumstances demanded, it turned to closed networks and to 'organisation in the shadows', defying illegality, with small meetings of eight to ten people. 'Measures of control and repression against actual or likely dissidents and rebels continued and were accentuated in the later 1870s.' Repression was severe, and some 15,000 workers were imprisoned (some for fourteen years). A thousand workers left Sanlúcar to avoid arrest.[462] Fermín Salvochea, who had emerged as a leading figure in the Canton of Cádiz, was captured by forces of General Pavia and sentenced to life imprisonment.[463] In some places, wages were cut by 20 per cent, in others by half.[464] Anselmo Lorenzo was to write that a tyrannical regime reigned in Barcelona and not even the smallest socialist labour demonstration was permitted.[465] The FRE called for a special levy to support strikers and migrants. Some workers were driven into exile and would contribute to the promotion of a radical labour movement overseas. Internationalists were treated in infamous fashion; some were deported to the Philippines where forty died, others to the Marianas Islands.[466] Radical seeds were also scattered in the Caribbean and in Latin America.[467]

The FRE was still able to print 17,000 copies of a manifesto in 1874.[468] That July a clandestine congress was held in Madrid; ten *comarcas* (regional structures) were created to facilitate co-ordination, and clandestine area meetings, but in several rural areas 'forces of order' entirely obstructed IWMA organisations. Defence units – *grupos para la acción revolucionaria socialista* – were set up (perhaps a precedent for the CNT-FAI defence units of the 1930s). Although the public organisation of the FRE was not so visible, a subterranean network survived and would grow vigorously when new opportunities arose in 1881. Mexican internationalists sent word through the FRE that they supported the federalist IWMA. The ongoing clandestine organisation of the IWMA in Spain in the later 1870s contrasted with the quasi-disorganisation of the IWMA in France and Italy and the anaemia of labour organisation in Germany. There was perhaps a price to be paid for the devolved *comarca* administration: each one might face particular challenges in its own circumstances, and, with fewer opportunities to meet other *comarcas* they may have been less ready to understand others' dynamics; also, financial hardship reduced the FRE's income. Over the next few years differences of opinion would emerge between the collectivist and communist libertarian currents.[469]

Italy

Discontent and protests grew in the early 1870s as food prices and taxes on grain increased. Strikes broke out in Florence, Ravenna, and Ancona.[470] The price of one kilo of bread might amount to a third of a day's pay. Misery was ever-increasing. In Rome, one father committed suicide because he could find no food for his five children.[471] Many workers emigrated. Young girls might be sold, and shipped off to London, Paris, or other cities, forced to hand over a regular quota to violent pimps.[472] Rebels thought hunger and the knowledge that food was being hoarded would spark anger. The number and intensity of protests increased, and rioters demanded lower bread prices.

Bagnolesi, Malatesta, Paganelli and other IWMA activists were still imprisoned in November 1873. A report was published on the recent regional and international congresses: *Atti del 6° Congresso Universale di Ginevra e del 2° Congresso Regionale Italiano di Bologna*. Membership for the Italian federation estimates from early 1874 varied between 26,000 and 30,000, organised in around 130 sections.[473] The Italian federation was served by several journals: *Capestro* in Fermo, *Comunardo* in Fano, *Fame* in Genoa, *Giustizia* in Girgenti, *Petrolio* in Ferrare, *Povero* in Palermo, *Risveglio* in Sienna, *Schiavo bianco* in Turin, and *Sempte avanti* in Livorno. Government action destroyed some papers but others emerged.[474]

A *Comitato Italiano per la Rivoluzione Sociale* was established early in 1874 and planned an uprising. We, it announced, are declaring war on every current facet of everyday life.[475] Bulletins declared that the time for peaceful propaganda for revolutionary ideas was past, and that it was time for vigorous propaganda, for barricades, and insurrection. Soldiers should join the people. For a time, it appeared that the Italian IWMA was progressing: *L'Ami du Peuple* (Liège, 5 April 1874) noted papers reporting new sections joining the International every week. The bulletins of the *Comitato* spoke for the 'we' who opposed and/or hated tyrants, starvation, and the church.

They might have hoped that they spoke for 'everyone', or at least for those who shared their anger – but although there was mass anger, not everyone was prepared to revolt. Beyond Italy, much of the federalist IWMA was not enthused about prospects for a popular revolt.[476] Two years later, at the Bern congress of the IWMA in 1876, Errico Malatesta said that given the popular mood, Italian members had no choice and had to join protests.

A revolt was attempted in Bologna, in August 1874, with the intention that it would spread across northern Italy. However, the government had kept a close eye on rebels. Scores were arrested, and the revolt failed to ignite.[477] When these rebels were put on trial, they were acquitted: perhaps indicating that they enjoyed a measure of respect and were not seen as evil or terrorists.

Bakunin had been present. He (and others) may have had little confidence in success but hoped for a heroic death. When the attempt fell apart, he escaped, disguising himself as a priest. The Italian federation was disrupted and did not attend the Brussels international congress in September 1874, writing that the public life of the IWMA was impossible. No regional congresses were held in Italy in 1874 or 1875. Repression increased: the Jura *Bulletin* of 27 December 1874 reported that 152,888 persons had been placed under *ammonizione* (police banning orders) and another 22,000 under special surveillance measures (*domicilio coatto*) and/or residence in internal exile, often in remote places. Some activists emigrated, and an IWMA group emerged in Alexandria (Egypt). Costa and many other activists were imprisoned.[478] Some activists retreated to the Ticino (Switzerland) and worked to re-organise the Italian federation from there. A correspondence committee began to function in Naples in 1876.

The events in Bologna were of little importance in themselves, but they marked the beginnings of a new tactic, which came to be called 'propaganda by the deed'.[479] It was a propaganda tactic: staging protests and demonstrations, peaceful or not so peaceful, designed to draw attention and seeking to win support.[480]

France and Switzerland

In France, the state kept a wary eye on labour organising. Camille Camet was arrested in November 1873. A grand trial was held in Lyon in April of the following year and 26 people were convicted. Henri Boriasse and Camet received prison sentences of three and five years, respectively.[481] IWMA activity was much reduced.[482] *Der Volksstaat* (28 November 1873) displayed its customary hostility, taking the view that these conflicts amounted to police fairy tales (*polizeimärchen*) 'decorated with a gush of Bakuninist phrases'.

Johann Philipp Becker continued working for Social-Democracy,[483] he reported that Perret[484] was no longer taking part in the Geneva section, and that work to build a federal organisation on a Swiss-wide, or French-Swiss basis had stopped.[485] Economic recession challenged the Swiss labour movement. Work discipline was often severe. Saddlers in Neuchâtel worked a thirteen or fourteen-hour day. Bakers in that city might get the food and lodgings but received only 7 or 8 francs a week. Ten were sacked when they asked for 11 francs a week.[486] In Geneva's watch and clock industry, there was a ten-hour day, and talking was forbidden. Skilled outworkers in the watch and jewellery trades sought to maintain and extend their control over work processes, fearing the introduction of new machinery and the employment of cheap, unskilled labour – women and children.* They sought to own technology and machinery, to prevent themselves being reduced into the 'slavery' of waged work as in England. There, they said, the proletariat was completely subjugated and crushed;[487] manual workers were forced to work long hours for poor pay as wage slaves, or white slaves.[488] Reports of harsh practice came in from several places. In Belgium, some workers had twelve-hour days.[489] One correspondent in Boston reported that in the USA workers were often paid in arrears on the tenth or twelfth of the following month, and employers never paid off those first ten or twelve days – a system of organised theft, (also prevalent in many large factories in German-speaking Switzerland). The economic crisis, rather than exciting the working classes, has beaten them down; 'there is now I believe no [press] organ to represent the principles of the International in America; there is the most complete calm.'[490] *La Federación* (18 October 1873) wrote of how the bourgeoisie might count profits, head off to the countryside stroll through the Swiss lakes, visit the beauties of the country, and squander funds accumulated from their 'slaves'. Their luxury insulted proletarians' humility and misery. Workers' homes in Switzerland were overcrowded, lacking hygiene or morality. Owners (thieves) could charge twenty-five pesetas a month for a room.

The Jura federation prospered in the year after the Geneva congresses and reached a peak membership of 250 to 300,[491] (adult French-speakers in Switzerland numbered some 300,000). It had some community influence – sections were lively. and members were active. It was developing a small syndicalist, workplace presence through the creation of resistance societies, meetings, and strikes; albeit that some new affiliations were brief.[492] Local

---

* The Jura *Bulletin* of 18 April 1875 reported that in the watch and industry 81% of workers were men, and 19% women.

area organising continued across trades. Adhémar Schwitzguébel wrote a short commentary on the economic crisis, *Les crises industrielles et leurs causes* on behalf of the Courtelary engravers' federation; it suggested strengthening labour organisations and other measures to attenuate the impact of the crisis.

The Jura Federation had some support in France and in the Alsace. The Jura congress of 1874 was attended by new sections– one had been founded recently in Bern. Fifteen sections were represented by delegates, and IWMA members attended in an individual capacity.[493] A section in Alsace had to overcome the close attention of the German police authorities. The *Bulletin* (14 December 1873) reported that socialists there were designated as separatists (*particularistes* or *sonderbündler*) if they refused to join the German Social-Democratic Workers Party, and the German government looked approvingly on them and was delighted to find allies for its policy of Germanisation.*

The federation was careful about motivating general strikes.[494] It reacted positively to demands for reduction of the working day coming from other labour organisations but insisted that these must be fought for by trade organisations; otherwise, the bosses of the electoral-political system would use workers as *Stimmvieh* (electoral cattle), and, in the absence of a strong labour organisation, 'leaders' would likely form alliances with the 'advanced' radicals. Reforms, even if they were enacted on paper, would become so much chaff – whatever the bourgeoisie choose to concede. To impose shorter working days and other improvements independent workplace labour organisation was needed. [495]

Labour's strength was dwindling,[496] but the federation had occasional successes. Workers in La Chaux-de-Fonds turned to the Jura federation for assistance when employers reacted to the economic downturn by reducing wages. Fritz Heng, a Jura member presided at a 2,500 strong meeting. It induced managers to withdraw the pay cut.[497] The *Bulletin* (18 January 1874) urged workers to look for a solution to the crisis: international solidarity was needed, an international league of labour to confront international economic problems. Co-operatives might be the organisational form after the emancipation of labour but they were not the means to accomplish that liberation.[498] The *Bulletin* (13 June 1874) supported the demand of the *Arbeiterbund* for a maximum ten-hour day.

Workplace conflicts continued in Geneva. There was a woodworkers strike in June 1874. The *Bulletin de la Fédération Jurassienne*, noted the

---

* A section of French speakers in Nottingham had also applied to join the Jura federation; but had been referred back to the British IWMA, *Eastern Post* 26 April 1873.

differential weight of solidarity funds raised: 285.75 francs had been forthcoming from Geneva itself, whereas 2755.10 francs had been raised in the rest of Switzerland and abroad. Why did the rich associations of the Geneva Fabrique give so little?

The *Bulletin* (19 April 1874) reported on the arrest of 50 building workers by the Geneva police: an altercation had broken out when some workers called others not to accept lower pay. The representatives of the bourgeoisie defended 'the freedom of labour' – *cheap* labour. Such things would not be happening if the IWMA had maintained the strength it had in 1869, wrote the *Bulletin*; at that time, the strength of the labour movement had enforced the going rate for the job. That strength needed rebuilding. The *Bulletin* of 26 April reported the success of a carpenters' strike in Neuchâtel and the outbreak of a carpenters' strike in Geneva. No carpenter should travel there it warned. The Genevans were asking for payment by the day at the rate of 0.50 francs an hour, and a ten-hour day. It was also reported the police had been empowered to deport from the area any workers without the means to support themselves – thus, any striking worker could be deported. The edition of 31 May noted that some seventy workers had been imprisoned and another twenty deported. 'Dead-beats, fat rentiers, parasites of all sorts and sizes; owners, pastors, and priests, can stroll around at their ease contemplating the just punishment inflicted on workers and idleness with a satisfied eye', wrote the *Bulletin*. Later that year the Geneva authorities insisted that the title *La Commune* could not be used for a journal, and a second issue came out without a title. [499] Subsequently Henri Perret took a position as a Geneva police *commisaire* with a 2,400-franc salary, and Mr Josseron, the president of the centralist congress became the police superintendent for morality (suppressing 'vice'). The Jura *Bulletin* commented: 'Ah, now we understand why the gentlemen fought against political abstention and sought to have their friends join the authorities!' Another IWMA journal commented: 'The ouvriers-bourgeois party was able to achieve its goal there: an alliance of some labour organisations with the radicals [Radical Party] was soon accomplished, and the leaders, who had intrigued to obtain this result were compensated with appointments and fat pay.' In their view, very little was being achieved by the Swiss *Arbeiterbund*: 'four years on from its beginnings the *Arbeiterbund* has become a docile instrument in the hands of the radicals and they use it when they need to solicit votes at an election; as for serious socialist demands, the *Arbeiterbund* views such things as utopian, the mere sight of a red flag frightens them, and they have quite banished it from their demonstrations.' [500]

The Jura *Bulletin* noted that the Swiss *Arbeiterbund* adopted a humble and subservient tone towards the Swiss state; as had Heinrich Oberwinder in Vienna and the *Arbeiterbund* had condemned him as a traitor; obviously it thought this *Bund* was far too humble.[501] Social-Democrats were aware that there had been a split in the movement in Austria-Hungary, and the confidential report of the New York General Council had said that this was a matter of 'personal brawling'; it wanted unity and dues.[502] There was in fact a policy dispute: Oberwinder's critic Andreas Scheu had sought links with Czech workers and Oberwinder had resisted that. The General Council had chosen to work with Oberwinder, suspecting Scheu of dissidence (the dreadful crime of 'Bakuninism').[503]

In July 1875, some 2 to 3,000 Italian miners building the Gotthard tunnel went on strike. Ventilation and working conditions were appalling. Three years later, a report cited 182 deaths and serious injuries: an average of five accidents per month.[504] The time taken to walk to the rockface, some 90 minutes per day, was unpaid. Pay was inadequate – 3 to 4 francs per day – and channelled through scrip, usable only at company stores,* where food was bad and expensive. The workers struck for better working conditions, and payment in currency. Managers offered 30,000 francs to have a militia unit sent in. Several workers were wounded and three killed. Eight workers were imprisoned and eighty more sacked.[505] Army recruits who had failed to join their units were fined. A fund was set up to help strike victims; it received donations from the Jura, Spain and elsewhere.[506] Swiss nationalism facilitated these killings, a certain disdain for foreigners was endemic. It was challenged by IWMA members in Vevey who resolved to print the names of the local government officials and officers who had ordered the shooting, so that their actions could be publicly deplored.[507] Two years later a law was passed that made it compulsory for workers to give employers two weeks' notice before going on strike.[508]

The Bulletin de la Fédération Jurassienne

The *Bulletin de la Fédération jurassienne*, edited by James Guillaume, enjoyed some pre-eminence among IWMA federalists. Its regularity and long life set it apart. Its geographical location and linguistic aptitude facilitated coverage of European issues. The presence of French refugees brought in new collaborators. 46 copies were sent to foreign subscribers (in Austria, Belgium, Britain, Egypt, France, Germany, Greece, Hungary, Italy, Mexico, the Netherlands, Portugal, Romania, Spain, Uruguay, and the USA),[509] but it had few contributors based abroad. The *Bulletin* (and other

---

* Similar systems were used by landlords in the American South. Scrip tied workers down and left them open to abuse and indebtedness.

journals allied with the Jura federation) carried many articles on movements of working peoples in Europe and America. For example, it noted that two members of the Miners' Union, were elected as Liberal-Labour members of the British parliament in February 1874: Alexander Macdonald for Stafford, and Thomas Burt for Morpeth. They defended trade unions and brought a whiff of working-class life into the House of Commons; however, it noted that the *Bee-Hive* criticised their participation in a Royal Commission. It doubted that they would promote any socialist agenda. Given that the recent trades union congress in Nottingham represented over a million workers, could the labour movement not be more energetic and less patient, it asked? Several reports were carried on strikes and trade union congresses. The *Bulletin* took a conciliatory line towards electoral tactics in Germany. Given the conditions there 'in their place we would act likewise'; however, it wrote that electoral-politics was a bad tactic for Switzerland, 'which would make the cause of labour retreat rather than advance'.[510] In another issue (8 December 1874) it summed up views on deputies and legislatures as follows:

> If a workers' deputy goes into a bourgeois assembly to work for negative politics – that is to say to refuse to join in parliamentary business and to protest against all its workings, that amounts to serving the proletariat. But if a workers' deputy enters a bourgeois assembly to take part in its work, to demand concessions, improvements or, in a word, to engage in parliamentarianism, then that is serving the bourgeoisie.

The *Bulletin* carried local news, for example that flooding was caused by the felling of forests which previously had retained rainwater; it blamed speculators who looked only to enrich themselves; two years later a forest law was enacted to prevent floods.[511] The *Bulletin* printed a letter at the request of the *Schweizerische Arbeiterbund* supporting a bookbinders' strike in Zurich, where workers were demanding pay of 40 centimes an hour and a ten-hour day, and warning workers not to take up job offers there; a month later it recommended a report on labour rates and hours.[512] Some eighteen months after the congress of 1873, the *Bulletin* (14 February 1875) noted an item in a programme proposed for the *Grütli* association, and a demand for 'The emancipation of the class of woman workers, through the payment of work by women on the same terms as men'. The *Bulletin* commented:

> This is something utopian, and one is astounded to find this under the name of a so-called practical man. Doesn't Mr Bleuler know that wage rates depend on the higher or lower costs needed to maintain a worker?

Women, being maintained at a lesser cost than men will always be paid less; only vain words can protest, against this unavoidable fate,* and one must bow one's head before 'the iron law of wages'– as Lassalle put it so well. To improve the position of women workers, there is only one real way, and that is to abolish waged-work through a social revolution.

The Jura Federation supported various publications:[513] it issued an annual *Almanach du peuple* between 1870 and 1874,** each of 40 to 50 pages. Contributors included Bakunin, Paul Brousse, Jules Guesde, Gustave Lefrançais, André Léo, Benoît Malon, Élisée Reclus and Adhémar Schwitzguébel. The *Almanach* was sold in Belgium and elsewhere, helping to spread federalist ideas. It published an occasional flyer in German, a *Social Demokratisches Bulletin*.

Bruno Gutsmann attended the federalist IWMA congress held in Bern in 1876, along with at least one observer from the new German Social-Democratic party. Their presence indicated some thaw in relations between socialist traditions.[514] That congress was held after the remnants of the centralist IWMA had declared their International dissolved, leaving the federalists as the sole surviving IWMA network.

Empires, labour, and armed forces

Slavery and indentured labour (largely of Chinese and Indian workers) continued in independent states (e.g. Brazil, and Peru), in many colonial territories, notably in the Caribbean, in eastern and southern Africa, Mauritius and in parts of the Islamic world.[515] Coolies built railways in Cuba and in the USA. Male workers were used on a mass scale as indentured or coolie labourers. Some women were brought over too. A contemporary comment by Leon Metchnikoff noted: 'Slaves on board slave-ships never had to suffer the treatment inflicted on coolies; an African had to be bought and in consequence represented quite a large sum in the eyes of an honest entrepreneur; a Chinese is worth less than 25 francs.'[516] There were high rates of mortality among indentured labourers. The *Neuer Sozial-Demokrat* (1 March 1874) reported that a set of Chinese investigators was being sent out to report back on ill-treatment in Cuba and Peru.

Empires were expanding and contracting, military conflicts were flaring. New areas of revolt were growing. In some European parts of the Ottoman empire rebels planned revolts, taking the Paris commune as a model.[517] There was an insurrection near Chalco in a south-eastern area of the state

---

* No doubt women workers rejected the view that unequal pay was an 'unavoidable fate'.
** *La Commune, almanach socialiste pour 1877* was published in Geneva, in late 1876.

of Mexico in 1868-9; one of its leaders was Julio López Chávez, a follower of the Greek anarchist Plotino Rhodakanaty; Chávez was killed shortly afterwards.[518] Strikes followed, and a *Gran Círculo de Obreros* began to organise.[519] *El Socialista, El Obrero Internacional*,[520] *La Comuna* and other labour journals reflected on the effectiveness of strikes. The first edition of the latter, published in 1874 told readers:

> The Commune lives on in France as in Mexico, the United States, Germany, China and in Arabia; but needs all men of good will to gather together to work for the consolidation of our principles, so that a new Koszciusko may be raised for the emancipation of Poland, a Kosuth for the freedom of Hungary, another O'Connell to snatch Ireland from the clutches of the British lion; a new Garibaldi to proclaim the Italian Republic; another Cespedes to make the Antilles independent; a great man for every idea, a political and religious Christ to redeem the world again; to erase the boundaries between peoples; to demolish the thrones of kings; to change words of hate into the kiss of peace ...[521]

And, three years later it was reported that

> A revolt of communists has just broken out among the Indians in Hidalgo state in Mexico. They want to recover land that whites took from them at the time of the conquistadors. They have chased away the landowners and have burnt [legal] papers establishing their property rights. But the army has come in to re-establish order ... that is to say, to re-establish in their properties the current successors of those who stole the land of old. The task is unfinished. Naturally, honest journals in Mexico do not forgo this new opportunity and accuse the 'Internationalists' of having exerted 'a fatal influence' on the Indians.[522]

A General Congress of Mexican Workers was convened in 1877. It defended women's rights and education, to prevent them being made into slaves.

Socialist and anarchist networks developed slowly in the Americas and parts of Asia and Africa, often spreading out from cities and ports. At first, refugees from the Commune and economic migrants from parts of Europe might be shaped by experiences in countries of origin, but later might adapt to new circumstances, coming to respect indigenous communities and developing new hybrid cultures. Foreign agitators were seen as responsible for strikes, and lands receiving migrants deported 'foreign trouble-makers'.

In Ontario, Métis communities were in one sense insiders, but in another sense were outsiders, in the eyes of the incoming Canadian state. They developed as a community of resistance confronting settlers' economic and political systems. In Cuba, the death of the Spanish republic and the restoration of the monarchy augured a revival of Spanish colonial power. Some white Cubans would develop links with the IWMA[523] and supported the abolition of slavery. Cubans rebelling against Spain came together from various ethnic communities, with diverse ideas about the future. There were conflicts in Africa too, as European forces intervened (against the Zulus, the Ashanti, the Berbers, and other peoples). Léon Hugonnet would write, in 1877, of the solidarity and egalitarianism that existed among Berber peoples in Algeria. Writing in *Le Travailleur*, he expressed regrets for 'our failure in not considering Algeria's barbarians as brothers; and being victims of our prejudice and egoism'.

Undeniably contemporary civilised people, educated amid social hatred and having been made blind by individualism are hardly prepared to bring about our desires and theories; only our descendants will see such things come about. Further, it seemed to me useful and encouraging to make known societies which, without having the least idea of European phraseology, possess in a most complete fashion customs of association; long practising a solidarity made necessary by the climate and nature of the earth in the north of Africa and untaught by masters. I have seen in these facts, which even our adversaries cannot dispute, a powerful argument against the reproach of unachievable utopianism which is constantly addressed to our aspirations. ... [N]othing gives such honour to a people as their protection of the weak. Moreover. the poor are fed by the community. ... [O]ur [French army] cut-throats made their apprenticeship in fire-raising and murder against the Algerians. The remedy for weakness in the face of an invader is to be found in the solidarity of peoples, and not as Mr [Ernest] Renan believes in a central power and a professional army.[524]

Hugonnet advocated respect for the rights of all the peoples in Algeria and for the autonomy of local communes. French legislation, introduced in 1873, facilitated the privatisation of communal lands in Algeria.[525] Later, Kropotkin in his work *Mutual Aid*, would write of how Kabyle (Berber) people shared food and prevented famine.[526] These authors were beginning to challenge Eurocentric and racist perspectives.

Elisée Reclus wrote that *Le Travailleur* was set up by friends seeking to create a forum for libertarian ideas. He recognised the growth of national forces, based on language and ethnicity. 'But' he wrote, 'this is only a stage. Superior interests, a higher morality will bring people together, following not languages or so-called origins – because we are all mixed by comings and goings – but depending on ideas of rights and duties. On the one side are those who seek to profit from inequality and injustice, on the other those who work for their own freedom, and the freedom of others.'

Certain delegates at the Geneva congresses had begun to see that there was something not quite right about the use of the word 'civilised', but African, American and Asian peoples were not present, and made little or no input into the IWMA at this time.[527] In metropolitan societies colonialism was widely portrayed as somewhat exotic and progressive: new technologies and cultures were being sent out to 'backward' peoples, and new colonial products were being made available back in the metropolis.

The Jura Federation was in touch with the Mexican *El Socialista*, but the situation of rural rebel *campesinos* – and their ideas (as in the *Manifesto a todos los oprimidos y pobres de Mexico y del Universo*) and thinkers (Julio Chávez López and Plotino Constantino Rhodakanaty) – appear to have been less well known.[528] Elisée Reclus would work over the next twenty years on the mammoth *La Nouvelle Géographie universelle, la terre et les hommes*. This work, and that of his brother Elie would go some way to challenge racist thinking. 'First of all, we must rid ourselves of every prejudice and of every sentiment of rage, disdain, and hatred which still divides peoples.'[529] He drew attention to the barbarous treatment of Jews and Moslems by the Catholic Inquisition since 1478, in Spain.

Armed forces evoked various perspectives. Some of the army rank and file might see service as a patriotic duty, others joined up under duress, and others resisted – avoiding or refusing call-ups or deserting once enlisted.[530] Radicals of all sorts might encounter the police, armed forces and Pinkertons (counter-gangs), when disputes and strikes erupted. Some causes attracted radicals (e.g. support for revolutionaries in Spain or for national liberation struggles in Eastern Europe and parts of the Ottoman Empire). Conversely, the prospect of service in repressive forces repelled radicals, and might encourage them to emigrate to avoid recruitment. Libertarians were among those who sought to undermine the loyalty of the forces to the governments of the day. Bakunin wrote that a soldier, once he had spent three, four, or five years in the army 'can only emerge from it as a monster'.[531] Evidently this was not always so; the Jura *Bulletin* publicised a case of soldiers thinking for themselves:

We, a group of under-officers of the Belgian army, we want to make this public declaration, so that you should be certain that among the military there are convinced men, men waiting with impatience for the hour of the soon-to-arrive social renovation. ... Many journals say that if a revolution comes soldiers will do their duty, if calling on them to shoot fathers brothers and friends can be called that. We reply to them, these 'gentlemen', that when the great day comes a large part of us will never fire on the people; on the contrary, we will help them.[532]

The libertarian press reported on army officers and their crimes and might lampoon 'civilised' armed forces. One satirical correspondent in Russia reported on imperial forces who organised a massacre in a campaign in Khiva and Tashkent (central Asia). The key goal of that Russian foreign policy was said to be:

quite naturally the propagation of 'civilisation' among the people of the East, who are much less susceptible to being civilised than European peoples, because they possess neither Krupp artillery, nor those instruments that have been invented and dedicated to the extermination of the human race – and that is why our 'civilised' government's attention has been directed towards them.[533]

Opinions were changing slowly, with some respect for cultures that might not be so economically developed but were convivial. *Le Travailleur* and some libertarians of European heritage were beginning to condemn barbarous colonialism, which reduced indigenous peoples to servants or slaves,[534] and coming to value conviviality. Much later Walter Rodney would write about the complexity of relations between races, classes, states, and armed forces, and note that it was very significant that 'stateless societies ... did not attack their neighbours [in Africa] in order to acquire captives for the benefit of the Europeans. It means that where there was an African society without a ruling class the Europeans had no one who could be their accomplices in the slave-trade.'[535]

The Jura *Bulletin* noted how numbers of soldiers in Europe had risen over 15 years, from 4.2 to 5.8 million. It reproduced the following table:

Nations General total of men	1859	1874
Germany	836,000	1,261,000
Austria	443,000	857,000
Belgium	80,000	93,590
Britain		479,000
France	640,000	978,000
Italy	317,000	605,000
Russia	1,224,000	1,519,000

These numbers were far from telling the whole story, because governments were doing all they could to increase the numbers of legalised butchers. Rulers sought to sow hatred – instead of the fraternity; it was the duty of workers to seek mutual understanding.[536] Social-Democrats did not entirely share libertarians' views on the armed forces. They commented on the vast sums spent on the army: military spending was too large, military service was too long, barracks were unhealthy, soldiers were badly fed and clothed.[537] Mostly, they focused on abuses and did not seek to challenge 'their' state. When the new party formed in Germany it proposed 'a people's army' (militia) instead of the regular army; declarations of war and peace should be made by representatives of the people. Libertarians had no faith in national 'people's' armies – knowing how strikers and outsiders were treated by the armed forces (in France, Switzerland or the USA). Centralist leaders might see 'brigands' or 'pirates', where libertarians recognised fellow rebels.

The USA

Woodhull & Claflin's Weekly claimed to be the only free press paper in the world. In the edition of 15 November 1873 it set out a prospectus that looked for a new political system, one for all adults, with a new land system and the free use of 'a proper proportion' of land; a new industrial system, in which each individual would remain possessed of production; a financial system, in which the government would be the source, custodian and transmitter of money, (without usury); a new sexual system; proper childcare and education, etc.

On 13 December 1873, the *Weekly* carried 'An Address to the people of the United States from the [Spring Street] Federal council of I.W.A. of North America'. The address called for paper money to kickstart projects:

'to start up all the public improvements, employing the laborers direct without the intervention of contractors, paying the laborer a fair price for his work and according proper hours.'

Legislation for an eight-hour day, for employees of the federal US government dated back to the summer of 1868; New York construction workers had succeeded in obtaining it after a prolonged strike in 1871-2. The *Eastern Post* (London, 24 May 1873) reported the American Federal Council advising European federalists that immigration authorities were keeping penniless migrants on Blackwell's Island, New York, to use them as strike-breakers. Italian workers who tried to escape had been beaten back with clubs, and some had died.[538] On 12 and 13 August 1873, the *Chicago Daily Tribune* had remarked that little by little employers were progressively flouting the law: 'Inquiry shows that in certain trades the eight-hour plan is almost entirely ignored.' 500 New York painters had gone on strike to prevent a return to a ten-hour day. On the 16th the *Workingman's Advocate* reported on a convention called to press for a ten-hour day in Massachusetts. Weaker unions found it difficult to defend gains, and business had deeper pockets than labour, when strikes threatened.

The bankruptcy of the Jay Cooke company in September 1873 signalled the beginning of the second worst crash in US economic history and weakened or reversed campaigns to extend the eight-hour day. The Jura *Bulletin* (28 December 1873) quoted a report in the New York *World* that there were 58,000 unemployed there – and this number may have risen to 100,000.[539] The value of wages declined, perhaps by half. In Chicago there were deaths from starvation. Further afield there were international repercussions when debts went unpaid. In Francophone Switzerland, the export trade in clocks and watches was severely reduced.[540] The recession brought evictions, riots and sharpened political tensions. It undermined labour organisations and both wings of the American IWMA. Wages were cuts, the length of the working day was extended to nine or ten hours, workers were laid off, and union membership fell. Both the Colored National Labor Union and the once-substantial National Labor Union disintegrated. Some members moved on to the Knights of Labor.

Over the winter of 1873-74 a wave of local strikes broke out on the railways. Organised and unorganised rail workers found support from surrounding communities and labour bodies.[541] Strikers were able to prevent services running, and in some cases destroyed infrastructure. Economic coercion, strike-breakers, and military force were deployed against them.

In November 1873, the centralist American Federal Council issued a manifesto, signed by secretary F. Bolte, calling for 'fair work, fair living';

for work to be provided, an eight-hour day,* relief in kind or money, and a halt on evictions from December 1873 to 1 May 1874.[542] The Spring Street sections also demanded measures to help the unemployed. On 11 December, 4,000 people crammed into a meeting at the Cooper Institute in New York (with an overflow outside) to be addressed in English and German. A banner over speakers' heads said we are dealing with serious affairs, politicians, please stay away. One demand was for an end to spending on government sinecures and soft jobs costing five million dollars. Theodore Banks, a leader of the Painters' union, presided. A Committee of Safety was formed with 48 men and two women. It was drawn from diverse bodies, and included: Banks, Benoît Hubert and others from the Spring Street network, exiles from France, some in a society of Paris Commune refugees including the Blanquiste/communard Élie May, and members of IWMA German section No. 1, including Friedrich Bolte and Karl Conrad. The latter had just fallen out with Friedrich Sorge.[543] William West was suspicious of the new committee and advised working people to act for themselves. A committee meeting of the Spring Street Federation recommended that the proposals of the 11th should not be accepted.[544]

In December 1873 and January 1874, the Federal Council of the Spring Street IWMA (Secretary G. W. Madox, President: W.A.A. Carsey based at State Street, Brooklyn) called on the government to issue $500 million of currency, to counter excessive interest rates. It would be a remedy – 'Government employ, i.e., the people through the instrument of government employ themselves.' It called for help to facilitate settlers getting land, to relieve starving citizens in the cities, 'whose condition to-day is worse than negro slavery ever was,' following the example set in Australia, Brazil and Canada. There were calls for land to be distributed: 'millions of acres of land [are] unimproved and now unproductive. We have in the city of New York alone one hundred thousand able-bodied men idle and homeless. Can we not utilize men and lands to the enrichment of both?' [545] Working people were urged to organise in the IWA, and in the 'United Order of Internationals'. The latter organised both secretly and openly, meeting at 234 Fifth street.[546]

The Committee of Safety sponsored protests, and on 13 January 1874 some 7,000 workers gathered in a freezing Tompkins Square.[547] They included P.J. McGuire, Victor Drury, Élie May, and some supporters of the German Tenth Ward network. Sorge (as in December 1871) and other moderate labour bodies did not lend support. Later Sorge commented:

---

* Similar demands were made in Chicago. Meetings were also organised in Cincinnati and Louisville. (*Chicago Daily Tribune*, 25 December 1873).

'*Die Arbeiter Zeitung* warned against them as before, that a premature and incomplete demonstration would break the thrust of the organization.'[548] The *New York Daily Herald* had reported on the 12th: 'The Committee of Public Safety is not recognized by the trade unions or adherents to the General Council.' It portrayed 'firebrands' seeking 'notoriety'.

Police authorities had been gathering information; they had ordered the arrest of anyone urging workers to stop work. 1,600 police were present. They attacked, killing one, arresting scores, and wounding hundreds. The initial reaction of *Woodhull & Claflin's Weekly* (24 January 1874) was guarded: 'though the *Weekly* would [prefer to] accomplish a revolution by more peaceful methods, it will never fail to stand up sternly to the front in demanding, even at the price of blood, the constitutional rights of all the citizens of the United States.' Five days later the *New York Herald* called demonstrators communists, and 'dangerous conspirators'. It said they were holding 'secret meetings'. These 'disturbing elements' were, said *The Herald*, demanding the equalisation of property and 'free love'; they had no religion and had no respect for persons or station; they upheld the red flag and spat on all other flags;[549] also, it wrote, they had failed to link up with Irish Catholics. In fact, there were some five Irishmen among those arrested alongside American, French, Italian, Polish, Swedish and many German workmen.[550]

The *New York Dispatch* (18 January 1874) was scathing. It noted that recent events had called public attention to the International, which it said, was a body of harmless idiots or blind enthusiasts; its most active persons were Theodore Banks, Patrick Dunn, and T. Maddox [Madox]. The *New York Herald* was concerned that with mass unemployment honest workers might lend an ear to 'wild theories' and 'incendiary balderdash'. Most agitators were foreigners who had no intention of becoming US citizens, it said. It looked to charity relief funds to avoid troubles.

Many people were appalled by the police violence. A women's committee and four defence units of a hundred men each were formed to protect future demonstrations, led by Élie May.[551] Arsène Sauva organised French-speaking defenders. Theodore Banks spoke at the Cosmopolitan Hall to some seventy or eighty people on the 17th; the *Herald* reported him saying:

> We are denied the right of even meeting in peace and quietness in this hall. Police guard all the entrances, and detectives have been placed in our midst to watch our every movement. This I consider even a greater outrage than the one which was perpetrated on Tuesday last; for they have even busied themselves in warning the workingmen to keep away, telling them

that if we met there would be trouble. The committee, however, have met here in defiance of the police. We are not to be terrified. We are not to be coerced into giving up our rights as citizens. Outrages such as these leave men no other remedy than military action and to be prepared militarily, in order that we can meet whenever we desire to exchange opinions and prepare for action. At Tompkins Square they prepared an ambuscade for us, and without a word of warning began an indiscriminate clubbing. Those who were endeavoring to run in order to escape laceration were clubbed unmercifully – one workingman being killed outright, and another now lies at the point of death. The time has come, and we must now prepare for the worst. We must resist as workingmen, and as such we must endeavor to put down all monopolies. Under the present laws which govern society how much better off are we than the former slaves in the South? (Voice in the audience – 'They were well fed.') Yes, they were well fed, and they were cared for and provided with work, which we are denied. We are not even as fortunate as were the negroes. Talk about free America and the Stars and Stripes! Why, the Stars and Stripes are in disgrace. We must prepare to fight those opposed to us. We are tired of political demagogues. We have had enough of them. They talk about the Communists. The Communists are the only ones who look after the rights of the workingmen. (Loud applause.) Nowadays the workingman who dares to say a word draws down upon his head the anger of the press. The competitive system in existence makes all the trouble. We want the system of universal co-operation, and to this opinion we must all incline. The man who does not labor robs the man who does. He hires you for his good only and robs you of the profit which belongs to your labor. Independent action on the part of the workingmen is the only way we can gain our ends, and if we cannot meet pacifically, we must organize militarily. We must have no sympathy for anybody but our families, and if the police will not allow us to meet quietly, we must go armed to our meetings.

The meeting passed the following resolutions:

Whereas we are passing through a great financial crisis which has thrown us suddenly out of employment; and whereas there is no destruction of the real wealth of the country, but speculation in gold, stocks and the people's lands, sanctioned by the government, has been the sole cause of the panic; and whereas we are industrious, law-abiding citizens, who wish to avoid all outrage on person or property, and deprecate violence or injustice in any form; and whereas we desire only the means of obtaining the necessities of life, not as objects of charity, but as law-abiding citizens, whose right it is to demand work of the government which we have always protected and supported; therefore, we are

Resolved. That we will not eat the bread of idleness nor starve in the midst of plenty; but that we demand work, and pay for that work, now and without delay.

Resolved. That we demand the rigid enforcement of the eight-hour system on all private as well as public work, and the instant and entire abolition of the whole government contract system.

Resolved. That if the government will not furnish work for the unemployed, we, through our Committee of Safety, will in this our time of need, supply ourselves and our families with proper food, shelter and clothing and will send all our bills for the same to the City Treasury to be liquidated, until such times as we shall obtain work and pay.

Resolved. That we demand an immediate and permanent reduction of twenty-five per cent on all house rents until the 1st of May to the unemployed of all classes.

Resolved. That, in the furtherance of the objects set down in the above resolutions, we will enroll our names and organize, not in the interest of any political party, but in the interest of all the people who are suffering from the present condition of affairs.

Resolved. That we will appoint from this mass meeting a committee of twelve workingmen, residents of the ward, to organize the working classes of the ward and co-operate with the German ward organizations.

Resolved. That we will support and sustain the Committee of Safety in its work of securing the above objects.[552]

Support had been organised already in German wards and further efforts were being made to organise in English-speaking areas. The Safety committee was empowered to convene a convention of representatives of US industry to study the interests of the entire people, and to elaborate a common plan of action. Its secretary was to network with all labour and agricultural organisations to promote harmony and unity of action. Granges were most powerful allies against the hydra of monopoly agriculture.[553]

The *New York Herald* noted mass homelessness. Ten thousand children were on the streets.[554] On the 28th it wrote that a reporter had been told that the Safety committee had recruited 11,000 men and it was in touch with similar bodies nationally. Five lawyers were engaged to defend persons arrested in Tompkins Square, and families were being supported. Legal arguments were made that authorities had violated the people's right to be in the square. On the 31st the same paper reported that a public meeting in the Cooper Union condemned the police action as illegal, brutal, and unconstitutional. On 13 February, a meeting of the Committee of Safety was held. A report, under the heading 'The Rights Of Citizen – A New Platform For The Industrial Party', said that New York workingmen had resolved:

> That the time of humble petitions or of energetic protest, to which our rulers answer only by silent disregard or violent clubbing and imprisonment, is now gone forever. That the time is come for combined action on the part of the toiling masses to enforce their rights ... that we shall also propose that all railroads, canals, telegraphs, mines, gas-works – in fine, all those industries that bear a character of public interest and monopoly, become the property of the people, to be held by the government in trust for the people, the profits accruing therefrom to replace taxation.[555]

The Committee did not last long, but some members helped form an ephemeral Industrial Political Party. The protests around Tompkins Square sparked a huge wave of interest for the International, and a brief revival of the federalists' *The Worker*, subsequently renamed as *The Toiler*.* A new weekly, *International*, also appeared in New York, edited by G.W. Madox.[556] There was no great revival of IWA organisations, although a French-language section of the IWMA did form in June 1874 (it met at 123 West Houston Street, New York and had Arsène Sauva as secretary correspondent). It published a *Bulletin de l'Union républicaine de langue française*. It attempted to revive the IWMA in the US and stressed armed struggle.[557] Other parts of the Spring Street federation were dissolving or moving on, and the centralists were engaged in bitter internal conflicts.

There was great support for co-operative labour organisations, operating in urban and rural areas and for cooperative stores or Granges. By 1874-5 there were 19,000 local Granges with almost a million members, operating in 32 US states and in parts of Canada. Many cooperatively-owned workshops were formed. Grangers varied in outlook, some former members of Spring Street joined, some demanded women's suffrage; others were not so progressive.[558] IWMA members were concentrated in cities and had little capacity to influence the greater part of American labour living in rural areas.** Cooperative stores might make wages go further.

* Published in English and German, from May to November 1873.
** An IWMA section in New Orleans showed an interest in establishing industrial and

Conflicts escalated in the centralist IWMA in New York, over money matters and the direction of the weekly *Arbeiter Zeitung*. There were demands that greater attention should be given to local concerns and it was said that the paper and its editorial board were drifting away.[559] Power struggles and internal conflicts flared between leading figures in New York sections, and through local New York networks, the Federal (USA) council and the (international) General Council. Power might swing one way or another, depending on how just four or five persons might vote and form a majority. Expulsions followed. The New York General Council was reduced to German-only membership. George Stiebeling a veteran Social-Democrat asked, rhetorically: 'Is it not the case that this lamentable result passes the most damning judgement on developments since the congress at the Hague?'[560] A resolution of the No. 1 (German) New York section, shows how much bitterness was present:

> that F. A. Sorge, ex-General-Secretary had lost the confidence of his colleagues, through his many failings towards the principles of labour, through his overt alliance with the leaders of US bourgeois parties and with the known agent of the Austrian government, Henry Oberwinder, in Vienna. He has shown himself as a perfidious and dangerous enemy of the working class, through his participation in the shameful attacks committed against the *Arbeiter Zeitung* and in consequence workers of every country were warned not to enter into correspondence of any sort with him, given that he used such correspondence only to cause damage to the working class, and to satisfy his ambition and his personal vexation.[561]

The General Council took over the functions of the USA Federal Council and dissolved it, in February 1874.[562] Three individuals, Bolte, Carl and Praitsching, were expelled from the International. Several sections withdrew or were suspended pending confirmation by a general congress.[563] Sorge wrote: 'No great work was ever begun by a majority'.[564] Earlier he had justified the actions of the General Council expelling six federations on the grounds that the New York General Council acted for the majority (at The Hague congress); now he treated fellow centralist critics as enemies.[565] The newspaper dispute led to lawsuits between the contending parties: F. Bertrand, Sorge, Spier, et al. vs. F. Bolte et al. A costly and long-drawn out legal dispute followed,[566] provoking this rebuke from one French New York IWMA section:

agricultural colonies.

We note, with sadness that, not content with having disorganised our federation through their authoritarianism, the same men, the same clique, now insult our entire Association by dragging it through this country's civil courts. To place the task of settling our differences among ourselves in the hands of our enemies is to disregard their constituents, who would be the best judges of this affair. It is more than negligence or cowardice. It is treason! It is an intentional crime.[567]

The Jura *Bulletin* thought old patterns were being repeated, Mr Sorge's ideal, it wrote, was emerging as 'an International in which every section is to be suspended, in which every [Regional] Federal Council is dissolved, and in which only the General Council remains!'[568]

The centralist US congress of Philadelphia (11-13 April 1874) had resolved to work for reforms: 'The political action of the Federation confines itself generally to the endeavor of obtaining legislative acts in the interest of the working class proper, and always in a manner to distinguish and separate the workingmen's party from all the political parties of the possessing classes.'[569] These legislative acts might involve working for an eight-hour day, accident compensation by employers, an end to child labour, health inspections, and the abolition of indirect taxes. The *Workingman's Advocate* of 11 April 1874 reported New York state legislation prohibiting children under 14 working over 60 hours a week. There was also a strike of cap-makers in New York (mostly German Jews). The centralists decided that their American federation was not to join political or electoral work until it was sufficiently strong to make a significant impact, then it might begin on a local scale. Meanwhile trade-union organising was the priority. Some sections disagreed and withdrew, joining the Social Democratic Workingmen's Party. Many short-lived, radical organisations emerged: co-ops, mutualist networks, Sovereigns of Industry, the United Order of Internationals, regional parties of Labor and Workingmen, the United Workers of America, etc. The Knights of Labor were unusual in having a longer life; they were founded in 1869, built underground especially in craft sectors, and later among coalminers, but only emerged in strength and in public in the 1880s.

Acrimony in the centralist remnant American IWMA resulted in Sorge resigning from the New York Council in August 1874. The *Arbeiter Zeitung* ceased publication in March 1875, and membership fell to around 360, very largely German speakers.[570] On 1 October 1875 diverse socialists and internationalists met in New York in an attempt to build a united organisation. What remained of the General-Council-IWMA in the USA was wound up in 1876 at a conference, when ten delegates came to an exhibition in Philadelphia;[571] some former members joined a new Socialist Labor Party.

Ethnic, social, and international conflicts were becoming ever more acute in these years. The possibility that employers might use imported labour to break strikes had been an important consideration in the decision of English and French workers to create the International Working Men's Association back in the early 1860s. When many workers were journeymen there was always a fear that an employer would use other journeymen to replace strikers. Ethnicity was another key factor. In the USA, there was at least one occasion, in Florida in 1873, when managers sought to use white workers to break a strike of African American lumber workers.[572] In the first half of 1873, employers supported by soldiers brought in African Americans from Virginia, and Italian immigrants from New York, to replace strikers at the coal mines of Ohio and Pennsylvania. Later, when the miners returned to work, the strike-breakers were sacked. There were further strikes at the mines: one bitter seven-month struggle ended in defeat in the summer of 1875. Owners sought to impose pay cuts and hired private Pinkerton 'detectives'. The strikes of the mid-1870s marked a turning point, accentuating awareness of class conflict. Albert Parsons, (later a Haymarket martyr) spread the message that the wage system was 'infamous' and saw hope in the building of a co-operative commonwealth. He worked with the Socialistic Labour Party to build workplace and electoral support.[573] There were some two million people unemployed in 1877, and workers began to emigrate *from* the USA to seek a better life elsewhere. In 1876, a report of starving workers in Montreal inspired this comment:

European workers should stop dreaming of emigration, they will find the same social question everywhere. Twenty years ago, workers hoped that they might create model societies[574] in the New World, based on justice; and that once their practice had been confirmed, their principles would then return to conquer peacefully the old world. Vain hope! Everywhere, the international association of exploiters has forestalled the international of labour. The real struggle is here.[575]

Samuel Gompers thought there were no more than 50,000 organised workers in all the Americas.[576] Labour organising was increasingly difficult. There was some exhaustion, and the diverse socialist organisations went their own way.[577] Much of the American press propagated anti-radical and anti-immigrant messages.

The Jura *Bulletin* had carried a letter in early 1874 addressing conflicts arising from managers employing 'cheap' Chinese slave-workers in the USA. The letter remarked: 'Everyone knows that these Chinese are the most sober-living people in the whole world, if they have a few handfuls of rice, they are the happiest of mortals, they are content to have the most minimal wage and let themselves be led.' The *Bulletin* commented: 'It is not in declaring war on Chinese workers that American workers will escape ruinous competition from them, but in building a solidarity of interests between these two categories of the exploited and in forming a common alliance against exploiters.'[578] There had been instances of Chinese railway construction workers going on strike for equal pay, notably a week-long strike in June 1867, broken when thousands of Chinese workers were starved back to work; and there were reports of them buying weapons for self-defence. There was precious little solidarity between 'white' and Chinese labour. In 1877 the *Bulletin* noted increasing social and political tensions. Property qualifications were put in place and universal male suffrage undermined.[579] In the 1876 elections the Socialistic Labour party demanded – among other things – an end to the [prison] contract labour and legal measures to prevent the Chinese migrating to the USA. The latter was soon passed into law. Samuel Gompers, active in a Cigar Makers Union,[580] had no sympathy for incoming Cubans[581] or the Knights of Labor. He opposed the immigration of Chinese labourers. He was to become a long-time union leader.

'Reconstruction' – the period after the American Civil War in which slavery had been abolished and some reforms begun, ground to a halt in the early 1870s; the election of Rutherford B. Hayes to replace President Ulysses S. Grant in 1877 formalised its ending. Army troops were removed from Louisiana and South Carolina. Segregation and white supremacy were extended and consolidated in the former Confederate states. White supremacy had been gaining ground for some time, implementing measures to prevent African American men from voting, controlling sharecroppers, developing convict labour systems, allowing intimidation and lynching. The sharecropping system encouraged indebtedness and made for a system of 'debt peonage'.[582] Violence was most extreme in the South but was also a fact of life in the North. Developments in the USA may not have been understood in Europe; for example, the Brooks–Baxter War in Arkansas was noted in the Jura *Bulletin* (7 June 1874), but the race and class dynamics involved were not explained. *Volksstaat* of 19 January 1877 carried comments on brutality, race, politics, and the US election, and noted that in Mississippi and South Carolina, the number of African Americans, was a key factor, and that whites sought to manage their vote.

In California and elsewhere many working people turned on Chinese immigrants and argued for their exclusion,[583] so too did some of the IWMA sections aligned with Sorge and his New York council. The attitude of the Colored National Labor Union was complex – it admitted Chinese members, but its 1869 convention opposed servile labour.[584] In contrast, *Woodhull & Claflin's Weekly* (27 December 1873) took another tack: 'we have shown enough to call public attention to the examination of the differences between the world's two grand forms of civilization … we may have much to impart to our Asiatic neighbors, we have also from them much to learn.' Similarly, the Spring Street journal *The Worker*, called for the defence of the Chinese and urged that they be encouraged to join the International.[585] The *New National Era* (Washington, D.C., 3 July 1873), a paper edited by Frederick Douglass, commented that Anglo-Saxons were slave-greedy tyrants who were now targeting Chinese people; it reprinted a proposal from Chinese residents in San Francisco, that if Americans would leave China, the Chinese would leave America. There was an attack on Chinese people in Chico (California) in February 1877 – three men were killed, and houses were burnt. Perpetrators served only short sentences. There were also many attacks on First Peoples. Overall, the groupings that might have supported progress in the USA remained fragmented, and no great coalition emerged. In 1877 an anarchist journal noted the limited success of mass strikes and suggested a lesson: that there was a vicious and egotistical side to trade organisation when its sole goal was defence of wages.[586] A broader agenda was needed, but decades would pass before new winds of change blew.

Marx, Engels, Social Democracy and the G.C. of the I.W.A

The New York General Council's report to the centralist congress (*The World*, 10 September) was published in the *Volksstaat* of 28 September 1873. It remarked on a cigar workers' strike, endorsing the 'spirit of solidarity' and presenting it as evidence that the 'attempt to destroy our organization by playing secession has miserably failed'. 2,000 Dutch cigar workers had sustained a strike in the summer of 1873. Solidarity had indeed flowed, between largely Dutch, English, German and Jewish workers, but it flowed irrespective of any opinion regarding 'secession', and without help from New York. John Hales and other 'secessionist' federalists had facilitated that solidarity and 33,000 guilders were provided by trade unions in London. One historian noted that once the General Council was established in New York, 'there is no record of workers approaching the General Council for help'.[587]

This report sought to inflate the reputation and achievements of New York General Council, taking credit for what others had done, while belittling and attacking enemies. Centralists had drafted proposals for the 1873 congress carefully, focusing on building 'unity' through national and international labour executives.[588] They had spelled out an ambitious scheme to centralise labour, through an alliance of political parties and trade unions, and the New York council had demanded that '[t]he central bodies – as referred to in the preseding [sic] [point] No.2 – shall be brought into [illegible] with the similar central bodies of all other countries through the medium of the G.C. of the I.W.A'.[589] I have seen no evidence that other organisations wanted the General Council to become the medium for international co-ordination. The idea that labour should want to organise through the medium of a General Council, a body that could not even afford postage stamps was ludicrous. It was pretentious for the centralist congress to endorse the creation a hierarchy of committees and leaders, when what links there were, had been developing without input from them.[590] The six or so men who ran the G.C. of the I.W.A. had evidently acquired delusions of grandeur. Honest and respectful foundations were needed: a cycle of meetings open to diverse viewpoints, the building of trust (between organisations and communities), regular exchanges of news and newspapers, mutual financial support, and work to prevent the recruitment of strike-breakers. The exaggeration, bad faith and delusion exhibited by the G.C. of the I.W.A. was an obstruction in the way of the building up of an honest, broad, democratic, and accountable international network.

Volksstaat's report on the Geneva congresses (see appendix five below), asserted that dilletantes at the federalist congress in Geneva merely repeated slogans.[591] It led readers to believe that the General Council had great support and that the federalists were merely a small collection of non-workers. It neither acknowledged that Geneva's centralists had split away, nor that seven federal regions supported federalism. A detailed report was promised, but never came. Bourgeois newspapers provided more detail.

Becker's reports turned to airy philosophy. He wrote: 'The IWMA did not create the Social-Democratic movement, on the contrary, it is a consequence of it'. Readers would have gathered that the IWMA was a party inspired by German Social-Democracy. (A party created in 1869). Becker was concerned not with historical accuracy, but with spinning a national creation myth, to follow on from his invention of congress delegates. He misled *Volksstaat* readers, obscuring that it was workplace organisers who had come together to found the International, back in 1864, and neglecting to mention that no IWMA federation had ever been created in Germany and no regular dues had been paid from there. Also, Becker's resolution on politics, as agreed by the centralist congress,* set out that any politics with a goal of labour emancipation might be supported. This was vagueness itself, leaving it to members in each country to act on a national level, as they thought best.**

The federalist congress was named as a 'Bakuninist' event, although Bakunin himself took no part in it.[592] 'Anarchism' was a term of abuse. Once upon a time, Marx had written that a spectre of communism was haunting Europe.[593] Twenty-five years on, 'Bakuninism' had become a spectre haunting the Social-Democratic party leaders. Whole pages of the *Volksstaat* were devoted to 'Bakuninism' and to the party's own national congress, but the reports on the two Geneva international congresses were philosophical and short.

For Marx, Engels and Sorge, the 1873 centralist congress was a disaster. Participants went their separate ways. The remnants of the Geneva Romande federation became mere adjuncts to bourgeois radicalism. Oberwinder would be repudiated. Remaining General Council supporters fell into further acrimony and isolation. History repeated itself: Marx and Engels had fought critics in London; later Sorge and Bolte and their respective allies fought each other over control of the New York Council.

Marx and Engels had been busy before the September congresses preparing partisan polemics. Their pamphlet *L'Alliance de la démocratie socialiste et l'AIT* (The Alliance of Socialist Democracy and the IWMA) was published just days before the congresses met. One vicious amalgam asserted that federalists had the *secret* aim of subjecting the IWMA 'to the "authoritarianism and dictatorship" of the Alliance and its permanent dictator, "Citizen B", [and] this would have gratified the desires of the European police, who wanted nothing more than to see the International forced to retreat'.[594] Marx and Engels hoped that *L'Alliance* would kill off 'Bakuninists'. The pamphlet was circulated to journalists and was quoted in several papers.[595] The phrases below, culled from the *Northern Whig*, show in what 'light' Bakunin and the Alliance were cast:

> He a native of Russia, and has been accused over and over again, long before the International was heard of, of being a paid emissary of that Power[596] ... In 1866 he was sent Siberia, where he enjoyed *faveurs exceptionelles*[597]

---

*   Page 319ff

**   Advice from any labour organisation framed in one national context might be altruistic, or self-regarding and self-serving. Even if it was well-intentioned, it might be inappropriate in another context.

... In 1861 was furnished with money by the Government of Siberia to make a pretended escape ... In 1868 Bakunin's connection with the International began, and it is said that until he was expelled the Congress of the Hague he has not ceased his intrigues to destroy its influence ... he created a secret junta ... 'Alliance of Socialist Democracy,' the members of which were bound to take their orders[598] from him alone ... divert attention from the fact that he was paid agent of Russia ... directs its blows, against the revolutionists[599] who refuse to trust in his orthodoxy or to obey bis commands. Two of his agents. Albert Richard and Gaspard Blanc, arc debited with the idea of plotting for a Bonapartist reaction to restore Napoleon III[600] ... The pamphlet is published in London by Darson, Oxford-street.[601]

Lies such as these were reprinted in journals in Germany, Switzerland and the USA. In the *Volksstaat,* polemics against Bakunin appeared over several issues, usually as the first substantive article on its front page and taking up to as much as a quarter of the space in an issue.[602] These polemics were part of a long-standing political war;* they sought to persuade readers that the practices of critics from 'backward' countries were disastrous, they prejudiced Social-Democratic circles in Germany, but had less impact elsewhere. They did not kill off 'Bakuninists'. Franz Mehring – an honest Marxist – later commented that the *Alliance* pamphlet was 'not a historical document, but a one-sided indictment whose tendentious character is apparent on every page'.[603] Evidently, it received little interest: Engels had advanced the £32 needed to print it, but his accounts in the year to September 1874, show that he recovered only £4 18s. for his outlay.[604] These were not trivial sums, given that the New York council was unable to afford even postage stamps.

In Germany the 'Marxist' discourse was challenged in *Der Neuer Sozial-Demokrat* (12 September 1873), the paper of the ADAV, the labour union inspired by Lassalle. It expressed the opinion that 'the current [federalist] International congress places itself, so we can see, within the optic of a rigorously democratic labour organisation, which the German General Labour Union [ADAV] endorses'. *Der Neuer* (17 September 1873) commented that Marx had tried 'to undermine it, [the ongoing IWMA] and in doing so used the same manoeuvre that has so often been applied in

---

* Accusations that Bakunin was an agent of the Russian state had first been published in the *Neue Rheinische Zeitung,* 6 July 1848, (edited by Marx). The IWMA congress of 1869 condemned Liebknecht for repeating such slanders; nevertheless, Marx and other Social-Democrats continued to repeat them. Victor Dave, 'Michel Bakounine et Karl Marx', *La Revue anarchiste* (Paris), August and September 1923.

vain against the ADAV, namely that of disparagement and fragmentation'. For *Der Neuer* the centralist congress had been a fiasco. It had met a week late, in contravention of IWMA statutes; some 25-30 'orthodox' delegates attended, but all but five of them lived in Geneva (four newspaper reporters and a fifth man from Stuttgart – a Marxist/ Social-Democrat). Not a single centralist federation was represented. So, '[f]or the so-called orthodox, it amounted to a funeral announcement'. *La Federación,* (Barcelona, 18 October 1873) called the Marxist congress a 'thorough fiasco'.

As the date of the centralist congress approached, Marx and Engels had come to realise that the Geneva internationalists had turned against them. A letter dated 30 August shows them deciding that neither they nor their agents should attend: 'there can be absolutely no question of going to Geneva on account of people like that, people who even refuse to accept mandates from English sections. I think *you would do well to send a counter-order.*'[605] They were not prepared to argue their case in circumstances that gave them no easy majority. They began to cast spin, describing the congress they had helped summon as a mere local event. Afterwards they too called it a 'fiasco'.[606] Marx expressed his private views on events in Geneva in a letter to Sorge on 27 September:

> the Genevans failed in their bid to gain control of the General Council, but they have, as you will be aware, *managed to nullify all the work done since the first Geneva Congress and even to carry through numerous measures running counter to the resolutions adopted there* ... As I view European conditions, it is quite useful to let the formal organisation of the International recede into the background for the time being, but, if possible, *not to relinquish control* of the central point in New York so that no idiots like Perret or ADVENTURERS like Cluseret[607] may seize the leadership and discredit the whole business ... for the rest not to give a jot for the Geneva local decisions, to simply ignore them.

Sorge followed Marx: the minutes sent on from Geneva were said to be in absolute disorder and were disregarded.[608] No official report was published. Although it had been called from New York 'in regular fashion',[609] and not by the Geneva or Swiss IWMA, all its careful international preparation and planning was obscured. The poor congress attendance arose out of choices made by Marx and Engels: they had pushed for the wholesale expulsion of federations (resulting in the poverty of their network), they had pushed for the relocation of the General Council to New York with the very predictable result that a gulf was created between the mass European membership and the leaders on the other side of the Atlantic. For the centralist camp, the most important consequence was the defection of the Geneva centralists. Henri Perret attempted to set up a League of Labour Corporations with contacts in Belgium and elsewhere. Marx now denounced him and his allies as 'idiots'.[610]

In August 1874, Sorge resigned his position as IWMA General Secretary. Engels wrote to him: 'With your resignation the old International is entirely wound up and at an end.' He went on to write: 'I think that the next International – after Marx's writings have had some years of influence – will be directly communist and will openly proclaim our principles.[611] The relocation of the General Council to New York had been motivated in terms of a rising class struggle in the USA with Marx saying he trusted Americans to help guide the IWMA. Now, two years on, Engels made clear that whatever leadership he and Marx exerted had depended on Sorge alone, and once he went, everything was at an end.

The American centralist IWMA was neither guide nor model. Indeed, insofar as it failed to confront the racism that targeted African Americans and the Chinese it was anything but a model. 'America', or rather a handful of German-speaking supporters in New York, mattered when Marx and Engels thought they could be used to maintain influence, but now, two years on, the resignation of one man, Sorge, was enough for them to consider the old International entirely wound up. Their reaction showed how much of the Marx/Engels' leadership depended on particular individuals and just how much the motivation for the relocation of the General Council had been a manoeuvre to maintain their power.

Marx, Engels and their allies had a strategic orientation; they had concluded that rebel uprisings should be avoided. French workmen were advised to do their 'duties as citizens',[612] i.e., co-operate with the incoming French republic, to be wise and calm, and not to rise up, as they had in 1792. Later he highlighted the dangers of 'idiots' like General Cluseret launching adventures. Years later he wrote that with common sense the Communards 'could have reached a compromise with Versailles useful to the whole mass of the people – the only thing that could be reached at the time'.[613] In the early 1870s Marx and Engels were concerned to promote 'legal' and electoral politics with labour working to influence radical bourgeois politicians. Much of the ongoing, federalist International realised that launching uprisings was untimely, but also recognised that circumstances might impel popular revolt; they might indicate new directions, even if they were not perfect socialist models.

Marx and Engels hailed the defeat of Napoleon III as useful because it helped promote 'our theory' (and organisation) as against that of Proudhon.[614] As Germany national unity was achieved, they wrote that inadvertently Bismarck was 'working for *us*'.[615] There was some delusion in this claim – and in other claims – for national* and social progress achieved vicariously. There was also delusion in the claim in respect or influence acquired vicariously through various labour leaders. It was easy to claim that the presence of one or another labour leader at an IWMA conference signified mass support, but most often these claims were misleading. For several years from its foundation leading members of the British trade union movement had co-operated with the IWMA and sat on its General Council. This co-operation was useful to both sides, but it came to an end with the outbreak of the Paris Commune and thereafter these leaders gave no support to the IWMA. Marx acquired some indirect influence working with such people, but no radical base was built up in the British labour movement through this collaboration, and sometime collaborators on the General Council became open enemies of rebelliousness and the IWMA. When this strategy of working with and through British labour leaders failed, Marx and Engels turned to exercising influence through German Social-Democracy and its outpost in New York.

Eccarius, Hales, Malon, Andreas Scheu, (and others), although they endorsed electoral politics, were cast out or termed 'Bakuninists' by Marx and Engels, because they had minds of their own and were not subservient. Critics were termed riff-raff, dupes and traitors. Conversely, turncoats, closet conservatives, and the odd racist nationalist (D'Entraygues, Van Heddeghem, Maltman Barry, Oberwinder), while they disfigured socialism and socialist organisation, were put to use. Marx and Engels pushed for the mass of IWMA members to be expelled, from what they saw as 'their' International, (an instrument *in our hands*). They quite deliberately retained records in their own possession. These practices indicate that Marx and 'General' Engels saw themselves (and appointed themselves and their friends) as commanders in an army waging political warfare, ready to cast off allies, use reactionary forces, insult and attack critics, and propagating lies and myths to establish their leadership and ownership of the labour movement.

As noted above,** James Guillaume had concluded that Marx 'cannot imagine an organisation in which nobody commands, and nobody obeys'. Engels, a former army officer and manager, viewed command as an inevitable

---

* Furthermore, the priority attached to the building of national electoral-political parties facilitated openings for nationalist agendas to trump internationalist commitments.
** See page 53.

function. Guillaume countered with another narrative, he practised mutual respect, (without it progress could not be made) and documented the perverse effects of 'Marxist' activities. There was a fundamental divergence here, both at this time and subsequently, as traditions emerged, libertarians sought to imagine and shape structures without command and subservience. The practices of Marx and Engels, focusing on 'utility' and on objects (people) filling a role, contradicted aspirations that Marx himself had helped to incite, and that had helped inspire the IWMA. Many working people were stirred by thoughts of fashioning freedom through their own organisations, learning from their own experience and directing things for themselves. The belief that the 'right man' should be put in the right place directing things, degraded that participatory aspiration. A letter from Engels to Bebel reveals how key Marxists sought to justify their role:

> ... *our concern* was not to delay the catastrophe but to take care that the International emerged from it *pure and unadulterated* ... if we had come out in a conciliatory way at The Hague, ...
>
> Then the International would indeed have gone to pieces – gone to pieces through 'unity'! Instead of this we have now got rid of the rotten elements with honour to ourselves – the members of the Commune who were present at the last and decisive session say that no session of the Commune left such an extraordinary impression upon them as this session of the tribunal which passed judgment on the traitors to the European proletariat.
>
> Incidentally, old man Hegel said long ago: A party proves itself victorious by splitting and being able to stand the split. The movement of the proletariat necessarily passes through different stages of development; at every stage part of the people get stuck and do not participate in the further advance; and this in itself, is sufficient to explain why the 'solidarity of the proletariat', in fact, everywhere takes the form of different party groupings, which carry on *life-and-death feuds with one another*.[616]

The argument was patently untrue. The supporters of the recent Paris Commune had diverse views. Many looked back to past Jacobin models, but this had not prevented them from supporting that revolt and maintaining a solidarity on their side of the barricade. Various trends had worked together despite differences; there was friction between them, but the life and death struggle was against the reactionary forces of Versailles. Likewise, faced with reactionary Carlist forces in Spain, bourgeois cantonalists and other radicals tended to work together, rather than carrying on life-and-death feuds with one another. 'General' Engels was speaking as a would be director of operations in the Social-Democratic army; seeking to destroy those outside his party, writing off other tendencies as inevitable casualties, in a political war.

Interestingly, just two years earlier the General had taken an opposite tack on unity and solidarity in a letter to Cafiero (1-3 July 1871): 'We know as well as he [Bakunin] does that inheritance is nonsensical, although we differ from him over the importance and appropriateness of presenting its abolition as the deliverance from all evil; and the 'abolition of the state' is an old German philosophical phrase, of which we made much use when we were tender youths. *But to put all these things into our programme would mean alienating an enormous number of our members and dividing rather than uniting the European proletariat.*'[617]

In this 1871 instance Engels was advocating proletarian unity, in 1873 his take on 'unity' implied things 'going to pieces'. Why this apparent change of direction? The first instance concerned the draft General Council resolution (rejected by the Basle congress of 1869) that inheritance should be *taxed*. A congress plurality had agreed with Bakunin and wanted a *ban* on the inheritance of capital.* The idea of banning the inheritance of capital would have affected chiefly Social-Democratic party candidates seeking influence in elections, usually in some form of alliance with liberal or radical parties. For most IWMA members it would have been only a declaration of intent, but for Social-Democratic partisans of electoral politics, any attack on property might impede prospects if liberal allies were antagonised. At one moment, 'unity' was to be built through a set of electoral politics with bourgeois radicals; two years later a 'pure and unadulterated' new start was advanced, *against* a false 'unity'. Evidently in each instance it was party building that was being prioritised, and not unity. Calls for unity might be used to disguise work to promote a particular partisan agenda.

The view that the working class should constitute itself as a single political party, with a universal electoral tactic was at odds with varied circumstances and experiences, and varied perspectives. Ideas-based organisations might come in various forms (an electoral party, a clandestine network, some form of association defined by a programme, a group of close friends). It was natural that there should be diverse views, and thus socialists faced the

---

* In the discussion at the Basle congress radical Proudhonists including Bakunin and his friends, and persons allied with the London General Council all opposed the inheritance of *land*. That measure might alienate landlords, but landlords would never support the IWMA, so this project would have no damaging electoral consequences. It might have had consequences for an alliance between urban labour, and rural peasants, and Bakunin highlighted possible consequences.

task of working to bring some harmony amongst themselves.

Where life-and-death feuds were viewed as a part of normal political life, where persons were purged and where attempts were made to 'beat the traitors out of the field', there were consequences.* Immediately, these acts of war damaged conviviality, reduced participation, and impeded solidarity.

Further consequences might follow: people and organisations subjected to abuse might waste energies if they descended to the level of their attackers and responded to abuse with abuse, in a downward spiral.[618] Smashing and political warfare caused damage among victims. Where 'organisation' and 'politics' was equated with these poisonous norms, radicals might go to opposite extremes and repudiate all forms of organisation and equate all forms of 'politics' with corrupt electoral fraud. Such exaggerated reactions hampered the development of useful participatory forms of organisation and a politics that facilitated social transformation. Fortunately, many radicals (of all sorts) would repudiate feuding, smashing and political warfare. Marx pushed the New York council to expel the mass of IWMA members, but the mass of IWMA members cared not a jot that Marx wanted 'the formal organisation of the International [to] recede into the background'; they carried on, disregarded Marx and his allies, and left them to stew in their sectarian misery.

It was natural that radicals of all sorts should seek to work together effectively without contradicting or undermining each other. But party 'unity' might be or become selfish and/or poisonous: parties involved some layers and repelled others, parties might encompass coalitions of interests, but some goals would be subordinated to others. Party leaders, where parties were formed of hierarchies of committees, were far removed from the grassroots, and they and their committee hierarchies substituted themselves for popular power, and obstructed grassroots participation. 'Pure and unadulterated' parties easily became partisan instruments. The workings of Marx, Engels and their allies were experienced by particular Social-Democrats in Germany, and by Eccarius, Hales and Jung in London, They saw many forms of manipulation: restricting agendas, changing times and dates, preventing unfriendly delegates from taking part in decision-making, fabricating blank credentials to manufacture majorities, fabricating congresses and records, deceiving, insulting, trashing, expelling – and worst of all seeing such behaviour as normal.

After the fiasco in Geneva, Marx and his allies did not dare attempt to organise another international congress. Marx and Engels were perceived as sectarian, egotistical and possessive. Critics recognised 'authoritarianism':

---

* See page 193.

a manipulative 'unity', built on political warfare and 'smashing'; this false-unity disrespected opponents, fostered a poisonous environment and repelled a mass membership. Through such doings Marx and Engels isolated themselves and were shunned. Where endemic 'life-and-death feuds' were taken as normal, there could be little solidarity. Where party-building became a self-serving and all-important activity there was often little energy left over to support social struggles. Ambitious would-be politicians were promising that, if elected, they would be able to reduce social conflict. Through their practices,[619] Marx, Engels, Becker and Sorge damaged labour solidarity in their own times, and bequeathed myths, lies and poisonous party-centric paradigms for the future.

The German-language left

Social-Democratic party leaders took advice from Marx and Engels and published some of their texts. They might pay lip service to the memory of the Commune, but in practice they were often law-abiding and law-respecting, working to influence or obtain reforms through working in existing political systems. Social-Democrat leaders were embarrassed by reports of their linkages to the International, and by claims that they were promoting industrial strife.[620]

The *Volksstaat* of 6 March 1874 denounced Heinrich Oberwinder;[621] naming him as an agent of the Austrian liberal bourgeoisie. The movement in Austria-Hungary had begun to split back in November 1871, when 300 people broke with him. 'This Oberwinder, a Frankfort journalist, had helped to introduce Lassallean Socialism in Austria; after some years, however, he leaned towards the Liberal Party and reduced the once vigorous Socialist movement to a mere suffrage question. At last, the great mass of the Party, headed by Andreas Scheu, rose against this, and Oberwinder's followers were soon reduced to a small and vanishing clique.'[622] Oberwinder and his supporters were ousted from leadership positions at the labour congress at Neudörfl, in April 1874; Germans and Czechs had some encouragement to build distinct networks. However, the period following congress offered no easy opportunities as the economy crashed: party organisations were hit by arrests and the membership of the trade unions all but collapsed. Oberwinder eventually returned to Germany. It became clear that he was a Pan-Germanist, an anti-Semite, and in the pay of Bismarck.[623]

Austria-Hungary and Germany were empires with many ethnic communities, but Oberwinder had focused only on German speakers, while his critic, Andreas Scheu, was more ready to work with the Czech people. In eastern borderlands relations between Germanic and Slav workers were often oppressive and sometimes ugly. In 1873, German was made the language of instruction, even in areas where Polish-speakers were a majority; later, the courts and other state offices were ordered to use only the German language. In Berlin in March 1877, a riot broke out when 'cheap' Silesian and Polish workers were hired to work on building tramways. 'Foreign' workers were sacked and replaced by local workers.[624] The least progressive Social-Democrats, especially the likes of Oberwinder, if they read in *The Communist Manifesto* of 'social scum, that passively rotting mass thrown off by the lowest layers of the old society' or if they read Engels' writing off of un-historic nations, converted such prideful undertones regarding industrial progress in 'civilised' lands, into nationalist and racist thinking. Where some Marxists saw rabble susceptible of becoming 'a bribed tool of reactionary intrigue', readers of Bakunin might have seen some potential progressive rebels. Conversely, where some Marxists saw settled citizen-artisans as good Social-Democrats, readers of Bakunin might have seen complacent liberals and conservatives.

In Germany, the General Labour Union (ADAV) inspired by Lassalle and its rival Social-Democratic party would together win some 350,000 votes (6.7%) in the national elections of January 1874, (men over 25 paying a minimum tax had the vote). Left candidates in Berlin attracted 12,000 votes out of 40,000. In Saxony, the left won 90,000 votes, some from working people, others from the middle classes, as against 50,000 for conservatives and 110,000 for liberals. Johann Jacoby, a veteran democrat allied with the Eisenacher socialists, was elected but refused to take his seat in the *Reichstag*, declaring: 'Being convinced that it is impossible to work through parliamentary means, to transform a military state into a popular state I cannot bring myself to take part in deliberations when I know that these will be useless from the very start.'[625] In March 1874, Johann Most, a Social-Democratic Reichstag deputy, was given a two year prison sentence, one of several arrests that year. Along with the unions of carpenters and masons, the ADAV was banned in Berlin, in March 1875.[626] It had 16,000 to 20,000 supporters. Because unions regulation varied a little from place to place, it moved to Bremen to set up new offices outside Prussia.[627] The persecution of critical editors[628] and workplace activists increased markedly after 1873. 87 members of the Lassalle labour union were imprisoned; their sentences amounted to 212 months.[629]

In the face of this increasing state repression some 25,700 followers of Lassalle and Social-Democrats came together in a merged party, the *Sozialistische Arbeiterpartei Deutschlands* (Socialist Workers Party), in May-June 1875.[630] The new party was united by its hatred of Bismarck and his aristocratic state; it was not so much the party of the industrial proletariat, but more a party for affluent, respectable artisan family men, hoping for progress and influence. Many unskilled and uneducated remained outside the party, and so too did many dependents and non-citizens. It elaborated the 'Gotha' party programme, seeking progress and a free state by any legal means. Marx and Engels felt cut off from this new party. It made male suffrage a key demand.[631] It advocated the development of a co-operative future: 'the establishment of socialist productive cooperatives with state aid under the democratic control of the working people.' It demanded a maximum ten hour working day, an eight hour day for women and workers under 18, and a ban on child labour. Marx sent a critique of this 'Gotha' programme to party leaders – Auer, Bebel, Bracke, Geib and Liebknecht – but they decided not to publish it.[632] Bebel wrote that Marx's tone was regrettable, reeking of 'personal hatred and jealousy'. Marx and Engels, although they disagreed sharply with the Gotha programme, did not publish their critique at this time. (The merger of the two left labour currents in Germany encouraged Austrian co-thinkers to reject action outside the law; in the USA, the German left gradually came together to build a party, the remnant IWMA was dissolved, and supporters moved on to merge with other groups and create a new Workingmen's Party).[633]

Marx's criticism had focused on the failure of the party to mention its aspirations for social transformation. He advocated the use of the word *Gemeinwesen* (commonwealth, commune) to indicate that aspiration. Marx wrote: 'That the workers desire to establish the conditions for co-operative production on a social scale, and first of all on a national scale, in their own country, only means that they are working to revolutionise the present conditions of production, and it has nothing in common with the foundation of co-operative societies with state aid.' This criticism challenged aspects of the Gotha programme but had little to say about the party's everyday practice and activity. Having made such remarks in private to his party, Marx was satisfied that he had done his duty and saved his soul.[634]

There were critics who thought that this party could not be saved, and that its praxis was destructive to socialist progress. In 1877, one critical journal suggested that the party had become a farm – for domesticated animals. Parliamentary action was the dominant theme: 'Electoral agitation, which at first was put forward as a means, has become today the sole goal of the party.' The presence of a few members in parliament did nothing to prevent workers' misery or stop the use of the military against them. 'It was dupery or criminal to lead the working masses on to the terrain of legal reforms.'

'Evidently the party of agitation and socialist propaganda limits itself to electoral propaganda; the labouring masses, blinded by the activity of their leaders, places its confidence in parliamentarianism, little by little forgetting its programme and demands.' Critics noted: 'the constant recommendation of these leaders is "slow march, step by step, patience".' The party rank and file were told to trust leaders and not encouraged to build their own capacity; for them it was all sterility and powerlessness.[635]

Some unions had been close to the Lassalle ADAV, others to the Social-Democrats. Before the two parties merged there had been some conflict between rival workplace bodies; after the party merger it took some time to unify unions with different traditions into a 'Free' union network, facing other labour networks of catholic and Hirsch-Duncker unions. These 'free' unions were sometimes described as a party pre-school. In repressive conditions most unions focused on basics and showed little interest in transforming production. Unions were stronger among skilled workers and artisans, leaving peasants aside. Large employers, such as the Krupp metal and armaments firm, worked hard to exclude unions and many industrial workers were unorganised. *The Times* reported that workplace organisers might repudiate the name of the International, because its very name was enough to frighten off patriotic workers.[636] *Le Travailleur* (May 1877) perceived a growing labour bureaucracy that impeded progress and fostered a largely passive membership. The economic recession reduced earnings and increased hours. Strike activity declined hugely. There were 352 strikes in the peak year of 1872, 88 in 1875, and a low point of 15 was reached in 1879.[637] Education was a factor credited with a capacity to avert conflict; so much so that 'in Germany strikes are rare', declared the *Huddersfield Chronicle* (4 November 1874). Unions strove to maintain a law-abiding political neutrality but might be treated as criminal organisations if they refused to hand over membership lists to the police. Bismarck attempted to introduce stronger breach-of-contract legislation, and, although this was not passed at first, many unions were effectively banned. In 1877 membership of the 'free' unions was around 50,000. Government repression hardened in 1878 and a ban was introduced against strike funds and benefits. Labour maintained some cohesion, however, not so much through national structures, but rather through informal local meetings and educational networks. Both the papers of the federalists, and the leading Social-Democratic journal *Volksstaat* carried notes on fund-raising to support strikers. There were frequent allusions to 'international' trades organisations in the German Social-Democratic press, but most often congress locations and organisations were in German-speaking areas.

The new *Sozialistische Arbeiterpartei Deutschlands* received friendly greetings from the Jura Federation. Bebel spoke in favour of contact with all sorts of socialists.[638] Nevertheless, libertarians criticised editors and leaders; they saw the goals and methods of the new party as aiming at little more than a reprise of the Jacobin constitution of 1793, with an agenda that was more bourgeois than socialist. Years later, in 1896, Wilhelm Liebknecht would argue, against anarchists, that some centralising force was necessary and had been directed by legislative assemblies (in the English civil war, with the execution of Charles I, and in the great French revolution).[639] Liebknecht was looking forward then to a 'democratic' parliamentary revolution in Germany, one that would sweep away anachronistic, feudalistic and Prussian forms of government, not one focusing on a socialist and social agenda for change. Libertarians hoped for a more explicit grassroots focus, and hoped that, in time, the new party might catch up with the federalism and socialism[640] – a forlorn hope, as later events would show. Over the coming decades the Social-Democrats' option for electoral politics appeared to be validated as the party won votes in larger and larger numbers. Already, it had sufficient income to finance eight full-timers and numerous others on an occasional basis. In the view of Diego Abad de Santillán, Social-Democracy had always been 'an appetising field for the aspiring living at the expense of workers' misery'.[641]

August Bebel, in his autobiography *My Life*, left a record of his electoral and parliamentary perspectives. He commented:

> The proletariat increases more rapidly than any army can be increased; and as an army increases, its Social Democratic elements also increase, all the more rapidly as the industrial proletariat furnishes an ever-larger proportion ...
>
> We know that our time approaches, that circumstances are developing in our favour, that with the disappearance of class antagonism, and the disappearance of the lower middle classes, who are being thrust downward into the ranks of wage earners, Social-Democracy will grow ever stronger, and will finally lay hands upon the supreme power.[642]

This outlook appeared to suggest that, gradually and inexorably, the state and its army would be transformed as proletarian numbers increased. Circumstances would ripen passively with the passage of time. For the time being the party would say that state reforms were insufficiently radical and would oppose them, but that opposition was tactical, momentary and opportunist and not a matter of principle – the party was playing the parliamentary game, even if it opposed Bismarck. The party leadership prioritised winning more votes and feared radicals who might threaten party unity if they acted prematurely and/or beyond the law. Critics noted that party editors and leaders disrespected ordinary party members. It had been a habit in meetings to have a question box so that the audience might ask questions anonymously, however some embarrassing questions came to be asked, and it was then decided that only signed questions would be taken.[643] Party authorities took measures to intimidate critics, going so far as to highlight the non-resident status of foreign critics to the police. Dissident activists, notably Johann Most, would be expelled from the party. Such behaviour, suggested critics, was controlling, and augured nothing good if ever such leaders achieved state power.[644] Furthermore, the ongoing practice of centralist discipline created a feedback loop: the grassroots were discouraged from thinking and acting for themselves.

Some nationalist colouring emerged along with the sentiment that German labour was 'better' organised than elsewhere. The view that Bismarck was working for 'us' in creating a centralised greater German state has been mentioned above. Leading Social-Democrats looked on their nation as a bulwark against reactionary Russian autocracy. There was a greater-Germanic twist to this 'internationalism';[645] it was somewhat disdainful of other peoples, and particularly of 'uncivilised' and Slav peoples.[646] Elsewhere, and among libertarian critics especially, expansionist Germany was seen as the leading reactionary power in Europe.[647]

The *Volksstaat*

The *Volksstaat*, the journal of the Social-Democratic Workers' Party, was published in Leipzig, but listed addresses in Hoboken (New York), and Chicago and quoted rates for posting to various destinations; it was said to have had 2,000 subscribers in 1870. It advertised London's German IWMA section at 81 Blue Post Newman street, Oxford street, and its secretary Friedrich Lessner (20 August 1873); also the IWMA New York first section, at 10 Ward Hotel, corner of Brooms and Forsyth Street, and in Paris the Café-Brasserie Suisse, at 35 rue de l'Arbre, a place where the *Volksstaat* could be read, and which offered food at all prices. *Volksstaat* offered texts to purchase: two by Bebel, four by Engels, twenty-four by Lassalle, four by Liebknecht, three by Marx, the IWMA statutes, etc.

Much of the *Volksstaat*'s space was dedicated to political overviews and comments on developments in Germany. It responded to criticisms from other papers in detail and published political analyses and polemics. Against political opponents its style was bitter; for example, it concluded its polemical texts against Bakunin (on 26 September 1873) with a reference to his 1870 text *K oficeram russkoj armii* (mentioned above) and writing that his demand for discipline was 'the only point on which Bakunin had not lied'. Such bitter belligerence served to demarcate respectable and legal electoral politics from outlaws and rebels. The paper proclaimed its support for *Internationalen Gewerksgenossenschaften* (International labour associations) on its masthead and carried occasional texts on labour outside Germany: notes on developments in Belgium (labour conflicts), Brazil (slavery), France (war records), Vienna (conflicts between Oberwinder and Scheu), Switzerland (the Gotthard strike), the UK (lockouts) and New York (noting the lack of work there). Information and notices about workplace organisations might also be found in every edition.

The tone of the *Volksstaat* report on the eighth IWMA congress in Bern in 1876 was factual rather than insulting. It was entirely different to the tone adopted by Becker in 1873, perhaps because the remnant centralist IWMA had been dissolved leaving only the federalists' International as a pole for 'German Internationalists'. The report noted a call for a congress to meet in 1877, open to all socialist trends. It recognised 'comrade Malatesta' and noted that state brutality necessitated secret forms of organisation – 'peaceful, legal tactics were quite impossible'. Differences remained, but they were not so great.[648] At this moment tactical diversity appeared to be back on the Social-Democratic agenda.

The ongoing IWMA

Shortly after the end of the 1873 congress, Bakunin sent a letter to the Jura Federation asking it to accept his resignation, due to age and ill-health:

> ... you have re-set the great IWMA on its way ... Your congress, a congress of freedom, brought together delegates of all the principal European federations, other than Germany. It loudly proclaimed and fully established, or rather confirmed, the autonomy and fraternal solidarity of workers of every land. The authoritarian, or Marxist congress, composed only of Germans and Swiss workers, who appear to have no respect for liberty, vainly tried to patch up Mr Marx's now ridiculous and broken dictatorship ... they ended up with a hybrid plant, one that no longer has untrammelled authority, as dreamed up by Mr Marx,[649] but one that still lacks freedom, and they parted, feeling discouraged and discontented both with themselves, and with others. Their congress was a funeral ... So, dear comrades, I retire full of respect for you, and fully sympathetic to your great and saintly cause – the cause of humanity. I will continue

to follow your every step with fraternal concern, I will salute your every new success. Until death, I am yours.[650]

Bakunin cast a note of caution for the future: the federalist congress may have been a success, but European working peoples were profoundly divided. The potential for international labour solidarity was much in doubt, given German Social-Democrats' espousal of legal and electoral politics and bitter hatred of non-electoral politics. Solidarity – as in an acceptance of diversity, and respect for varied tactics and ethnicities – had been gravely undermined and Labour Movement coherence, such as it was, had been further degraded. Those who continued to promote the International through a broad-based congress offered a different model of organising and, at best, disagreed in more respectful ways.

Bakunin himself pursued two courses of action. He announced his withdrawal from politics and told the *Journal de Genève* that henceforth he would 'bother no one'. He also took advantage of money provided by Carlo Cafiero to buy a villa 'La Baronata', near Locarno. Land ownership might give him some legal protection against the threat of deportation back to Russia. Residents at the villa divided up everyday tasks more or less equally, with men working more outdoors in gardens and women more indoors. It was intended that the villa would serve as a refuge for internationalists. Bakunin participated in discussions with Cafiero, Andrea Costa, Malatesta, Francesco Pezzi and Giovanni Zirardini, with a view to organising a rising in northern Italy.

For James Guillaume, the outcome of the two congresses must have afforded him great satisfaction.[651] Along with Bakunin, he had been expelled by the gerrymandered congress at The Hague; now, a year later, seven federations had repudiated that decision. Bakunin may have inspired some delegates, but it was Guillaume who developed a more practical course. He and the Jura Federation worked for co-operation with the other regional federations, including federations in the UK and the USA which were more open to electoral party politics. While they disagreed with electoral party politics they tried to avoid antagonism.[652] Guillaume urged for recognition where 'adversaries do something good', as against the view, often propounded in the Social-Democratic press, that enemies were bad through and through. This broad policy – determined but respectful – would prevail over the next few years at the IWMA congresses held in Brussels in 1874,[653] and Bern in 1876. In quiet times advocates of radical transformation might seek to avoid wasting human resources, to reflect on past shortcomings, and to think through better ways of doing things.

The federalists had shown caution in their discussion of the general strike. A set of libertarian politics was emerging, but it did so in a period in which energies were declining. Setbacks in Spain and Italy might be used to suggest that all non-parliamentary left activity was ill-fated and misconceived, and for lack of anything better, socialists should prefer electoral politics. Elisée Reclus, a member of the Vevey IWMA, wrote to Bakunin in April 1875: on one level he was no longer confident in the inevitability of progress – we may be beaten because we have only a weak spirit of cohesion, whims but not resolve. On another level he was more hopeful: 'what reassures me is the scientific movement in these times' (e.g., in sociology and Darwin's ideas of evolution). 'I do not say, like some sort of apostle, that the "truth will make us free", but it will get us at least half-way there'.[654] Bakunin concluded that for the time being 'revolution' had gone to bed.[655] He tried to think through key problems in working for socialism in countries where there was some freedom to speak and organise. He looked at ways to encourage participation (in some forums chatting, a restraint on formality and speech-making), preventing insider committee men lording it over outsiders; he advocated involving the mass of working people (women, peasants, the urban 'rabble' as against restricting activity and limiting it to certain urban, skilled, semi-bourgeois citizenry). He looked for methods of organisation fit for the socialist purpose, for preparations and finding ways to act promptly when momentous moments arrived, developing the IWMA and bodies of intimate friends who might find means and strategies, undermining armed forces, building a general staff for the people-as-an-army, empowering persuasive 'generals'* who could negotiate mass social 'squalls', ensuring that these generals (or other experts) should retire, and crucially countering the drastic effects of 'leave-it-to-us' professional politicians whose hierarchical norms and strategies inhibited change. And he did all this although he was sick, aged, and beset by family and monetary problems. He died in 1876.

An Anarchist International? A new International?

Did the federalist congress make a new start and was a new, 'Anarchist International' founded in 1873? The federalist delegates stressed continuity and did not see themselves starting a new International. For them it was the sixth congress of IWMA that met, not the first congress of a new International. They rejected any change of title for the IWMA and maintained the considering preamble clauses to its statutes almost word for word, in the form approved by the first IWMA congress.[656] Guillaume worked hard to

* See below p. 290.

win over IWMA members in the UK, Belgium, the Netherlands and the USA, where federations did not embrace the more libertarian perspectives that prevailed in Italy, the Jura and Spain – and won Bakunin to that approach.

Federalist forms of organisation sought to socialise decision-making, to rotate leadership and to prevent the consolidation of managerial power.[657] The IWMA statutes were clarified, the autonomy of sections and federations was asserted, and the General Council abolished. If some changes were made, this did not, in the view of most internationalists, amount to the creation of a new, distinct International. Federalists observed that, once again, many centralist delegates had not been appointed in democratic fashion and did not report back to sections.[658] The federalist congress avoided such abuses and reaffirmed the International's pluralist identity. The ongoing, federalist International breathed through its press, through its series of congresses, and through discussions and report-backs before and after congresses. FRE delegates, for example, had 500 copies of a *Memoria* to help report about the Geneva congress, and local bodies were invited to comment. The federalist congress delegates were realists; they neither pretended that their congress was perfect, nor wanted to legislate and impose views on others.

Marx and Engels had recognised the role of the IWMA press and, as noted above, had attempted to muzzle it in 1871. They feared and accused Bakunin of controlling several papers and were all too aware that they themselves had no such influence. Their 'leadership' was conducted largely through private communications to their friends and allies, and through press releases sent to the bourgeois press. In that respect the General Council was relatively impotent, as compared with the diffuse leadership of the IWMA in continental Europe, articulated through an IWMA press.

The IWMA lived on without Marx and Engels. Sections and federations worked to support each other when strikes broke out, journals spread news and discussions,[659] networks met in congresses, the anniversary of the Commune was celebrated. It was a period of economic crisis, and if the ongoing IWMA and labour struggles did not prosper greatly, it was largely because this crisis, coupled with repression, weakened labour and grassroots organisation of all sorts, and obstructed progress, and not because the ongoing IWMA suffered through the lack of the Marx/Engels leadership. Marx had argued that without the General Council 'the International would be nothing but a confused, disjointed "amorphous" mass,' but things did not turn out so in September 1873. It was the federalists who brought real delegates to their congress, while about half the delegates at the centralist event were fakes.

The federalist IWMA congress of 1873 was not an anarchist event. This is shown most clearly by the fact that federations in the UK and USA supported forms of electoral politics. Libertarians did not attempt to cajole them into withdrawing from electoral activity. The congress functioned democratically, discussing experiences, exchanging views, and respecting the IWMA precepts of truth, justice and morality.[660] Furthermore, it was often the practice of the ongoing IWMA to attempt some conciliation with other socialists and internationalists, through inviting them to be observers at IWMA congresses and events. Anarchism was defined by some delegates not as disorder, but rather as 'organised order'.[661] Many members focused on building an organisational base around the workplace. Journalists might portray Italian and Spanish delegates and French refugees as 'pure anarchists', suggesting that after doing away with the General Council, they would go on to destroy every regional and local executive commission,[662] but this expectation was not fulfilled. There was nothing chaotic about the federalist congress.

The ongoing federalist IWMA did contain many members with a broad libertarian and anti-parliamentary identity – and it had seeds of syndicalism and anarchism, but it contained a variety of other seeds as well, including people who rejected 'anarchism' outright. The events of 1873 did not amount to a re-making of the ongoing federalist IWMA as an Anarchist International. Indeed, many delegates called themselves federalists, or revolutionary socialists, rather than 'anarchists' and this would be the case for some years to come.[663] Many former members of the Paris Commune were working with the federalists. They found in the ongoing federalist IWMA practices that chimed with their experience. Real solidarity persisted, as reports above showed; it flowed from workplace to workplace, federalists raised funds for strikers of all persuasions. Centralists may have practiced solidarity within their own circles, but there are few records of that solidarity going further. Libertarians stressed workplace solidarity: 'the greater unity of the International is founded, not on the artificial and always maladroit organisation of some centralising power, but rather, on the one hand on the real identity of the aspirations and interests of the proletariat of every land, and on the other hand on the absolutely free federal networking of the free sections and federations of every land.'[664] Adhémar Schwitzguébel was to write:

The interests of the masses can be safeguarded, determined, and discussed only by the masses themselves, not by masses in a chaotic state in the confused shape of a plebiscite; but rather by the masses returned to themselves, networked together in autonomous groups; groups that understand their own needs, knowing well what they want, contracting with neighbouring groups, forming free federations of communes, within which, without the intervention of any official tutor, working people will themselves construct safeguards for their collective and individual interests.[665]

For libertarians, socialism made progress when working peoples developed their own capacity; that capacity was built largely through workplace organising and solidarity,[666] but also through education, discussion, publishing, and local organising – work sometimes carried out by groups of freethinkers, and/or by local propaganda sections of the IWMA. The rebel Paris Commune suggested signposts for many radicals, and sketched aspects of grassroots democracy that might be filled out and developed. It was an inspiration worldwide, helping to spark building of capacity at the grassroots. The organising of a socialist future was to be prefigured in current practice where possible. Decision-making might be facilitated by a congress, but matters were to be aired in grassroots bodies before and after a congress, and grassroots bodies might endorse or reject congress resolutions. Partisans of electoral politics wrote off such thinking as impractical and 'utopian'.

As noted above, the General Council was abolished by the federalist congress, and the system of voting at international congresses was changed. In the past the complexion of each congress was affected by its location. The General Council had planned a congress in Mainz in 1870. The location of the fifth congress at The Hague was then chosen to make it easy for delegates from Britain and Germany to attend, while it was much further and more costly for delegates from southern Europe to come. The federalists' decision to have voting by federation had the effect of preventing the undue weight of nearby sections. It also prevented a central authority fabricating a congress majority for itself through faking mandates or choosing an advantageous location.

Centralists presented devolution as disorganisation. Some Social-Democratic politicians viewed devolution and grassroots responsibility as anarchy. In their discourse, the labels 'anarchist', or 'Bakuninist' were used to mobilise the 'us', against 'them' ('disorganisers'). They sought to define a project subservient to the law, hence the party paid no dues to the International. Their internationalism was a largely ethereal project, in contrast to the practice of the great majority of internationalists who affiliated and paid dues, whatever the law might have to say.

In the early 1870s, and for the most radical, politically conscious persons in and around the IWMA, rather than the terms 'anarchism' and 'Marxism', the appropriate antinomies were federalist internationalism as against Social-Democracy, and respect for rebelliousness as against deference to the state and the law. Bakunin and Marx both bequeathed texts that would have some influence in defining the shape of ideas-based organisations in later years, but in 1873 their influence was limited. In the later 1870s and after, some federalists gradually adopted forms of anarchism. Bakunin worked on programmes for diverse ideas-based bodies on many occasions, but he thought programmes would differ, and that there might be as many ideas-based organisations as there were programmes. He once couched his thinking on leadership in these terms:

> What we all want is living unity, one that is really powerful, one that is created by freedom, through free expression, *in lively diversity*; expressing itself in struggles, as every living force looks for harmony and equilibrium. I can understand how a General of a regular army division adores the deathly silence that discipline imposes on a crowd. Your Generals, our Generals, the people's Generals have no need or the silence of slavery; being used to living and leading in the midst of squalls they are never so tall as when they face those squalls. Popular life, as it loses its shackles, is punctuated by squalls – only they can blow away the established world of inequality.[667]

Federalism and Centralism

The congress of the first of September had recognised that the component parts of the IWMA should be autonomous, with each one deciding a path for itself, but united by bonds of mutual solidarity. Congresses might act as sounding boards and federations might learn from each other,* but no attempt would be made to legislate one policy on all. The form of organisation agreed was described as a contract between federations, a contract that was voluntary. Discipline was self-imposed. When a body supported a policy, it was expected to do so in practice and not just in words.[668] This was not anarchic dis-organisation, but federalist organisation, working through differences of opinion, towards consensus and united action. Matters of principle might be debated but would not be subjects for legislation. Any part might suggest a policy or perspective, but no part – not even the congress or Federal bureau – could tell other parts what to do. Cohesion

* See for example, the resolution adopted on 5th September, that the IWMA should consider experience in Spain, it proposed, but did not insist.

depended on collective agreement and that could not be legislated.

Federalists sought to restore and practice respectful procedures and processes in fashioning priorities and perspectives. In 1873 and 1874 they discussed the role of a general strike and attitudes to state-provided services (the post, railways, etc.). The federalist IWMA congresses *hosted* discussions on such controversial matters but avoided *legislating* an international policy. They promoted international congresses as meeting places for solidarity and discussion.[669]

As regards organisational and administrative matters, a key decision concerned how the federalist IWMA was to be run. As for administrative matters, the congress rejected both voting by a head count of delegates present, at a congress, and a proposal for a 'card vote', with votes weighted in proportion to the number of IWMA members represented by a particular delegate. The London *Daily News* (6 September 1873) commented that had such a system been adopted, the Spanish Federation with its 36,000 members, would have swamped all the others. Delegates chose instead a voting system allowing one vote for each IWMA federation. This was seen not as a perfect system, but as the one that had the fewest inconveniences, with a corollary that should be as little voting as possible to minimise these defects.

Another less obvious change concerned the rights of the co-ordinators of the IWMA. The General Council had exercised its rights to appoint several delegates for the congress of The Hague. The effect of this and other procedures was that 21 of the 65 congress delegates were members of the General Council. In contrast, the federalist IWMA gave no rights at all to its Federal Bureau, and that bureau could neither appoint its own IWMA congress delegates, nor 'pack' a congress. Leaders might emerge – in all sorts of organisations – but federalists stressed responsibility to the grassroots, reacting against manoeuvres that promoted central authority. For federalists, the grassroots were key; for Marx it was the reverse, and the General Council must have its 'prerogatives'.

Many delegates at the centralist congress had also been unhappy about the excessive power of the General Council; it resolved to greatly reduce its powers – but to no effect – as that New York council decided to not publish its resolutions, disregarded them, and affirmed that resolutions of The Hague congress should remain binding. The Jura *Bulletin* noted that the US centralists' congress of April 1874 had resolved to call an international IWMA congress for 1875, with a venue not in Zurich, as decided by the centralists' Geneva congress, but rather somewhere in England. It commented: 'A fine example of what is called cavalier action. Mr Sorge, on his own authority annuls the acts of *his own* congress of Geneva and declares that he will continue to act on those from The Hague. Is he having a laugh at the expense of his own people?'[670] (Sorge wrote that he and his friends carried on to prevent things falling into 'unworthy hands'.)[671] The centralists' general congress, slated to meet in Zurich (and then in England) in 1875, never met.

The General Council, in its report to the Geneva congress of 1873, (see texts from *The World* and *La Liberté* above), had highlighted centralisation and suggested that if their 'lessons' were not learnt repeated disasters were bound to follow, implying that central leadership was the only alternative to 'disorganisation'. This form of politics was perhaps binary and vertical: vertical in that central authorities decided policy and corrected those who strayed; binary in that the 'sensible' policy of the leadership was counterposed to another less rational or irrational policy, implying that there was only one sensible choice. Bebel did not see things in a top-down light: he once wrote: 'The party does not exist for the leader, but the leader for the party.' A leader might be deposed if he strayed.[672] Federalists chose not disorganisation but accountable, co-ordinated, contractual organisation; respecting the fact that conditions differed from place to place. They sought to socialise leadership rather than choosing leaders. The federalist delegates wanted to prevent an executive or General Council exercising power; they discussed methods of preventing authority and the power of individuals – showing incidentally that there were different views among them on the meaning of such terms as anarchy, collectivism, and individualism.[673] Solidarity was key in federalist organising, it was the energy exciting a mass organisation such as the IWMA. It operated in the workplace and community and from one workplace and community to another; it was the glue that balanced diversity and autonomy. Solidarity was not to be taken for granted,* nor decreed, but had to be discussed, understood, agreed, motivated, defended, expanded and revived after setbacks.

Federalism implied a respect for responsible democratic practices, the responsibility of regional federations to their own members, regional autonomy,[674] and voluntary contractual relations between federations. Federalist organisation was described thus: 'a *contract* is an engagement which only links contracting parties; *law* is the will of a few imposing itself on all.'** For federalists, decision-making was to be a process: formally

---

* Note the caveat expressed above by the Spring Street federation: 'It must be clearly understood ... [See page 111]

** See comments by Verrycken in the tenth session of the congress on the nature of contracts between federalists.

speaking this would come from a chain; through regional discussions, regional delegates being appointed, General Congress discussions, reporting back and lastly ratification of General Congress decisions by regional congresses and sections. Informally, opinions might be shaped through the press – especially IWMA journals.

The federalists set up a bureau to facilitate communication on an international scale, but they gave it no powers. Federations might contact each other directly; exchanges of journals and letters went back and forth between them. One might describe the IWMA as largely a horizontal network. The IWMA's (international) Federal Bureau was not set in one place permanently and was tasked with co-ordination and gathering the agenda for international congresses. The Jura federation came to this conclusion:

So, the question now dividing the International may be resumed in two projects: federalism or centralism. Two projects for social renovation are present: one conceives of future society in the form of *a centralised popular state* (a *Volksstaat*); the other defines it on the contrary as *a free federation of freely associated agricultural and industrial associations*. These two programmes are mutually exclusive, [but] are perhaps destined to be achieved in the future, side by side, in different regions; but as for the International, that is to say, an actual grouping of labour societies, the latter can exist only on the basis of federative principles. Centralism will kill it; federalism will save it.[675]

The Jura federation may have hoped that solidarity was growing and spreading, but if so, that hope was not so well founded: economic and political conditions were such that solidarity did not grow so much, or so easily, and without that glue, the international was in peril however it was organised. Federalist organisations were resilient but were subject to outside pressures.

Consequences

What, in the world of labour, were the consequences of the 1873 events?

The largest labour body of the era, the British labour movement, represented by influential trade union leaders and labour and radical newspaper editors, saw little in continental Europe to attract them towards re-affiliating and supporting the International. Trades councils might support counterparts when strikes occurred, but the level of institutional support for an International of Labour, as enjoyed back in 1864, was no longer on the cards. Social-Democracy had never given much thought or support to the International. Federalist insurrectionaries were weak; radical syndicalism might perhaps have been glimpsed but had not yet taken solid shape. Circumstances such as these provided poor material for strengthening a labour International.

An electoral coalition of sorts was built up in Germany. The left won 350,000 votes in January 1874, and Engels asserted that this had 'placed the German proletariat at the head of the European workers' movement'.[676] Most federalists would have disagreed. In terms of party-building and winning votes, Social-Democracy was certainly prominent, but was it advancing the end goals of the IWMA? The party programme* was challenging aspects of a feudal state and pursuing democratic reforms. But there was little if any socialism in these demands, and little everyday socialist organising. Workplace union organising in Germany was divided between liberal, Catholic, and 'free' networks. These bodies were growing weaker, strike activity was in decline, and the space for public political debate was diminishing. German states were hardening the application of combination laws. In other countries workers' unions joined the International despite state repression, but this was not so in Germany, even among the 'free' union networks. Labour made progress where there was strength, determination, will, numbers and capacity, in the workplace and in grassroots, social and cultural organisations.[677] Measured thus, the organisation of labour in Germany was not so strong, and the accumulation of votes was a symptom of a weak and shackled labour movement taking to the electoral urns as an easier option. Other channels of protest were illegal, and few were ready to defy the state. Moreover, party-building and vote winning activities were already becoming priorities in themselves. Social-Democracy in Germany pursued a distinct path, publishing some Marxist texts and paying lip service to 'internationalism', but prioritising a national agenda and remote parliamentary structures.

Among working people (of all shades of opinion), there was a common desire for shorter working hours, better pay and better lives. All might have agreed with a sentence penned by Marx: 'that hitherto all struggles have failed, for want of solidarity between workers of various trades within each country, and for the lack of fraternal unity between the workers.' But clearly there were disagreements as to how unity and solidarity were to be built, about the scope of a progressive agenda (short-term or long-term), as regards gender equality, respect for all ethnicities and peoples, about the focal points and places where labour should organise, and

* See page 282.

about organisations' forms and methods. Federalists and libertarians were expressing doubts on the likely destination of Social-Democracy: their experience led them to believe that although Social-Democracy might be Jacobin and collectivist, it was not socialist; layers of officials would be empowered, rather than the grassroots.* All internationalists aspired to build socialism, but the programme of German Social-Democracy excited little enthusiasm in other industrial countries. Social-Democratic demands were somewhat progressive, in relation to the militaristic German state, or other autocratic states, but they were not so progressive in relation to countries where feudalism had been partially or wholly eliminated (Britain, France, Switzerland, or the USA), where anti-capitalist and socialist demands were being developed – to that extent the claim that the German proletariat was 'at the head of the European workers' movement' was inept.

Many German radicals and Social-Democrats unhappy with their party emigrated. Johann Most and Wilhelm Hasselmann moved over to work with libertarians and federalists in the USA. They were unable to change the course of Social-Democracy, either there or back home. The narrow perspectives that characterised much of the German American left persisted and were fed back to the homeland. For example, in 1891-92 Friedrich Sorge reviewed the story of the German labour in the USA and its role managing the centralist IWMA, for the *Neue Zeit*, the theoretical organ of the German Social-Democratic Party. He disregarded the racial oppression of African Americans and Chinese workers and located campaigners for women's suffrage among a petty bourgeoisie which had 'a chaotic effect on the discussion of social questions'.[678]

Conflicting viewpoints – Social-Democracy/'Marxism' as against Federalism/'Anarchism' – were shaping rather different forms of solidarity. The 1873 IWMA federalist congress was a forum working to build solidarity and participatory politics. Its conduct conveyed a message: one could disagree respectfully. Critics were allowed to speak and were countered by reason and argument. Delegates' credentials were checked on 1 September 1873, but these checks resulted in the exclusion of only one man, a police spy. At The Hague in 1872, checking credentials took two and a half days: the heart of that congress had been the effort to construct a majority, attempting to beat, silence and/or exclude IWMA 'enemies'.[679] The construction of parties changed the overall shape of Labour, but they were neither a substitute for the International, nor a new stage of development emanating out of the

---

* Libertarians feared the practice of cohabitation with capitalism and the building of alliances (of sorts) with radical liberals but could not know how long such practices would endure, or what effects they might bring over time.

International.

In Germany, the International had never had a substantial membership. New national electoral-party organisations did not emerge from or replace substantial organisations working through the International. Rather, the development of electoral party organisations was an alternative path. National electoral parties did not usher in a dynamic, new era of labour organising. What began, and what was expressed in the hundreds of thousands of votes garnered by German Social-Democracy, was something of limited scope, in limited arenas, with a limited agenda, something quite uninspiring for much of the ongoing International.

Tens of thousands of IWMA members went on organising without them, encouraged by the growth of the International's organisations in Italy and Spain. The ongoing IWMA sought to encourage solidarity, most crucially in workplace disputes, over and above differences in political perspectives. Federalists sought to create a convivial atmosphere at their congress. Delegates recognised that no one line could be appropriate for the varied circumstances. Federations and sections would deal with disputes and set priorities; no international forum could properly understand and judge local and regional conditions. In the final analysis, it was the sections that might respect and implement insights developed in IWMA congresses, and no leadership, party executive, congress, or General Council, could (or should) force sections to act against their will.

Leaders in the Jura federation appeared to believe that effective solidarity was a complex, multifarious, and demanding process, requiring mass action on multiple fronts and patient dialogue to help build tolerance, support and coalitions. A precondition for broad coalitions for change was that mutual respect should be encouraged between various tendencies and organisations. Solidarity was easier to find in the workplace, but less easy in the realm of ideas.

At the congresses of the ongoing IWMA, up to Bern in 1876, and in their journalism, federalists strove to reforge convivial norms to sustain the ongoing International, building firm but respectful policies, at best seeking to broaden the impact of a progressive labour movement. Federalists sought to build open and horizontal structures for international decision-making. Such structures were fractious, but friction was inevitable given varied circumstances.[680] Libertarians had leadership of a sort – one that strived to facilitate decision-making through respecting a measure of diversity. This practice, upholding 'truth, morality and justice' came to be seen as a 'method of freedom', a method bringing no easy solutions or instant results. IWMA federalists sought to build coalitions of workplace resistance, working to overcome differences in their own ranks and differences with other labour entities. They recognised that dialogue would help to remedy disagreements, facilitate organisation, and build solidarity and unity; their commitment to federalism acknowledged diverse views and facilitated a respect that was a step towards overcoming differences. Some would go on to challenge Eurocentrism, racism and sexism.

Centrifugal forces were at work, particularly in Belgium. Among various building trades there was strong support for federalism, but many Belgians, led by César de Paepe moved towards viewing the state as a neutral actor, and chose to work in electoral political parties.[681] Some Italians supported demonstrative actions, hoping that one insurrection might incite another. The Jura federation steered a course between these extremes.[682] Fragile workplace structures were weakened in the economic depression. The shape of the IWMA gradually changed as the weight of radical workplace organisations declined, leaving behind smaller networks that discussed politics but were not so rooted in mass movements.

IWMA federalists held international congresses in 1874 and 1876.* The congress in Brussels in September 1874 charged the Jura federation with responsibility for forming the next Federal Bureau.** The congress considered four questions: 1) In a new social organisation how should public services be delivered, and by whom?[683] 2) the matter of political action of the labouring classes.[684] 3) Was there a need for a manifesto to explain the fundamentals of our association? 4) the choice of a universal language? As usual, there were reports on the situation of labour in various countries.[685] Two Lassalleans from Brussels were present and supported electoral politics as a legal way to press for change, while other ways were illegal.

Eccarius was the sole British delegate and was a correspondent for the *Times* of London and the *World* of New York. This congress and the next two attracted few delegates from outside the host country. This reflected the new voting system. No longer could the location of a congress be swayed by the undue weight of local delegates. Now that voting rights were allocated to federations rather than sections, there was less incentive for far-away sections to pay for expensive travel costs for many delegates, and perhaps a greater incentive to discuss matters beforehand and to instruct delegates in the light of those instructions. The Jura federation allocated 300 francs for the travel costs of its delegate to the Brussels general congress of September 1874 – and decided that it was enough to pay for just one delegate there

---

* The congress scheduled to meet in Barcelona in 1875 had to be cancelled because of the political situation in Spain.
** It remained there for three years.

(several sections contributed sums of 15 to 50 francs).[686]

The Bern congress of 1876 was remarkable. It met after the dissolution of the centralist remnant IWMA, lending this congress an opening to present itself as the undisputed, entire IWMA. It was attended by federalist of various sorts, and by Social-Democrats from Germany and elsewhere. The respectful tone of the report in the *Volksstaat*, mentioned above, contrasted entirely with the sneering, and jibing of Becker's report of three years earlier. Differences emerged in the exchanges of viewpoint there, but the congress showed that despite these, one could proceed without viciousness and dishonesty, and without seeking to corral supporters and exclude opponents.

Labour faced an uphill struggle given economic circumstances – the economic downturn of 1873. Reaction was at work, even in 'civilised' lands: churches attempted to extend their influence, conservatives attempted to restrict discussions of sex and gender equality, imperialists and racists sought influence. Governments might seek to shape labour through a discourse of citizenship as a privilege (in an empire that had privileges – so much better than autocratic states or 'savagery'), while employers sought to undermine labour solidarity by turning workers against workers. There were mainly setbacks and defeats, and few successes even for reformists at this moment. In some districts Australian workers won the eight-hour day[687] but in others Chinese workers were harassed. The central German government was seeking to promote a regime of labour passivity; it sought to shape workplace organisations that did not discuss political issues, restricting political discussion within its ineffectual parliament. The conflicts within Spain, leading to an army coup and the overthrow of the Republic, coupled with failed attempts at insurrection in Italy, signalled that, for the present, the fire of Commune ideas had been smothered. Remembrance of the Paris Commune spread but its echoes became feinter. Revolution, even in Spain and Italy, went to bed.[688] At the 1873 federalist congress, Ostyn had observed that authoritarian rule and repression had consequences – after the twenty years spell of domination by Napoleon III initiative was lacking.

If, at this time, one contrasts 'Marx' and 'Bakunin', (ideological networks associated with these names) some telling themes emerge. For 'Marx' the possession of ideological clarity trumped all and motivated the purge of 'his' instrument (his International). For 'Bakunin', a programme and an ideas-based body would only draw in perhaps a few thousand people in the whole of Europe.[689] Hence the importance of the IWMA and of building mass solidarity, beginning, but not ending, in the workplace where it was most natural. By 1873, neither current thought that socialist movements had good prospects, but while the one urged caution and supported activity within the law, the other did not respect the law. Habitually, those who chose electoral activity entirely repudiated rebels and illegal activities, while others, however they themselves might chose to act, would not condemn rebels. Both the 'Marx' and the 'Bakunin' current addressed the more active minorities, begging questions about how these minorities should relate to the wider labour movement. For 'Bakunin', rebels could not easily be all of one mind, but rebel coalitions, the Paris Commune for example, were possible, and the actions of minorities might test potential and encourage greater activity, or perhaps counsel prudence.* 'Marx' encouraged communists to believe that through ideological clarity they had acquired the capacity and the duty denied to others to lead. As Ostyn hinted, there would be long-term consequences as different forms of action and inaction created feedback, which subsequently would influence organisations and their aspirations.

In and around 1873, few members chose to be in the centralist remnants alongside Marx, rather more chose the ongoing federalist IWMA alongside Bakunin, some repudiated both and very many more knew nothing of either or cared nothing for either. Even the ongoing IWMA was diverse: it was a coalition, including both electoralists, and non-electoralists. This coalition was not all 'Bakunin', though it pleased Marx to label all his radical internalist opponents as Bakuninists. A sense of proper proportion is needed: the remnants of the centralist IWMA might be counted in hundreds,[690] IWMA federalists and Social-Democrats in tens of thousands, but working people had to be counted by the million. On a worldwide scale, IWMA supporters (even if one includes Social-Democrats who almost never paid IWMA dues) were a few drops in the ocean of working people.

After some years of depression there was an economic revival. Workplace organisations and unions recovered. In Europe, some attempts would be made to build an international of union networks. A 'Universal' socialist congress was organised in Ghent in 1877. It provided a forum where Wilhelm Liebknecht and other Social-Democrats were able to work together with Hales and de Paepe; Liebknecht crossed swords again with James Guillaume, but they did agree that where was disagreement, there should be no personal abuse.[691]

Bismarck brought in anti-socialist laws in 1878. Party organisations were destroyed, the membership of the 'free' trade unions plummeted, so too did strikes. Prohibitions were extended to bodies seeking to subvert

---

* Audacity in 1870 at Lyon and in 1874 in Bologna. Some federalists did not encourage the attempted rebellion of 1874.

the state, social order, public peace or 'amity between classes'. Innkeepers, booksellers, and librarians might be convicted if they circulated banned publications and the police had powers to ban meetings. After some decline, Social-Democracy gradually rebuilt its electoral base. Beginning at the conference at Chur in 1881, it gradually and cautiously constructed a new International, avoiding revolutionary rhetoric which might have given rise to increased repression. Social-Democrats promoted the formation of a Second International that insisted on the priority of electoral politics, rejected extra-parliamentary action, and attempted to define socialism in terms of law-abiding parliamentary politics. Federalists and libertarian socialists would challenge them; they would focus on the passivity of labour within the Second International and look to build labour autonomy through participatory organisations.

Internationalists might respect the autonomy of various communities of resistance, but it did not follow that such respect was easily returned. IWMA members felt affinity with Irish Fenians, but the image of the IWMA as a bunch of atheists obstructed their support for the International. Many communities of resistance went each their own way and only a few worked explicitly for cultural respect and mutual solidarity. Within labour movements nationalist, racial and cultural splintering would have long-term damaging effects. Nationalism and imperialism would facilitate support for armed forces. In Europe, a sense of pride in belonging to a progressive and civilised nation would grow more readily than empathy for non-European cultures and a broader internationalism. In the USA racism held sway, shattering labour solidarity for almost a century.

Religious, national, racist, liberal and other sentiments were very present, and supporters of radical sentiments were often marginalised and disorganised. Working people of all sorts were targeted by regulation, or much harsher measures, and might instinctively support fellow workers and rebels, whatever their views. For the bulk of the IWMA, solidarity was key often expressed in terms of helping to support strikers, refugees and victims fleeing military service or state repression. However, the small networks of radical internationalists were relatively powerless and were polarised between those seeking some form of grassroot class autonomy, and organising for workplace and community power, and electoralists seeking to obtain parliamentary reform and prepared to cohabit with capital and the state.

The historiography of the IWMA and the Paris Commune is a controversial field. Marx, Engels, Sorge and Becker strove to appropriate the legacy of the International for themselves as they distanced themselves from the ongoing

IWMA. Many liberal and Marxist writers have followed them uncritically, and have spread fallacies in their histories, presenting developments in terms of a Marx/Engels 'guiding leadership', labelling centralists as 'proletarian' and writing off critics as petty bourgeois or bourgeois. Some of their texts assimilate 'Marxist' supporters with the modern industrial proletariat, and libertarians with backwards, pre-industrial rebels, although in continental Europe radicals of all sorts had limited influence in industry and in the labour movement. Editors of the *Collected Works* of Marx and Engels, for example, presented the history of the International through a lens that focused on Marx/Engels activities in and around the General Council. They asserted that 'Bakuninists steered a course towards splitting the movement',[692] a claim that relegated diversity to the background, that disregarded the IWMA's mass membership and the press organs that they relied on to understand developments. This 'Marxist' discourse focused on the decisions at the one gerrymandered congress (at The Hague), while largely disregarding others. Most IWMA members did not regard a remote General Council as any sort of leadership; for them IWMA organisation was articulated primarily through their local sections and their local and regional press. They knew little of what the General Council discussed or did. In large majority they did not follow it when it adopted an electoral party-building strategy, and in 1873, they chose delegates to have it abolished. 'Marxist' texts spread untruths: that the International died after the congress at The Hague, and that anarchists sought disorder and chaos. Some recent texts refute this distorted historiography.[693]

The nature of radicalism, the balance between types of organisation and the strength of spirit of international solidarity, waxed and waned over time and from place to place. Progress might perhaps have come through the development of coalitions, but if this was so, then how were coalitions to be built? Some radicals grappled with such questions, but overall, no successful socialist answers were forthcoming. Various forces were at work after 1873 and helped transform the ongoing IWMA and other networks. Depression and repression took their toll. In the deepening economic crisis, wages were reduced, health suffered, and many workers were thrown into the ranks of the unemployed. Many workplace organisers focused on bread-and-butter priorities. In places there was a process of mutation as mass organisations withered and as remnants became ideas based groups. Various states worked hard to ban IWMA organisations. The conjunction of all these factors (working on the International from without) was largely responsible for ending the progress that had helped develop and expand solidarity, momentum and the International. But the International was also weakened from within, as setback followed setback, as the practice of electoral politics became little more than an occasional exercise in harvesting votes, and as differences of opinion turned to antagonism and hatred. Federalists had much greater support than centralists, but they were still a minority, active but not strong enough alone to incite mass offensive action. Except where they were strongest (in Spain and Italy), they had had only a limited capacity to support working people or their organisations. In Britain: workplace (economic) organisations were strong but radical influence was negligible, and the Liberal party was drawing in representatives of labour. In Germany, Social-Democrats attracted votes by the hundred thousand, but Social-Democracy was perhaps more a passive dissident community working to adapt that system, and rather less an active community working actively to replace and transform it.

The long-term consequences of the 1873 congresses lay in the ideals, tactics, models and perspectives of political organisation and behaviours bequeathed to future generations of socialists – among them both libertarians and Marxists (of various sorts). Individual IWMA members were working to broaden the socialist agenda, seeking to understand, value and incorporate broader interests but the International had not yet brought in both genders or all peoples. The 'leave it to us' practice of electoral parties gravely weakened the potential counter power of rebel coalitions. Legacies might be evaluated, re-evaluated, distorted or fabricated. Past motifs might be challenged, as experience and changing circumstances made clear that they were inappropriate. As years went by, patterns of thinking and traditions changed, often losing touch with the context – and historical veracity – of the circumstances and premises which had first shaped them.

Over the next twenty years federalists would evolve through various fragments: some took on new forms in anarchist-communist and anarcho-syndicalist structures, each defending federalist models that harked back to examples from the 1870s and spreading to Latin America, parts of Asia and Africa. Over those years, German Social-Democracy would inspire electoral political parties and electoral coalitions, and these would become something of a model in the Second International, also spreading into new regions. Both traditions would influence left, libertarian and socialist politics in the 1880s and beyond.

Appendices

Appendix 1

Hermann Jung's speech to the congress of the British Federation on 26 January 1873.[694]

[Supporters of the IWMA in Britain split up in the course of 1872. On the one hand was a network around John Hales, with widespread support in East London and from branches in Hulme and Liverpool. On the other hand, centralists strongest in Manchester and among German exiles. Hales accused the 'Marxists' of wanting to turn the association 'into a secret one, with an infallible pontiff at the head of it, who shall thunder excommunications against all who shall dare to enquire or doubt'. A congress held on 26 January 1873, drew in veterans (Eccarius and Weston), besides Hales and Jung, only eleven delegates in all, 'a miserable affair'. Several provincial branches were demoralised or 'did not know what to do'.[695] Earlier in December meetings in London had been manipulated and sabotaged – meeting times were changed, and/or rooms locked to exclude certain members.][696]

Citizens, I consider it necessary to make a few remarks to explain my position. You are all aware that I have for a long time been intimate with Marx. Formerly he used to consult his friends about what was to be done, when any question of importance turned up, and we always agreed before things were brought on in the open Council Meetings. After Engels came to London that was no longer done, and hence it often happened that we were divided in the open meetings, and by this Marx gradually lost the confidence of his old friends. He then introduced a new element into the Council (the Blanquists) and adopted a wavering policy, sometimes leaning to one side, sometimes to another. In the sub-committee* I was in the opposition, if anything was said it was noted upon at once. I wanted inquiry and was called the reactionist. One day I found a man named Weiler, who had said something, and Marx asked him to repeat it. It was something

---

* Given the lack of language skills among members of the General Council foreign correspondence was considered by a sub-committee which edited the documents brought to the full council.

about what Hales had said at the [British] Federal Council. I heard Foster's report of the same meeting in the morning, which differed altogether from Weiler's. Marx and Engels insisted that Hales be dismissed at once, I was for suspension, for the purpose of instituting an inquiry. In this I succeeded and that was the way in which I voted for the suspension of Hales.

But no matter whether Hales had done wrong or not, Dupont was sent to the [British] Congress, and ordered to oppose everything that Hales might do, whatever it was, that was all the instruction he had. Engels was for getting a majority to smash the opposition, I was for arguing the question and to smash the opposition by argument. Engels reckoned upon the sections, and the delegates they were likely to send, for the purpose of outnumbering the opposition. I opposed it, which widened the breech between me and Marx. I have always given opponents more time to speak than my own side. If they are wrong no smash will convince them, if right they are sure to triumph in the long run. Dupont and Serraillier used to disagree with Marx as much as I did, but they did not oppose him, they only came to me to complain.

In the Spanish affair Engels had written and demanded an answer to certain questions by return of post, if not the [Spanish] Federal Council was to be suspended and this without any orders from anyone. Four days after the despatch of his letter he proposed the suspension. It takes two days for a letter to reach Spain, and there was no time for an answer to come back, and there was no time to reply. I asked him how he got the information he acted on, he said he had it from Lafargue,* not a secretary of section or an official of any kind. My opposition had the effect of bringing the matter before the Council, and the policy was counteracted, but the Federation was lost.

At all the former [International] Congresses I and Eccarius had been the exponents of Marx's doctrine, but I could not vote for his new policy, and rather than vote against him I resolved to stay away. A few days before the Congress [at The Hague] some news arrived had arrived which made it doubtful whether the [General] Council would have a majority. Marx and Engels came to me to urge me to go. I refused giving as my reason that I had sacrificed too much already. The next day they came and said, I must go, it might depend on one vote, I replied, you can easily buy that. They offered to pay the costs, if it was £20. Engels said you are the only one who can save the Association. I replied I can only go if you and Marx step away.

The last meeting before the [Hague] Congress I wrote a resolution in

* Jean Grave met Lafargue in prison. He asked him about his publication of the names of members of the Alliance, which had resulted in their imprisonment. Lafargue prevaricated. 'Like all good followers of Jules Guesde, he was, in discussion with anarchists, generally of bad faith.' Jean Grave, *Le Mouvement libertaire sous la IIIe République*, Paris: Les Œuvres Représentatives, 1930, pp. 83-4.

several languages, proposing the removal of the General Council from London. Marx and Engels were dead against it. I wanted the General Council removed to Switzerland or Belgium. At Zurich there are many able men in the Association. I could see that no new Council could be formed in London.

At the New York [American] Congress Sorge and Dereure were elected as delegates for the Hague and then Sorge demanded blank credentials to take with him, and when objected to Sorge showed a letter from Marx. I received news of this and went to Marx and he said if Sorge had done that he is *ein dummer kerl* [a stupid fool]. [Maltman] Barry had one of these blank credentials[697] filled in.*

I gave Johannard a letter to read in which I declined being re-elected [to] London should [it] again be selected as the seat of the General Council. When Dupont returned from The Hague he came to me to complain how Marx had served him. On the road out Marx said to Ranvier he must be president of the Congress. Ranvier objected and said that he knew only one language. That did not matter said Marx, everything was arranged. On the first day at the Hague, Marx persuaded Dupont to accept the presidency, and then within Dupont's hearing he went to Brismel [Brismée] of Brussels telling him that he must be president. Dupont expressed his surprise at this conduct, and then Marx turned around and said, 'The French would not like you on account of your violent temper'.

Serraillier had credentials from different parts of France and to compel Marx to pronounce himself he threatened to give credentials to Lissagaray and others to form a party of his own against the Blanquists. To prevent that Marx consented to the removal of the General Council.

When New York was proposed as the seat of the General Council, Johannard said that was only to get it in the hands of Sorge, the tool of Marx. Sorge had made himself so obnoxious that no one would have voted for him, and Marx promised that he should not be on the Council. A few vacancies were left to be filled up at New York, and the first thing the new council did was to install Sorge as General Secretary. Thus, the man who, in the opinion of Marx is a stupid, has been made the head of the General Council, Marx has deceived and betrayed all his old friends. I have written to many of them about it and told them what I thought of it. Mrs Marx

---

* *The Eastern Post* (15 February 1873) published notes on the means used to fix the majority at The Hague congress: it was not convened according to the rules, it was 'packed', credentials were accepted from a section that did not exist, and from at least one man who were not a member; credentials were offered to men 'upon condition that they would vote in a certain way' (indignantly refused); blank credentials were brought over from America, etc.

came once and Miss Marx twice, and Dupont and Lafargue have been after me to go to Marx, I refused.

After the [Hague] Congress I made up my mind to have no more to do with the International, but from letters of members of the foreign section of Manchester, I found that Engels was writing letters everywhere, giving people advice who to elect as delegates and who not. This induced me to alter my mind, and I joined the [British] Federal Council. I joined to prevent the English Federal Council falling into the arms of the Backouninists as such my objective was to prevent a split and organise here the movement to counteract the Hague Congress.

Had the political question been fairly argued out with the abstentionists we could have converted them. We killed the opposition on the land question with argument, we should have succeeded in this. I have known Schwitzguébel since he was a boy, he is an honest fellow, and open to argument, we might have converted them.

Feeling rather indisposed, and not being able to attend the meetings regularly, I was going to resign, and had written my resignation, when [Samuel] Vickery broke up the meeting, but upon that I determined to remain. Marx and Engels say I turned because the council is no longer here, and that I head the opposition. I have not written to any one abroad, but they are writing abroad against me everywhere, and now I shall write too.

On the morning of the opening of the Congress at the Hague a friend of mine who had paid for the Hall was told by Marx that he would have to leave the room but if he liked to remain Marx would give him credentials. The credentials were refused. On the previous day, the same man went to Rotterdam to meet Marx and Engels and knowing the disposition of the opposition he advised caution. Caution be d – d. was the reply, "We have the majority, and we'll smash the opposition," but the majority broke to pieces in the smash.

The congress unanimously passed the following resolution:

Considering that the Hague Congress was illegally constituted, the majority present being a fictitious one, created for the purpose of swamping the true representatives of the members of the Association. That the resolutions passed thereat were subversive of the 'Fundamental Pact' of the Association, which recognized the right of every Federation to decide upon its own action. That the programme for that Congress had not been previously submitted to the cognizance of the branches as required by the General Rules, Administrative Regulations Art. 1, Rule 10. This Congress of British delegates repudiates the action taken at the Congress of the Hague, and its nominee the so-called General Council of New York.[698]

Appendix 2

Report on the Public Meeting held in Geneva on the evening of 4 September.[699]
[*The Daily News* (edition of 8 September) reported:

… the room was crowded, The Russians were again present, and there was a good sprinkling of Germans, who were supposed to be favourable to the other party; but the bulk of the audience consisted of men whose dress and sunburnt skins sufficiently proved that they belonged to the ranks of labour.' There were effective speeches by Lefrançais and Costa. Eccarius spoke in German. *The Times*, 4-17 September 1873, noted that Lefrançais, a French refugee (not a delegate), spoke at length. He noted new banks, factories, railways, telegraphs – all international institutions. Yesterday's national principles were challenged by international trade and competition. Eccarius, remarked on changes in the IWMA. It had been formed by London political trades unionists and non-political Paris Proudhonists. In 1869, at Basle, collectivism had entered and Proudhonism had been voted out. The London trades-union element had gradually disappeared but in Paris the trades-union element had displaced the Proudhonists. The Franco-Prussian war had prevented the next congress meeting and then the shape of the General Council had changed: The co-option of members had turned the balance of the Council.]

The meeting intended for workers of Geneva, advertised, and convened by public bills and posters, was held on Thursday evening. A dense crowd filled the congress hall. A large number of speakers, among them comrades Dave, Lefrançais, Verrycken, Costa, Joukovsky, Van den Abeele and Farga, addressed the two issues on the agenda: the principles, goal and means of action of the International, and the principle of federative organisation.

Comrade Eccarius, having noted a certain number of German [-speaking] workers in the hall, took advantage of that circumstance to explain in a speech in German, the origins of the cleavage which came about at the congress of The Hague, and the motives which he considered had obliged him to take sides with the federalists. This speech provoked some violent objections from a small group of dissidents belonging to the *Schweizerische Arbeiterbund* (whose journal is the *Tagwacht*) and from citizen Gutsmann – the same who had presided at the congress of Olten,[700] came up the rostrum to reply to Eccarius. Notwithstanding all that had been said in the meeting, the citizen seemed to be entirely ill-informed about the International's current affairs and had taken into his reckoning not a jot of the true value of that congress [at The Hague]. He was able to respond, with arguments that had only such weight as these:

Eccarius, has declared himself against the General Council out of vexation, because he is no longer a member thereof. Some have pretended that the General Council no longer exists, because twenty men declared it abolished. These twenty men, who represent only themselves, had no right to take such a decision, thus the General Council continues to exist now, as it did before the Geneva congress. Lastly, the Jura Federation, which talks so much of the principles of the International, does not put them into practice. Indeed, it knows how to find money to print pamphlets, but when strikes break out in Geneva, it doesn't send a penny.

Referring to this last assertion, Guillaume, replied to Gutsmann that, as regards the Neuchâtel section that he represented, it was indeed true that over the last two years it had not come to the aid of any strike in Geneva, but there were reasons for that, namely, at the time of the strike of painters and plasterers in Geneva in 1870, i.e. shortly after the cleavage in the [former] Romande Federation, the Neuchâtel section, wishing to show the spirit of fraternity which it felt towards them, despite the divisions that had broken out on certain matters of principle, hastened to send its contribution to the strikers. Two sums of 50 and 24 francs were sent off, on 11 and 14 June, to the address of de M. Saulnier, president of the strike committee; the despatch of that money is recorded by postal dockets, but the treasurer of the Neuchâtel was never able to obtain a receipt from the recipient. Well, given such facts, and until it becomes known what view should be taken concerning the morality of certain committees in Geneva, the Neuchâtel section decided not to send off any further sums to Geneva.

Joukovsky, in turn, recalled the attitude of Jura sections regarding various strikes in Geneva and showed by plain facts just how much Gutsmann's assertions were slanderous and mendacious. At the time of the great construction strike in 1868, the Jura Mountain sections showed themselves to be the first to come to the aid of their brothers in Geneva. And the section of Le Locle alone, gathered up the sum of 1,500 francs. Later, when the roofers and tilers strike of 1870 broke out, the mountain sections sent their delegates to the meeting in Vevey, where one of them, comrade Spichiger, proposed an immediate collection should be made. Some weeks later, on the occasion of the painters' and plasterers' strike, which soon developed into a general construction workers' strike, the federal committee of the Jura Mountain's [federation] sent an urgent appeal to its sections for them to come to the aid of workers in Geneva. This appeal was recognised, and considerable sums were sent, Guillaume has just reminded us that the section in Neuchâtel, sent 74 francs on its own account, and had never received a receipt. Lastly, very recently – and despite the events of The Hague – the jewellers strike* was another occasion for many Jura sections to prove to Geneva's workers their practical solidarity;[701] they opened subscriptions and imposed on themselves a mandate for extraordinary dues. As for what Gutsmann said about a meeting of twenty persons voting to abolish the General Council, that is quite simply ridiculous. These twenty men represent not themselves, but the whole organised proletariat of Europe and America, with the exception of a few dissident groups remaining loyal to the General Council; they are then not a clique, but rather the millions of workers who form the International, who have just now declared, through their delegates, the banishment of Authority, an irrevocable deposition, and authority is, abolished in the International for good and all.

The lateness of the hour obliged the meeting bureau to end the session, just at the moment when the discussion had become most interesting, nevertheless, we believe that this exchange of views on the matter of scission, a matter as yet still very badly understood in Geneva, may have been able to open the eyes of many of those who attended.

Appendix 3

Discussion on the General Strike 3-4 September 1873

[The matter of General Strikes had been considered before the congress. For example, one paper serving the Spanish IWMA had reflected that it might be:

> an act that that have always been seen as the precursor for the liquidation of this unjust society ... from the depths of conscience we believe that the life and future of the Association perhaps turns on this subject. ... A general strike supposes a long and appropriate period of propaganda among the popular masses, as yet not affiliated to the International; further it presupposes some conscious study of all aspects of labour statistics, and lastly, that which is most important: the character and consciousness of the labouring masses, their temper and readiness ...

El Condenado asked: was the European proletariat, outside the International, ready for that battle against the old society? Is the political situation fitting for success, for such things in the near future? We believe neither the former nor the latter. 'We go slowly because we do not wish to stumble or fall, after advancing so far.[702] A proposal arising from the Belgian regional congress in Antwerp (15-16 August 1873) on solidarity and the

---

* A nine-hour day was won; strike funds went were paid back only after two years.

general strike (suggesting that partial strikes should not be encouraged) elicited the following Spanish comment, recognising difficulties that might ensue: '... above all the obstacles presented by workers who, as yet, do not yet have an awareness of their position, of their mission and of their rights, and make themselves into instruments of the bourgeoisie, lacking in their duty of solidarity towards other exploited people ...'[703] After the congress there was a discussion in *La Federación*, (20 and 27 September 1873); among other points it commented on goals, noting that individual freedom would be guaranteed by economic-social institutions. It remarked that the status of women would be elevated – and each sex would have the same rights and duties. Four years later *Le Travailleur* (Geneva, September 1877, pp. 12-13) reflected on a strike wave in the USA. It suggested that for progress to be achieved, a general strike would need to spread and escalate into revolution. It wrote that when battle was joined a vanguard formed from revolutionary groups might push things along, until the entire army of working people joined in the struggle.

The Geneva congress came to a rather hesitant conclusion, 'having in mind the current state of organisation of the International'. Delegates were aware that whatever they might agree, strikes were a matter for broader circles, and that, as yet many workers were not minded to join or follow a lead from the IWMA.

This appendix sketches the debate on the general strike which the congress decided should *not* be published in the *Official Report*. Guillaume published this text some thirty years later in *L'Internationale: documents et souvenirs 1864-78*.[704]]

* * *

Congress addressed next the question of the general strike. In this session Joukovsky, the reporter of the commission was heard, then successively Manguette, Verrycken, Alerini, Guillaume, Costa, Brousse, Bert, Viñas, Ostyn, Spichiger and Hales. Given the congress decision just agreed, this discussion was not published in the *Report*, but I am able to provide an analysis, from the manuscript which was left and remained with me.

Joukovsky, reporting for the Commission, said that it thought that the question of a general strike is a matter subordinated to the lesser or greater spread of regional and international organisation of trades' bodies; and to the statistical work that the International must prepare in view of such a strike. Also, a general strike being nothing other than a social revolution – because it would be enough to suspend work for ten days for the existing order to collapse – the Commission thinks that this question is not going to receive a solution from this Congress, and all the more so because a discussion would put our enemies in the picture as to those means we might intend to use for social revolution.

Manguette and *Verrycken* explained that Belgians considered the general strike as a means to bring about a revolutionary movement. 'If the Spaniards and the Italians tell us that in their countries it isn't a useful way to accomplish a revolution, which is no reason for us to reject it – in those lands where workers are used to resorting to strike action. What we would like to consider is the possibility of spreading the movement and making it international. We would like it if, when workers in one country come out in a revolt – be it in the form of a general strike or in some other form – that other peoples should combine their effort with those of a country in revolt.'

Verrycken noted that if a general strike had been possible at the time of the Paris Commune, one would doubtless have been able to prevent the victory of the reactionaries. During the last Spanish revolution, the general strike would have been an efficacious means of paralysing Prussia and preventing it isolating the Spanish revolutionary movement.

Alerini cited events in Alcoy as an example of what might be obtained through a general strike, even if these events were restricted to just one area. In that town, workers of certain trades' bodies were on strike and were about to succumb and be forced to restart work, without obtaining anything. Then the Spanish Federal Commission, (which was based in Alcoy) proposed the launching of a general strike of all trades in the town, all committing themselves so that no trade organisation would resume work until all had achieved satisfaction. This general strike led to an armed struggle, in which workers overturned the local authorities; prominent bourgeois were arrested as hostages; and, when General Velarde presented himself before Alcoy with the army, he was forced to negotiate; hostages offered themselves up as mediators: the provincial government promised that there would be no reprisals taken against the insurgents; that the conditions that strikers demanded from their managers were to be accepted, and that a tax would be imposed on the bourgeoisie, the product of which was to be used to pay for the days lost during the strike. In consequence, Alerini is a convinced partisan of the general strike as a revolutionary means.

Guillaume commented that the idea of a revolutionary general strike was on the agenda. It was the logical consequence of the practice of partial strikes. People recognised that one should work to generalise strikes, given that partial strikes allowed only incomplete and momentary results.* To

---

* A year later, in the *Bulletin de la Fédération Jurassienne*, (20 December 1874), Guillaume wrote that the usefulness of a strike was not just in the small material advantages obtained

succeed a general strike should be international. But is it necessary that it should break out everywhere, at the same time, on a fixed date following some order? No, such a question should not be pressed, nor should one encourage the supposition that such things might arise in that way. Revolution must be contagious. It should never be the case, in a country when a spontaneous movement is about to break out, that one should seek to defer an explosion using as an excuse that one should wait for other countries to be ready to follow.

Costa said that while the general strike was an excellent revolutionary method, partial strikes have been just dust to throw into workers' eyes. It was not sensible however for congress to issue an opinion on the matter – it might only give the bourgeoisie something to mock.

Brousse thought that although in some countries the general strike was a practical measure; elsewhere – such as in in Italy and France for example – it was an impractical measure. Why, in France – where the general strike was impossible – shouldn't revolution be made in the form of a movement of communes?*

Bert submitted the following draft resolution:

Considering that a general strike is a strike of every sort of trade in every location. Every partial general strike will be organised in such a way that only one set of trades should be on strike in various places, and that those on strike should be sustained by the solidarity and support of all other trades. The benefit of the wage rise obtained through an initial success should contribute to the support of a second set of trades which might go on strike next, and so on, until victory is complete.

Brousse affirmed that such propositions would [amount to] the defeat of organised workers.

Costa had a different proposition, namely:

Considering that a general strike is an excellent and practical measure to secure a social revolution and – in view of the declarations of delegates – while this measure may serve some federations and help promote the success of the revolution, it is an impossible and impractical means for others. Congress declares that it confines itself to noting these diverse opinions and leaves it to each federation to review how they should

(and lost in days following), but rather in the agitation that is created, in more lively feelings of solidarity, and in consciousness that is born among previously indifferent workers, seeing that their interests and those of management, do not coincide. Marianne Enckell, *La Fédération jurassienne*, Genève: Éditions Entremonde, 2012, p. 94.

* An administrative area.

organise, to find those means which might lead on, most soon and most surely, to the emancipation of labour.

Alerini objected that it would be unwise to publicise a declaration conceived in such terms, which is to say, pushing overtly for a social revolution.

Costa observed that he was not demanding that the resolution should be published.

James Guillaume made the following proposition, avoiding use of the expression 'social revolution':

Considering that workers can get only momentary and illusory relief from partial strikes, given that wages are always and essentially restricted to [providing only] the measure strictly needed to prevent workers starving to death. Congress, without believing in the possibility of renouncing partial strikes completely,* recommends workers to dedicate their efforts to building international organisation through trades' bodies, which would allow them, one day, to launch a general strike, the only really effective strike that might bring about the complete emancipation of labour.

Viñas was not a supporter of strikes. In his view, it was strikes that had diverted labour away from the revolutionary movement. Perhaps labour in Spain, if it had not been absorbed by numerous strikes, might have moved on better towards its complete emancipation. Some people say that the general strike is a revolutionary means – Viñas denies that.** To achieve as much, striking workers would have to be conscious that revolution was a necessity. So, one must work to have the exploited masses understand that necessity, and only then will they make the revolution, without a strike being needed as a pretext.***

*   As some Belgian delegates had demanded at the Verviers [Belgian IWMA] congress on 14 April 1873. (Note by James Guillaume). *Solidarité Revolutionnaire* (Barcelona), 14 August 1873 and 1 September 1873, reported that the Belgian IWMA congress of 15-16 August had decided: 'All federations and sections should work assiduously to organise a general strike, and should abandon partial strikes except in cases of legitimate defence'.
**   Viñas was thinking of workers of Barcelona, who, in July 1873, had held a peaceful general strike, instead of an insurgency (Note by James Guillaume). The usefulness of general strikes was to be debated by the FRE, a congress resolution of June 1874 advised fewer partial strikes; see: Anselmo Lorenzo, *El proletariado militante*, op. cit., Vol. 2, chapter 7; George R. Esenwein, *Anarchist Ideology and the Working-Class Movement in Spain 1868-1898*, University of California Press, 1989, p. 58-59.
***   *The Times*, 8 September, reported Viñas saying: 'The Internationalists of Barcelona had determined upon a General Strike, to show their solidarity with the people of Alcoy. They had organized a strike, but the mass of the people had not followed them. There had been no thought of revolution. At Barcelona the men not belonging to the International had received arms, the Internationalists had not. No Strike would result in anything

Ostyn believed that the International is and should remain a grand and practical school of social and political economy, something that many workers did not understand. The real means to achieve the emancipation of labour is through the enhancing and enlightening of spirits.

Spichiger thought that partial strikes should not be condemned; in his view one should take advantage of these movements – even if they could not bring about immediate satisfaction. No doubt we should endeavour to work to have workers understand that only a general strike might liberate labour; but for that extended propaganda is needed, and meanwhile, we should be careful, and should be against [allowing ourselves to be drawn into] opposing partial movements or diverting those workers who are not, as yet, revolutionary, away from strikes.

Joukovsky said that the first question to be decided was that of knowing if congress wanted to vote for a resolution about general strikes. On that point, the president (Verrycken) asked delegates if they wished to set out a view on the following question: 'Does the congress wish to adopt a resolution on the subject of the general strike?' Every delegate replied 'yes', except Hales, who replied 'no', and Van den Abeele, who abstained, because the Dutch Federation, at its congress of 10th August had voted to wait for the decisions of the General Congress on the general strike, in order to discuss and adopt something, if it was appropriate.

In the eighth (private) session on the morning of Thursday 4 September, the discussion on the general strike was continued and concluded. The commission, through the agency of Joukovsky, had proposed a somewhat badly drafted declaration, the first part of which insisted on the necessity of regional and international organisation of trades' bodies; [while its] second part said: 'The general strike being nothing other than the social revolution, because the suspension of all work, even for just ten days, would suffice to make the current order die off entirely, and therefore, the question is to be set aside.'

Manguette and *Van den Abeele* rejected this draft declaration, while *Cyrille* and *Joukovsky* defended it. *Hales,* for the first time (to my knowledge) employed an expression which has since become well known in Germany (*Generalstreik, Generalunsinn*) [General Strike, general nonsense].[705] He expressed himself as follows: 'The general strike is impractical and is an absurdity. To have a general strike, one would first of all have to organise

practical in that direction. A general Lock-out might stir up the workpeople. Unless the mass of the workpeople were conscious of wanting a revolution, a General Strike would be of no use, and if they were conscious of the necessity and ready for the social revolution, they would have no need of resorting to the equivocal opportunities offered by a General Strike.'

everywhere with this in view, and if and when labour organisation was completed, the social revolution would be accomplished.' After a somewhat confusing discussion in which Alerini, Bert and Farga spoke again, the commission, reconsidering things, presented a draft resolution which it had just reworded, instead of the declaration that it had proposed earlier. It was *Costa* who read it out the draft text:

> Congress, considers that, having in mind the current state of organisation of the International, no complete solution can be given to the question of a general strike, and it urgently recommends workers to organise international unions of each trade.

Farga proposed that a phrase be added, recommending 'active socialist and revolutionary propaganda'. Verrycken supported Farga's amendment, subject to the deletion of the word 'revolutionary', which he said, 'is very often understood as meaning battles in the streets and is a word that would not be understood in Belgium'. Farga replied that he was very willing to delete the word 'revolutionary'.

The new text of the commission, completed by Farga's amendment was then adopted unanimously, in the following form (which was made known in the afternoon public session):

> Congress, considers that, having in mind the current state of organisation of the International, no complete solution can be given to the question of a general strike, and it urgently recommends workers to organise international unions of each trade, as well as active socialist propaganda.

Appendix 4

The Two Congresses, report in the Bulletin de la Fédération Jurassienne, *28 September 1873*

Now that the federalists and the authoritarians have each held their congresses in Geneva, and now that we have exact information on the two gatherings, we will use a few lines to set them side by side. Our readers will find it easy to draw their conclusions.

The international congress of 1st September convened by the federalists, was formed by the following federations: England (21 sections), Belgium (8 area federations: Antwerp, Gent, Brussels, Borinage, Centre-Hainaut, Charleroi, Liège, and Vesdre valley; each composed of numerous sections); Spain (270 local federations, formed from 557 resistance sections and 117 mixed-trades sections; also 11 regional trade unions, comprising all together

447 resistance sections); France (numerous sections spread over several departments, some of them already forming departmental federations); the Netherlands (4 local federations: Amsterdam, The Hague, Rotterdam, Utrecht); Italy (a hundred or so sections, mostly grouped into local and provincial federations); Jura (14 sections in the Swiss Jura plus sections in Alsace and France).

In addition, the federal council of Spring Street, New York,[706] around which around half of the American sections have remained,* sent their support to the congress – and not just a simple or platonic affiliation, but also material support, in the form of money sent over, intended to cover the Americans' share of the congress costs.

In view of the above listing, let us see what the gathering of Marxists amounted to. Initially, a noisy lot of delegates were announced – from Italy, Spain, Portugal, France, England, and America. Today, reading the report of the Marxists themselves, *it is plain that not one delegate from these lands attended the congress.* If one can believe the *Tagwacht* of 13 September there were 39 Marxist delegates; according to last Sunday's *Tribune du peuple*[707] the number was 30, which were divided up as follows: 1 German delegate, 10 Austro-Hungarian delegates, 4 from German-speaking Switzerland, 1 from Moutier, 1 from Locco (Ticino), 12 from Geneva, and 1 from the Netherlands.

The Dutch delegate was none other than Van den Abeele, who, having attended the congress of 1st September, and having voted for its every resolution, went on, on behalf of the Dutch federation, to place an ultimatum before the Marxists. When, as might well have been expected, this ultimatum was rejected, Van den Abeele withdrew, which did not prevent the Marxist gentlemen, with their usual bad faith, from counting him as one of their own.

As for the Austrians or Austro-Hungarians, the story of Mr Schwartz and his mandates is well known.[708] These so-called Austrians were all, save one, Germans based in Geneva. This so-called *Universal and International Congress* was therefore composed, as these gentlemen confessed, of 29 delegates (we do not count Van den Abeele), i.e., of 21 persons from Geneva, of 6 other Swiss, of one German and one Austrian (Mr Schwartz).**

No one represented the New York General Council!

One could not dream up a more complete fiasco, or a more ridiculous

---

* According to a letter in the *Bulletin de la Fédération Jurassienne,* 20 July 1873, the anti-authoritarians had held a congress in Philadelphia on 9 July 1872 where sections numbered 3, 9, 12, 17, 22, 26, 31, 35, 48, 50, 51, 52, and 53 were represented.
** Oberwinder – alias 'Schwartz.'

disaster. Also, the Marxist congress produced just the effect that we might have wished for. It opened the eyes of even the most blind to the real state of things. It showed that the entire International, less a few dissidents, was with the federalists. Regrettably, this demonstration came a little late to produce an immediate and substantial impact in Geneva, given that in the last three years no good has been achieved by the Marxist gentlemen, and had at least almost succeeded in killing off the International completely in this city. The *Tagwacht* of Zurich appears to have been discomforted and shocked by this ridiculous congress. Having first published pompously some texts to announce the opening sessions, it ceased entirely to speak of it. The silence spoke volumes.

* * *

The congress of 1st September abolished the General Council. The Marxist congress maintained it for its own and located it once again in New York, for a two-year period. So, Mr Sorge will continue to reign over Geneva, Moutier, Zurich, and the friends of Mr Schwartz. What fun!

Leaders in Geneva greatly desired to see the General Council relocated to Geneva; they have gone somewhat cool on Marx, so it seems, and it appears that there were two currents in the authoritarian congress – one representing the French-speakers of Geneva, the other the German-speakers of Geneva and proper Germans – and the latter prevailed. They also prevailed on the question of politics. Geneva's French-speakers wished that the congress should not express an opinion on this point, so that all labour forces might concentrate on the economic question; but by grace of the (contraband) Austro-Hungarians and the German-Swiss, the famous resolution of the congress of The Hague, making [electoral] political action both centralised and compulsory, was placed within the statutes just adopted by these Marxists.

So, as can be seen, certain people in Geneva are moving closer to us. We note with pleasure that experience over the last few years has not been without some use as far as they are concerned.

A detail, concerning decisions taken as regards the next congresses, may serve as a touchstone to indicate the strength and seriousness of the two parties – the federalists and the authoritarians. The federalist international will hold its next congress on the first Monday in September in 1874, in Brussels, among one of the best organised regional federations. That congress, all things suggest, will be one of the best yet staged by our Association; it will be the first great public demonstration of the International after its adoption of the federative principle and after its abolition of authority in all its workings.

And what will the Marxists do? Alas, that year the Marxists will have no congress. The oven of Geneva was too much of a setback, and another grilling next year might kill them off entirely. So, no congress in 1874. They are to meet again in Zurich, in German territory, only two years hence. One might have been pleased to suppress congresses entirely, but to do so would have amounted to admitting defeat all too clearly. So, it was resolved for form's sake to hold out for one more at least. A showing less sparse than 1873 might be prepared over two years, and it might be hoped that, on this occasion Mr Sorge might perhaps cross the Atlantic to allow his person to be seen by the faithful.

Let us end with a review from the *Journal de Genève*, which is not without interest. This worthy journal has shown the Marxists its charming face and has reserved all its insults and condemnation for us. Instinctively it sees in us the only serious opposition to the bourgeoisie. In its issue of 19th September, it strives to show the authoritarians that their principles are fundamentally *bourgeois*;[709] and it regards them as friends, adding that there is an abyss between the Marxists and the *anarchists* (that is the name they give us). Their logic leads them to the conclusion that the Marxists are no longer internationalists, and consequently one must allow them the indulgence that is accorded sinners who repent; whereas one must prosecute and fight anarchists, 'who are logical internationalists,' and allow them neither grace, nor rest. These are the final words of the *Journal de Genève*:

Anarchy – that is the name the logicians of the International have adopted for their flag – with such sincerity and with such unparallel naïveté! And they are in the right. The real dissidents, are the authoritarian internationalists, today seeking to apply the brakes on the downward slope, because they have seen the abyss and fear the void. They have been called *bourgeois*, and, if it is true that the name of bourgeois is a synonym for conservative, that is the description that they deserve. Between them, and the all-out revolutionaries, those who want devastation for devastation's sake (they have us in mind), those who are fanatics of social upheaval (us again), there is such a distance that no fancy words can hide things for long. Orthodox internationalists (Marxists), be on your guard. You are out there, on the road to reaction, and you know enough of your former friends the anarchists, to know that, from them, neither pity nor moderation can be expected.

Except for those last words, this is all clear, and let us add, quite correct. The *Journal de Genève* wants to use *anarchists* to symbolise terror, and it wants to draw Geneva's workers back into the bosom of the good bourgeois family – but really, they ['we anarchists'] are not so ferocious, and they [we] ask for nothing more than to be allowed to tender the hand of friendship to everyone who struggles for labour's emancipation. This resolution, voted unanimously by the congress of 1st September, is a proof; it particularly targeted workers who still follow Marxist leaders:

The congress of the International Working Men's Association, meeting in Geneva on 1st September 1873, believes it is its duty to declare that this Association intends to practice solidarity towards all workers of the world, in the struggle against capital to achieve the liberation of labour, *whatever organisation they may adopt.*

Appendix 5

On the Geneva conpgresses, Der Volksstaat, *5 and 8 October 1873*

[The editions of 5 and 8 October carried a report by Johann Philip Becker, *Ueber die kongresse zu Genf,* dated 29 September. The federalists were named as *Sonderbundler* – a name that resonated with the secessionist confederates in the American civil war, or the conservative Catholics of the brief Swiss Sonderbund civil war of 1847.[710]]

In recent weeks, the bourgeois press has once again set itself a-shouting; this time it is joyful, rather than fearful as before. In its desire to conjure illusions, it is mixing together causes and effects in a comforting manner, and it shows no proof of understanding, even partially, the socialist labour movement as a whole, or the elements and organs that constitute it.

In former times, the bad conscience of exploiters and oppressors made them view the IWMA as a horrible monster, one as large as the entire world; their teeth chattered, and they screamed out in pain. Today, in contrast, the thought of the happy news of the death of the International, makes them believe in the possibility of calmly returning to the old order of things, taking comfort in imaginations and beliefs: 'The International is dead, completely dead,' that is the joyful cry that resonates in the pages of 'well-informed' papers.

What is dead, is something that never existed (except in brains tortured by bad conscience), and those older and fearful screams were better founded than today's joy. The IWMA did not create the Social-Democratic movement, on the contrary, it is a consequence of it. Furthermore, it will live as long as the latter, it is an emanation of it, its living form, and its institutional cadre, and the socialist movement will live on, as long as there are oppressors and the oppressed, exploiters and the exploited, and so long as there is domination by princes, priests or social classes, and so long as the law of equal benefits, justice for all, goes unrecognised. Its objective is not new. The history of civilisation has never known anything else, even if it might be in a less clear form, or one generally less conscious than in our days. Naturally, it is only the oppressed class, the only one to be interested in that information, which possesses historic initiative, and, as the reign of capital is international, and as oppression and exploitation are identical throughout the civilised world, in consequence its aspirations are always international, and everything that is human, and everything that touches on its humanity is morally implicated.

Now, Social-Democracy is still in its adolescence, it will have to pass through many phases of development; as its force matures, as its consciousness becomes clearer; it will have to change its habits often, installing its organisation and constitution in line with its tastes and needs. It goes without saying that this still young movement, which finds itself in opposition to traditional history, in the field of religion, politics and society, will not be entirely free from deficiencies, prejudices, national fads, racisms, supernatural beliefs, etc., of the generation in which it evolves; on the contrary, it conceals within its midst numerous contradictions which it will have to eliminate in the course of its evolution. It must be its own pupil, and its own school, just as its task must be the collective work and the common property of all. Just as every advance in civilisation is the sum of material and intellectual activity of all places, and just as every new progressive step relies on previously acquired knowledge, and on already existing reality, wherein every man is drawn into the cycle of evolution to contribute and go on contributing in some fashion – more or less important – according to the strengths and capacity owed to the community. Even the most genial brain and the most skilled hand, despite every admiration that it might otherwise merit, will not pretend to seek personal privilege. The principles that serve as its foundation and that determine its direction within the processes of historical development, cannot be *invented* because they are already present, narrowly rooted in the essence of things, but only *discovered* and as is well understood formulated ever more exactly and more readily accessible to everyone. As regards the 'Lassalle principles' for example, one cannot consider those that are in conformity with authentic reality, and which act within the sense of the history of civilisation but only those that are contrary to reality, conceived of only in relation to situations which have now been left behind us in the past, good only to make spirits fanatic, pushing them into sectarianism, more or less arbitrarily invented, and belonging properly to their author; it might be very appropriate to say, where applicable, that correct principles are not those of Lassalle, and that the principles of Lassalle are not correct. It is the same for the 'principles' of Schulze-Delitzsch, Proudhon, Fourier, Mill, Marx, etc. Very rarely have thinkers and independent researchers acted like Marx, who himself has never had the pretension to have invented principles, but only to have discovered them, that is to say, to have scientifically proved their presence in the processes of social-economic evolution. How absurd, on the other hand, is the fashion of the press of the economically satisfied ruling class, as it judges the great movements of our time, and treats the principles mentioned above, which have become more and more generalised, and notably in the events that came to the fore in the congress of Geneva! The liberal press sometimes reasons as if one was still in the epoch in which civilisation was entangled in theocratic dress, draped in theological capes, where the 'Holy Spirit' came only from above, where every good idea was considered as the gift of grace of some mystical providence, and where the denominations of religious-parties – such as Christians, Moslems, Lutherans, Calvinists, and other sects named after persons were entirely in their place. However, it is instructive or rather revolting to see the spiritual correspondent of the *Journal des Débats*, in its report on the congresses held in this city, imposing the 'collectivism invented by Bakunin' to the communism 'represented by Marx' and adding Marx is the true father of the communist doctrine called after Lassalle! But what should one say, when one finds even in the socialist camp, the members of a great association which, either out of ignorance or fanatical pride, or as a selfish ruse, adopts the name of Lassalleans, and to them counterposes the sectarian cachet? Is there not there the most pitiless criticism of Lassallean action, already nearly entirely tied up in the corset of its dogmas? In calling the adepts of international socialism (freely emerged from the cultivated ground of science) 'Marxists', the bourgeois press, though acting out of the ignorance demonstrates bad taste, and that much more damaging in that it acts to counterpose them to the senseless sect of 'Bakuninists', which, for its part, carries its very ironical and mocking name as a well-merited punishment. But, when one has read the news of the congress, as presented in that widely presented daily (all so touching in its moralising vigour), the *Journal de Genève*, one is tempted to believe that one is facing a systematic confusion of notions. This so proud paper, which is so jealous of its honour and its journalistic dignity, contents itself with presenting through extracts from the French press everything that it finds so confusing on this subject and even reproduces from the *Landbote* of Winterthur a very severe criticism of the secessionists and their congress, written by one of our comrades, and this to show to the rest of the world – just imagine! – how, with such pertinence, Switzerland appreciates and condemns the activity of the IWMA, and vice versa!

Let us now come to the two congresses one of which, that of the secessionists, had been announced by wall-posters as the 'Congress of the International' and not of the IWMA. That congress brought together six French and one Russian delegates, all resident in Geneva, (of these seven, four delegates represented the 'Revolutionary Socialist Propaganda Section' of the city and its fifteen members, the other three France), six Jura delegates representing some 150 members, three Italians (many sections but many imaginary ones, 300 members) five Spanish, one Belgian, one Dutchman (the latter had been mandated to participate equally both in this and in the following congress, and to observe a conciliatory attitude toward both sides), and two only from England (Hales and the well-known German worker Eccarius), who, as they themselves said, had managed to obtain mandates from bodies which they did not even know up close, in order to be easy to act as journalists at the congress. In all this assembly, there were only seven manual workers, (workers here even allege that there were only four), and thus there were nineteen 'mind-workers' as they modestly called themselves: former teachers, former journalists, and other scribblers and one student. Bakunin was wise enough to stay away. French was the language of the congress, Spanish and Italian were spoken a little, nothing in German or English – and there was a lot of talk. Phrases about social revolution, and slogans – 'anarchy', 'the absence of authority and a state', 'withdrawal from politics', 'not to leave a stone standing from the old world' – stood out, all without consideration of the conditions needed for such a radical remodelling of organisation. Public participation was very limited, and working people in particular were entirely absent, although there were several socialist dilettantes present, with the recently arrived French émigrés contributing a considerable contingent, and a proper squad of Russian women students who came from Zurich, who effectively aided the chatter. Thus, the speakers drew some satisfaction from their pseudo-revolutionary verbiage. Anyone who have read the recently published *Allianz der Sozialistischen Demokratie* (Hamburg, Otto Meissner),* can have at least a rough approximation how busily the Holy Ghost of Anarchy as a World Redeemer was buzzing in plain sight around the heads in the

---

* The first column of the *Volksstaat* of 19 September 1873 carried an announcement for the pamphlet.

Schiess bear-hall, logically, anarchy could not signify organisation, and organisation could not signify anarchy.

The most robust organisations, tyrannies with their rifles and machine-guns, the reign of capital with all its wizardry, disciplined and hierarchical power of its clerics and recourse to heavenly help and holy stupidities, all that will be blown away, by any wind like so much chaff, and disappear into nothingness, if nothing organised. Yes, yes, that is the way of things, didn't God create the world out of nothing; now, in the same way, the Bakuninists will make a nothing-world, out of nothing! But *nihil ad rem*, nothing comes from nothing, and meanwhile, let us leave them to float away in their nothingness just as they wish, and let us move on to something more real, the sixth congress of the IWMA of the Hotel de la Navigation.[711]

The latter congress had 31 delegates, all but four of them manual workers, of these eighteen were German (Germans and German-Swiss), nine French (French and Swiss), two Italian, one Dutch and one Serbian.[712] Among them were two women, one a German, the other a French speaker. The countries represented were Switzerland, Germany, France, Austria, Hungary, Italy, and the Netherlands. Letters had arrived from Serraillier, the representative of the General Council, and from the English Federal Council, according to which, at the moment of departure of these delegates (four persons), there had been obstacles which made it inopportune for them to participate in the congress, and expressing the wish that the congress should maintain the decisions of the London conference of 1871 and of the Congress at The Hague of 1872 and sanction the location of the leadership and administration in New York. The delegate who had been expected from Lisbon did not arrive; he sent a sympathetic telegram, and others then arrived from several Swiss towns, and a confraternal letter came from Bordeaux.

The opening of the congress was on 7th September and took the form of a general popular meeting with participation of a mass of workers. As delegates from the opposing congress spoke, feeling their theories attacked (beyond which there was no salvation); the event took on a slightly fractious tone, but on the whole, it did not lack a useful effect on the workers of Geneva. Monday and Tuesday there were closed sessions, dedicated to validation of mandates and the election of a bureau; but thereafter there were public sessions, or put another way, three sessions a day. The posing of philosophical positions and ideological exaggerations in the previous congress was such that it created a sober ambiance, one which almost went to the other extreme, and especially among the delegates of Geneva, who, in an effort to be practical, sometimes lost sight of theory. Of course, the unanticipated absence of delegates from the General Council and of English delegates was, in the first few days the cause of much disquiet, and that circumstance did nothing to encourage spirits. Despite it all, one can say entirely truthfully, that without a thought being given for the circumstances that would be needed to achieve it, the 'autonomists' did not cease to speak of revolution in their congress, while the latter congress thought much about how to work to create its preconditions, without speaking much about revolution. Organise unions, bring them into federations, centralise them! – that was the solution. The debates were directed with much tact and skill by a Geneva goldsmith, citizen Duparc and conducted in German and French. As usual in international congresses, Germans took on the written and oral translation work. The number of listeners in public sessions was exceptionally strong, especially in evening sessions. The General Council's annual reports – one public (which has already been published in the organs of our party), the other confidential with a financial part – were approved by unanimity less one, the Dutchman. The confidential stressed financial poverty and the need for raising funds; it listed persons appointed with mandates for particular countries and their tasks. There was a request that Congress should formally expel the Jura Federation 'for utter want of party discipline' and for bringing the IWA into disrepute – a request which appear to have fallen by the wayside. The report ended with a request that the General Council be relocated to Europe. Reports from the delegates excited a lively interest. They painted, in the first place, a picture of the state of their sections and federations and more generally of the labour movement in their respective countries. But, one did not proceed as the earlier congress did, where the Spaniards and Italians above all behaved as if every one of the associations or societies they listed belonged to their particular tendency, which is a long way from being so, according to other news received in the course of the last few weeks (last week, three Italian unions asked to be affiliated to our association). A friendly evening in the nearby garden, marked the culmination of the congress week, a mass of workers' families participated, and there were in turn speeches, readings, music, singing and fireworks. It finished with a banquet and was closed on Saturday evening after midnight. I will not present the essential resolutions here which will be the object of a detailed report in the soon to be published minutes. It should however be noted even now that the commission revising the regulations and statutes, in which almost every nuance of the party was represented, has already been able to achieve a general agreement on the modifications to be made, so much so that its tact incited other congress members, to abstain from any tricky opposition; and as the dominant tendency was in any case to display as much unity as possible to the public, and to the congress of the secessionists, the propositions of this commission were adopted without excited discussion, only with minor modifications and editing. However, spirits were raised when the discussion on the location of the General Council and of the next congress were raised; in the end New York and Zurich were voted by a great majority. Other decisions have already been communicated in *Volksstaat*.

To conclude, let us glance at the radically opposed tendencies in the two congresses.

Proudhon's baroque sauce, that 'anarchy was the best of governments', had, deplorably turned the heads of the apostates, it has placed them in the uttermost opposition to the fundamental principle of socialism, and has transformed them into *Sonderbundler* (secessionists). Their logic ends with the breaking down of every social entity into its very atoms; in placing the individual above the collective, and in combatting organisation and centralisation, it deprives society of the strength and means needed for destructive work – revolution – which they embrace more in their hearts, and which they love with such a passion. Another idea, all too attractive to the over-excitable and fanatical elements, but yet contradicting their theory and practice, is the one that pretends that the IWMA has, above all, a mission to force social revolution, in the briefest predetermined period, (but without due organisation!!), to destroy the existing world, and to abandon whatever remains to make the future, which means in their language: to now total anarchy. Even if one admits that this tendency might be inspired by the best of intentions to serve humanity, it cannot win through action that is demagogic and undemocratic, and which through club chatter, with the lumpenproletariat of great cities, this product of class rule, always ready for destruction and vengeance – and more; its success among the lumpenproletariat can only be temporary, and thus artificial, because it is the most unstable army in the world. Being without principles, it belongs always to whoever promises the most, and even places itself in the service of reactionaries, if opportunities arise. For money, it will not hesitate at the first opportunity, to hang the chiefs that it has earlier applauded and acclaimed, it will applaud and salute traditional oppressors as the idols of the day, thus creating some variety in anarchism – thus, through the science of its preconceived ideas of anarchism, it will become the most perfect abscess of the civilised world. Is it not true that NCOs and in part even the officers of certain regular armies, this human scourge, are recruited from this lumpenproletariat?

One should also add that the abstention of our *Sonderbundler* from all 'political activity', were it to be generalised, would deprive working people of all political education, and may undermine the development of the skill needed to destroy the evil, without speaking of the creation of anything better. It is certain that the basic principle of socialism – solidarity – will resist a senseless phrase if these teachings were to be generalised, and if the fraternity they exalt was not erected into an imperious duty, if it is made concrete in the law of a community – failing which it will fall back into personal selfishness, and the demoralising regime of charity, as in the past. Despite all this, the partisans of this tendency imagine that they are pushing history, while they are the ones being pushed, if not cruelly pushed aside.

What then is wanted by the other tendency – the IWMA – on the other side? Placing itself on realistic and scientific foundations, it seeks to develop and build respect for reason and justice. It recognises the labour movement as a cultural and historical entity, a powerful, thorough revolutionary force. According to the times, locations, and circumstance it adopts an offensive or defensive attitude, and as it sees the dominant economic system collapse, it is driven by the consciousness of its mission and by its regenerative energy. It organises, builds, disciplines, moralises; when the moment comes for the final collapse of the old social edifice, it relies on installing its own house in place of that devastation, ready to be lived in and to be improved. In taking an active part in political life, it seeks to adopt a firm position as regards matters of instruction and education; because it is through teaching and education that it aims to undermine despotism and its instruments of blind obedience. Energetically, it demands freedom of action, it wishes to destroy political despotism, wherever and everywhere where it can, by every means possible, to conquer political power for the working class, in order to accelerate and complete its workings – suppressing the dualism of State-Society, working so that society is the state, and the state is society – to place unity in life. Yes, it wishes to abolish disorder, to put in place real order, instead of current disorder, instead of anarchy in production and consumption, instead of the right of the strongest in the economy, instead of an arbitrary State, with its deceitful façade of constitutional forms, this State of class and princely domination.

Suggestions for Further Reading

Documents of the International

Freymond, Jacques, *La première internationale*, (Four volumes), Geneva: Droz, 1962-1972.

And online:

(1) 1866 and 1868: *The International Working Men's Association, London: Resolutions of the Congress of Geneva, 1866, and the Congress of Brussels, 1868.* http://archive.org/stream/resolutionsofcon00inte/resolutionsofcon00inte_djvu.txt Archive.org has also reports on the congress at The Hague, https://archive.org/details/firstinternationalvol6.

(2) 1869: *Compte-rendu du IVe Congrès tenu à Bâle en septembre 1869,* Brussels, Imprimerie Désirée Brismée, 1869. Available online: on http://books.google.co.uk/

Report of the Fourth Annual Congress of the International Working Men's Association, held at 'Basle, in Switzerland, from the 6th to the 11th of September, 1869; Published by the General Council, 1869; available via http://hdl.handle.net/10622/B6E656DD-15BA-4E47-A6F7-B7132F4544C3

(3) 1873: *Compte-rendu officiel du sixième congrès général de l'Association Internationale des travailleurs tenu à Genève du 1er au 6 septembre 1873*, https://helda.helsinki.fi/handle/10138/153643; reports to the centralist congress, e.g. *Confidential report General Council 1873*, IISG, Hermann Jung Papers, Inventory number 78; https://access.iisg.amsterdam/universalviewer/#?manifest=https://hdl.handle.net/10622/ARCH00698.78?locatt=view:manifest; https://search.iisg.amsterdam/Record/ARCH00698/ArchiveAccessAndUse#tabnav

(4) 1876: *AIT: Compte-Rendu, Congrès, Bern, 1876* http://gallica.bnf.fr/ark:/12148/bpt6k5544648f/f6.pleinepage.langFR see also: *Vorwärts*: 8 and 10 November 1876.

Bibliography

https://syndikalismusforschung.files.wordpress.com/2015/06/1_internationale_quellen_erweitert.doc

Other texts

Antología Documental del Anarquismo Español, http://www.cedall.org/Documentacio/IHL/Antologia%20Documental%20del%20Anarquismo%20espanol_V%20I.pdf

Archivo Obrero, various journals, https://archivo-obrero.com/
    hemeroteca/

Bebel, August, *My Life*, University of Chicago Press, 1913;
    https://ia800209.us.archive.org/26/items/cu31924032592077/
    cu31924032592077.pdf

Bensimon, Fabrice; Deluermoz, Quentin & Moisand, Jeanne, Eds, *Arise
    Ye Wretched of the Earth: The First International in a Global Perspective*,
    Leiden: Brill, 2018. (Also online.)

Berthier, René, *Social-democracy and Anarchism in the International
    Workers' Association*, 1864-1877, Talgarth: Merlin Press, 2015.

Bulletin de la Fédération Jurassienne, https://archivesautonomies.org/spip.
    php?article75

Du Bois, W. E. Burghardt, *Black Reconstruction*, New York: Harcourt,
    Brace, 1935. (Also online.)

Eckhardt, Wolfgang, *The First Socialist Schism: Bakunin vs. Marx in the
    International Working Men's Association*, Oakland: PM Press, 2016.

Federación, (Spanish IWMA journal) Available online http://mdc2.cbuc.
    cat/cdm/search/collection/federacion/ https://arca.bnc.cat/arcabib_pro/
    ca/publicaciones/numeros_por_mes.do?idPublicacion=651&anyo=1873

Friedrich-Ebert-Stiftung, *Der Neuer Sozial-Demokrat, Der Volksstaat,* (and
    other German papers), http://fes.imageware.de/fes/web/

Gallica, digital library of the Bibliothèque nationale de France, https://
    gallica.bnf.fr Journals and books, e.g.: *Journal des débats politiques et
    littéraires*; Gustave Lefrançais, *République et Révolution*.

Guillaume, James, *L'Internationale: documents et souvenirs 1864-78*, Paris:
    Societé nouvelle de librairie et d'éditions, and Stock. (Four books: 1905,
    1907, 1909 and 1910). Available online: http://fr.wikisource.org/wiki/
    Auteur:James_Guillaume.)

Haithi Trust, https://babel.hathitrust.org

International Institute of Social History (IISG) Amsterdam, papers
    of various activists, especially the collection of Hermann Jung and
    Friedrich Lessner; clippings from newspapers and reports of various
    sorts, available online: e.g., https://search.iisg.amsterdam/Record/
    ARCH00698

Jstor, https://www.jstor.org/

Léonard, Mathieu, *L'émancipation des travailleurs*, Paris: La Fabrique,
    2011.

Lorenzo, Anselmo, *El proletariado militante: Memorias de un internacional*,
    various editions, online at: https://www.solidaridadobrera.org/ateneo_
    nacho/libros/Anselmo%20Lorenzo%20-%20El%20proletariado%20
    militante.pdf

Marxist website: http://www.marxists.org Texts by Marx, Engels, on the Paris Commune and on the International: https://www.marxists.org/history/international/iwma/index.htm

Mehring, Franz, *Karl Marx: The Story of his Life*, London: Allen & Unwin, 1939. (Available online).

Mémoire Présenté par la fédération jurassienne de l'Association Internationale des Travailleurs à toutes les fédérations de l'Internationale, Sonvilier: Au siége du Comité fédéral jurassien,1873.

Messer-Kruse, Timothy, *The Yankee International: Marxism and the American Reform Tradition, 1848-1876*, Chapel Hill: University of North Carolina Press, 1998.

Nettlau, Max, 'Marx and Engels and the IWMA' *Freedom*, February-April 1907, https://www.libertarian-labyrinth.org/bakunin-library/max-nettlau-marx-and-engels-and-the-iwma-1907/

--, *Bakunin e l'Internazionale in Italia: dal 1864 al 1872*, Geneva: Edizione del Risveglio, 1928. https://www.liberliber.it/mediateca/libri/n/nettlau/bakunin_e_l_internazionale_in_italia/pdf/nettlau_bakunin_e_l_internazionale_in_italia.pdf

--, *La première Internationale en Espagne*, Dordrecht: D. Reidel, 1969.

Scheu, Andreas, *Briefe und Auszüge aus Briefen von Joh. Phil. Becker, Jos. Dietzgen, Friedrich Engels, Karl Marx u. A. an F. A. Sorge und andere*, Stuttgart: J.H.W. Dietz Nachf, 1906, https://ia800906.us.archive.org/24/items/bub_gb_lLIDAAAAYAAJ/bub_gb_lLIDAAAAYAAJ.pdf

The Times (London), https://www.thetimes.co.uk/archive

Le Travailleur (Geneva), 1877, https://archive.org

Woodhull & Claflin's Weekly (New York), http://iapsop.com/archive/materials/woodhull_and_claflins_weekly/

NOTES

Three references below have been abbreviated:
Arise for *Arise Ye Wretched of the Earth: The First International in a Global Perspective*, edited by Fabrice Bensimon, Deluermoz Quentin & Jeanne Moisand, Eds, Leiden: Brill, 2018, p. 273. Timothy Messer-Kruse
BFJ for the *Bulletin de la Fédération Jurassienne*
CW for volumes of Marx & Engels, *Collected Works*, London: Lawrence & Wishart, 1975-2004.

1   Michel Cordillot, 'Socialism v. Democracy? The IWMA in the USA, 1869–1876.' in *Arise*, p. 273. Timothy Messer-Kruse, *The Yankee International: Marxism and the American Reform Tradition, 1848-1876*, Chapel Hill: University of North Carolina Press, 1998, pp. 100ff.

2   *Le Révolté* (Geneva), 1 April 1882, quoted figures of 60,917 imprisoned and 30,113 killed.

3   35 of them according to the *New York Herald*, 18 December 1871, other sources say 180.

4   Jeanne Moisand, 'Revolutions, Republics and IWMA in the Spanish Empire (around 1873)', in *Arise*.

5   *New York Daily Herald*, 18 December 1871; *Chicago Tribune*, 21 December 1871; *The Buffalo Commercial*, 19 December 1871.

6   Some two months earlier there had been an even larger demonstration in New York. 25,000 had marched for the eight-hour day, including African Americans and 200 people from the French IWMA section No, 2. Keona K. Ervin, *The Black Worker*, Vol. 2, Philadelphia: Temple University Press, 1978, pp. 279, 281-2. (Jstor).

7   *The World* (New York), 18 December 1871; Timothy Messer-Kruse, *The Yankee International*, op. cit., p. 196; Ronald Creagh, *Histoire de l'anarchisme aux Etats-Unis d'Amerique*, Grenoble: Editions La Pensée Sauvage, 1981, pp. 147-8.

8   Benoît Hubert, a maker of surgical instruments, joined French New York IWMA section, active in the Spring Street federation, the Sovereigns of Industry and Knights of Labor.

9   Sorge reported that the event had produced quite a stir, and that 'the daily press was full of statements and reports about the "International."' Ronald Creagh, *Histoire de l'anarchisme*, op. cit., pp. 147. Samuel Bernstein, *The First International in America*, New York: Aug. M. Kelley, 1965, p. 90.

10   See introductory remarks, etc, in Philippe Corcuff & Michaël Löwy (Eds), 'Changer le monde sans prendre le pouvoir? Nouveaux libertaires, nouveaux communistes', *Contretemps*, No. 6, Paris: les éditions Textuel, 2003, p. 9.

11   Wolfgang Eckhardt, *The First Socialist Schism*, Oakland: PM Press, 2016, pp. 382ff.

12   See minutes of 3 September below.

13   Charles Alerini, Camille Camet, Andrea Costa, Victor Cyrille, Victor Dave, George Eccarius, James Guillaume, John Hales, Nikolai Joukovsky, Raphaël Farga Pellicer, Jean-Louis Pindy, Henri Van den Abeele. *The Daily News* (London), 5 September 1873.

14   James Guillaume (1844 -1916) was present at the first IWMA congress in 1866 and

was influential in the Jura and in French libertarian networks over fifty years.

15   The congress at The Hague voted to expel Bakunin and Guillaume.

16   George Eccarius (1818-1889), German tailor, active in the Communist League, sometime IWMA general secretary.

17   Hales (1839-?) had been the General Secretary of the London General Council in 1871-72. He worked to build up an English or British regional federation.

18   Charles Thomann, *Jean Louis Pindy*, La Chaux-de-Fonds: Imprimerie Coopératives, 1951.

19   Charles Alerrini, Édouard Andignoux, Alfred Andrié, Jean and Émilie Baptiste, Paul Brousse, Camille Camet, Aristide Claris, François Dumartheray, Jules Montels, Charles Ostyn, Antoine Perrare.

20   *Hague Congress of the First International September 2-7, 1872: Minutes and Documents*, Moscow: Progress Publishers, 1976, pp. 113-15. Delegates based in Germany appear to have been B. Becker (Brunswick, Chemnitz), J. Dietzgen (Dresden), Kugelmann (Celle, Hanover), Ludwig (Mainz), Milke (Berlin) and Schumacher (Solingen). Hepner, editor of *Volksstaat*, had a New York mandate. Others had German mandates, but were not based there e.g., Cuno (Düsseldorf and Stuttgart).

21   Auguste Serraillier (1840-1891) active in the Paris Commune and sentenced to death in absentia, exiled in the UK, collaborated with Marx, appointed the General Council's plenipotentiary for France.

22   Friedrich Sorge (1828-1906), a professional musician, active since the 1848 German revolution. Spent many years in exile in New York, he lived off rents from a boarding house in Hoboken and was rich enough to travel first class. He attended the congress at The Hague, was a loyal follower of Marx and served as General Secretary of the New York council from 1872 to 1874.

23   Nikolai Utin (1845-1883), Russian radical involved in the Land and Freedom network, sometime editor of *l'Égalité* of Geneva, returned to Russia and requested a government pardon.

24   Johann Phillipp Becker (1809-1886) a brush-maker turned small businessman, active in the German revolutions of 1848, then in exile in Geneva, a Marx ally.

25   *Der Bund* (Bern), 14 September 1873. Andreas Scheu and other radicals criticised Oberwinder over his support for liberal electoral reforms and demanded his resignation from the *Volkswille*. The *Linzer Volksblatt*, 4 September 1873 wrote of workers being used as toys by the liberals.

26   For example, Aristide Claris, a former communard, had to contend with surveillance by Belgian and Swiss authorities.

27   L. Bertrand, *Histoire de la Démocratie et du Socialisme en Belgique*, Vol. 2 Paris: Cornély, 1906, p. 227

28   Ibid., p. 182,

29   John W. Boyle, 'Ireland and the First International', *Journal of British Studies*, Vol. 11, No. 2, 1972, p. 61.

30   See notes in the *Eastern Post*, 15 February 1873.

31   Jacques Rougerie, 'Sur l'histoire de la Première Internationale: Bilan d'un colloque et de quelques récents travaux', *Le Mouvement Social*, No. 51, 1965, p. 33. (Jstor); Errico Malatesta, 'La Prima Internazionale', *Pensiero e Voluntà*, No. 18, September 1924.

32   Giuseppe Mazzini (1805–1872), Italian revolutionary (Catholic).

33   Bakunin drafted a critique of Mazzini, 'Agli Operai delegati al Congresso di Roma', for a conference that met in November 1871. The text was sent to London, and praised by Engels, who was unaware who had written it. Mikhail Bakunin, *Selected Texts 1868-1875*, London: Anarres, 2016, pp. 184-86.

34   Carlos Fontes, *Anarquismo em Portugal (1796-2022)*, https://colectivolibertarioevora. files.wordpress.com/2022/11/anarquismoemportugal.pdf

35   Marx's *Capital* was 'written subjected to a preconceived system … whereas a real scientific method would have checked facts, over and beyond any systemic preoccupation … Marx believes that he is a materialist; in reality he is not,' *BFJ*, 15 June 1872.

36   'Carlo Cafiero accomplished an important work in drafting this summary of *Capital*, approved and looked over by experts and even by Marx himself …' https://www. marxists.org/archive/cafiero/1879/summary-of-capital.htm The anarchist journal *L'Avant-garde* (La Chaux-de-Fonds), 28 June 1879 welcomed its publication.

37   Pier Carlo Masini, *Storia degli anarchici italiani, da Bakunin a Malatesta (1862-1892)*, Milano: Rizzoli, 1972, pp. 62-63; Max Nettlau, *Bakunin e l'Internazionale in Italia*, op. cit., pp. 560, 493ff.

38   See Mathieu Léonard, 'Carlo Cafiero and the International in Italy', op. cit.

39   Marc Vuilleumier, 'Sur quelques proscrits de la Commune', *Le Mouvement social*, No. 44, 1963, p. 71.

40   Auguste Blanqui (1805–1881), French socialist insurrectionist. His followers cooperated with Marx and Engels for a brief period in 1872, but lost confidence in them, and deserted the IWMA.

41   'La Première Internationale', http://commune1871-rougerie.fr/ internationale%2Cfr%2C8%2C103.html

42   Liberal Hirsch-Duncker unions sought co-operation with management, see: https:// www.gewerkschaftsgeschichte.de/neue-gruendungswelle-gewerkschaftsidee-breitet-sich-aus.html; A figure around 19,000 is quoted in: Dick Geary, 'Socialism and the German Labour before 1914,' in Dick Geary, Ed, *Labour and Socialist Movements in Europe before 1914*, Oxford: Berg, 1989, pp. 101-2.

43   Nunzio Pernicone, *Italian Anarchism: 1864-1892*, Oakland: AK Press, 2009, p. 83; Julius Braunthal, 'Die Stärke der Ersten Internationale: Legende und Wirklichkeit', *International Review of Social History*, Vol. 5, No. 2, 1960, pp. 249–64.

44   Jan Moulaert, *Le mouvement anarchiste en Belgique*, Ottignies (Belgium): Quorum, 1996, p. 22.

45   Peter Kropotkin, *Memoirs of a Revolutionist*, Boston: Houghton, Mifflin, 1889, p. 177.

46   *Documents of the First International*, (5 volumes), Vol. 5, London: Lawrence & Wishart, 1962, p. 462.

47   Max Nettlau, *La première Internationale en Espagne*, op. cit., pp. 171-72; 181-82.

48   Jean-Charles Buttier, 'James Guillaume et l'usage des statistiques: un savoir au service de l'émancipation', *Cahiers d'histoire. Revue d'histoire critique*, No. 138, 2018, pp. 41-58.

49   Adriana Dadà, *L'anarchismo in Italia fra movimento e partito: Storia e documenti dell'anarchismo italiana*, Milan: Teti Editore, 1984, document 5, pp. 165-170.

50   Pier Carlo Masini, *Storia degli anarchici italiani*, op. cit., pp. 82-84.

51   The May 1873 edition of the *Bollettino della Federazione Italiana della Associazione*

Internazionale dei Lavoratori, reports various activities and strikes.

52   Celso Ceretti (1844-1909) had been a Garibaldi supporter before joining the Italian IWMA. Later that year he volunteered to fight in Spain against the Carlists.

53   Pier Carlo Masini, *Storia degli anarchici italiani*, op. cit., pp. 77-85.

54   *Daily News*, 5 September 1873.

55   Max Nettlau, *Bakunin e l'Internazionale in Italia*, op. cit., p. 634.

56   Errico Malatesta, *Le Réveil* (Geneva), 12, 26 January, 9 February 1929. Malatesta wrote that libertarians began as a network of dozens. The IWMA constituted then no more than an infinitely small minority, unknown in many regions.

57   Élisée Reclus, (1830–1905), French geographer and anarchist, served in the Paris Commune's national guard and was sentenced to deportation for life.

58   *La Federación* (Barcelona), 22 November 1873.

59   Kropotkin wrote that over 80,000 Spaniards paid regular dues to the IWMA. *Memoirs of a Revolutionist*.

60   The Belgian IWMA federation had a peak membership of six to seven thousand members, Jan Moulaert, *Le Mouvement Anarchiste en Belgique*, op. cit., p. 22.

61   A membership of 10,000 (exaggerated?) is mentioned for Geneva, https://bge-geneve.ch/iconographie/personne/association-internationale-des-travailleurs

62   Max Nettlau, *La première Internationale en Espagne*, op. cit., pp. 140-41.

63   See 'On Leaders and Politics', in Mikhail Bakunin, *Selected Texts 1868-1875*, op. cit., pp. 119-20.

64   Max Nettlau, *Bakunin und die russische revolutionäre Bewegung in den Jahren 1868-1873*. In: Archiv für die Geschichte des Sozialismus und der Arbeiterbewegung, (Carl Grünberg Ed.), Leipzig: Hirschfeld, 1915, Vol. 5, p. 410.

65   Peter Lavrov (1823-1900), Russian, teacher, IWMA member, socialist; in Paris in 1871, in Zurich in 1872-3; Alan Kimball, 'The First International and the Russian Obshchina', *Slavic Review*, Vol. 32, No. 3, 1973, pp. 491-514; Graham John Gamblin, 'Russian populism and its relations with anarchism 1870-1881', University of Birmingham. Ph.D thesis, 2000, pp. 164-65.

66   Florian Eitel, *Anarchistische Uhrmacher in der Schweiz*, Bielefeld: Transcript Verlag, 2018, pp. 256-57.

67   *La Federación* (Barcelona), 18 October 1873.

68   Pindy, had served as a colonel in the army of the commune; sentences of death had been passed on other delegates: Charles Alerini, Jules Montels, Charles Ostyn; and deportation on Édouard Andignoux, Antoine Perrare). https://maitron.fr

69   Gustave Lefrançais (1826–1901), a teacher, Communard, member of the Jura Federation, anarchist; he attended the Saint Imier IWMA congress and spoke at public sessions of the federalist congress of 1873.

70   French authorities were also helped by counterparts in London.

71   *La Federación*, 18 October 1873.

72   Zamfir Ralli, alias Z. K. Arbore, (1848-1933), medic, worked with Bakunin up to 1873, moved to Geneva. later a Romanian senator.

73   *BFJ*, 15 April 1873.

74   Paul Avrich, *Bakunin and Nechaev*, London: Freedom Press, 1987.

75   *Neue Zürcher Zeitung*, 27 September 1872; Woodford McClellan, 'Nechaevshchina: An Unknown Chapter', *Slavic Review*, Vol. 32, No. 3, 1973, pp. 546–53.

76   Bakunin, *Les Ours de Berne et l'Ours de Saint-Pétersbourg*, Neuchâtel: G. Guillaume, 1870.

77   *The Times*, 10 September 1873.

78   *The Daily News*, 5 September 1873.

79   *London Evening Standard*, 1 September 1873.

80   Richard Hostetter, *The Italian Socialist Movement*, Princeton: Van Nostrand, 1958, p. 314.

81   *The Times*, 10 September 1873, (report dated the 6th).

82   For contrasting perspectives see: Marcello Musto, ed., *Workers Unite! The International 150 Years Later*, London: Bloomsbury, 2014, chapter XI; and a critical review: anarchism.pageabode.com/anarcho/review-workers-unite-international-150-years-later.

83   He hoped that if the FRE continued to grow. Max Nettlau, *La première Internationale en Espagne*, op. cit., p. 175.

84   Probably written by Johann George Eccarius.

85   See also: Henry Collins, 'The English Branches of The First International', in Asa Briggs & John Saville (Eds), *Essays in Labour History*, London: Macmillan, 1960.

86   Adhémar Schwitzguébel (1844-1895) was a key figure in the Jura Federation. He had travelled to Paris to help Commune rebels find a refuge in Switzerland. A congress motion at The Hague to expel him from the IWMA was defeated.

87   He never came.

88   Errico Malatesta, 'La Prima Internazionale', *Pensiero e Voluntà*, No. 18, September 1924.

89   Jacques Freymond, *La première internationale*, Geneva: Droz, 1962, Vol. 2, p. 109.

90   See note 382.

91   Julius Braunthal, 'Die Stärke der Ersten Internationale', op. cit., p. 262.

92   The delegates did begin to discuss the pros and cons of national electoral party politics. Judging by the record of this discussion, more delegates opposed electoral politics. See René Berthier, *Social-democracy and Anarchism in the International Workers' Association, 1864-1877*, Talgarth: Merlin Press, 2015, pp. 169-72.

93   Developments in the IWMA between 1869 and 1872 are dealt with at greater length in Wolfgang Eckhardt, *The First Socialist Schism*, op. cit., and in René Berthier, *Social-democracy and Anarchism in the International Workers' Association*.

94   Adopted by the Hague Congress September 1872; see: https://www.marxists.org/history/international/iwma/documents/1872/hague-conference/resolutions.htm

95   K. Steven Vincent, *Between Marxism and Anarchism: Benoît Malon and French Reformist Socialism*, University of California Press, 1992, p. 49.

96   The *Eastern Post*, 1 and 15 February 1873, reported on the congress of the British I.W.A. (London 26 January 1873; it was reported that at The Hague 26 copies of balloting papers were unmistakably copies. IISG, Hermann Jung Papers number 160; *La Federación* (Barcelona), 15 March 1873.

97   *La Federación*, 18 January 1873. Short report on congresses of the Belgian Federation appeared in the *BFJ*, 15 January, 15 May, 15 July, 24 and 31 August 1873. *The Times* (London), 5 September 1873. Léon-E. Halkin, 'Liège, la Première Internationale et la Commune', *Revue belge de philologie et d'histoire*, Vol. 44, No. 4, 1966, p. 1171.

98   A text written in 1872 and 1873, in *CW*, Vol. 23, pp. 421-25.

99   Marx: 'the distribution of general functions has become a routine matter which entails no domination', *CW*, Vol. 24, pp. 519-20.

100 The King of Prussia had been overthrown as Prince of Neuchâtel, but still had supporters there. Dr Coullery sought an electoral alliance with this royalist party. Once elected, Coullery and his ally 'never said a word about socialism', *BFJ*, 3 May 1874; James Guillaume, *L'Internationale: documents et souvenirs 1864-78*, Paris: Societé nouvelle de librairie et d'éditions, Book 1, 1905, p. 61.

101 Detlev Mares, 'Little Local Difficulties?' in *Arise* p. 51.

102 Henry Collins, 'The English Branches', op. cit., pp. 249-51, 264.

103 Marc Vuilleumier, 'La Suisse', *International Review of Social History*, Vol. 17 (1), 1972, pp. 290. A hundred years would pass before Swiss women could vote. Foreign workers, a quarter of the labour force, are disenfranchised.

104 Ibid, p. 297.

105 Mikhail Bakunin, *Selected Texts 1868-1875*, op. cit., pp. 117, 119-20, 144-46.

106 In the USA many people of African and Chinese descent could not vote. In Geneva, strikes by building workers came to be seen, by Utin and other centralists as impediments to electoral prospects. Many strikers were non-citizens, who had no electoral prospects. Kropotkin, *Memoirs of a Revolutionist*, op. cit. pp. 178-79; Wolfgang Eckhardt, *The First Socialist Schism*, op. cit., p. 32n.

107 *L'Ami du Peuple*, 6 July 1873.

108 1 November 1870; *Documents of the First International*, Vol. 4, op. cit., p. 81.

109 *Bulletin*, 15 February 1873; *The Workingman's Advocate* (Chicago), 27 September 1873.

110 Mark A. Lause, 'The American Radicals & Organized Marxism: The initial experience, 1869–1874', *Labor History*, Vol. 33, No.1, 1992, p. 76.

111 Samuel Bernstein, *The First International in America*, op. cit., pp. 65, 87.

112 Keona K. Ervin, *The Black Worker*, Vol. 2, op. cit., pp. 272, 276-77; Henry Louis Gates (Jr), *Stony The Road: Reconstruction, White Supremacy, and the Rise of Jim Crow*, New York: Penguin Press, p. 15.

113 Russell Maroon Shoatz, *Autonomous Resistance to Slavery and Colonization*; notyrcister press, https://libcom.org/files/autonomousresistancetoslaveryandcolonization.pdf; Haley Markbreiter, *An Interview with Saralee Stafford and Neal Shirley, Dixie Be Damned, But Damn Everything Too*, June 2017, https://thenewinquiry.com/dixie-be-damned-but-damn-everything-too/22

114 Hermann Schlüter, *Die Internationale in Amerika*, op cit., Chicago: Deutsche Sprachgruppe der Sozialist. Partei der Ver. Staaten, 1918, pp. 152, 155, 164. (https://archive.org/details/18schluterdieinternationaleinamerika/page/n165/mode/1up?view=theater).

115 Mark A. Lause, 'The American Radicals & Organized Marxism', op. cit., pp. 67, 111. See also Timothy Messer-Kruse, *The Yankee International*, op. cit., pp. 166-70, 148, 'immoral and self-defeating'.

116 Ibid., p. 134.

117 Ibid., p. 31.

118 'Their demands of woman suffrage and woman's rights, said Bolte, were not of great moment to the labor movement.' Samuel Bernstein, *The First International in*

America, op. cit., pp. 116-22.

119   Stan Nadel, The German Immigrant Left in the United States, in Paul Buhle & Dan Georgakas (Eds), *The Immigrant Left in the United States,* New York: SUNY Press, 1996; Timothy Messer-Kruse, *The Yankee International,* op. cit., p. 152.

120   Timothy Messer-Kruse, *The Yankee International,* op. cit., pp. 121-22.

121   *New Orleans Republican,* 9 February1873.

122   *BFJ,* 20 July 1873.

123   Report on the Congress of 19 January 1873, in *BFJ,* 1 April 1873. Max Nettlau's analysis of the intent of various IWMA supporters to promote socialism and the IWMA can be found in *La Protesta* (Buenos Aires), 23, 24, 26 November 1922.

124   The General Council condemned the Spring Street federation because fewer than two-thirds of its members were manual workers. Eccarius rejected their exclusion and noted that by that criteria the General Council was itself deficient. Ronald Creagh, *Histoire de l'anarchisme aux Etats-Unis,* op. cit., p. 150.

125   Timothy Messer-Kruse, *The Yankee International,* op. cit., pp. 204-205.

126   Hermann Schlüter called it a humbug convention: *Die Internationale in Amerika,* op. cit., p. 165.

127   Timothy Messer-Kruse, *The Yankee International,* op. cit., p. 201.

128   Ibid., pp. 14, 119-20.

129   Mark A. Lause, 'The American Radicals & Organized Marxism', op. cit., p. 78. Bernstein says the premise of the Woodhull *Weekly* was co-operation between capital and labour. Samuel Bernstein, *The First International in America,* op. cit., p. 113. See also: Ronald Creagh, *Histoire de l'anarchisme aux Etats-Unis,* op. cit., p. 135. The *Weekly* published the *Communist Manifesto* in its edition of 30 December 1871, and Marx's *Civil War in France.*

130   The issue of 20 September 1873 carried an article on 'Colored people' combining to buy and run land. The ongoing persecution of Africa-Americans was given less attention.

131   Friedrich Sorge, 'Die Arbeiterbewegung in den Vereinigten Staaten', in Miriam Frank & Martin Glaberman, 'Friedrich A. Sorge on the American Labor Movement', *Labor History,* Vol. 18, No. 4, 1977, p. 602.

132   John R. Commons, et al. (Eds), *A Documentary History of American Industrial Society,* Volume IX, Cleveland Ohio, Arthur H. Clark, 1910, p. 372.

133   *The New York Herald,* 3 & 10 March 1873.

134   Samuel Bernstein, *The First International in America,* op. cit., p. 141.

135   *New York Daily Herald,* 19 August 1872; Michel Cordillot, 'Socialism v. Democracy? The IWMA in the USA, 1869–1876.' op. cit., p. 276.

136   *Eastern Post,* 11, 16, (with the comment from New York) 29 March, 18, 19 April 1873.

137   *New-York Tribune,* 20 January 1874, Samuel Bernstein, *The First International in America,* op. cit., p. 195.

138   *Eastern Post* (London date unclear, 1873), IISG, Hermann Jung Papers, Inventory number 161, https://hdl.handle.net/10622/ARCH00698.161

139   *The Workingman's Advocate* (Chicago), 9 July and 27 September 1873; *Woodhull & Claflin's Weekly,* 9 May 1874.

140   *The Redwood Gazette* (Minnesota), 31 July 1873.

141   Francis Kessler, 'L'émergence des conventions collectives de travail en Allemagne au

XIXe et au début du XXe siècle', *Revue d'histoire moderne et contemporaine*, Vol. 36, No. 3, July-September, 1989. p. 512.

142   *Der Volksstaat*, 10 October 1873.

143   *Mémoire Présenté par la fédération jurassienne de l'Association Internationale des Travailleurs à toutes les fédérations de l'Internationale*, Sonvilier: Au siége du Comité fédéral jurassien, 1873, p. 284(n).

144   Hermann Schlüter, *Die Internationale in Amerika*, op. cit., p. 265; there is a record that German Social-Democrats remitted $25.92.

145   See: Anselmo Lorenzo, *El proletariado militante: Memorias de un internacional*, (Bilbao: Zero, 1974, first published 1901, various editions); https://theanarchistlibrary.org/library/anselmo-lorenzo-the-conference-in-london

146   *CW*, Vol. 43. p. 475.

147   *Reynolds's Newspaper* (London), 28 July 1872, comments on the extent of IWMA presence in Britain. Wolfgang Eckhardt, *The First Socialist Schism*, op. cit., p. 393.

148   *Daily News*, 5 September 1873.

149   Royden Harrison, 'Marx, Engels, and the British Response to the Commune', *The Massachusetts Review*, Vol. 12, No. 3, 1971 978-3-643-91223-7. (Jstor).

150   Henry Collins, 'Karl Marx, the International and the British Trade Union Movement', *Science & Society*, Vol. 26, No. 4, 1962, pp. 415ff. (Jstor)

151   On the IWMA in Britain in 1872 see *BFJ*, 15 February 1873; Duncan Bowie, 'The British Labour Movement and European nationalism and socialism in the nineteenth century', *Socialist History*, No. 57, 2020.

152   See Nicolas Delalande, 'Transnational Solidarity', in Fabrice Bensimon, et al, *Arise Ye Wretched*, op. cit., p. 69.

153   See: Antony Taylor, '"Sectarian Secret Wisdom" and Nineteenth-Century Radicalism: The IWMA in London and New York', in *Arise* p. 295; David Burbank, in *Reign of the Rabble: The St Louis General Strike of 1877*, New York: Augustus M Kelley, 1966, p. 34 and *CW*, Vol. 23, p. 284. A letter of Engels of 5 October 1872 suggests that the General Council, had it been left in London, would have come under the control of followers of Blanqui, or 'corrupt men used to selling themselves to the liberal bourgeoisie'.

154   Henry Collins, 'The English Branches', op. cit., p. 244.

155   See also appendix one; Henry Collins, 'The English Branches', op. cit., pp. 256-59. Universal Federalists objected to the 'centralizing and despotic power' in the IWMA. Jung supported electoral politics, believing that the next great step for the labour movement was to get working men into the legislature, 'in the first instance [this] requires combinations and alliances with the advanced men of the middle classes.' *Eastern Post*, 9 February 1873; 26 May 1872, and several rebuttals, dated June and after; also the *Daily News*, 20 September 1872. (Jung collection, IISG).

156   *Spain and the World*, 15 May 1937. See also: Detlev Mares, 'Die englischen Publikationsorgane der Internationalen Arbeiterassoziation', MEGA-Studien 1998/2, pp. 24-48.

157   Hales's proposition was defeated. *Documents of the First International*, Vol. 5, op. cit., pp. 248-52.

158   21 July 1873, 'The Alliance', *CW*, Vol. 23., op. cit., p. 556. 'in Marx's opinion the responsibility for drafting and enforcing a common theoretical programme

– compulsory for all – lay with the General Council where he set the agenda …',
Wolfgang Eckhardt, *The First Socialist Schism*, op. cit., p. 82. For an assessment of
the Federal Bureau set up instead of the General Council, see: Miklós Molnár, 'La
Fédération jurassienne comme siège du Bureau fédéral', *Actes de la Société jurassienne
d'émulation*, Vol. 75, 1972.

159 The Sonvilier congress (November 1871), also passed statutes setting out that:
'No authority is invested in the [Jura] Federal Committee.' James Guillaume,
L'Internationale: documents et souvenirs 1864-78, Paris: Societé nouvelle de librairie et
d'éditions, 1907, Book 2, Part 4, Chapter 1, pp. 236, 239-44.

160 In the USA American centralists had an organisational structure described as a
pyramid, with a supreme Federal Council, at its tip. Its delegates at The Hague were
mandated to press for strong centralisation, Samuel Bernstein, *The First International
in America*, op. cit., pp. 143-44.

161 *Documents of the First International*, Vol. 4, op. cit., p. 270.

162 *CW*, Vol. 21, pp. 84ff.

163 *CW*, Vol. 22, pp. 421-24, emphasis added; Vol. 23, p. 411-12.

164 See also chapters on the London conference and its aftermath in: Wolfgang Eckhardt,
The First Socialist Schism, op. cit.

165 Letter, 11 September 1867, *CW*, Vol. 42, p. 424.

166 *CW*, Vol. 22, p. 614, e,g,: 'The trades unions can do nothing by themselves…'

167 *Mémoire Présenté*, op. cit, and James Guillaume, *L'Internationale*, op. cit., Volume 1,
part 1, pp. 10ff.

168 https://www.marxists.org/archive/marx/works/1871/09/politics-resolution.htm

169 Letter to Jenney Marx, 23 September 1871.

170 James Guillaume, *L'Internationale: documents et souvenirs 1864-78*, op. cit., book 3,
part 3, chapter 12, pp. 222-23.

171 *BFJ*, 8 June 1872.

172 César De Paepe (1841-1890), medical doctor, a veteran Belgian IWMA activist, later a
Social-Democrat.

173 Hermann Jung (1830-1901), Swiss watchmaker, active in the German revolutions of
1848, then moved to London; General Council member and IWMA corresponding
secretary for Switzerland 1864-1872.

174 Franz Mehring, *Karl Marx: The Story of his Life*, London, Allen & Unwin, 1939,
chapter 9.

175 See Marx's letter to Engels, 4 November 1864. https://www.marxists.org/archive/
marx/works/1864/letters/64_11_04-abs.htm

176 *Documents of the First International*, Vol. 5, op. cit., p. 271

177 Bakunin formed successive fraternal networks. Max Nettlau, *La première
Internationale en Espagne*, Dordrecht: D. Reidel, 1969, pp. 53-67.

178 Letter to Engels, 27 July 1869, and envisaging his expulsion from the IWMA, *CW*,
Vol. 43, pp. 332-33.

179 *CW*, Vol. 22, pp. 79, 411-12; 472-73.

180 *La Révolution Sociale*, November 1871, quoted in Erich Gruner, 'La Suisse et le
tournant historique de 1870-1871', *Revue d'Histoire Moderne & Contemporaine*, Vol.
19-2, pp. 235-45.

181 André Léo, (alias of Victoire Léodile Béra, 1824–1900) exiled to Geneva, wrote with

other communards for *La Révolution Sociale.*

182 K. Steven Vincent, *Between Marxism and Anarchism*, op. cit., p. 47.

183 *CW*, Vol. 23, 1985, p. 95.

184 *CW*, Vol. 22, p. 417; CW, Vol. 44., p. 307.

185 *Hague Congress of the First International September 2-7, 1872: Minutes and Documents,* Moscow: Progress Publishers, 1976, p. 532.

186 Minutes of 5 March 1872 record that Marx related only salient points of the French text to the General Council. Documents were habitually sent out 'signed' with the names of all its members, even where members had been absent at meetings that approved them or had not read them. Maltmann Barry said he did not wish to endorse a document he did not understand. *Documents of the First International*, Vol. 5, op. cit., pp. 119-20; Edmond Villetard, *Histoire de l'Internationale*, Paris: Garnier, 1872, p. 249.

187 Marianne Enckell, *La Fédération jurassienne*, Genève: Éditions Entremonde, 2012, p. 105; *La Liberté* (Geneva), 13 October 1872; *La Antorcha*, (Buenos Aires), 11 January 1924.

188 It also published a letter from Lafargue, and reply.

189 *BFJ*, 15 June 1872.

190 For critique of the gap between certain Anglophone (Marxist) and Francophone (Anarchist) perspectives see: René Berthier, '"Science & Society", Mr A. H. Nimtz & Bakunin', https://www.academia.edu/39262714/_Science_and_Society_Mr_A_H_ Nimtz_and_Bakunin.

191 Hales was accused of making irregular contacts with the American Spring Street federation.

192 Eugène Dupont wrote to Engels and described horizontal communication as 'treason'. Henry Collins, 'The English Branches', op. cit., p. 262.

193 *Reynolds's Newspaper* (London), 28 July 1872.

194 See chapter on the Sonvilier Circular in: Wolfgang Eckhardt, *The First Socialist Schism*, op. cit.

195 James Guillaume, *L'Internationale: documents et souvenirs 1864-78*, Paris: Stock, 1909, Vol. 3, part 4, chapter 5, p. 304; part 5, chapter 3, pp. 67, 82. One edition of *Volkswille* was seized, after it protested against the expulsion of Paris communards from Austria-Hungary.

196 Wolfgang Eckhardt, *The First Socialist Schism*, op. cit., p. 393.

197 The paper, run by a small Madrid network allied with Marx and Engels, had published the names of IWMA supporters, setting them up for arrest.

198 Max Nettlau, *La première Internationale en Espagne*, op. cit., pp. 164-65.

199 Timothy Messer-Kruse, *The Yankee International*, op. cit., p. 162.

200 August Bebel (1840–1913) and Wilhelm Liebknecht (1826-1900) long-serving German Socialist activists and Reichstag deputies.

201 *Der Volksstaat*, 2 July 1873.

202 It was true that odd former members of the IWMA worked for Napoleon, but it was a blatant lie that 'Revolution ist also diesen Bakunisten identisch mit Bonapartismus', *Volksstaat*, 19 October 1873, p, 2.

203 *BFJ*, 2 and 30 November 1873.

204 Ibid, 14 December 1873.

205   20 September and 5 April 1873; https://permalinkbnd.bnportugal.gov.pt/serials-titles/item/6528-o-pensamento-social

206   Engels wrote to Sorge to request a subsidy for *La Plebe*; Samuel Bernstein, *The First International in America*, op. cit., p. 173.

207   Marianne Enckell, *La Fédération jurassienne*, p. 95.

208   *Der Volksstaat*, 18 June 1873; Jacques Freymond, *La première internationale*, Geneva: Droz, 1972, Vol. 3, p. 151.

209   Eckhardt, *The First Socialist Schism*, op. cit., p. 368.

210   The response of the Italian federation was similar, *La Federación* (Barcelona, 1 February 1873)

211   *Woodhull & Claflin's Weekly* (New York), 26 April 1873.

212   See also a letter of James Guillaume, June 1876, in: Pier Carlo Masini, *Storia degli anarchici italiani*, op. cit., pp. 291-93.

213   This edition also remarked on workers facing hunger, cold, having no political or social rights, no right to life or to work, having no freedom of speech.

214   Max Nettlau, *La première Internationale en Espagne*, op. cit., p. 170.

215   A loan from Engels perhaps, Samuel Bernstein, *The First International in America*, op. cit., pp. 149-50.

216   *CW*, Vol. 22, p. 414; Vol. 44, p. 220. Summary of Financial Administration etc, in *Hague Congress of the First International September 2-7, 1872*: Moscow: Progress Publishers, 1976, pp. 659ff. See also: R.P. Morgan, *The German Social Democrats and the First International*, Cambridge University Press, 1965, p. 183; Wolfgang Eckhardt, *The First Socialist Schism*, op. cit., pp. 86ff.

217   For example, see a communication from the English to the Belgian IWMA, suggesting the replacement of the General Council, noting that the resolutions of The Hague were null and void, and raising such points as a change of name for the IWMA; another from the Spanish IWMA called for the reassertion of integrity and the principles of freedom and federation: *L'Internationale, Organe des sections Belges de AIT* (Brussels), 4 May 1873.

218   The British Congress of 26th January 1873 concluded that in 1872 at The Hague: 'That the programme for that Congress had not been previously submitted to the cognizance of the branches as required by the General Rules, Administrative Regulations Art. 1, Rule 10'; it repudiated 'the action taken at the Congress of the Hague, and its nominee, the so-called General Council of New York.' It saw resolutions passed at The Hague as subversive of the Fundamental Pact of the IWMA which recognised the right of every Federation to decide upon its own action. *The Eastern Post*, 9 February 1873; see also *BFJ* of 1 March 1873, p. 4.

219   Letter, Engels to Sorge, 3 May 1873, in *CW*, Vol. 44., op. cit., pp. 490-94. Wolfgang Eckhardt, *The First Socialist Schism*, op. cit., p. 358.

220   Hermann Schlüter, *Die Internationale in Amerika*, op. cit., p. 256.

221   *BFJ*, 1 December 1872.

222   Hermann Schlüter, *Die Internationale in Amerika*, op. cit., p. 230.

223   Letter, Sigismund Borkheim to Frederick Engels, 9 October 1872, in *The Hague Congress of the First International: Reports and letters*, Moscow: Progress Publishers, 1978, p. 557.

224   *Der Zeitgeist: Organ für das arbeitende Volk* (Munich), 18 September 1873. In 1876, a

key party committee had over 50,000 marks available to spend on propaganda.

225 Wolfgang Eckhardt, *The First Socialist Schism*, op. cit., pp. 299-301.

226 '[T]he General Rules adopted by the Hague Congress stressed that the General Council was a body answerable to all the members of the Association.' *The Hague Congress of the First International*, op. cit., p. 22. The article on the IWMA in England, mentioned here is in the *BFJ*, 15 February 1873; it quoted a General Council circular number 34, published in the *International Herald* to the effect that political action was obligatory.

227 The New York council received dues from sections in North America and occasionally from Europe. Hermann Schlüter, *Die Internationale in Amerika*, op. cit., p. 230.

228 General Council instructions to Auguste Serraillier, 18-22 July 1873?, IISG, Hermann Jung Papers, Inventory number 77.

229 *CW*, Vol. 44, p. 523.

230 Jacques Freymond, *La première internationale*, Vol. 1, Geneva: Droz, 1962, p. 404; not universally welcomed! *CW*, Vol. 43, op. cit., p. 101; see also letter to Bebel, Vol. 45, p. 62.

231 Heiner Becker, 'Johann Most in Europe', *The Raven* (London), No. 4 1988, p. 293.

232 *Der Hochverraths-Prozeß wider Liebknecht, Bebel, Hepner vor dem Schwurgericht zu Leipzig vom 11. bis 26. März 1872. Mit einer Einleitung von W. Liebknecht*, Berlin: Vorwärts, 1894.

233 *Der Volksstaat*, 22 August and 28 September 1873.

234 *Le Travailleur* (Geneva), July 1877, p. 23.

235 *La Emancipación* (Madrid), 3 July 1871

236 *La Federación* (Barcelona), 1 March 1873; Anselmo Lorenzo, *El proletariado militante*, op. cit.;

237 *L'Internationale, Organe des sections Belges de AIT* (Brussels), 12 October 1873. *Volksstaat* 8 October 1873.

238 Edmond Villetard, *Histoire de l'Internationale*, Paris: Garnier, 1872, p. 142.

239 *Freedom* (London), September – October 1900, emphasis added.

240 Michel Bakounine, letter, 'Aux Frères de l'A[lliance] en Espagne', Locarno, 12-13 June 1872.

241 French translation: 'Aux officiers de l'armée russe', Geneva, January 1870; text 70003, Michel Bakounine, *Oeuvres complètes* (CD), Amsterdam: International Institute of Social History, 2000.

242 *Eastern Post*, 3 May 1873. *The World* (New York), 1 February 1873.

243 *BFJ* 15 April 1873; see also Samuel Bernstein, *The First International in America*, op. cit., p. 164; *Der Volksstaat*, 18 June 1873, carried a note from the New York council denying that he had been appointed.

244 Report on the Geneva congress in *The Times* (London), 5 September 1873.

245 Marx, to Bolte: 'what is needed above all is vigorous action from the General Council', 12 February; and to Sorge: 'Postponing the Congress is absolutely out of the question; it would mean abandoning the field to the other side', 14 June 1873, *CW*, Vol. 44, pp. 476, 507.

246 The New York General Council declared that 'all persons and societies who refuse to recognise congress resolutions or who deliberately fail to fulfil duties imposed

on them by general regulations and statutes place themselves outside the IWMA and cease to belong to it'. (*Volksstaat*, 26 January, and 30 May 1873). See also: handwritten minutes in the IISG Jung collection; James Guillaume, *L'Internationale: documents et souvenirs 1864-78*, Paris: Stock, 1909, part 5, Chapter 3, p. 58; and René Berthier, *Social-democracy and Anarchism*, op. cit., p. 91.

247   *BFJ*, 15 June 1872.

248   See speech by Hermann Jung, appendix one below, and a resolution of the British federation.

249   A process often used in factional struggles: 'With such an honest conscience, one takes over the arguments of an adversary, one warps and deforms them, and rapidly one makes any confrontation and dialogue impossible.' Marc Vuilleumier, 'La correspondance du peintre Gustave Jeanneret', *Le Mouvement social*, Paris, No. 51, May-June 1965, pp. 80-81.

250   *CW*, Vol. 44, op. cit., pp. 231, 256, 269, 297, 298, 475, 512, 527.

251   'Report of the General Council', August-September 1872, https://www.marxists.org/history/international/iwma/documents/1872/hague-conference/hague-report.htm

252   'The Internationals. Election of agents to the approval of Karl Marx', *The World*, (New York, report dated 10 January 1873), called for IWMA bodies to send names and addresses of potential agents to New York and Karl Marx, published 1 February; Hermann Jung Papers number 135; https://access. iisg.amsterdam/universalviewer/#?manifest=https://hdl.handle.net/10622/ ARCH00698.135?locatt=view:manifest).

253   Letter of 18 January 1872, quoted in *Le Mouvement social*, No. 51, Paris, May-June 1965, p. 98, (Jstor).

254   'Les trois socialismes, réformistes, communistes et anarchistes' *Almanach du people*, 1872 ; Adhémar Schwitzguébel, *Quelques écrits*, Paris: Stock, 1908, pp. 71-73.

255   The author concluded that a future course of action should be guided by facts and experience; emphasis added.

256   Prosper Olivier Lissagaray, *Histoire de la commune de 1871*, Paris: E. Dentu, 1896, p. iii.

257   Federico Ferretti, 'Anarchist geographers and feminism in late 19th century France: the contributions of Elisée and Elie Reclus, *Historical Geography*, Vol. 44, 2016, p. 74.

258   See texts of 1871, published as 'Socialism and the Paris Commune' and 'On Discipline', in Mikhail Bakunin, *Selected Texts 1868-1875*, op. cit., pp. 95, 101-112.

259   Victor Prosper Considerant (1808-1893), French democrat.

260   Pierre-Joseph Proudhon (1809-1865), French libertarian socialist, his works were most influential in the early years of the IWMA. *BFJ*, 15 June 1872.

261   https://maitron.fr/spip.php?article154757

262   *The Bee-Hive*, 7 January 1865, emphasis added.

263   Anthony Zurbrugg, 'Bakunin, the Franco-Prussian War and After', *Anarchist Studies*, Vol. 29, Issue 2, London: Lawrence & Wishart, 2021, p. 18.

264   James Guillaume was aware of Joseph Déjacque (1821-1864), a revolutionary critic of Proudhon had lived in the USA for several years and advocated a socialism that confronted sexism and racism.

265   Michel Bakounine, (James Guillaume, Ed.), 'Fédéralisme, Socialisme et Antithéologisme' (1867-68), in *Oeuvres*, Volume 1, Paris: P. V. Stock: 1895, pp. 157-

158. Bakunin thought that Asian and African peoples might also join the IWMA, but that that development was many years off. 'Circulaire à mes amis d'italie', (1871), *Oeuvres*, Volume 6, p. 392.

266 'La Première Internationale', http://commune1871-rougerie.fr/internationale%2Cfr%2C8%2C103.html

267 https://www.ainfos.ca/en/ainfos44892.html

268 Carolyn J. Eichner, 'Civilization vs Solidarity: Louise Michel and the Kanaks', *Salvage*, 2017. A revolt of Kanak people broke out in New Caledonia in 1878.

269 *The Times* (London), 13 September 1873; see also comments on Austria, in Guillaume, *L'Internationale*, op. cit., part 5, chapter 3, pp. 93-94. Engels wrote in a letter to Sorge. 3 May 1873 saying he endorsed Oberwinder's tactics because: 'in Austria feudalism has only partly been overcome ...' *CW*, op. cit. Vol. 44, p. 491; Sorge complained that some of Oberwinder's allies were too close to the bourgeoisie. See also: Gian Mario Bravo, 'Nel Centenario Della II Internazionale: Le Origini Del Socialismo Nell'impero Asburgico', *Studi Storici*, Vol. 30, No. 3, 1989, p. 647. (Jstor)

270 Report dated on the 10th, *The Times*, 13 September 1873.

271 Nikolay Joukovsky (Zhukovsky, Žukovskij, 1833-1895), teacher, libertarian, Russian revolutionary, lived in exile in Geneva. 'a brilliant, elegant, highly intelligent nobleman, a favourite with the workers ...' Kropotkin, *Memoirs*.

272 On politics in Geneva see 'On the Alliance', [Rapport sur l'alliance, August 1871], in Mikhail Bakunin, *Selected Texts 1868-1875*, op. cit., pp. 142ff.

273 'there could be no foreigners in the International': Bakunin, *Selected Texts*, op. cit., p. 167.

274 *La Liberté* (Paris), 11 September 1869.

275 Bakunin, *Selected Texts*, op. cit., pp. 182, 217.

276 *Documents of the First International*, Vol. 5, op. cit., pp. 253-55.

277 William Kenefick, 'Confronting White Labourism: Socialism, Syndicalism, and the Role of the Scottish Radical Left in South Africa before 1914', *International Review of Social History*, Vol. 55, No. 1, 2010, pp. 29–62, (Jstor).

278 10 Ward Hotel club statutes, quoted in Friedrich A. Sorge, 'Die Arbeiterbewegung', op. cit.

279 *Chicago Tribune*, 21 December 1871. Douglas papers, April 1856, quoted in Henry Louis Gates, *Stony The Road: Reconstruction*, op. cit., p. 11.

280 Eugene Genovese, *Roll, Jordan, Roll: The World the Slaves Made*, New York: Vintage, 1976, p, 155.

281 Timothy Messer-Kruse, *The Yankee International*, op. cit., pp. 194-95.

282 https://en.wikipedia.org/wiki/Marching_Song_of_the_First_Arkansas; David Roediger, 'Making Solidarity Uneasy: Cautions on a Keyword from Black Lives Matter to the Past', *American Quarterly*, Vol. 68, No. 2, 2016, pp. 223-48, (Jstor).

283 W. E. Burghardt Du Bois, *Black Reconstruction*, New York: Harcourt, Brace, 1935, pp. 685, 680, 674.

284 Ibid., p. 684-85.

285 Press Association Intelligence information: publications appeared 18 April to 3 May.

286 W. E. Burghardt Du Bois, *Black Reconstruction*, op. cit., p. 685.

287 Booker T. Washington, *Up From Slavery: An Autobiography*, New York: Doubleday, 1901, pp. 83-84.

288   The issue was raised at a congress of sections, held at the Tenth Ward Hotel, 6-8 July 1872. 'It left undefined its position on the question of Chinese labor, raised by a section in San Francisco. The delegates were content to reject slavery – in any form, including indentured Chinese labor, and urged the enactment of legislation to prevent it.' Samuel Bernstein, *The First International in America*, op. cit., p. 143.

289   'Platform' point 7, *Workingman's Advocate* (Chicago), 21 September 1872.

290   David Goutor. '"Stand by the Union, Mr. Arch": The Toronto Labour Establishment and the Emigration Mission of Britain's National Agricultural Labourers' Union', *Labour / Le Travail*, Vol. 55, Athabasca University Press, 2005, p. 26, (Jstor). Racism was invoked to motivate attacks on Chinese workers on behalf of 'white Australia', in Clunes (Victoria), in December 1873.

291   'Report of the North American Federal Council to The Hague Congress', *The Hague Congress of the First International*, op. cit., pp. 224-27, 49.

292   *CW*, Vol. 23, op. cit., p. 255.

293   In August 1869, a National Labor Union convention had heard an appeal for fair treatment from an African American activist, Isaac Myers. The convention decided that Black workers should be allowed to join but should be kept in separate labour organisations. Herbert Hill, 'The Problem of Race in American Labor History', *Reviews in American History*, Vol. 24, No. 2, 1996, pp. 193-94.

294   *Proceedings of the Colored National Labor Convention*, Washington DC: Offices of the New Era, 1870, p. 3; https://omeka.coloredconventions.org/files/original/395c8b166607f33e1fadeb7eec6e67af.pdf

295   Antony Taylor, '"Sectarian Secret Wisdom" and Nineteenth-Century Radicalism: The IWMA in London and New York', in Fabrice Bensimon, et al, in *Arise*, p. 293.

296   Mark A. Lause, 'The American Radicals & Organized Marxism', op. cit., p. 74.

297   Walter Rodney, *How Europe Underdeveloped Africa*, London: Bogle-L'Ouverture Publications, 1983, p. 99.

298   *Reynolds's Newspaper* (London), 28 July 1872.

299   'This was the charter of the land, And guardian angels sang this strain: "Rule, Britannia! rule the waves: "Britons never will be slaves."' Africans were forced to sing as much. Walter Rodney, *How Europe Underdeveloped Africa*, op. cit., p. 110.

300   *Proceedings of the Colored National Labor Convention*, op. cit., p. 31.

301   See also: *La Federación* (Barcelona), 8 November 1873) reporting from South Carolina (Charleston?) describing splendid results for agricultural workers who cultivated collectively, sharing all their produce,

302   Henry Louis Gates, *Stony the Road*, op cit.; Timothy Messer-Kruse, *The Yankee International*, op. cit., p. 207.

303   See: Engels 'The Prussian Military Question and the German Workers' Party', 1865.

304   *Le Mirabeau* (Verviers), 24 October 1873, quoted in: George Alter, *Family and the Female Life Course: The Women of Verviers, Belgium, 1849-1880*, University of Wisconsin Press, 1988, p. 124.

305   Point four of four, 'to be discussed by the women delegates of Verviers', meeting called for 13 July, *L'Ami du Peuple* (Liège), 6 July 1873; Antje Schrupp, 'Die Genfer Frauensektion der Ersten Internationale', op. cit.

306   *BFJ*, 15 November 1874. *Woodhull & Claflin's Weekly*, 20 September 1873, p. 7, pointed to Comstock hypocrisy and an Indianapolis brothel advertising its services

for 'merchants, lawyers, judges, aldermen, statesmen, gentlemen of elegant leisure and the very best classes of society'.

307 James Guillaume noted that some specialised jewellery trade workers opposed women working, the use of machines, and the trend to minutely defined work. They feared current development in industrial production. Guillaume, *L'Internationale*, op. cit., part 5, chapter 4, p. 103.

308 James Muldoon, Mirjam Müller & Bruno Leipold: 'Aux Ouvrières!': socialist feminism in the Paris Commune', *Intellectual History Review*, 2022.

309 *La Sociale*, No. 39, 8 May 1871.

310 She condemned both marriage and prostitution, seeing all-too-common domination in relations between men and women. *Alternative Libertaire*, 17 August 2020.

311 Federico Ferretti, 'Anarchist geographers and feminism' op. cit., p. 71.

312 Temma Kaplan, *Anarchists of Andalusia, 1868-1903*, Princeton University Press, 1977, pp. 61-62.

313 Mari Jo Buhle, *Women and American Socialism 1870-1920*, Urbana: University of Illinois Press, 1978, p. 12.

314 November 1874; Hermann Schlüter, *Die Internationale in Amerika*, op. cit., p. 301. The current demands of German Social-Democrats included votes for men over 20, women were not mentioned, *Der Volksstaat*, 10 October 1873.

315 *Le Travailleur* (Geneva), November 1877, p. 15.

316 Susanne Mutert, 'Une intégration ambiguë: Femmes et syndicats en Bavière 1868/69-1892', *Clio. Histoire, femmes et sociétés*, No. 3, 1996.

317 https://maitron.fr/spip.php?article185958

318 An IWMA 'Section des dames' (Ladies' section) had existed in Geneva c. 1868 but fell apart in 1872, Antje Schrupp, 'Die Genfer Frauensektion der Ersten Internationale', http://www.antjeschrupp.de/die-genfer-frauensektion

319 Nunzio Pernicone, *Italian Anarchism: 1864-1892*, op. cit., p. 79

320 *Bollettino della Federazione Italiana della Associazione Internazionale dei Lavoratori*, May 1873.

321 https://www.treccani.it/enciclopedia/luisa-minguzzi_(Dizionario-Biografico); 'There are hundreds or thousands of [Italian] working-class women who were active in the International who still deserve their historian...' Carl Levy, 'The Italians and the IWMA', in *Arise*, p. 215.

322 Florian Eitel, *Anarchistische Uhrmacher*, op. cit., p. 451.

323 Ibid., the *Fédération ouvrière du Vallon* may not have joined the Jura Federation.

324 Laurence Marti, 'Entre exclusion et hésitations. Femmes et syndicalisme dans l'horlogerie au 19e siècle, *Cahiers d'histoire du mouvement ouvrier*, No. 29, 2013, Lausanne: Association pour l'étude de l'histoire du mouvement ouvrier, pp. 13-14, 21.

325 See congress report, (pp. 74-75), http://www.cgtvalencia.org/wp-content/uploads/2014/09/actas_congreso_fai_1872.pdf, also Joel Delhom, 'La difícil inclusión de las mujeres en los sindicatos españoles: de las resoluciones de los congresos al caso de las trabajadoras del calzado en Barcelona (1870-1931)'; *I Congreso de Investigadorxs sobre anarquismo*, Buenos Aires: CeDInCI – IDAES /UNSAM, 2016.

326 Anselmo Lorenzo, *El proletariado militante, Memorias de un internacional*, Vol. 1, chapter 27; P. Carcoma, 'Amazonas Rojas [1868-1874]: Arquetipo Revolucionario

Feminista'.

327 'Bardina: Itinéraire d'une populiste, 1853-1883', *Cahiers du Monde Russe et Soviétique*, 1975, p. 323-352 ; Florian Eitel, *Anarchistische Uhrmacher*, op. cit., pp. 256. 260-61. A person named Noro served as an assessor at the federalist 1873 congress, but James Guillaume, *L'Internationale*, Part 5, chapter 5, p. 108, does not specify whether it was husband Jean Baptiste or wife Émilie. Virginie Barbet was a member of the Geneva *Section de propagande et d'action révolutionnaire socialiste* that helped organise the federalist congress but was not a delegate. She had been active in the IWMA in Lyon and Le Creusot, she advocated the suppression of inheritance – it being very disadvantageous for women – and she opposed military service.

328 Barbara Alpern Engel & Clifford N. Rosenthal, *Five Sisters: Women Against the Tsar*, London: Allen & Unwin, 1975, pp. 9, 20-23.

329 Similar to words in *The Russian Government Herald*, 21 May 1872.

330 *BFJ*, 1 March 1873. The General Council, in March 1872, had refused to recognise it, saying it was a student body. *CW*, Vol. 23, p. 126.

331 Florian Eitel, *Anarchistische Uhrmacher*, op. cit., p. 256.

332 Alan Kimball, 'The First International and the Russian Obshchina', *Slavic Review*, Vol. 32, No. 3, 1973, pp. 502-04.

333 In 'Les russes à Zurich', 1931, https://archivesautonomies.org/spip.php?article4673; Bakunin, *Œuvres complètes*, Paris: Editions Champ Libre, 1978, Vol 6, pp. 471-75.

334 Max Nettlau, *Geschichte der Anarchie, Vol. 2, Der Anarchismus von Proudhon zu Kropotkin 1859-1880*, Berlin: Verlag Der Syndikalist, 1927, p. 203.

335 Richard Stites, *The Women's Liberation Movement in Russia: Feminism, Nihilism, and Bolshevism, 1860-1930*, Princeton University Press, 1978, p. 137.

336 Marie-Claude Burnet-Vigniel, 'Bardina', op. cit., pp. 333-34. The programme forms the second appendix in Bakunin's *Statism and Anarchy*.

337 *Le Travailleur*, September 1877, p. 28.

338 Laurence Marti, 'Entre exclusions et hésitations', op. cit., p. 11ff.

339 Antje Schrupp, 'Bringing Together Feminism and Socialism in the First International: Four Examples', in *Arise*, pp. 343-54.

340 *The Times*, 12 September.

341 Regarding the first IWMA congress of 1866, James Guillaume wrote: 'Among other things one question interested me: it had been said that the International Association preached women's emancipation, the abolition of the family; I wanted to hear a clear explanation of that issue. Well, these were the conclusions of a memoir read by one Paris delegate. The family is the foundation of society, women's place is in the home, not only do we not want her to abandon it to take a place in a political assembly, or to give a speech in a club, but also, we would not even wish, were it possible, that she should desert it to accept industrial work. Through its applause the assembly showed its unanimity and that it shared this viewpoint.' James Guillaume, *L'Internationale: documents et souvenirs 1864-78*, Paris: Societé nouvelle de librairie et d'éditions, and Stock, 1905, Vol. 1, part 1, p. 7.

342 James Guillaume, *L'Internationale: documents et souvenirs 1864-78*, op. cit., part 5, chapter 5, p.116.

343 *BFJ*, 5 July 1874.

344 The Extraordinary Congress of Saint Imier in September 1872 had refused to admit

Terzaghi. He was expelled from the Italian Federation in March 1873. Nunzio Pernicone, *Italian Anarchism: 1864-1892*, Oakland: AK Press, 2009, pp. 46, 73. He was welcomed by Engels and his allies; only later did they realise they were dealing with another police agent. (*CW*, Vol 47, pp. 154, 583.) In that text he is falsely described as a Bakuninist.

345 *La Federación* (Barcelona), 18 January 1873;'Asociación Internacional de los Trabajadores, III Congreso Obrero de la Región Española, Celebrado en Córdoba del 25 de diciembre de 1872 al 2 de enero de 1873 … Actas y apéndices'.

346 On these conflicts, see chapter 10 of Max Nettlau, *Miguel Bakunin, la Internacional y la alianza en España (1868-1873)*, online via https://sites.google.com/site/bibliolibertaria/acervo; Juan Gómez Casas, *Anarchist Organisation: The History of the FAI*, Montreal: Black Rose, 1986, p. 41.

347 Práxedes Mateo Sagasta was a constitutional/conservative prime minister; Francisco Candau was the conservative minister who proposed the dissolution of the IWMA.

348 Rebels held the town for a month. Temma Kaplan, *Anarchists of Andalusia*, op. cit., pp. 104ff; Max Nettlau, *La première Internationale en Espagne*, op. cit., pp. 199-208.

349 Some weeks later a judge fined a master mason who sought to have Alcoy labourers work a nine-hour day, breaking a convention that had set an eight-hour day. The judge explained that this fine was needed to prevent any repetition of the July events. (*BFJ*, 18 October 1873.)

350 General Pavía was the commander appointed by the Madrid government against the cantonalists.

351 Juan Torres Fontes, 'La acuñación de moneda cantonal en Cartagena', in *Murgetana*, XLII, Murcia, 1975, pp. 95.

352 The Junta surrendered in January 1874.

353 *BFJ*, 1 September 1872.

354 On 27 August 1873, the Portuguese Federation sent a letter protesting against the lies told about events in Alcoy; later it was announced that the federation had been definitively reconstituted. (*La Federación*, 4 October 1873). See also: Max Nettlau, *La première Internationale en Espagne*, op. cit., p. 157.

355 The editors of the *BFJ* published comments from the German socialist press; see for example the edition of 31 August 1873. Some Lassalleans maintained contacts with the Jura, but no formal alliance ever resulted.

356 There was some rapprochement between the Portuguese and Spanish IWMA, but the former's journal, *O Pensarmento Social* was hostile to persons associated with the Alliance and with Bakunin. João Lázaro, Associação Internacional dos Trabalhadores em Portugal', *Revista Mundos do Trabalho*, Florianópolis, Vol. 11, 2019, pp. 15-17

357 An extensive report on this Congress was published in the *BFJ*, 1 May 1873.

358 One section in Moutier (Jura) attended the centralist congress.

359 *BFJ*, 1 and 15 June 1873; Guillaume, *L'Internationale*, op. cit., part 5, chapter 3, pp. 74-78.

360 See also *The Times* (London), 5 September 1873.

361 See Mikhail Bakunin, *Selected Texts*, op. cit., pp.184ff

362 Founding documents can be found online: http://bibliotecaborghi.org/wp/wp-content/uploads/2016/01/Prog-e-regol-della-Federazione-italiana-della-Associazione-internazionale-dei-lavoratori-1872.pdf

363   A picture of pre-industrial economic and political shapes is painted in the *BFJ*, (7 December 1873).

364   There is a report in the edition of 6th July.

365   A memoir by Hubert, dated 1 December 1872, and outlining conflicts in the American section, was published in the *BFJ*, 1 and 15 February, 15 March, 1 April and 20 July 1873. See also Timothy Messer-Kruse, *The Yankee International*, op. cit.

366   The Spanish federation had three representatives at The Hague as against six from Germany and regarded its voting system as unfair. *The Hague Congress of the First International*, op. cit., pp. 56-57, 203.

367   The *Journal de Genève*, 10 September 1873, wrote that Hales had good sense and that the Italians and Spanish delegates dreamt only of upheavals and revolution.

368   *The Times*, 10 September reported that the Americans sent 25 francs to the federalist congress.

369   The congress report has a German original text (omitted here) and a French translation.

370   *The Times* of 6 September carried a report on the discussion of the 2 September (misdated to the 3rd).

371   Buonarotti, Grachus Babeuf, and Anarcharis Cloots were radical activists in the Great French Revolution that began in 1789.

372   See appendix three.

373   A reference to the creation of delegates at the previous congress at The Hague, Wolfgang Eckhardt, *The First Socialist Schism*, op. cit., pp. 290ff.

374   The Romande Federation had at one time encompassed most sections in French-speaking Switzerland. See also the report published in *The Times*, 13 September 1873, noting that the old French-Swiss Federation had been dissolved, on account of the difficulty of knowing who belonged to it. Some sections had dwindled, others had left, others merely existed on paper.

375   See also: 'On Leaders and Politics' in Bakunin, *Selected Texts*, Merlin Press, op. cit., pp. 113ff.

376   Guillaume named Henri Perret, Grosselin, Duval, etc. In his book *L'Internationale*, Guillaume noted that this was a reference to Utin and his Russian entourage, (part 5, chapter 5, p. 126.)

377   Gustave Bazin, (1842-189?) Jewellery worker, active in the Commune and participated in various IWMA and left networks.

378   Sorge had written on behalf of the General Council to bar Dutch delegates. Wolfgang Eckhardt, *The First Socialist Schism*, Oakland: PM, 2016, p. 405.

379   See also Samuel Bernstein, *The First International in America*, op. cit., p. 174.

380   'Don't Set the Time Machine for 1873!', https://www.bostonfed.org › ledger › ledger2003PDF

381   Becker told Sorge that the leading elements belonged exclusively to 'our International' and that many sections stood on our side – but exaggerated. Letter, 14 June 1873, *Briefe und Auszüge aus Briefen*, p. 113.

382   IISG archive.

383   See also comments in the *BFJ*, 14 December 1873 – co-ops needed to be inspired and re-inspired by socialist solidarity, if they were to avoid becoming self-satisfied.

384   There are brief notes on these reports in *Der Bund* (Bern), 14 September 1873.

385   The Rules and Regulations of the Geneva section of the Alliance of Socialist Democracy are in Bakunin, *Selected Texts*, Merlin Press, op. cit., pp. 155-56.

386   The Basle congress passed a resolution against *land* inheritance. A resolution against the inheritance of *capital* received a plurality of votes; it would have passed if abstentions had not been counted as votes against. The inheritance proposal of the General Council was rejected by a majority but was nevertheless printed in its Basle congress report. René Berthier, *Social-Democracy and Anarchism in the International Workers Association*, op. cit., p. 8.

387   This *London Evening Standard* journalist was in error: neither Henri van den Abeele (delegate from The Hague), nor Wilhelm (Zurich delegate) were members of the Alliance.

388   Michael Bakunin, (Arthur Lehning, Ed.) *Selected Writings*, London: Jonathan Cape, 1973, pp. 166ff.

389   Substantial extracts were also printed in the *Journal de Genève*, 19th September 1873.

390   Labourers in Dorset, and East Anglia, were demanding higher wages and faced a backlash from farmer landlords. Some were evicted from tied cottages. Emigration was proposed, but some Ontario trade unionists saw a system of legalised robbery in Canada.

391   *Journal de Genève*, 14 September 1873.

392   The *BFJ*, 20 November 1872, carried reports on members refusing to serve on the General Council. Édouard David wrote that its members were devotees of Karl Marx.

393   There were articles in British papers such as the: *Globe, Lloyd's Weekly Newspaper, Reynolds's Newspaper, Leicester Daily Post, Sheffield Daily Telegraph, The Shipping and Mercantile Gazette*, and the *Western Morning News*.

394   *La Liberté*, 6 September 1873.

395   Ibid., 8th September 1873.

396   *Le Figaro*, 10 September 1873.

397   Ibid., 16 September 1873.

398   *The Bee-Hive*, 27 September, had critical responses from Eccarius and Hales.

399   *Neue Freie Presse*, 14 and 15 September 1873.

400   Jürgen Schmidt, 'Global Values locally transformed the IWMA in the German States, 1864–1872/76', in *Arise*, p. 139.

401   See: Frederick Engels; 'To the General Council of the International Working Men's Association', 15 April 1873. *CW*, Vol. 23, pp. 437-38.

402   *The Times*, 13 September 1873; *Le Travailleur*, June 1877, p. 23.

403   Bruno Gutsmann (1848-1913), a German exile in Switzerland, a prominent figure in the labour and Social-Democratic organisations. He served as the German-language secretary of the 'Marxist' congress. Previously he had been a long-term activist in the Lassalle workers' organisation in Germany.

404   Hermann Schlüter, *Die Internationale in Amerika*, op. cit., p. 236.

405   *The World*, 11 September 1873; confidential report, p. 7, IISG, Hermann Jung Papers, Inventory number 78; https://access.iisg. amsterdam/universalviewer/#?manifest=https://hdl.handle.net/10622/ ARCH00698.78?locatt=view:manifest

406   *CW*, Vol. 45, op. cit., p. 29.

407   Ibid., p. 274; Edmond & Ruth Frow, *The International Working Men's Association and*

the Working Class Movement in Manchester, 1865-1885. Der Volksstaat, 4 July 1873.

408   Emphasis added, Andreas Scheu, Briefe und Auszüge aus Briefen von Joh. Phil. Becker, Jos. Dietzgen, Friedrich Engels, Karl Marx u. A. an F. A. Sorge und Andere, Stuttgart: J.H.W. Dietz Nachf, 1906, ibid., pp. 119, 124-26, 130-31. In later letters Becker reported to Sorge that the president and secretaries of the congress were no longer in Geneva.

409   Jacques Rougerie, 'Sur l'Histoire de la Première Internationale', op. cit., p. 34.

410   Max Nettlau, Der Anarchismus von Proudhon zu Kropotkin, op. cit., p. 211.

411   BFJ, 14 March 1875.

412   La Federación (Barcelona), 13, 20, 27 September and 4 October 1872; Anselmo Lorenzo, El proletariado militante, Vol. 2, op. cit., chapter 5; Albert Garcia-Balañà 'Transnational and Local History in the Formation of the FRE-IWMA' and Jeanne Moisand, 'Revolutions, Republics and IWMA in the Spanish Empire (around 1873)', both in Arise. Max Nettlau, La première Internationale en Espagne, op. cit., 1969, Chapter IX.

413   Temma Kaplan, Anarchists of Andalusia, op. cit., pp. 87-90.

414   Max Nettlau, La première Internationale en Espagne, op. cit., p. 179.

415   Jason Garner, 'El cooperativismo de consumo y el anarcosindicalismo en Cataluña (1898-1939) ¿Herramienta burguesa o anarquista?', I Congreso de Investigadorxs sobre anarquismo, Buenos Aires: CeDInCI – IDAES /UNSAM, 2016; http:// congresoanarquismo.cedinci.org/wp-content/uploads/2017/03/Actas-Final-con-indice_final.pdf

416   Eastern Post, 24 May 1873.

417   The New York Herald, 31 August 1873.

418   Max Nettlau, 'El anarquismo en España', La Protesta (Buenos Aires), 20 February 1929.

419   La Comisión Federal, Alcoy, 24 February 1873.

420   Guillaume once wrote that he opposed electoral work to establish a Volksstaat but would accept labour candidates on 'condition that they lead towards an-archy'. L'Internationale, op. cit., part 5, chapter 3, p. 86., pp. 60-61, 152.

421   Perhaps an echo of the thinking of the Saint Imier congress? La Solidarité Révolutionnaire was edited by former supporters of the Paris Commune now in exile. In Spain, the defeat of the Commune had provoked thinking that it would be best to encourage concerted action and to avoid piecemeal revolts.

422   Max Nettlau, La première Internationale en Espagne, op. cit., p. 169ff.

423   Max Nettlau, Der Anarchismus von Proudhon zu Kropotkin; seine historische Entwicklung in den Jahren 1859-1880, Berlin: Der Syndikalist, 1927, p. 206.

424   George R. Esenwein, Anarchist Ideology and the Working-Class Movement in Spain 1868-1898, University of California Press, 1989, p. 75.

425   La solidarité révolutionnaire, (Barcelona), 10 June 1873.

426   La Federación (Barcelona), 1 March 1873, Document 17, in Antología Documental del Anarquismo Español, op. cit.

427   Federación 26 August 1873.

428   Jeanne Moisand, 'Revolutions, Republics and IWMA in the Spanish Empire (around 1873)', in Arise, pp. 244-45.

429   Juan Torres Fontes, 'La acuñación de moneda cantonal en Cartagena', in Murgetana,

XLII, Murcia, 1975, pp. 95. Friedrich Engels described persons released from prison as the 'worst robbers and murderers', 'The Bakuninists at Work', *CW*, Vol. 23, pp. 595ff.

430 *La Federación*, 20 September 1873.

431 There was opposition to war in Cuba: '¡Abajo la Guerra!', *El Corsario* (La Coruña), 22 August 1896, document 27 in: *Antología Documental del Anarquismo Español*, op. cit.

432 *L'anarchisme à Cuba*, Paris: Éditions CNT-Région parisienne, 2004; Kirwin Shaffer, *Anarchist Cuba: Countercultural Politics in the Early Twentieth Century*, Oakland: PM Press, 2019, pp. 4-5.

433 Ibid, document 19, 'Los sucesos de Alcoy', *La Federación*, Barcelona, 19 July 1873; *BFJ*, 17 August 1873.

434 Temma Kaplan, 'De l'émeute à la grève de masse: conscience de classe et communauté ouvrière en Andalousie au XIXe Siècle.' *Le Mouvement Social*, No. 107, 1979, p. 33. (Jstor)

435 Édouard Waintrop, *Les Anarchistes Espagnoles, 1868-1981*, Paris: Éditions Denöel, 2012, p. 49.

436 Engels presented the *junta* as a government, writing that Bakuninists had betrayed their principles: 'The Bakuninists at Work', *CW*, Vol. 23, pp. 595ff. The *Bulletin*,16 November 1873, carried extracts from Engels, and accused him of changing tack shamelessly, to attack federalists and libertarians.

437 Lead article, *BFJ*, 9 November 1873.

438 Document 19, 'Los sucesos de Alcoy', *La Federación*, Barcelona, 19 July 1873.

439 Diego Luis Fernández Vilaplana, 'Alcoi, julio de 1873', https://anarkobiblioteka.files. wordpress.com/2016/08/alcoi_julio_de_1873_-_diego__luis_fernc3a1ndez_vilaplana. pdf

440 Anselmo Lorenzo, *El proletariado militante*, op. cit., Vol. 2, chapter 6.

441 Miklós Molnár, 'A propos de l'insurrection cantonaliste de 1873 en Espagne: L'attitude des anarchistes et la critique d'Engels', in *Anarchici e anarchia nel mondo contemporaneo*: Atti del Convegno Torino, 5, 6 e 7 dicembre 1969, Turin: Fondazione Luigi Einaudi, 1971. Texts in *La solidarité révolutionnaire* suggest that in this crucial period the political debates were between libertarians and republicans. See section I.3 'Ideologia', *Antología Documental del Anarquismo Español*, op. cit.

442 Max Nettlau, *La première Internationale en Espagne*, op. cit., p. 211.

443 Jeanne Moisand, 'Revolutions, Republics and IWMA in the Spanish Empire', *Arise*, pp. 241ff; Guillaume, *L'Internationale*, op. cit., part 5, chapter 3, pp. 86.

444 Co-ordination was lacking and libertarians learnt little from these events. César M. Lorenzo, *Les Anarchistes et le Pouvoir*, Paris: Éditions du Seuil, 1969, pp. 21-27.

445 Clara Lida, *Anarquismo y revolución en la España del XIX*, Madrid: Siglo XXI, 1972, pp. 200-201, quoted by Joël Delhom, La Fédération espagnole de l'Internationale et la Commune de Paris (1871-1874)', in Gilbert Larguier & Jérôme Quaretti, Eds, *Commune de 1871: utopie ou modernité ?* Presses Universitaires de Perpignan, 2000.

446 Paul Brousse (1844–1912), a French exile in Spain and Switzerland, he helped edit the *BFJ*, later veered from anarchism to possibilist Social-Democracy.

447 Charles Alerini, (184-1901), teacher, joined the Marseille Commune insurrection in 1871, condemned to death, an FRE delegate at The Hague in 1872, joined a French section in Barcelona in 1873 and was imprisoned in 1875-6 in Cadiz. After

participating in the French IWMA federal congress in 1877 appears to have ceased political activity.

448 Camille Camet (1850-1917), weaver, French army deserter, exile in Spain and Switzerland, arrested in 1873, released 1879, later veered to support French Socialists (Guesde).

449 José García Viñas (848-1931), a medic, worked for *La Revista Social,* a key figure in the FRE and the *Alianza* up to 1880. Attended IWMA congresses in 1876 and 1877.

450 George R. Esenwein, *Anarchist Ideology and the Working-Class Movement in Spain,* op. cit., p. 48.

451 Clara E. Lida, *Anarquismo y revolución,* quoted by Joël Delhom, 'La Fédération espagnole de l'Internationale et la Commune', op. cit.; Engels wrote 'Barcelona did not raise a finger…' *CW,* Vol. 23, p. 587. (Carlists had bases near Barcelona). Max Nettlau, *La première Internationale en Espagne,* op. cit., pp. 196ff;

452 Max Nettlau, noted a lack of internal FRE documentation on these choices; *La première Internationale en Espagne,* op. cit., p. 176,

453 Texts written in September-October 1873 and published shortly after in *Der Volksstaat, CW,* Vol. 44, p. 583, emphasis added.

454 Ibid., p. 598. See also Guillaume, *L'Internationale,* op. cit., Part 5, chapter 6, p. 151ff.

455 Bakunin wrote he had as much power over events in Spain as over weather! Letter to the *Journal de Genève,* 25 September 1873.

456 The *Bulletin* of 16 November 1873 reprinted extracts from *Volksstaat* (2 and 5 November) to illustrate contradictory points in its polemic. Emphasis added.

457 Max Nettlau, *La première Internationale en Espagne,* op. cit., p. 138.

458 Ibid., pp. 216-17.

459 Clara E. Lida, 'Para repensar a Mano Negra: El Anarquismo Español durante la clandestinidad', *Historia Social,* No. 74, 2012, p. 12.

460 *BFJ,* 4 January 1874.

461 George R. Esenwein, *Anarchist Ideology and the Working-Class Movement in Spain 1868-1898,* op. cit., p. 65; Clara E. Lida, 'Para repensar a Mano Negra' op. cit., pp. 3–22.

462 Clara E. Lida, *La mano negra: anarchisme rural, sociétés clandestines et repression en Andalousie (1870-1888),* Montreuil: Éditions L'échappée, 2011, p. 86; Max Nettlau, *La première Internationale en Espagne,* op. cit., p. 239.

463 He was born in a privileged family, and in and out of prison supported radical and libertarian causes; some 50,000 people attended his funeral.

464 Temma Kaplan, *Anarchists of Andalusia,* op. cit., pp. 108-09.

465 *El proletariado militante,* op. cit., Vol. 2, chapter 7.

466 *BFJ,* 3 January 1875; Juan Gómez Casas, *Anarchist Organisation: The History of the FAI,* Montreal: Black Rose, 1986, p. 43.

467 Max Nettlau, 'A Contribution to an anarchist bibliography of Latin America', http:// dwardmac.pitzer.edu/Anarchist_Archives/bright/nettlau/NettlauLABib.html

468 *BFJ,* 12 April 1874.

469 Clara E. Lida, 'Sobrevivir en secreto. Las conferencias comarcales y la reorganización anarquista clandestina (1874-1881)', *Cahiers de civilisation espagnole contemporaine,* 2015, pp. 25-27. For a critical perspective on the Spanish Federation, see: Anselmo Lorenzo, *El proletariado militante, Memorias de un internacional,* op. cit.; in this view

some libertarians were excessively pushy, and it might have been more effective, had they adopted more patient practices.

470   Pier Carlo Masini, *Storia degli anarchici italiani*, op. cit., p. 86.

471   *BFJ*, 15 March 1874.

472   Ibid., 4 April 1875.

473   32,450 in April 1874, Nunzio Pernicone, *Italian Anarchism: 1864-1892*, op. cit., pp. 75-78; Giampietro Berti, *Errico Malatesta e il movimento anarchico italiano e internazionale 1872-1932*, Milan: Franco Angeli, 2003, pp. 34-35.

474   *BFJ*, 4 January and 7 June 1874.

475   Pier Carlo Masini, *Storia degli anarchici italiani*, op. cit., p. 73.

476   Nunzio Pernicone, *Italian Anarchism: 1864-1892*, op. cit., pp. 85-95.

477   Pier Carlo Masini, *Storia degli anarchici italiani*, op. cit., pp. 87-91.

478   *Le Travailleur*, April-May 1878, p. 20-24.

479   Max Nettlau, *La première Internationale en Espagne*, op. cit., pp. 215-17. Viñas cast doubt on the efficacy of strikes. *Solidarité Révolutionnaire* (14 August 1873) sketched a project for a nationwide insurrectionary general strike. Paul Brousse promoted forms of direct action. Giampietro Berti, *Errico Malatesta e il movimento anarchico italiano e internazionale 1872–1932*, Milan: Franco Angeli, 2003, p. 37; also: Guillaume, *L'Internationale*, op. cit., part 5, chapter 3, pp. 97-98.

480   *BFJ*, 5 August 1877, commented that certain recent action were simply 'acts of propaganda'; see also Mathieu Léonard, 'Carlo Cafiero and the International in Italy', in *Arise*, pp. 373-74; René Berthier, *La rupture avec le bakouninisme et la fin de l'AIT*, Paris: Editions du Cercle d'études libertaires – Gaston-Leval, 2013; Caroline Cahm, *Kropotkin and the Rise of Revolutionary Anarchism, 1872-1886*, Cambridge University Press, 1989, pp. 76ff.

481   Florian Eitel, *Anarchistische Uhrmacher*, op. cit., p. 247.

482   *The Guardian* (London), 1 May 1874; Jean Maitron, *Le mouvement anarchiste en France*, Vol. 1, Paris: Gallimard, 1992, p. 92.

483   He attended the Chur congress of 1881 that began the process of founding a Second 'electoralist-socialist' International.

484   *BFJ*, 2 September 1877

485   *Briefe und Auszüge aus Briefen von Joh. Phil. Becker*, op. cit., p. 125.

486   *BFJ*, 3 May 1874.

487   Ibid., 13 July 1873, ('Le Congrès des monteurs de boîtes').

488   Ibid., 26 October 1873.

489   Ibid., 20 December 1874.

490   Ibid., 1 February 1874.

491   Marianne Enckell, *La Fédération jurassienne*, p. 79; a figure of 150 was mentioned by Becker, *Der Volksstaat*, 5 October 1873.

492   Marianne Enckell, *La Fédération jurassienne*, op. cit., pp. 93-94.

493   Ibid., 10 May 1874 ; Charles Thomann, *Le Mouvement anarchiste dans les Montagnes neuchâteloises et le Jura bernois*, La Chaux-de-Fonds: Imprimerie des Coopératives Réunis, pp. 77, 82. Economic depression began to hit the federation in 1874.

494   Caroline Cahm, *Kropotkin and the Rise of Revolutionary Anarchism*, op. cit., p. 225.

495   *BFJ*, 1 November 1874.

496   Marianne Enckell, *La Fédération jurassienne*, op. cit., p. 80.

497   Charles Thomann, *Le Mouvement anarchiste,* op. cit., pp. 81-82.

498   Jura (Romande) congress resolution of 1870, in *BFJ,* 8 February 1874.

499   *BFJ,* 24 May 1874.

500   *L'Avant-Garde,* 1 July 1877.

501   *BFJ,* 20 December 1874. The edition of 10 May reported on the Jura congress of April 1875.

502   Article on splits in Austria in *Der Volksstaat,* 14 June 1873; Herbert Steiner, 'Die Internationale Arbeiterassociation und die österreichische Arbeiterbewegung', *Archiv für Sozialgeschichte,* No. 4, 1964, p. 512.

503   *CW,* Vol. 44, p. 520.

504   *L'Avant-garde* (La Chaux-de-Fonds), 18 November 1878.

505   *BFJ,* 8 & 15 August, 28 November 1875. *Le Révolté,* 10 July 1880, commented on managerial corruption that 'wolves' do not feed on each other... only paltry fines resulted.

506   629.45 francs were raised: *BFJ,* 12 August 1877.

507   Guillaume, *L'Internationale,* op. cit., part 5, chapter 7, p. 295

508   *Le Travailleur,* October 1877, p. 7-8; June 1877, pp. 22-25.

509   Florian Eitel, *Anarchistische Uhrmacher,* op. cit., pp. 357-58.

510   Ibid., 24 October 1875.

511   *BFJ,* 9 August 1874.

512   Ibid., 28 December 1873, and 18 January 1874.

513   For a list see: Florian Eitel, *Anarchistische Uhrmacher,* op. cit., 373ff.

514   René Berthier, *Social-democracy and Anarchism,* op. cit., pp. 104-119.

515   Slave numbers were estimated at one million in Brazil, and 269,000 in Cuba. 'Négres et Coolies', *Journal des Economistes* (Paris), October 1873, p. 106. This article reviewed slavery and forced labour in parts of Africa, Asia, and elsewhere. See also: Ron Ramdin, *The Making of the Black Working Class in Britain,* Aldershot: Wildwood House, 1987, chapter 3. Also: *The Hague Congress of the First International,* op. cit., p. 261.

516   *Le Travailleur,* April-May 1878, p. 18.

517   Yavor Tarinski, 'The Commune and the Balkans: The Case of Bulgaria', *Freedom,* 6 June 2022; https://baerenkiental.ch/kontakt/https://freedomnews.org.uk/2022/06/06/the-commune-and-the-balkans-the-case-of-bulgaria/

518   *La Protesta,* (Supplement, Buenos Aires), 1 May 1924.

519   Amanda Rosales, Sergio Chávez y Mario Gijón, *La huelga en México (1857-1880),* online edition, 2003, http://www.antorcha.net/biblioteca_virtual/historia/huelga/huelga.html#7

520   http://www.antorcha.net/index/hemeroteca/obrero_internacional/obrero_internacional.html

521   'Nuestro programa', *La Comuna* (Mexico City), 28 June 1874; https://revistamemoria.mx/?p=2724

522   *Le Travailleur,* October 1877, pp. 9-10; John M. Hart, 'Agrarian Precursors of the Mexican Revolution: The Development of an Ideology', *The Americas,* Vol. 29, No. 2, p. 136. *La Internacional* (Mexico City), No. 2, 11 July 1878.

523   Joan Casanovas, 'Slavery, the Labour Movement and Spanish Colonialism in Cuba, 1850-1890', *International Review of Social History,* Vol. 40, No. 3, 1995, pp. 379.

524 One rebel leader, Mohamed Ben-Ali, was exiled to New Caledonia, *Le Travailleur*, September 1877, pp. 16ff.

525 Socialism was said to be the 'natural law' of Algeria. Ibid, October 1877, p. 15-16.

526 Chapter 4.

527 The article, 'L'Internationale et les Chinois', in *Le Travailleur*, March-April 1878, remarked: 'We know the issue of labour is serious everywhere, in China, as elsewhere… there is solidarity between the oppressed of the east and west, drawn from the common struggle against misery…' (pp. 22ff, 29) A further article appeared in the April-May issue.

528 *BFJ*, 24 December 1876.

529 Ibid., 13 June 1873; and two articles by Federico Ferretti: 'The murderous civilisation: anarchist geographies, ethnography and cultural differences in the works of Elie Reclus', *Cultural Geographies*, 2017, Vol. 24, No. 1, p. 111-129; and '"They have the right to throw us out": Élisée Reclus' New Universal Geography'. *Antipode*, 2013, Vol. 45, No. 5, p. 1337-1355.

530 *BFJ*, 26 October 1873 reported on the prospect of the Belgian army being used to break railway strikes.

531 Bakunin wrote: the German army was 'prepared to suppress or cut down anything on earth and to commit every conceivable atrocity, at home or abroad, at the mere nod of its king-emperor.' The troops 'used against the Paris Commune were pure French, but they committed in a few days more crimes and atrocities than the German army did in the entire war.' *Statism and Anarchy*, chapters 1 and 3.

532 *BFJ*, 14 December 1873.

533 Ibid., 18 April 1875.

534 'Indigenas y Hacendados', *La Internacional* (Mexico City), No. 6, 11 August 1878.

535 Walter Rodney, *West Africa and the Atlantic Slave-Trade*, Historical Association of Tanzania / East African Publishing House, 1967, p. 9.

536 *BFJ*, 25 June 1875.

537 *Der Volksstaat*, 13 August; 21 November 1873.

538 IISG, Hermann Jung Papers, Inventory number 192.

539 Michel Cordillot, 'Socialism v. Democracy?: The IWMA in the USA, 1869–1876.' op. cit., p. 276; Samuel Bernstein, 'American Labor in the Long Depression, 1873-1878', *Science & Society*, Vol. 20, No. 1, 1956, pp. 66-67. (Jstor)

540 *BFJ*, 4 January 1874, reported economic slowdown in the Jura, caused by unpaid bills and financial disorder in America. Swiss exports of watches and clocks to the USA declined hugely.

541 Herbert G. Gutman, 'Trouble on the railroads in 1873–1874: Prelude to the 1877 crisis?', Labor *History*, Vol. 2, No. 2, 1961, pp. 225ff.

542 *New-York Tribune*, 30 January 1874.

543 Sorge had proposed that ties to the Public Safety Committee should be broken. Hermann Schlüter, *Die Internationale in Amerika*, op. cit., pp. 279-80.

544 Bolte and Conrad complained that Marx and Engels sought to direct the New York council and had refused to pass on IWMA records, *BFJ*, 1 & 8 February 1874. An account of the meeting of the 11th and its resolutions is in *Woodhull & Claflin's Weekly*, 27 December 1873. The next issue of 3 January 1874 recorded opposition in Spring Street meetings held on 14 and 21 December.

545 *Woodhull & Claflin's Weekly*, 17 and 24 January, 14 February 1874.

546 The Spring Street federation discussed secret organisation at a meeting on 10 August 1873; *Woodhull & Claflin's Weekly*, 30 August 1873, 17 and 24 January and April 1874; *New York Daily Herald*, 6 January.

547 John R. Commons et al., *History of Labour in the United States*, Vol. II, New York: Macmillan, 1918, p. 220.

548 Miriam Frank & Martin Glaberman, 'Friedrich A. Sorge on the American Labor Movement', *Labor History*, Vol. 18, No. 4, 1977, p. 603.

549 *New York Herald*, 18 January 1874.

550 *New York Tribune*, 14 January 1874.

551 Michel Cordillot, 'Les Blanquistes à New-York (1871-1880)', *Revue d'Histoire du XIXe siècle*, No. 6, 1990, p. 82.

552 Ibid.: Banks's speech was reproduced in the *BFJ*, 8 February 1874.

553 *BFJ*, 1 February 1874 ; Guillaume, *L'Internationale*, part 5, chapter 6, p. 163. Samuel Bernstein, *The First International in America*, op. cit., p. 163.

554 *New York Herald*, 22 January 1874.

555 *Woodhull & Claflin's Weekly*, 28 January 1874.

556 Mark A. Lause, 'The American Radicals & Organized Marxism', op. cit., p. 70. *The Worker* had survived for only eight issues. Samuel Bernstein, *The First International in America*, op. cit., pp. 185-86; *Woodhull & Claflin's Weekly*, 7 February and 28 March 1874. (I have been unable to read the press of the Spring Street federation and *The World*.)

557 Michel Cordillot, 'Les Blanquistes à New-York (1871-1880)', *Revue d'Histoire du XIXe siècle*, No. 6, 1990, p. 83

558 *New York Herald*, 4 February 1874; *Woodhull & Claflin's Weekly*, 28 January 1874; John Curl, *For All the People: Uncovering the Hidden History of Cooperation, Cooperative Movements, and Communalism in America*, Oakland: PM Press, 2012, pp. 79-80; Timothy Messer-Kruse, *The Yankee International*, op. cit., pp. 238-39.

559 It had a circulation of 3,000. *Briefe und Auszüge aus Briefen von Joh. Phil. Becker*, op. cit., p. 133; John R. Commons (et al.), *History of Labour in the United States*, Vol. II, op. cit., p. 217.

560 George C. Stiebeling, *Ein Beitrag zur Geschichte der Internationale in Nord-Amerika*, New York: Möhring, 1874, pp. 8ff, 17; Hermann Schlüter, *Die Internationale in Amerika*, op. cit., pp. 17, 296. Hermann Schlüter, *Die Internationale in Amerika*, op. cit., pp. 253ff, 296.

561 *BFJ*, 27 December 1874.

562 George C. Stiebeling, *Ein Beitrag zur Geschichte der Internationale in Nord-Amerika*, op. cit., p. 12

563 Ibid., pp. 13-17; Guillaume, *L'Internationale*, op. cit., part 5, chapter 10, pp. 245-46; Samuel Bernstein, *The First International in America*, op. cit., pp. 263-65. Hermann Schlüter, *Die Internationale in Amerika*, op. cit., pp. 238ff, 334.

564 Samuel Bernstein, ed., *Papers of the General Council of the International Workingmen's Association*, Milan: Feltrinelli, 1961, p. 74.

565 Timothy Messer-Kruse, *The Yankee International*, op. cit., p. 146.

566 Andreas Scheu, *Briefe und Auszüge aus Briefen*, op. cit., p. 142.

567 *BFJ*, 21 March 1875.

568 Quoted from the *BFJ*, 14 June 1874; Timothy Messer-Kruse, *The Yankee International*, op. cit., p. 247.

569 Samuel Bernstein, *The First International in America*, op. cit., pp. 261-65.

570 Only representing Germans, in the view of George C. Stiebeling, *Ein Beitrag zur Geschichte der Internationale in Nord-Amerika*, op. cit., p. 17.

571 Letters had been sent to centralist sections in Europe, a few replies came from Switzerland and from London. Andreas Scheu, *Briefe und Auszüge aus Briefen*, op. cit., pp. 144, 147, 149-51. Miriam Frank & Martin Glaberman, 'Friedrich A. Sorge on the American Labor Movement', *Labor History*, Vol. 18, No. 4, 1977, pp. 605-06; *Verhandlungen der Delegirten-Konferenz zu Philadelphia, 15 Juli, 1876*, New York, 1876.

572 Jerrell H. Shofner, 'The Labor League of Jacksonville: A Negro Union and White Strikebreakers', *Florida Historical Quarterly*, Vol. 50: No. 3, 1971.

573 Paul Avrich, *The Haymarket Tragedy*, Princeton University Press, 1984, pp. 34, 40.

574 See for example, *Voyage en Icarie* and Etienne Cabet: https://www.marxists.org/subject/utopian/cabet/icarus.htm

575 *BFJ*, 23 January 1876.

576 *Le Travailleur* (Geneva), August 1877, p. 8. Other sources quote higher numbers of unemployed. See also *L'Avant-Garde* (La Chaux-de-Fonds), 15 July 1877. David Burbank, *Reign of the Rabble: The St Louis General Strike of 1877*, New York: Augustus M Kelley, 1966, pp. 4-6; five million?; the 50,000 figure is mentioned in Samuel Bernstein, 'American Labor in the Long Depression', op. cit., p. 68.

577 Max Nettlau, *Der Anarchismus von Proudhon zu Kropotkin*, op. cit., p. 214.

578 *BFJ*, 14 February 1874; James Guillaume, *L'internationale, documents et souvenirs*, op. cit., Vol. 3, Part 5, Chapter 11, p. 264; and Elisée Reclus, 'Les Chinois et l'Internationale', *Almanach du Peuple pour l'année 1874*, Le Locle: Propagande socialiste, 1873.

579 *BFJ*, 5 August 1877.

580 At one point three out six centralists on the American Federal Council members were cigar workers (two Germans, and a Swede).

581 Gompers thought Cubans were concerned with winning independence, and neglected the cause of the union; Jeanne Moisand, 'Revolutions, Republics and IWMA in the Spanish Empire (around 1873)', in *Arise*.

582 Henry Louis Gates, *Stony the Road*, op. cit., p. 17.

583 Rob Weir, 'Blind in One Eye Only: Western and Eastern Knights of Labor View the Chinese Question', *Labor History*, Vol. 41, No. 4, 2000, pp. 422-23.

584 *Proceedings of the Colored National Labor Convention*, op. cit., pp. 11, 13; Timothy Messer-Kruse, 'From Crusaders to Bystanders?: Recent Reinterpretations of Labor's Role in the Chinese Exclusion Movement', *Race Traitor*, No. 15, 2001, p. 108. Timothy Messer-Kruse, *The Yankee International*, op. cit., pp. 210-11.

585 Ibid., p. 213.

586 *L'Avant-Garde* (La Chaux-de-Fonds), 11 August 1877.

587 Ad Knotter, *Transformations of Trade Unionism Comparative and Transnational Perspectives on Workers Organizing in Europe and the United States, Eighteenth to Twenty-First Centuries*, Amsterdam University Press, 2018, p. 97; Henry Collins, 'The English Branches', op. cit., p. 266; British federalists reported on the strike in the

Eastern Post (London, 24 May 1873), IISG, Hermann Jung Papers, Inventory number 192. *Der Volksstaat,* 12 October 1873.

588   John R. Commons, et al., Eds, *A Documentary History of American Industrial Society,* Volume IX, Cleveland Ohio, Arthur H. Clark, 1910, p. 375.

589   *Beschluss und Resolution des Generalrats betr. die Vorbereitung des Kongresses.* (Decision and resolution of the General Council regarding preparations for the Congress), IISG, Hermann Jung Papers, Inventory number 76.

590   A proposal, very similar to the one put to the centralist congress in Geneva, had been aired by the centralist British Council (dated 8 May 1873 and published in *The Hour*). See document 168, 'The International and the Trade Unions', in H. Jung IISG collection – misdated April 1873. Samuel Bernstein, *The First International in America,* op. cit., p. 168. The *BFJ,* 25 January 1874, commented that practical work was needed to facilitate the project of international resistance.

591   *Der Volksstaat,* 5 October 1873, p. 2.

592   Bakunin was busy with writing and publishing projects, especially *Statism and Anarchy: The Struggle of the Two Parties in the International Working Men's Association* (first published 1873). It was smuggled into Russia and where it had had an enormous impact. Paul Avrich, 'Review', *Slavic Review,* Vol. 27, No. 4, 1968, p. 651.

593   The opening line of the *Communist Manifesto* (1848).

594   *Hague Congress of the First International September 2-7, 1872: Minutes and Documents,* Moscow: Progress Publishers, 1976, p. 533.

595   It was republished as *Ein Komplott gegen die Internationale Arbeiter-Association,* Braunschweig: Bracke, 1874. See: 'The Alliance of Socialist Democracy and the IWMA', *CW,* Vol. 23, pp. 454-580; for James Guillaume *L'Internationale,* op. cit., appendix to Vol. 3, notably p. 328, comments: 'Marx wittingly deceived the commission of enquiry'.

596   *Northern Whig,* 8 October 1873. Excerpts were published in various journals, e.g., the *Derry Journal,* 10 October 1873 and the *Enniskillen Chronicle,* 16 October. The *Yorkshire Post and Leeds Intelligencer* (29 September 1873) was more moderate – merely saying the Bakunin was suspected of being a Russian police spy. See also *CW,* Vol. 23, p. 558.

597   *CW,* Vol. 23, p. 556.

598   Ibid., p. 554.

599   Ibid., p. 458.

600   Ibid., p. 555.

601   Bakunin had raised the matter at the Basle Congress in 1869, Liebknecht was censured but slanders did not stop. *La Antorcha,* (Buenos Aires), 4 and 11 January 1924; Wolfgang Eckhardt, *The First Socialist Schism,* op. cit., pp. 37-45, 202-208, 409-415.

602   Pamphlet extracts were also published in *the Journal de Genève* (19th September), the *Boston Globe* (23 October 1873), and the New York *Arbeiter Zeitung* between October 1873 and January 1874. *Der Volksstaat* carried an anti-Bakunin polemic over several issues in September 1873.

603   Franz Mehring, *Karl Marx,* op. cit., Chapter 15.

604   *CW,* Vol. 44, p. 521; Vol. 45, p. 45.

605   *CW,* Vol. 44, pp. 523-28, emphasis added.

606   Ibid, p. 534.

607   A member of the Commune administration, previously a general in the American civil war.

608   Becker wrote to Sorge in early November saying that he would send firstly, a transcript of the resolutions and revised statutes, and some ten days later the congress protocols; he wrote subsequently apologising for the delays, a packet to Sorge was finally sent on 25 November. *Briefe und Auszüge aus Briefen von Joh. Phil. Becker*, op. cit., pp. 125-6, 130.

609   George C. Stiebeling, *Ein Beitrag zur Geschichte der Internationale in Nord-Amerika*, op. cit., p. 7.

610   Perret, Bazin and others set up an ephemeral *Ligue des corporations ouvrières* publishing a journal *Union des travailleurs*. James Guillaume, *L'Internationale*, op. cit., part 5 chapter 5, p. 139.

611   Letter, Engels to Friedrich Adolph Sorge 12 September 1874.

612   *CW*, Vol. 22, pp. 267-269.

613   Letter to Domela Nieuwenhuis, 22 February 1881.

614   'the German working class is superior to the French both theoretically and organisationally. Their predominance over the French on the world stage would also mean the predominance of our theory over Proudhon's, etc.' Marx to Engels, 20 July 1870, *CW*, 1989, Vol. 44, p. 3; Vol. 22, p. 262; also, Marshall Shatz (Ed), Bakunin, *Statism and Anarchy*, Cambridge University Press, 1990, pp. 189ff.

615   Marx to Friedrich Sorge, 4 August 1874, *CW*, Vol. 45, p. 30.

616   Letter, Frederick Engels to August Bebel, 20 June 1873, in *The Hague Congress of the First International: Reports and letters*, op. cit., pp. 603-06. Emphasis added. In contrast, see Engels' declaration against Mazzini, 6 December 1871, in which he condemns a narrow Bakunin programme which would exclude the vast majority of IWMA members. *Documents of the First International*, Vol. 5, op. cit., pp. 350-51.

617   *CW*, Vol. 44, p. 163.

618   For example, a peaked Bakunin abused Germans and Jews. Friends urged him not to publish them and desist. Anselmo Lorenzo, *El proletariado militante*, Vol. 1, wrote that anarchists should repudiate anti-Semitic comments. Anselmo

619   See appendix one, also Engels to Wilhelm Liebknecht, 12 February 1873, CW, Vol. 44, op. cit., p. 477.

620   R.P. Morgan, *The German Social Democrats and the First International*, op. cit., pp. 218-20.

621   The controversy spread to the USA; some centralist IWMA members condemned Sorge's relations with Oberwinder. The New York General Council condemned Oberwinder towards the end of 1874. Gian Mario Bravo, 'Nel Centenario Della II Internazionale', op. cit., p. 648. James Guillaume, *L'Internationale*, op. cit., part 5, chapter 5, p. 139.

622   Max Nettlau, 'Marx and Engels and the IWMA', *Freedom* (London) March-April 1907; *Linzer Volksblatt*, 20 September 1874; Zdenek Solle, 'Die Sozialdemokratie in der Habsburger Monarchie und die tschechische Frage', *Archiv der sozialen Demokratie*, Vol. 6/7, 1967, pp. 319-27.

623   Oberwinder was named as an agent of Bismarck (*La Révolte*, 21 January 1888). He opposed translation of the *Communist Manifesto* into Czech. See: Robert S. Wistrich,

'Socialism and Antisemitism in Austria before 1914', *Jewish Social Studies*, 37, No. 3/4 (1975), pp. 323-32.

624   *BFJ*, 1 April 1877.

625   *BFJ*, 15 February 1874.

626   *Cardiff Times*, 27 March 1873.

627   Claimed in the *Neuer Social-Demokrat*, 10 September 1873.

628   August Bebel, *My Life*, University of Chicago Press, 1913, pp. 271-74

629   James Guillaume, *L'Internationale*, op. cit., part 5, chapter 8, pp. 191-92

630   August Bebel, *My Life*, op. cit., pp. 278-86.

631   Marx expected that women would be given the vote only, 'when we take over'. *CW*, Vol. 45, op. cit., p. 197.

632   Letter, Engels to August Bebel, March 18-28, 1875; *CW*, Vol. 24, op. cit., p. 67. For Marx and Engels, it was a case of 'our party' utterly denying respect for 'the principle that the workers' movement is an international one'. Their critique only became known in 1891.

633   http://www.slp.org/pdf/slphist/wmp_1876.pdf

634   Karl Marx, *Critique of the Gotha Programme*, (1875) section III, and appendix (online https://www.marxists.org; Letter, Engels to August Bebel, 18-28 March, 1875, op. cit., pp. 70-71.

635   *Le Travailleur*, June, July, August 1877; *L'Avant-Garde*, 15 June 1877. Vernon L. Lidtke, *Outlawed Party: Social Democracy in Germany*, Princeton University Press, 1966, pp. 46-53.

636   *The Times*, 16 September 1873, (on the centralist congress).

637   Figures from: https://www.gewerkschaftsgeschichte.de/downloads/tab_entwicklung_der_arbeitskaempfe.pdf, quoting laus Tenfelde & Heinricb Volkmann (Eds), *Streik. Zur Geschichte des Arbeitskampfes in Deutschland während der Industrialisierung*, Munich: Beck Verlag, 1981, p. 294.

638   The new party, worked within the law and could not join an International; it 'had to take note, it is true, that in the current situation in Germany, an International organisation is not possible. But what can be done – and should be – is to start a friendly correspondence between representatives of various socialist organisations, and to take advantage of opportunities arising in meetings to exchange views so that *a moral link* between ourselves and our brothers in other countries is created.' Bebel, quoted in René Berthier, *Social-democracy and Anarchism*, op. cit., pp. 128, our emphasis.

639   'Our congress', *Justice*, 29 August 1896.

640   *BFJ*, 28 March 1875; see also congress reports, 13, 20 and 27 September 1874.

641   *La Protesta* (Buenos Aires, Supplement), 1 September 1924.

642   August Bebel, *My Life*, op. cit., pp. 239, 293.

643   *Le* Travailleur, July 1877, pp. 27-28 ; August pp. 27ff.

644   *L'Avant-Garde*, 15 June 1877, commented that goals were relegated to some far way future. 'In two words a grand goal, with sadly [limited] means. The whole, moreover, while remaining always on the terrain of strict legality.' The party bureaucracy 'acted with touching agreement, carefully shutting the door against any abstentionist current. Any attempt, wherever it might be, *to act* or to make any propaganda for anything other than parliamentarianism, was slandered and emasculated.' This

colossus had feet of clay. *L'Avant-Garde* 12 January 1878. See also: *L'Avant-garde,* 4 November 1878; and *Le Travailleur* (Geneva), May 1877, pp. 19-22. August 1877, pp. 27-28.

645 Back in 1870 Bakunin had written of the Eisenacher Social Democrats: 'It was the creation of an exclusively German state that was posed in the first article of their programme as the main and supreme aim of the SDWP. They are above all political patriots'. 'Letters to a Frenchman', August-September 1870, in Bakunin, *Selected Texts,* op. cit., p. 85.

646 Roman Rosdolsky, 'Engels and the "Nonhistoric" Peoples: The National Question in the Revolution of 1848', *Critique, Journal of Socialist Theory,* No. 18-19, 1986.

647 Anthony Zurbrugg, 'Bakunin, the Franco-Prussian War and After', op. cit., pp. 17-24.

648 *Volksstaat,* 8 and 10 November 1876.

649 James Guillaume noted that Bakunin was referring to the centralist congress resolutions that reduced the powers of the General Council. Guillaume, *L'Internationale,* op. cit., part 5, chapter 5, p. 146.

650 The Jura *Bulletin,* 12 October 1873, and translated in *La Federación* (Barcelona), 1 November 1873.

651 Working in concert with Bakunin, writes Max Nettlau, *Geschichte der Anarchie,* Vol. 2, op. cit., p. 203.

652 German Social-Democrats do not follow our path, 'but it is for each people to choose their own way..,' *BFJ,* 8 February 1874.

653 A report by a *Times* correspondent (*Bradford Observer,* 12 September 1874), notes different perspectives on public services. See also chapter 13, Max Nettlau, *Der Anarchismus von Proudhon zu Kropotkin;* op. cit.

654 Elisée Reclus, *Correspondance,* Vol. 2, Paris: Schleicher, 1914, p. 170.

655 Mikhail Bakunin, *Selected Texts,* op. cit., pp. 251-2.

656 The sixth clause of the preamble had read: 'That the present revival of the working classes in the most industrious countries of Europe,' The two words – of Europe – were deleted.

657 For a discussion of managerial power see: Pat Walker (Ed.), *Between Labour and Capital,* Boston: South End Press, 1979.

658 Max Nettlau, *La première Internationale en Espagne,* op. cit., p. 213.

659 *The Times* (London, 10 September 1873) carried a report saying that in Spain the [ongoing] IWMA had no less than eight weekly papers, the Belgians had one in Flemish and three or four in the French language, and the Swiss several, some of them being [illegally] imported into France.

660 Marx to Engels, 4 November 1864: 'I was obliged to insert two sentences about 'duty' and 'right', and ditto about 'truth, morality and justice' in the preamble to the rules, but these are so placed that they can do no harm.' Marx to Engels, 4 November 1864; *CW,* Vol. 42, op. cit., p. 18.

661 *La Federación,* 20 September 1873.

662 For example, *Le Temps* (Paris), 9 September 1873.

663 In 1877, the journal *Le Travailleur* of Geneva, edited by Joukovsky, Alexander Oelsnitz, Charles Perron, and Elisée Reclus, defined itself as revolutionary socialist; it also discussed the term an-archist,

664 Extract from a resolution of the IWMA congress of St Imier, 15 September 1872. See

also Fabbri, in *La Protesta* (Buenos Aires, Supplement), 4 August 1924.

665   Adhémar Schwitzguébel, 'Gouvernement et Administration', in *Almanach du Peuple pour l'année 1874*, Le Locle: Jura Federation, 1874, p. 8; quoted in Florian Eitel, *Anarchistische Uhrmacher*, op. cit., p. 419.

666   See also 'On Leaders and Politics', in Mikhail Bakunin, *Selected Texts 1868-1875*, op. cit., especially pp. 132-35.

667   Mikhail Bakunin, *Selected Texts 1868-1875*, op. cit., pp. 205-06.

668   For example, see the call for a levy to support strikers – and the warning: 'Sections that do not fulfil their duties with respect to the practice of economic solidarity, will not have the right to the solidarity cooperation of the others in the event of a strike, while they have not paid the dividends indicated.' (Paragraph 2 of the additional article of the Statutes of the Spanish Federation). Document 18, Circular No. 12, 'La Comisión federal a todos los Consejos de las Uniones de la Región', in *Antología Documental del Anarquismo Español*.

669   Marianne Enckell, 'Bakunin and the Jura Federation', in *Arise*, pp. 363-64.

670   *BFJ*, 14 June 1874; see also Guillaume, *L'Internationale*, op. cit., part 5, chapter 5, p. 139 and the letter to Sorge of 27 September 1873, *CW*, Vol. 44, p. 534.

671   Miriam Frank & Martin Glaberman, 'Friedrich A. Sorge on the American Labor Movement', *Labor History*, Vol. 18, No. 4, 1977, p. 604.

672   August Bebel, *My Life*, University of Chicago Press, 1913, p. 184.

673   Viñas 'said the Spaniards understood by anarchy the abolition of the present state of society, not the abolition of order. True order could not come until the present state of society was abolished. Society should be based on economic science'. *The Daily News*, 6 September 1873.

674   See letter from Hales, November 1872, in Wolfgang Eckhardt, *The First Socialist Schism*, op. cit., p. 389.

675   *Mémoire Présenté*, op. cit., pp. 284-85.

676   Engels to Wilhelm Liebknecht. 27 January 1874, *CW*, Vol. 45, p. 6, emphasis added.

677   Errico Malatesta would ask: 'And how could these workers provide for the urgent needs if they were not already accustomed to meet and deal together with the common interests…?' 'L'organizzazione,' *L'Agitazione* (Ancona) 1, Nos. 13-15 (4, 11, and 18 June 1897), in Errico Malatesta, (Davide Turcato, Ed.), *The Method of Freedom*, op. cit., p. 244.

678   Friedrich Sorge, 'Die Arbeiterbewegung', op. cit.; Timothy Messer-Kruse, *The Yankee International*, op. cit., p. 195.

679   William West, 'report of citizen West…', *Woodhull & Claflin's Weekly*, 22 March 1873. West, then married to Woodhull, travelled to the congress at The Hague for section 12 in New York, but had his credentials rejected. Mark A. Lause, 'The American Radicals & Organized Marxism', op. cit., p. 73. Terzaghi was allowed to address the federalist congress in 1873.

680   Marianne Enckell, *La Fédération jurassienne*, p. 95.

681   See texts in Daniel Guérin, *Neither God nor Master*, Edinburgh: AK Press, 2005, pp. 221ff.

682   Andrew R. Carlson, *Anarchism in Germany: the early movement*, Metuchen, NJ: Scarecrow Press, 1972, p. 82.; *Woodhull & Claflin's Weekly*, 17 October 1874; René Berthier, *Social-democracy and Anarchism*, op. cit., pp. 104-140, 188-194. Notes on

events in Belgium late in 1880, when some thirty groups resolved to join and support a revived IWMA, can be seen in *La Persévérance* (Verviers), January 1881, https://drive.google.com/drive/folders/1WAzAyPAXF3a2vCaQBl2S0FKSR6HYonzj

683   Some Belgian socialist took the view that the state might provide public services in a disinterested manner. In June 1877, *Le Travailleur* commented: wolves would not make useful laws for sheep.

684   Policy was to be decided by each federation or party, considering local conditions. René Berthier, *Social-democracy and Anarchism*, op. cit., pp. 104-5.

685   James Guillaume, *L'Internationale*, op. cit., part 5, chapter 5, pp. 212ff; Max Nettlau, *Der Anarchismus von Proudhon zu Kropotkin*; op. cit., pp. 214-17 ; *BFJ*, 13, 20 and 27 September 1874; see also chapters 9 and 10 on labour struggles in Caroline Cahm, *Kropotkin and the Rise of Revolutionary Anarchism*, op. cit.

686   Guillaume, *L'Internationale*, op. cit., part 5, chapter 8, pp. 197.

687   *Der Volksstaat* (Leipzig),16 April 1873.

688   'L'organizzazione,' *L'Agitazione* (Ancona) 1, Nos. 13-15 (4, 11, and 18 June 1897), in Errico Malatesta, (Davide Turcato, Ed.), *The Method of Freedom: An Errico Malatesta Reader*, Oakland: PM Press, 2014, p. 244.

689   Mikhail Bakunin, *Selected Texts 1868-1875*, op. cit., p. 212.

690   Few centralists met or corresponded with Marx and Engels, after the congress at The Hague.

691   *Le Travailleur*, October 1877, asked: May we hope that in future polemics between the various organs of the socialist party [all sort of socialists] will not be made venomous by personal issues?

692   Introduction, *CW*, Vol 23., p. xxix.

693   Notably: René Berthier, *Social-democracy and Anarchism in the International Workers' Association*, op. cit.; Wolfgang Eckhardt, *The First Socialist Schism*, op. cit.

694   *Eastern Post*, 8 and 15 February 1873? (The previous edition of 1 February had carried a report on the first congress session of 26 January, and on correspondence received.) IISG archive. *La Federación*, 8 and 15 March 1873, carried further comments.

695   Henry Collins, 'The English Branches', op. cit., pp. 269-70.

696   *BFJ*, 15 February 1873.

697   Maltman Barry was admitted to the congress although he was a journalist expelled by the British Federal Council in 1872. The delegate of the Spring Street federation was excluded because it was said to be less than two-thirds working-class. *The Hague Congress of the First International*, op. cit., p. 261.

698   Wolfgang Eckhardt, *The First Socialist Schism*, op. cit., p. 392

699   *BFJ*, 14 September 1873.

700   A report on the congress is in the *BFJ*, 15 June 1873; see also James Guillaume, *L'internationale, documents et souvenirs*, op. cit., Vol. 2, Book 3, pp. 74-79; and https://hls-dhs-dss.ch/de/articles/017398/2012-11-27/

701   More cordial exchanges between the Jura Federation and the *Arbeiterbund* came a month later, regarding solidarity and fundraising for a strike in Central Hainaut (Belgium) – support was promised.

702   Article of *El Condenado*, Madrid, 11 August 1873, quoted in: Max Nettlau, *La première Internationale en Espagne*, op. cit., p. 182.

703   See: 'Memoria des délégués sur le Sexto Congreso General celebrado en Ginebra

(Suiza) del 1° al 6 de setiembre de 1873', in Max Nettlau, *La première Internationale en Espagne*, op. cit., pp. 185-86.

704   Guillaume had preserved the congress minutes. James Guillaume, *L'Internationale: documents et souvenirs 1864-78*, op. cit., part 5, chapter 5, pp. 116-21. See also: *The Times*, 8 September. The *BFJ*, 21 & 29 June 1874 carried an article reviewing strikes and factors making for their success.

705   James Guillaume is referring to disputes in the German labour movement circa 1905. Libertarian syndicalists were promoting the concept of a general social strike, while the more right-wing labour leader, Karl Legien, articulated the view that a General Strike was a 'general nonsense'. A. W. Zurbrugg, *Anarchist Perspectives in Peace and War*, 1900-1918, London: Merlin Press, 2018.

706   See also, *La Federación*, (Barcelona), 4 October 1873.

707   A liberal journal, later the organ of the Union démocratique du Jura.

708   Wolfgang Eckhardt, *The First Socialist Schism*, op. cit., pp. 404-05.

709   *Journal de Genève*, (19 September 1873, https://www.letempsarchives.ch/page/ JDG_1873_09_19/2),

710   See also Jacques Freymond, *La première internationale*, Vol. 3, Geneva: Droz, 1972. pp. 239-247.

711   End of first instalment, the second part below was published on 8 October 1873.

712   The Dutchman mentioned, Van den Abeele, walked out of the congress.

INDEX